# The New
# Woman's Day
# Cookbook

# The New

### Simple
### Recipes

# Woman's Day

# Cookbook

### for Every
### Occasion

## ELIZABETH ALSTON AND THE EDITORS OF WOMAN'S DAY

### filipacchi
publishing

*Woman's Day* Food Department

Food Editor: Nancy L. Dell'Aria
Managing Food Editor: Marisol Vera
Associate Food Editor: Ellen Greene
Associate Editors: Susan F. Kadel, Terry Grieco Kenny,
Donna Meadow
Test Kitchen Assistant: Dionisia Colon
Administrative Assistant: Kristie Cherry

Copyright © 2007 Filipacchi Publishing USA, Inc.

First published in the United States of America by
Filipacchi Publishing in 2005
1633 Broadway
New York, NY 10019

*Woman's Day* is a registered trademark of Hachette Filipacchi
Media U.S., Inc.

Design: Patricia Fabricant
Proofreading: Kimberly Walker
Indexing: Cathy Dorsey

ISBN: 1-933231-32-7

Printed in the United States of America

# Contents

# A Word from *Woman's Day*

BY JANE CHESNUTT, EDITOR IN CHIEF

For me, it's the Roasted Red Snapper with Coconut-Ginger Sauce (page 110). For Brad Pallas, *Woman's Day*'s creative director, the Brown Sugar–Baked Chicken (page 62). And for our food editor, Nancy Dell'Aria, it's the Shrimp Pad Thai (page 31). These are the *Woman's Day* recipes that we turn to time and time again, that never let us down or fail to give us pleasure. Here we've happily collected these, along with 352 others from our pages, into our newest cookbook.

All of these recipes were developed in our test kitchen, which in many ways is as different from a real kitchen as it could be. Sitting on the 42nd floor of a large midtown Manhattan office building, it's made up of four individual kitchens in one large room, a pantry (which is itself larger than most kitchens) and a dining room with sweeping views of the Hudson River, the Empire State Building and, off in the distance, the Statue of Liberty.

What goes on there, however, has nothing to do with the soaring skyline and everything to do with how America likes to cook and eat. In the 10 years since our last big cookbook, so much has changed. Go into most supermarkets today and the produce section will not only be stocked with a wide array of fresh fruits and vegetables, but also with such wonderful conveniences as greens washed and bagged, ready for a salad, and cut-up melon just right for a child's lunchbox.

Our tastes have changed, too, as America has moved far beyond meat-and-potatoes to embrace everything from sushi to Thai food. The way we filled our plates for years—that big piece of meat, the hearty serving of potatoes and a smaller side of a green vegetable—has gone the way of vinyl LPs and rotary-dial phones. Now we know that, whether for maintaining a healthy weight or preventing disease, whole grains, fruits and vegetables should take up most of the room on a plate.

The food pages of *Woman's Day* don't just reflect these changes but help lead the way. Our philosophy is simple: to produce foolproof recipes that have as few ingredients as possible, that you can get on the table quickly and that are, above all, delicious.

Speaking of delicious, I'm willing to bet you'll find a favorite among the dessert recipes we've collected here. It's no accident that more than half of our covers in a year feature desserts: Whether it's the always-popular cheesecake or apple pie or something a little fancier, like the Chocolate Truffle Pie (page 298), people love them. When you make a homemade dessert, there's not only the pleasure of preparing it but the satisfaction that comes from sharing it, and that, when you come down to it, is what cooking is all about.

Brad originally made the chicken drumsticks because he needed a quick and easy recipe one night and had all the ingredients on hand. Now the two little girls he first served it to are away at school and ask him to make it for them when they're back because it tastes like home. Believe it or not, it's not uncommon for us to get requests for *Woman's Day* recipes from the '40s because the original is so worn out it can't be read any longer. Nothing thrills us more than to hear that a recipe has been torn from the pages of the magazine, because then we know we've done our job, that we've created something useful and meaningful, that helps provide not only sustenance, but something a little more, something that becomes part of your everyday meals or special occasions. I hope you find a new tradition here.

Bon appétit!

# In the *Woman's Day* Kitchens

BY ELIZABETH ALSTON

It has been a daunting task selecting just 355 recipes from well over a thousand published in *Woman's Day* magazine over the last 4½ years.

I tried to select a variety of recipes you will find useful, easy and, most of all, delicious. In the chicken chapter, for example, you will find recipes for a whole bird, but also for breasts, legs, drumsticks, thighs and so on. The line under the recipe title lists the cut. We've also listed what you need: a baking dish, a grill (outdoor or stovetop), your oven, or a slow cooker (we know slow is hot again so we've included many slow-cooker recipes in this book). Ordinary pots and pans are not in the listing because we feel everyone has a selection of pots; nor does that line indicate if the recipe is cooked stovetop because we feel you are willing to turn on the stove, if not always the oven. With those crucial bits of information you can make a quick decision: to read the recipe further, or find another that suits your needs.

There are of course lots of great ideas for quick, weeknight dinners, because that's where everyone tends to get stuck in a rut. I hope you will find some that become family favorites. But there are also hearty recipes for when guests come over and for special occasions such as Thanksgiving and the Fourth of July. All the recipes have been developed and tested in the *Woman's Day* test kitchen. Testing includes not only the cooking, but also getting approval from some very discerning palates—those of our colleagues. And after that, the recipes have to be written and edited so you, the reader, can make them without hesitation or questions. Anticipating some of your questions, we've collected the following:

My purpose here is to make sure we are on the same track. Experienced cooks will say, "I know that," but beginners may not. At the risk of sounding naïve, here goes:

## EQUIPMENT

Many of our recipes call for a large skillet or a large, deep skillet. Using the right size and shape is important. The *Woman's Day* test kitchen recommends the following:

| IF THE RECIPE CALLS FOR A | USE ONE |
| --- | --- |
| Large skillet | At least 10 in. across the bottom with sides at least 2 in. high |
| Large deep skillet | At least 10 in. across the bottom with sides at least 3 in. high |

Checking the diameter across the bottom is essential because what may be described on the label as a 10-in. skillet may be 10 in. across the rim but not across the bottom where most of the cooking gets started. A wide bottom means you can brown more pieces of meat, fish or chicken, or meatballs at a time (see Browning, page 15). Or if you are cooking greens in the skillet more of the leaves will be exposed to heat, getting cooking off to a fast start.

Your best bet, if you are in the market for a new pan, is to look for what is called a sauté pan. It has straight sides and comes with a lid.

## CHECK FOR

- A NONSTICK FINISH, preferably integrated into the material of which the pan is made (rather than a coating). A nonstick finish allows you to use less fat for browning meat and vegetables.

- A HEAVY BOTTOM that will distribute heat evenly and help prevent burning.

- A COMFORTABLE HANDLE, ideally one that can also go into the oven or under the broiler. A small "helper handle" opposite the main one is good for lifting the pan in and out of the oven, or off the stove.

- A LID, PREFERABLY GLASS, so when food is cooking covered you can check progress without lifting the lid. (Lifting the lid reduces the temperature and slows cooking.)

Last, but not least, to keep a nonstick pan in good condition, use silicone or wooden tools (not metal, no matter what the manufacturer says) and (repeat: no matter what the manufacturer says) keep nonstick pans out of the dishwasher.

## SAUCEPANS

When a recipe calls for a "small" saucepan, choose one that holds about 1 qt (4 cups) liquid. For a "large" saucepan, one that holds about 3 qt (12 cups).

## FOIL

When a recipe suggests lining a pan with foil "for easy cleanup," you may omit the foil and wash the pan when cooking is done.

## BLENDER & FOOD PROCESSOR

If a recipe says "blender or food processor," either will work and the recipe has been tested both ways. A blender produces a smoother and finer purée (for soup, for example) but may not work when there's little or no liquid. Putting any liquid or at least semi-liquid ingredients (such as tomato sauce, preserves or yogurt) that the recipe calls for in the blender first may work, but not always. While a blender will happily make a smoothie or chop a small amount of nuts at a time it cannot handle chopping fat into flour for a crust, a task a food processor does in seconds.

## BAKING SHEETS

What used to be called cookie sheets or even jelly roll pans are now more often labeled "baking sheets," which is the term we use. For cookies, a rim on one or two sides is helpful for lifting the sheet in and out of the oven. For roasting vegetables or meat, a baking sheet rimmed on all four sides is important.

## KNIVES

It often amazes me how people will have a fancy kitchen, a high-tech computer or the latest car, but the worst kitchen knives. Unlike a car or computer, a good kitchen knife won't go out of date, won't need repairs, will last a lifetime or two and won't cost you dearly.

If your current knives make you blush, start with the following:
- One chef's knife (also called a cook's knife)
- A small paring knife

You can forget the paring knife to start with. Just go to a cookware store and ask for a "full-tang chef's or cook's knife." Ask what full-tang means; ask about brand differences; heft two or three sizes of knife in your hand these choose one that feels comfortable for you. Buy one knife and one simple sharpener, hand or electric. By the way, do not store your jewel of a tool in a kitchen drawer where it rubs against other tools; find someplace else, such as a magnetic strip placed well beyond the reach of children.

With slicing, dicing and chopping, as with so many skills in life, the more you do, the greater speed and confidence you will gain. Don't just watch those chefs on television!

# BASIC VEGETABLE PREPARATION

Again, experienced cooks will do much of this preparation without thinking. But a newer-to-the-kitchen cook may wonder what to peel and what not to peel.

## VEGETABLE PREP

The following are always peeled, unless a recipe specifies otherwise. Work quickly with a swivel-blade vegetable peeler and peeling will go fast:

> All-purpose potatoes
> Butternut (winter) squash
> Carrots
> Jicama
> Parsnips
> Sweet potatoes
> Yellow turnips, also known as rutabagas

It is not necessary to peel very young carrots or new potatoes from a store or farmer's market (or your garden, for that matter). Give them a good scrub and scrape with a small knife; the skin will loosen and come right off.

Butternut squash requires pressure to peel if you use a swivel-blade peeler; some people prefer to use a knife (see Peeling Butternut Squash, page 21). Because of their ridged or bumpy exterior other winter squash such as acorn, kabocha or Hubbard are nearly impossible to peel. Cut them in half or in wedges and bake or microwave until tender. Serve in wedges, or scoop out and mash the cooked flesh.

## SCRUB BUT DO NOT PEEL

- New potatoes
- Red-skinned potatoes (also blue or purple potatoes)
- Zucchini, lita, patty pan yellow and other soft-skinned summer squash

## OTHER BASIC VEGETABLE PREPARATION
*(not mean to be comprehensive)*

### CELERY

Cut a slice off the root end, then separate the stalks. Wash before cutting. Celery is easy to slice. It is also easy to dice: Cut a stalk lengthwise in 4 or 5 long pieces. Hold the pieces together and slice crosswise from one end to the other. Result: chopped or diced celery.

### CUCUMBERS

Unless a recipe specifies it, there is no need to peel a cucumber. Some people like to peel regular cucumbers because they may have been waxed (to retain moisture). Others like to peel Kirby cucumbers when the skin has tiny bumps. If you choose to peel a cucumber a swivel-blade peeler does a fast job. Seedless cucumbers (the long ones that are often individually wrapped and are sometimes called English or hothouse) do not need to be peeled.

### FENNEL

Often (incorrectly) labeled anise (it does have an anise flavor), fennel has a thick white base that ends in long green stalks and green fronds. By the time fennel gets to market the stalks have been trimmed to a few inches in length. A bulb of fennel just needs a thin slice cut off the root and the two coarse outer "leaves" removed. Fennel may be thinly sliced for a salad or quartered and roasted. It is also good just to munch on.

### GARLIC

Break off as many cloves of garlic as you think you might need. Either pull off the papery skin with the help of a small paring knife, or put the cloves on a chopping board, hold the flat side of a chopping knife on top of them and rap the knife firmly with the other hand. The garlic cloves should split open, making it easier to pull off the peel. Chop finely or slice, depending on what the recipe calls for.

A garlic press works well, too, and there's no need to peel the garlic first.

Finely chopped garlic packed in a jar has a somewhat stale flavor.

## GINGER
See page 382.

## JALAPENOS AND OTHER HOT PEPPERS
Cut the peppers in half lengthwise. Pull out and discard the stem, core and seeds. Then chop or cut as the recipe directs. Be careful not to touch eyes or other sensitive areas before thoroughly washing your hands.

## LEEKS
Leeks, which look like oversize scallions, are also a member of the onion family and related to garlic. Leeks tend to be expensive because they take a while to grow and require extra labor to produce the white bottom half. Leeks have one problem: The leaves tend to trap earth. To prepare them for cooking, cut off the roots and pull off any torn or very tough-looking outer leaves. Cut off any very coarse-looking green part from the tops. You will be left with the tender white base (rarely is dirt trapped in those tightly-wrapped leaves) and a good, but not quite so, tender green part. Cut the leek as the recipe directs. Wash in two or three changes of cold water and drain thoroughly. (A salad spinner works well if you are washing a lot of cut-up leeks.)

## ONIONS
Cut a thin slice off the root end and pull some of the skin off with the slice. Continue pulling off layers of skin until you reach onion.

Onion is chopped most easily in an organized way that takes advantage of its form. It is easiest if you can get someone who knows to show you

how to chop one, but if that's not possible peel a large onion and take a practice run. Essentially you are going to slice the onion (while keeping it together) in three different directions. As you slice in the third direction chopped onion will appear.

Use an 8- or 9-in. chef's knife, whatever size feels that feels comfortable. Cut a large peeled onion in half from stem end to root end. Put one half cut side down on chopping board. Hold with palm of left hand (if right-handed), with stem end pointing to your right. Cut off and discard a thin slice from the stem end. Turn knife so it is parallel to board and cut 8 horizontal slices from stem end to root end without cutting through the root; the root will hold the onion together. Next, turn knife so you're cutting down through onion toward the board and make 8 side-by-side cuts from stem end to root, again stopping just short of cutting through the root. Finally, make 8 cuts across. As you do, chopped onion will fall from beneath your knife. You're there.

Now chop the other half of the onion. By varying the space between the slices you end up with coarsely chopped, finely chopped or even minced (very finely chopped) onion. The closer the spaces between the slices the more finely chopped the onion. If this is a new experience for you will find that with a little practice you can do a very neat job of chopping an onion.

## PEPPERS, RED, GREEN, YELLOW
Before chopping or dicing peppers (sometimes called bell peppers) cut them in half lengthwise and pull out the stem, core and seeds. If the peppers are to be grilled or roasted whole, there's no prep. For stuffed peppers, cut a slice off the top of the pepper then pull out the seeds and core.

## SCALLIONS
Trim root ends with a small knife. Pull off and discard any mushy or very torn leaves. Use the white part and most of the green part. Scallions are

sometimes cut into 2-in. lengths and then cut lengthwise into strips, but more often recipes call for scallions to be sliced: Hold several together close to the white end and with a chef's knife cut thin or thick slices (as recipe calls for), starting at the white end and gradually moving your fingers back toward the green part. A recipe may call for the sliced green and white part to be kept separate because they are added to a dish at different times or because the green is used as a garnish.

## BUYING SALAD GREENS & GREENS FOR COOKING

Today every market carries a wonderful array of prewashed greens for salad and cooking, many prepacked in plastic bags. You may wonder why a recipe calls for 6 oz baby spinach or 8 oz coleslaw mix, instead of a 6-oz bag of baby spinach or 8-oz bag of coleslaw mix. Baby spinach, coleslaw mix and myriad salad greens mixes are also available packed in rigid, clear-plastic containers. They may even be sold loose. Bag, container or loose, any option works.

## NUTRITIONAL INFORMATION

For each one of the recipes in this book we feature a complete nutritional profile, including data on calories (cal), protein (pro), carbohydrates (car), fiber, fat, saturated fat (sat fat), cholesterol (cho) and sodium (sod) content. Please remember that all nutritional data is approximate and based on averages. One piece of beef is not exactly the same as another, nor is one carrot just like another. But taken as a general guide the nutritional information can help you appreciate the relative merits of each recipe so that you can decide whether it's appropriate for you and your family. If you're watching fat intake, remember that what counts is not the percentage of fat in any one dish, but rather the total number of grams of fat you eat over the course of a day or a week.

## FAT ATTACK

### MEAT

Calorie and fat data is based on well-trimmed meat. (Although with cuts such as short ribs a relatively high amount of fat is unavoidable.) If meat you buy comes with excess fat, cut it off. In many of our chicken recipes the skin is removed before the chicken is cooked. While boneless, skinless chicken breasts have practically no visible fat, chicken thighs often have a lot, which becomes more visible when the skin and/or bone is removed. Remove as much as you can before cooking; kitchen scissors do a good job.

### MILK

Unless a recipe specifies whole milk, it was tested with 1% lowfat milk.

Using whole milk instead rarely creates a cooking problem. But depending on the recipe and the proportion of milk called for, using lowfat milk instead of whole may yield a noticeably thinner, less creamy taste and texture.

## RUN A CLEAN KITCHEN

Without becoming a clean freak you should be aware of some things that help keep undesirable germs in their place and your family healthy:

- Refrigerate meat, milk, eggs and other perishable foods promptly. You'll find advice on length of storage for meat and poultry on page 59.
- Don't store raw meat, fish or poultry where juices can drip into other foods, especially other foods that will be eaten raw.
- Thaw frozen meat in the refrigerator. If you thaw it in the microwave cook it right away.
- Wash all produce before cutting or cooking, even foods such as melon or oranges where the skin is not eaten. The hands that hold and the knife that cuts a melon will almost certainly touch both the skin and the flesh.

- Use one board for cutting raw meat, another for cutting fruits and vegetables that will be eaten raw. Buy cutting boards that can fit in your dishwasher or give the boards a good scrub with detergent and a thorough rinsing after use, plus an occasional soak in a chlorine bleach bath. (Check before you put good chef's knives in a dishwasher.)
- Refrigerate eggs in their original carton (not in the door). Take out just as many as you need at a time.
- Cook eggs thoroughly—but that doesn't mean you should overcook them. Fry eggs just until the yolk thickens; cook scrambled eggs and omelets until the last bits of liquid are just set, but no more than that. Don't use recipes that include uncooked eggs.
- Always be alert for possible sources of cross-contamination. For example, if you take raw meat to the grill on a platter, don't put the cooked meat back on the unwashed platter, where the cooked food will mingle with raw meat juices. Don't use the marinade from a chicken dish as a sauce. After a casserole that included raw egg is baked, don't cover it with foil that touched the raw egg before baking.
- Keep hot foods hot and cold foods cold, especially when you are giving a party. Don't add more pasta salad to the dish of pasta salad that has already been on the table for 2 or more hours. Remove the first dish and put out a completely fresh dish.
- Wrap and refrigerate leftovers promptly. Also refrigerate soups, stews and other foods that you may have made ahead. No need to let them cool at room temperature first.
- Last, but most important of all, wash your hands before you start to cook and often while you are cooking.

# A Few Notes About Some Ingredients

## BREAD CRUMBS

"DRIED" BREAD CRUMBS refers to packaged bread crumbs that come plain or flavored for example Italian-seasoned.

"FRESH" BREAD CRUMBS are made by you with fresh bread (see *Fresh Bread Crumbs*, page 66). Cut or pull off crusts (or not, as you prefer), rip the bread into shreds and pulse it in a food processor until it is in crumbs. If you have extra bread, make it into crumbs and freeze them for another day. Making bread crumbs is also a good way to use up French or Italian bread, which dries out very quickly.

## CANNED BEANS

Most recipes that include canned beans call for rinsing and draining them. Pour the contents of the can into a strainer held over the sink. Rinse the beans with cold water and gently shake the strainer to drain.

## FLOUR

Unless otherwise specified, use all-purpose flour. In baking recipes you will always see the words all-purpose before flour in the ingredients list. But all-purpose flour is also used for all savory dishes and sauces in this book, even though not specified. Occasionally a recipe will call for "cake flour (not self-rising)." That is because cake flour can be purchased with or without baking powder added. "Not self-rising" means no baking powder has been added. To use self-rising flour plus baking powder called for in a recipe could create a very over-risen cake with a bitter aftertaste from too much leavening. Cake flour is made from a softer wheat with less gluten than all-purpose flour and helps give cakes a finer, lighter texture. If a recipe calls for cake flour and you don't have it, measure the same amount of all-purpose flour then remove 2 Tbsp from each cup called for.

## OIL

When a recipe calls simply for "oil," you can use any vegetable oil including canola, corn or soy. Usually olive oil will be fine, too.

Olive oil is often specified for the flavor it adds and occasionally peanut oil is, too. If you want to keep only one kind of olive oil on hand choose virgin. Its flavor is slightly more fruity than plain olive oil and less than extra-virgin.

# WEIGHTS & MEASURES

You'll find detailed information on measuring ingredients on pages 400-401, but the following information often comes in handy. You might be surprised at how many professionals don't know there are 3 teaspoons (tsp) in 1 tablespoon (Tbsp).

## TEASPOONS, TABLESPOONS, CUPS, PINTS, QUARTS AND GALLONS

3 tsp = 1 Tbsp

4 Tbsp = ¼ cup

8 Tbsp = ½ cup

5 Tbsp plus 1 tsp = ⅓ cup

2 cups = 1 pt (16 fluid oz)

4 cups  = 1 quart (2 pt, 32 fluid oz)

4 qt = 1 gallon (16 cups, 128 fluid oz)

## ELECTRONIC SCALE EQUIVALENTS

While recipes specify the amount of some ingredients (such as meat or produce) in pounds and ounces, most stores use electronic scales, which display (and print out on labels) ounces as fractions of pounds. Electronic scales are digital so a weight will seldom read any of the following figures exactly. Use them as a guide to make sure you buy what you need.

| WHEN A RECIPE CALLS FOR | A DIGITAL PRINTOUT WILL READ |
| --- | --- |
| 4 oz (¼ lb) | .25 lb |
| 8 oz (½ lb) | .50 lb |
| 12 oz (¾ lb) | .75 lb |
| 1 lb (16 oz) | 1.00 lb |
| 1 lb 4 oz (1¼ lb) | 1.25 lb |

## DRY WEIGHT AND FLUID MEASURE, POUNDS AND OUNCES VERSUS METRIC

The labels of most packaged food and beverages now show contents in metric as well as avoirdupois. For the metrically impaired, liquids are given in fluid ounces (fl oz) or liters (l); solids in pounds and ounces (lb and oz) or grams (g). usually minor confusions can occur in semi-solid products such as jam; the label may say "Net weight 12 oz," and you may think that is 1½ cups, just what the recipe calls for, but in fact a 12-oz jar of jam is only about 1 cup.

# Tips From Our Kitchen

## Pasta & Rice

### PESTO

Pesto is the Italian word for "pounded" and is used to mean an uncooked sauce (paste, really) of fresh basil, olive oil, pine nuts, garlic and Parmesan or Pecorino cheese. There are other pestos, including ones made with mint or cilantro. Pesto is wonderful tossed with pasta or stirred into a vegetable soup. A close relative, "pistou," is made in the South of France, also from basil, garlic and olive oil, with the occasional addition of grilled tomatoes. When fresh basil is in season, make several batches of pesto and freeze them. In addition to making a soup or pasta dish special, pesto makes a great dip or sandwich spread. Mixed with mayonnaise it is a delicious dressing for chicken salad.

Spread basil pesto on slices of Italian bread and dunk the bread in a bowl of vegetable soup.

### BEYOND THE GREEN

If you're cooking rice or pasta, cook extra and refrigerate it. (First toss the pasta with a teaspoon of oil to keep it from clumping.) Later in the week turn it into a filling salad by adding one or more raw or cooked vegetables (carrots, green peas, sugar snap or snow peas, broccoli, radishes, cucumber) and a dressing. Canned beans or chickpeas, drained and rinsed, can also be tossed with rice or pasta.

## Meat, Poultry & Fish

### NO GRILL? NO PROBLEM

If you don't have a barbecue grill but want your food to look and taste grilled, use a stovetop grill pan. Most have a baked-on black finish that resists sticking and leave "grill" marks that would fool anyone. The ridges also keep foods above much of the fat that may drip off.

Allow time for your pan to get good and hot (either gas or electric ranges work fine), lightly brush it with oil, then grill as the recipe directs. Stovetop grilling can be smoky, so turn on the fan in the stove's hood and keep a window open.

### OUTDOOR GRILLING SAFETY TIPS

- Do not use grill during high wind conditions.
- Put grill in an open area, away from house.
- Do not leave grill unattended.
- Do not pour starter fluid on hot coals.
- Make sure grill vents are open and free of ashes.
- To extinguish coals, close all vents and cover with lid.
- Check coals in a charcoal grill several hours later to make sure they are completely extinguished.

### MARINATING

Marinate foods in a glass, ceramic or stainless steel container, or in a ziptop bag. Most marinades contain acidic ingredients, such as lemon juice or vinegar, which can react with metal other than stainless steel and impart an off taste to the food. Although most of our recipes suggest a ziptop bag for convenience (especially if the food is being transported in the marinade), you can always use a bowl instead. Bowl or bag, be sure to turn the food often, so it is evenly exposed to the marinade.

## BROWNING POINTS

When a recipe calls for browning the meat as a first step, it is to add flavor and color to the finished sauce or gravy. (Browning does not seal in the juices.)

Heat the pot or skillet over medium to medium-high heat, then add any oil called for. Here's the most important thing about browning: Don't crowd too many pieces of meat or chicken in the bottom of the heated pan at one time. If you do, the pan will quickly cool and, instead of browning, the meat will steam, exude water and toughen. Leave space between each piece of meat. As pieces brown on one side, turn them over with a spatula or tongs.

## BROWNING GROUND MEAT

The first step in a quick skillet meal is often to "brown" the meat in a hot skillet, or to stir it over medium-high heat until it has browned. Especially if you are using very lean meat the meat may not actually acquire brown patches. Usually it will just lose its raw pink color. This is fine.

## HANDS ON

Hands are the best tool for shaping burgers and patties (no difference in shape, but anything other than a hamburger is sometimes called a patty). For moist, tender burgers, meat needs to be handled with a light touch, not pummeled into shape. If spices or other ingredients are being mixed into meat before shaping and you are going to use your hands to shape the burgers, use them, or a wooden spoon, to mix in the spices. Again, handle lightly. It almost goes without saying that hands need to be thoroughly washed both before and after handling raw meat. Keep a nailbrush at the kitchen sink and unscented soap. If you don't like touching raw meat, slip on a pair of disposable gloves first.

## BUYING AND STORING FISH

Fillets are the meaty sides of the fish cut off either side of the backbone (and more or less boneless) while steaks are slices cut across the bone. Larger fish such as salmon or halibut are available either way. If a steak is very large, it can be cut in half and the bone removed before cooking, but it may be simpler to cook the fish with the bone in and then insert a knife and ease the cooked fish away from the bone. The meat of tuna, swordfish and other very large fish is cut into boneless steaks.

Freshness makes all the difference in the way fish tastes. Look for firm-textured, moist, pearly flesh, with no sign of dryness. Odor, if any, should be mild and fresh, never strong and fishy. Pools of liquid in packaged fish generally indicate the fish has been around too long.

Refrigerate fish as soon as you get it home. Use it within 1 to 2 days, or freeze it. The colder the storage temperature the less rapidly the fish will spoil. If you have a fisherman in the house, it's good to know never to store ungutted fish, which spoils quite rapidly. Non-oily fish such as flounder, sole, red snapper and tilapia freeze best. Wrap individual fillets in plastic wrap before freezing them spread out on a baking sheet. When fish is frozen hard, pack several fillets in a ziptop bag. This allows you to easily take out just one or two fillets at a time. Freeze fillets for up to 6 months.

In most cases, fish should be thawed in the refrigerator, although thin fillets can be thawed at room temperature in half an hour. Try not to refreeze fish once it has thawed because each freezing and thawing leads to a mushy texture. If you do refreeze fish (and we all have times when plans change) cut it in small pieces and use it to make a chowder.

# Sausages

More than 200 varieties of sausages and luncheon meats can be found in supermarkets, delicatessens and specialty food shops throughout the United States. Every shopping trip seems to reveal a new variety of chicken or turkey sausage.

The name "sausage" comes from the Roman word "salsus," which means salted or, literally, preserved meat. So popular was sausage at wild festivals that it was banned there as the Christian era began. After the reigns of several Christian emperors, the ban was finally repealed.

By the time of the Middle Ages, sausagemaking was practiced by "wurstmachers" who became famous for their skill in spicing and processing distinctive types. Gradually their products became known by the town of their origin: Frankfurt-am-Main in Germany, Bologna and Genoa (salami) from Italy.

## A GUIDE TO SAUSAGES

FRESH SAUSAGE is made from uncooked fresh meat, mainly pork, chicken and turkey and occasionally beef. Fresh sausage is perishable; refrigerate it promptly and use within a few days (or freeze it). Cook thoroughly before eating.

UNCOOKED SMOKED SAUSAGE is much like fresh sausage but the meats used have been cured and smoking gives it a characteristic flavor and color. Treat as fresh sausage.

COOKED SAUSAGE is prepared primarily from fresh, uncured meat (occasionally cured meat are used). If smoking is part of the flavoring process the smoking takes place after the cooking process is completed. Cooked sausage is ready to serve and may be served cold or quickly grilled or fried for extra flavor.

COOKED SMOKED SAUSAGE, again, is prepared from uncooked meat, smoked and cooked fully. Although refrigeration is essential, any frying, grilling or heating in soup may be short, since the sausage has been fully cooked.

DRY AND SEMI-DRY SAUSAGES are made in highly technical and carefully controlled curing and drying processes. Bacterial fermentation is often used to develop flavor and to act as a preservative. Dry sausages may be smoked or not. They are ready to eat. Most hard dry sausages belong to the salami family and are air-dried from one to six months during which time about 35 to 40% of the moisture is lost. The texture of the sausage becomes very firm, or hard, and the flavor intensifies. Certain salamis are cooked and are air-dried for a much shorter period. These belong to the cooked sausage group and must be refrigerated. Semi-dry sausages are cooked while in the smokehouse, but only partially dried compared to hard dry sausages. They are ready to eat. An Antipasto Platter (see page 320) is a good opportunity to serve several different kinds of hard, dry sausages and to compare flavor and texture.

# Eggs

## BUYING AND STORING EGGS

Buy Grade AA or Grade A eggs and only from refrigerated cases, then get them in a refrigerator as soon as possible after purchase. If the weather is very hot, or if you have a long way to drive home, put the eggs and other perishable foods in a cooler with ice or an ice pack.

Leave the eggs in the cartons, where you should find them packed with the wider end up. Do not put them in the refrigerator door where the temperature would fluctuate each time the door is opened.

Eggs keep well if they are stored properly, at least three weeks beyond the expiration date printed on the carton.

## MAKING THE GRADE

Most of the eggs on the market are sold by grade and size. Standards for grade and size are established by the U.S. Department of Agriculture. The grades, in descending order, are Grade AA, Grade A and Grade B.

Grade AA eggs spread less and have a slightly firmer and higher yolk and white that Grade A eggs. Eggs that are Grade B will spread more than the other two grades and have a flatter yolk. Almost no Grade Bs find their was to the retail supermarket. Some go to institutional egg users such as bakeries or food service operators, others to "egg breakers" for use in egg products.

Eggs are also sold by size: Jumbo, Extra Large, Large, Medium, Small and Peewee. They are sized according to the minimum weight per dozen: Jumbo (30 oz), Extra Large (27 oz), Large (24 oz), Medium (21 oz), Small (18 oz) and Peewee (15 oz). The price differences are based largely on egg size, with larger ones costing more per dozen than smaller ones. The egg sizes most often available at retail are Extra Large, Large and Medium.

## EGG SAFETY

Proper care and handling of eggs is important in order to prevent the growth of potentially harmful bacteria such as salmonella.

- Select clean eggs from a refrigerated case. Don't buy dirty, cracked or leaking eggs because they may have become contaminated with harmful bacteria.
- Slightly move each egg in the carton to make sure it isn't stuck to the bottom because of egg leaking through a crack that you cannot see.
- Refrigerate eggs in their cartons as soon as you get home. Storing eggs in the carton keeps them from losing moisture and absorbing odors.
- Do not leave eggs in any form at room temperature for more than 2 hours including preparation and serving.

- When cracking eggs, try to avoid getting any eggshell into the raw eggs, just in case there are harmful bacteria on the shell. It's a good idea to crack the egg into a custard cup where you can easily remove any shell particles before slipping it into a skillet for frying or poaching.
- Use an egg separator to separate egg whites and yolks for soufflés, meringues or cakes, rather than passing the yolk back and forth between broken shells.
- Since any stuck egg probably had a hairline crack through which egg leaked into the carton, it is best to use those eggs for baking or in a dish where they will be thoroughly cooked.

## COOKING EGGS SAFELY

While it is important to cook eggs thoroughly it is not necessary to overcook them to be safe. A poached or fried egg is done when the yolk thickens. Scrambled eggs should be just set. An omelet can be slightly moist when it is folded over because the residual heat will finish cooking it.

## WHEN FRESHER IS NOT BETTER

Eggs that are hard cooked when very fresh can be impossible to peel because the fresher the egg the more the shell membranes cling to the shell. If you want to make egg salad or lots of deviled eggs for a party, the best solution is to buy and refrigerate eggs a week to 10 days before hard cooking them. During this time the eggs will take in air, which helps separate the membranes from the shell. Once you have hard cooked the eggs, crackle the shells all over so there is a very fine network of lines. When the eggshells are in tiny pieces they usually come off much more easily and without tearing the whites.

## HOW TO HARD COOK EGGS PERFECTLY

An unattractive, greenish-black ring around the yolk of a hard-cooked egg is the result of over-cooking. Follow this procedure for perfect hard-cooked eggs.

Put eggs to be hard cooked in a saucepan in a single layer. Add cold water to come at least an inch above the eggs. Cover and bring to a boil over moderately high heat. As soon as water comes to a full rolling boil remove the pan from the heat. Let stand, covered, 12 minutes for Medium, 15 minutes for Large eggs and 18 minutes for Extra Large (set a timer). Immediately pour off the hot water and fill pan with cold water (add ice if handy). When eggs are completely cool, crackle shells all over by tapping gently against sides of pan. Roll eggs gently between hands to loosen shell. Then peel off the shell, starting at the larger end, dipping the egg in water to help ease off the shell. Refrigerate the eggs until needed. If you are going to use the eggs the next day, refrigerate them in the crackled shells and peel just before using.

# Cooking Spray Safety

Using cooking spray in pressurized cans is a fast and efficient way to grease skillets as well as cake pans. A one-second spray can effectively coat a skillet and the actual amount of fat used is miniscule. In addition to saving time, this aspect also makes the sprays helpful when watching the amount of fat in a diet.

However, it's a good idea to reread the instructions on the cans now and then and remind yourself and family members of safety precautions. The contents of the can are under pressure and are flammable. Do not use spray near an open flame or hot grill. Never spray into a hot oven, or heated broiler; remove the food to be sprayed first. Be careful not to put the can on a hot cooktop or near a gas flame.

# Slow Cookers

## SLOW BUT GREAT

In these days of "get-dinner-on-the-table-fast," perhaps the popularity of the slow cooker is surprising. But not when you consider that it removes a major symptom of pre-dinner stress: trying to decide what dinner will consist of. What's on hand in the freezer, refrigerator or pantry? With the slow cooker, dinner is decided and cooking before you leave the house for work in the morning. We have eliminated the pre-browning so there are no extra pots to clean. Just fill the cooker, plug it in and let it do all the work. Most slow cookers even have a removable crock that is handsome enough for serving at the table.

## GET TO KNOW YOUR SLOW COOKER

You may be surprised at the wide range of cooking times in our slow-cooker recipes, for example, 4 to 7 hours. Slow cookers, we have found, vary considerably in temperature level and therefore the speed at which food cooks.

Plan to try a new slow cooker, or a new slow-cooker recipe, on a day you will be around to keep an eye on what's happening. Observe how the time the food takes to cook jibes with the cooking time in a recipe. Don't keep lifting the lid to look inside, as every time you lift the lid you add 20 minutes to the cooking time. Do this a couple of times and you will have a much better idea of how your slow cooker functions with our, or other, recipes.

Some foods, large pieces of meat for example, may be fine if cooked at too high a temperature for too long. Others may end up dry. Slow cookers are wonderful timesavers, but you do need to learn to live with the one you have.

## HOW TO USE YOUR SLOW-COOKER
• The cooker should be at least half full and no more than three quarters full.

- Don't be tempted to add more liquid than called for. Foods give up quite a bit as they cook and anything extra dilutes the flavor.
- There is no need to stir or turn food, and because it cooks evenly it won't stick or burn.

# Soups

## FREEZING SOUP

Most soups can be frozen. Freeze them in airtight containers (perhaps some in individual portions) leaving room at the top for the soup to expand when it freezes. Soups also freeze well in ziptop freezer bags: Turn the top of the bag back and put the bag in a bowl or large measuring cup. Pour or ladle in soup. Close the bag almost all the way then, holding onto the ziptop and bending it back slightly, lay the bag almost flat on the counter, letting most of the air out. Close ziptop. Freeze bag in flat position; it will thaw more quickly.

## STORING SOUP

Many soups taste even better the second or third day, once the flavors have time to fully develop. However, many soups thicken when chilled. To thin, stir in some extra broth, water, cream, milk or vegetable juice, depending on what the soup has in it.

Constant reheating does not help flavor, so only reheat as much soup as you need at a time.

## CHILLED SOUPS

On hot summer days when nobody feels like cooking, or even eating, a refreshing cold soup can be the perfect solution. Cold soups are great for summer eating because they can be prepared in quantity in the cool of the day. Keep a cold soup in the refrigerator for snack-seeking children (adults, too). Most chilled soups will keep for at least 3 days.

# Vegetables

## STORING LEAFY GREENS

Leafy greens, including chard, kale, collard, mustard and turnip greens and broccoli rabe, keep better if they are not wet. Damp greens can quickly turn to a soggy black mess if they are wet from rain or have been sprayed with water in the store. If the greens are wet, wrap them in paper towels before putting them back in plastic bags from the store. Use within 2 or 3 days.

## MESCLUN

A mixture of very young leaves, mesclun has become widely available. It may be called gourmet mix, spring mix or even world blend. There is no standard combination but among the young leaves often found are green and red leaf lettuce, lolla rosa, green and red oak leaf lettuce, arugula, tatsoi and mizuna.

Packets of mixed seeds, or planters with the seeds already growing, can often be found at garden centers. Mesclun is harvested (scissors work well) when the plants have just two or three leaves.

## SELECTING CORN

Choose ears of corn that feel heavy for their size. The stem end should look freshly broken or cut and feel slightly damp. The silk tassel should be moist and golden where it emerges from the husk and dry and brown at the ends. Fresh corn is best cooked on the day it is picked. If that's not possible, refrigerate it as soon as possible.

When buying fresh corn at a farmer's market do not peel back the husk, even at the very tip, as it hastens aging.

## AVOCADOS

Although there are many varieties of avocado, ranging from round to pear-shaped, the two most widely marketed are the Hass, with a pebbly textured dark green skin that is almost black when the fruit is ripe, and the brighter green Fuerte which has a thin, smooth skin.

Not counting the tiny cocktail avocados that weigh about 1 oz, an avocado can weigh as little as 3 oz or as much as 4 lb, depending on the variety. For obvious reasons (they could turn to guacamole on the way home), few avocados are found ripe at the market. Avocados grow on trees but like many fruits they ripen best off the tree. Look for firm ones that feel heavy for their size. At home, put them in a paper bag with an apple, close the bag and leave it at room temperature, checking daily to see how the ripening is going. When they darken and yield to gentle pressure, they are ready. When ripe, avocados should yield to gently pressure and can then be stored, whole or mashed, in the refrigerator for 2 to 3 days.

TO PREPARE: Cut the avocado lengthwise around the seed. Hold a half in each hand and twist in opposite directions to separate. Insert a small (tea) spoon between the seed and the fruit and work the seed out.

If you are going to mash the avocado (for guacamole), use the same spoon and scoop the avocado away from the skin. If you want to slice or dice the avocado, put the halves cut side down on a cutting board and peel off the skin. Then cut as the recipe specifies. To store ripe avocados for later use mash the fruit, adding 1 tsp lemon juice for each avocado to bring out the flavor and prevent browning.

Mash the fruit in a storage container, or pack it in after mashing, pushing mixture down to eliminate air bubbles. Place plastic wrap directly on the mashed avocado, then cover container tightly. You can also mash the avocado in a quart-size ziptop bag (close the bag and mash with your hands) then lay the bag on its side and press out all air before closing the bag again. Refrigerate mashed avocado for up to 2 days, or freeze for up to 2 months.

## TOMATOES

Think of tomatoes as fruit (they are actually berries). Depending on the source and season, you may need to buy them a few days ahead and let them ripen at home—just as you would bananas or avocados. Try to eat them at their peak; overage tomatoes lose nutrients.

Choose smooth, unblemished ones that feel heavy for their size and have firm, not mushy, flesh. Plum tomatoes are often the best choice for cooking. They contain less water and have fewer seeds and more sugar than other tomatoes.

Never refrigerate tomatoes. Cold temperatures kill flavor and stop the ripening process in its tracks. Instead, leave unripe tomatoes in a basket on a counter, stem side up and away from direct sunlight. Or put them in a closed paper bag or special ripening bag to speed up the process.

When tomatoes are in season, it's hard not to buy too many. Chop some and add to soup made from a can or a mix. Add them to stews or pasta sauces. Purée in a blender with a splash of balsamic vinegar, a pinch of salt and a drizzle of olive oil, and serve in a glass or mug as a refreshing cold soup.

## HEIRLOOM TOMATOES

Old varieties of tomatoes are turning up more frequently in farmer's markets and specialty stores. Too delicate to travel long distances, they are worth trying. Not every variety is worth the cost, but a plate of overlapping slices of three or four kinds looks beautiful and goes well with grilled meats. Heirloom tomatoes can be more affected by rainfall, leading to scars and cracks. Rinse the tomatoes, cut out scars and cracks and use a sharp knife to slice them.

## PEELING BUTTERNUT SQUASH

First cut a thin slice off the top and bottom with a knife. Now, if you have a good, strong swivel-headed vegetable peeler, use that; hold the squash tightly, work fast (you may have to go over the same territory more than once) and peel from middle to top, then turn the squash around and peel from middle to bottom.

Cut the squash in two at the bottom of the neck; then cut the part holding the seeds in half from top to bottom. Scoop out the seeds. The squash is now ready to cut into chunks or slices.

If your vegetable peeler isn't up to peeling hard squash, cut the squash as described here for peeled squash. Then take a small knife and carefully cut off the skin.

The peeled and cut surfaces of butternut squash, indeed of most winter squashes, tend to be slightly slippery, so be careful. A damp towel under your cutting board will prevent the board from sliding and if the squash slides while you are cutting it put it on a towel or paper towel.

## POTATOES: TO PEEL OR NOT TO PEEL?

There is no need to peel smooth-skinned potatoes and new potatoes of any kind. Just give them a good scrubbing with a vegetable brush and rinse them well.

Baking potatoes and sweet potatoes are not peeled, unless a recipe specifies.

Wash and peel all-purpose potatoes, unless a recipe specifies otherwise. A swivel-head vegetable peeler does the job quickly. Rinse the potatoes after peeling and if not to be used immediately submerge them in a bowl of cold water to prevent browning.

## GRATING LEMON PEEL

If you are still grating peel with a box grater, treat yourself to a rasp. It makes the task so fast and easy that it changes most cooks' attitude about grating lemon peel from negative to positive. A lemon rasp (there are similar tools for cheese and other foods) looks like something from a woodworking shop, which is where, in fact, the idea originated. The important point about grating lemon peel or zest, as some prefer to call it, is that you grate with a light touch and take only the bright yellow part. The white pith underneath tends to be bitter. If you need lemon juice for a recipe (or perhaps iced tea) and not the peel, take a minute and grate the peel first. Wrap tightly, label and freeze. You will be glad to have it another day.

## SHREDDING

When a recipe calls for shredded cheese or carrots and you are going to shred the food yourself, use the large holes on a four-sided box grater, or a food processor with the shredding disk.

To shred an apple, peel, but do not cut it. Grate down to the core using the large holes on a box grater. To shred lots of apples, peel, quarter and core; use food processor with shredding disk.

Cooked chicken or other meat is shredded differently. Pull or tear the cooked chicken (usually breast meat) into uneven, bite-size pieces about 1½ in. long. The tools? Your fingers or two forks.

# Pasta

Thomas Jefferson is credited with introducing macaroni to this country because he wanted to enjoy again a certain dish he had eaten in Naples. The man who drafted the Declaration of Independence and became the third President of the United States would surely be delighted to know how popular pasta has become in his native land. In many homes it is the main event at dinner almost once a week. (Jefferson also promoted pasta's later frequent partner, the tomato.) Every busy cook needs recipes for popular standbys such as Spaghetti with Meatballs and Baked Macaroni & Cheese, and we have excellent ones for both. There are also rich sauces for company or a spoil-the-family day: Beef & Mushroom Ragù and Farfalle with Mushroom Ragout. Several sauces feature fish: mussels, clams, tuna and smoked salmon. And plenty, of course, call for chicken. When you feel like baked ziti, but don't have the time to make it, whip up our Stovetop Ziti. And when tomatoes are at their flavorful best, be sure to make the Fresh Tomato & Basil Sauce with Pasta.

# Spaghetti with Meatballs

## GROUND BEEF · RIMMED BAKING SHEET

SERVES 4
**TOTAL TIME:** 30 minutes

**PER SERVING:** 784 cal, 38 g pro, 87 g car, 4 g fiber, 31 g fat (10 g sat fat), 133 mg chol, 1,288 mg sod

**MEATBALLS**

- 1 large egg
- 2 slices white sandwich bread, torn in small pieces
- ¼ cup (1 oz) grated Parmesan cheese
- 2 Tbsp chopped fresh or dried parsley
- 1 tsp salt
- ½ tsp pepper
- 2 tsp minced garlic
- 1 lb lean ground beef

12 oz spaghetti

**SAUCE**

- 2 Tbsp olive oil
- ¾ cup chopped onion
- 1 Tbsp minced garlic
- 28-oz can crushed tomatoes in purée
- ¼ tsp salt
- ¼ tsp freshly ground pepper

SERVE WITH: **grated Parmesan cheese**

TIP: Both sauce and meatballs can be made ahead; just reheat the meatballs in the sauce. If you prefer a smoother sauce, let it cool slightly, then purée in a blender.

**1** Heat oven to 425°F. Line a rimmed baking sheet with foil (for easy cleanup).

**2** MEATBALLS: Lightly beat egg with a fork in a medium bowl. Add bread, Parmesan, parsley, salt, pepper and garlic; stir until blended. Add beef and mix with your hands or a wooden spoon until blended. Form into sixteen 1½-in. balls. Place on prepared baking sheet and bake 12 minutes or until cooked through.

**3** Cook pasta as pkg directs. While Meatballs bake and pasta water comes to a boil, make Sauce: Heat oil in a large saucepan over medium heat. Add onion; cook 5 minutes, stirring often, until translucent. Add garlic, tomatoes, salt and pepper; bring to a boil, reduce heat and simmer 8 minutes or until slightly thickened (see Tip, left).

**4** Drain pasta in a colander; return to pot. Add about half the Sauce; toss to coat.

**5** Stir meatballs into remaining sauce. Spoon over pasta in bowls. Serve with grated cheese.

# Beef & Mushroom Ragu

## GROUND BEEF · SKILLET

YOU CAN MAKE THE SAUCE AHEAD AND ALSO SERVE IT ON SPAGHETTI.

2 Tbsp olive oil

8 oz white mushrooms, each cut in quarters

1 cup (1 large) chopped onion

1 Tbsp minced garlic

1 lb lean ground beef

28-oz can Italian peeled tomatoes

1 Tbsp tomato paste

1 tsp Italian herb seasoning

1 tsp sugar

½ tsp salt

¼ tsp freshly ground pepper

1 lb cheese-filled refrigerated or frozen ravioli

SERVE WITH: grated Parmesan cheese

**SERVES** 6
**TOTAL TIME:** About 40 minutes

**PER SERVING:** 551 cal,
28 g pro, 43 g car, 4 g fiber,
29 g fat (11 g sat fat), 122 mg
chol, 1,034 mg sod

**1** Heat 1 Tbsp oil in a large nonstick skillet over medium-high heat. Add mushrooms, onion and garlic; cook about 6 minutes, stirring often, until onion is soft. Remove mixture to a plate or bowl. Add beef to skillet and, breaking up clumps with a wooden spoon, cook about 6 minutes or until no longer pink.

**2** Add mushroom mixture, tomatoes, tomato paste, Italian seasoning, sugar, salt and pepper.

**3** Bring to a boil, reduce heat, cover and simmer 15 to 20 minutes until sauce has thickened and flavors have blended.

**4** While sauce cooks, cook ravioli as pkg directs. Drain in a colander and return to pot. Add remaining 1 Tbsp oil and toss to coat. Spoon into a serving dish; top with the meat sauce.

## PARMESAN CHEESE

Parmesan cheese is essential to the flavor of many pasta dishes, even when just sprinkled on at serving. A good Parmesan does not cut into neat slices and has a granular texture. The tiny crystals your tongue will detect are not, as you might think, salt, but are amino acids. The gold standard is Parmigiano-Reggiano from Italy, where Parmesan is typically aged 2 years or longer. Break off small chunks and eat them just as they are. To grate Parmesan, use a box grater, a Microplane grater or a food processor with the metal blade. A rotary grater also works well. Grate more cheese than you need and refrigerate it in an airtight container or buy the refrigerated kind.

# Cavatelli with Chicken & Broccoli

## CHICKEN CUTLETS · SKILLET

FRESH (REFRIGERATED) AND FROZEN PASTAS COOK MUCH MORE QUICKLY THAN DRIED.
OTHER SHORT-CUT PASTA SHAPES CAN BE SUBSTITUTED FOR CAVATELLI.

**SERVES** 4
**TOTAL TIME:** 30 minutes

**PER SERVING:** 571 cal, 30 g pro, 71 g car, 4 g fiber, 18 g fat (4 g sat fat), 38 mg chol, 439 mg sod

**DRIED VERSUS FRESH**
Fresh pasta is turning up more frequently in supermarkets, but it's not always the better choice. Fresh pasta is suitable for lighter sauces, while dried pasta complements robust, full-bodied ones. Fresh does cook much more quickly than dried. Most pasta today is made from 100% durum wheat flour (also known as semolina), a hard-wheat flour that produces high-quality pasta. Look for "enriched" on the label; it means that B vitamins and iron lost in the milling have been added back.

16-oz bag frozen cavatelli (short shells) or 12 oz dried cavatelli pasta

8 oz boneless chicken cutlets, cut in half lengthwise, then across in ½-in. wide strips

2 Tbsp flour

SAUCE
  4 Tbsp olive oil
  1½ Tbsp minced garlic
  8 oz (4 cups) fresh broccoli florets
  1 cup chicken broth
  ¼ tsp crushed red pepper (optional)

⅓ cup grated Parmesan cheese, plus additional to serve at table if you wish

**1** Cook pasta as pkg directs.

**2** While water comes to a boil and pasta cooks, put chicken and flour in large plastic food bag. Shake to coat chicken evenly.

**3** Heat 1 Tbsp oil in a large nonstick skillet over medium-high heat. Add chicken; cook 2 to 3 minutes, stirring often, until browned and cooked through. Remove to a plate. Reduce heat to low.

**4** Heat remaining 3 Tbsp oil in skillet. Add garlic; cook 30 seconds until fragrant. Stir in broccoli, broth and crushed pepper (if using). Bring to a boil, reduce heat, cover and simmer 5 minutes or until broccoli is tender.

**5** Drain pasta in a colander; return to pot or put in a bowl. Add Sauce, chicken and cheese; toss to mix and coat.

# Penne with Chicken, Asparagus & Lemon Alfredo Sauce

ONE-POT DINNER.

1 lb penne rigate (penne with ridges) pasta

1 lb asparagus, woody ends snapped off, spears cut in
     1½-in. lengths

SAUCE

     12 oz chicken tenders, cut diagonally in ½-in.-wide strips
        (see *Tenders and Tendons*, page 48)

     ½ tsp salt

     ½ cup flour

     1½ Tbsp olive oil

     16- or 17-oz jar Alfredo pasta sauce

     1 Tbsp freshly grated lemon peel

     3 Tbsp fresh lemon juice

     ¼ cup (1 oz) grated Parmesan cheese

1 large tomato, diced (1½ cups)

¼ cup chopped chives

Freshly ground pepper, to taste

> **SERVES** 6
> **TOTAL TIME:** 25 to 30 minutes
>
> **PER SERVING:** 576 cal,
> 29 g pro, 73 g car, 3 g fiber,
> 14 g fat (7 g sat fat), 86 mg
> chol, 1,192 mg sod

**1** Cook pasta as pkg directs, adding asparagus 4 minutes before pasta is done.

**2** While water comes to a boil and pasta cooks, sprinkle chicken with salt, then toss with flour to lightly coat.

**3** Heat oil in a large nonstick skillet over high heat. Add chicken; cook 3 minutes, stirring once or twice, until golden and just barely cooked through. Add Alfredo sauce, lemon peel, lemon juice and cheese. Bring to a simmer and cook 1 to 2 minutes until chicken is cooked through.

**4** Drain pasta and asparagus in a colander; return to pot or put in serving bowl. Immediately add Sauce, tomato, chives and pepper. Toss to mix and coat.

# Orzo with Chicken & Mint

## COOKED CHICKEN

ALTHOUGH ORZO PASTA IS THE SHAPE OF A GRAIN OF RICE, THE WORD TRANSLATES FROM THE ITALIAN AS "BARLEY." WHATEVER ITS LINGUISTIC IDENTITY, ORZO COOKS VERY QUICKLY, IN ABOUT 9 MINUTES. "RISI" IS A SIMILAR RICE-SHAPED PASTA YOU CAN USE INSTEAD.

**SERVES** 4
**TOTAL TIME:** About 20 minutes

**PER SERVING:** 403 cal, 21 g pro, 46 g car, 2 g fiber, 15 g fat (4 g sat fat), 44 mg chol, 342 mg sod

1¾ cups (12 oz) orzo (rice-shaped pasta)
1 large tomato, diced (1½ cups)
1½ cups (8 to 9 oz) diced cooked chicken
½ cup (2 oz) crumbled feta cheese
¼ cup olive oil
¼ cup chopped fresh mint
3 Tbsp fresh lemon juice
½ tsp salt
½ tsp freshly ground pepper

**1** Cook pasta as pkg directs.

**2** While water comes to a boil and pasta cooks, put tomato, chicken, feta, oil, mint, lemon juice, salt and pepper into a large bowl and toss to mix.

**3** Drain pasta in a colander; add to bowl and toss again.

# Farfalle with Chicken & Red Pepper-Basil Sauce

## CHICKEN BREAST · BLENDER OR FOOD PROCESSOR · SKILLET

**SERVES** 6
**TOTAL TIME:** About 30 minutes

**PER SERVING:** 459 cal, 28 g pro, 63 g car, 2 g fiber, 10 g fat (5 g sat fat), 70 mg chol, 596 mg sod

1 lb farfalle (bow-tie) pasta
12-oz jar roasted red peppers, drained
1 cup light cream
1 Tbsp olive oil
1 lb skinless, boneless chicken breast, cut in small chunks
1 Tbsp minced garlic
¼ cup chopped fresh basil
½ tsp salt
⅛ tsp crushed red pepper (optional)
GARNISH: basil sprigs

**1**  Cook pasta as pkg directs.

**2**  While water comes to a boil and pasta cooks, put roasted peppers and cream in a blender or food processor; process until almost smooth.

**3**  Heat oil in a large nonstick skillet over medium-high heat. Add chicken and garlic; cook 6 to 7 minutes, stirring 3 or 4 times, until chicken is browned. Stir in puréed pepper and cream, basil and salt. Simmer 3 to 4 minutes, until chicken is cooked through.

**4**  Scoop out ½ cup cooking water from pasta pot. Drain pasta in a colander; return to pot. Add chicken and sauce, the ½ cup of pasta cooking water and crushed red pepper (if using); toss to mix and coat. Garnish with basil.

# Straw & Hay with Prosciutto & Peas

### PROSCIUTTO · SKILLET

GOLDEN EGG FETTUCINE PLAYS "STRAW" AND SPINACH FETTUCCINE "HAY"
IN THIS TRADITIONAL ITALIAN DISH.

9 oz refrigerated spinach fettuccine (see FYI, right)
9 oz refrigerated egg fettuccine (see FYI, right)
2 cups (10 oz) frozen green peas
1 Tbsp olive oil
8 oz sliced mushrooms
4 oz sliced prosciutto, torn in strips (see *Specialty Hams*, page 135)
16- or 17-oz jar Alfredo pasta sauce.
½ cup (2 oz) shredded or grated Parmesan cheese
½ tsp freshly ground pepper

SERVES 4
TOTAL TIME: 15 minutes

PER SERVING: 763 cal,
35 g pro, 89 g car, 5 g fiber,
30 g fat (13 g sat fat), 217 mg
chol, 1,912 mg sod

FYI: Fresh, refrigerated pasta cooks much more quickly than dried.

**1**  Bring a large pot of lightly salted water to a boil. Add fettuccine and peas; cook as pasta pkgs direct.

**2**  While water comes to a boil and pasta cooks, heat oil in a large nonstick skillet over medium-high heat. Add mushrooms and cook about 6 minutes, stirring often, until lightly browned and tender. Stir in prosciutto strips and Alfredo sauce; heat through.

**3**  Drain pasta in a colander; put back in pot or in serving bowl. Add mushroom sauce, Parmesan cheese and pepper. Toss to mix and coat.

# Linguine with Clams & Parsley

CANNED CLAMS (AND PASTA) ARE GREAT TO HAVE ON HAND FOR THOSE TIMES THERE'S NOTHING IN THE HOUSE TO EAT. ALTHOUGH THE GENEROUS AMOUNT OF PARSLEY HAS A LARGE IMPACT ON THE FLAVOR, IF YOU DON'T HAVE ANY THE SAUCE WILL STILL BE GOOD.

**SERVES** 4
**TOTAL TIME:** 20 minutes

**PER SERVING:** 439 cal, 25 g pro, 72 g car, 3 g fiber, 3 g fat (0 g sat fat), 32 mg chol, 607 mg sod

12 oz linguine pasta
½ cup dry white wine or chicken broth
½ cup finely chopped onion
2 Tbsp minced garlic
Two 6.5-oz cans chopped clams, drained; juice reserved
    (see *Mussels and Clams*, page 34)
1 cup chicken broth
¾ cup chopped fresh parsley
2 tsp freshly grated lemon peel
3 Tbsp fresh lemon juice
½ tsp salt
⅛ tsp freshly ground pepper

**1** Cook linguine as pkg directs.

**2** While water comes to a boil and pasta cooks, put wine, onion and garlic in a medium saucepan over medium heat and bring to a simmer. Cover and cook 5 minutes or until onion is soft.

**3** Add reserved clam juice and chicken broth. Bring to a simmer and cook uncovered 3 to 5 minutes for flavors to blend. Stir in clams; heat through.

**4** Drain pasta in a colander; return to pot. Add clam sauce, parsley, lemon peel, lemon juice, salt and pepper. Toss to mix and coat.

### FISH SAUCE
A pungent, salty seasoning, fish sauce is know throughout Southeast Asia. Made from fermented salted fish, it varies in quality. Like extra-virgin olive oil (the first pressing of the olives), the first liquid poured off from the salted fish is considered the finest. Don't be put off by your first sniff; you will find that fish sauce, when used judiciously, adds wonderful flavor to food, especially dressings like the one here.

# Pad Thai

## SHRIMP · SKILLET

LOOK FOR RICE STICKS, FISH SAUCE AND RICE OR RICE WINE VINEGAR IN THE ASIAN FOOD SECTION OF YOUR MARKET. THE RICE STICKS WILL STILL BE A BIT STIFF AFTER SOAKING BUT WILL SOFTEN UP DURING COOKING. SERVE THIS REFRESHING DISH WARM, RIGHT AFTER YOU'VE ADDED THE LIME-JUICE DRESSING.

8 oz ⅛-in.-wide flat rice sticks (see *Rice Sticks*, right)

¼ cup rice vinegar

¼ cup fish sauce (see *Fish Sauce*, facing page)

2 Tbsp fresh lime juice

1 Tbsp sugar

3 Tbsp peanut oil or other vegetable oil

1 lb raw, peeled and deveined shrimp (any size) (see *Deveining Shrimp*, page 103)

1 Tbsp minced garlic

2 large eggs

8 thinly sliced radishes

4 scallions, cut in 1-in. lengths

¼ cup dry-roasted unsalted peanuts, finely chopped

¼ cup finely chopped fresh cilantro

**SERVES** 4
**TOTAL TIME:** 30 minutes

**PER SERVING:** 568 cal, 31 g pro, 63 g car, 1 g fiber, 21 g fat (4 g sat fat), 279 mg chol, 1,198 mg sod

**RICE STICKS**
These flat noodles, about ⅛ in. wide, are translucent white and are made from rice flour. They do not require boiling. After soaking them in hot water for 20 minutes drain, then toss with a stir-fry in a skillet to soften more or add to a hot soup. Almost hair-like rice noodles are sometimes deep-fried and scattered on top of a cold salad.

**1** Soak rice sticks in warm water to cover 20 minutes until softened. Drain.

**2** Meanwhile, mix vinegar, fish sauce, lime juice and sugar in a cup.

**3** Heat 1 Tbsp oil in a large nonstick skillet over medium-high heat. Add shrimp and garlic; cook 1 to 3 minutes, stirring two or three times, until cooked through. Transfer to a plate.

**4** Heat remaining 2 Tbsp oil over medium-high heat. Add eggs; stir just until set. Add radishes, scallions, drained rice sticks and vinegar mixture. Cook, stirring, 1 minute or until rice sticks soften and wilt.

**5** Place on a serving platter; top with shrimp, peanuts and cilantro. Toss to mix.

# Pasta with Shrimp & Eggplant

SHRIMP · SKILLET

**SERVES** 4
**TOTAL TIME:** 30 minutes

**PER SERVING:** 474 cal, 32 g pro, 63 g car, 8 g fiber, 13 g fat (4 g sat fat), 159 mg chol, 998 mg sod

8 oz whole-wheat or regular spaghetti

2 tsp olive oil

1½-lb eggplant, cut in ¾-in. chunks

1 red pepper, cut in thin strips

1 yellow pepper, cut in thin strips

¾ cup thinly sliced red onion

1 tsp dried oregano

1 lb raw, peeled and deveined large shrimp (see *Deveining Shrimp*, page 103)

10 pitted kalamata olives, halved

¾ cup (3 oz) crumbled feta cheese

Garnish: chopped fresh parsley

## FIBER AND PASTA

Whole-wheat pasta contains about 4 times the fiber of regular pasta and slightly more protein, vitamins and minerals. Try mixing whole-wheat pasta with regular pasta. Choose matching shapes so they'll cook in the same amount of time in the same pot.

**1** Cook pasta as pkg directs.

**2** While water comes to a boil and pasta cooks, heat oil in a large nonstick skillet over medium-high heat. Add eggplant; cook about 6 minutes, stirring several times, until almost soft.

**3** Add pepper strips, onion and oregano. Cook about 6 minutes, stirring often, until crisp-tender. Stir in shrimp, cover and cook about 3 minutes, stirring once, until shrimp are just done.

**4** Just before draining pasta in a colander, scoop out ½ cup cooking water. Put pasta back in pot, add ½ cup cooking water and the eggplant mixture. Toss to mix and coat. Pour into a serving bowl. Add olives, cheese and parsley. Toss again just before serving.

Pasta with Shrimp & Eggplant *(page 32)*

Spaghetti with Meatballs *(page 24)*

Baked Macaroni & Cheese *(page 40)*

Ham & Cheese Lasagna *(page 42)*

# Sicilian Pasta with Tuna

## CANNED TUNA

There are days in a magazine test kitchen when no one is testing recipes. Editors are either writing recipes at a computer or prepping and packing for a photo shoot. Going out to get a sandwich isn't even an option. On one of those days an editor put together this simple and satisfying dish.

12 oz linguine fini pasta
26-oz jar green and black olive pasta sauce (Puttanesca)
6-oz can solid white tuna in oil, drained and flaked

**SERVES** 4
**TOTAL TIME:** 20 minutes

**PER SERVING:** 544 cal, 25 g pro, 77 g car, 7 g fiber, 14 g fat (3 g sat fat), 7 mg chol, 1,209 mg sod

**1** Cook pasta as pkg directs.

**2** When pasta is almost cooked, heat pasta sauce in a medium saucepan over low heat, stirring occasionally. Add tuna; simmer about 2 minutes to blend flavors. Spoon over pasta; toss to mix and coat.

# Fettuccine with Smoked Salmon

## SMOKED SALMON

Equally good for family or company.

12 oz fettuccine
4 oz smoked salmon, cut in strips
6.5-oz container cucumber-dill spreadable cheese
⅓ cup sliced scallions
⅓ cup chopped fresh dill
1 Tbsp capers, rinsed
¼ tsp freshly ground pepper

**SERVES** 4
**TOTAL TIME:** 20 minutes

**PER SERVING:** 453 cal, 20 g pro, 68 g car, 2 g fiber, 11 g fat (5 g sat fat), 37 mg chol, 790 mg sod

**1** Cook pasta as pkg directs. Scoop out ½ cup cooking water before draining pasta in a colander.

**2** While water comes to a boil and pasta cooks, put salmon, cheese, scallions, dill, capers and pepper into a large serving bowl. Add pasta and the ½ cup cooking water; toss to mix and coat.

# Spaghetti with Mussels

MUSSELS · DUTCH OVEN

Farmed mussels are now easily available refrigerated in plastic bags. There are no "beards," the silky filaments the mussels use to latch onto stones, to pull off. And scrubbing is no longer necessary; rinse the shells well with cold water and discard any open ones that don't close when you tap them on the counter.

SERVES 4
TOTAL TIME: 25 to 30 minutes

PER SERVING: 567 cal,
24 g pro, 77 g car, 4 g fiber,
14 g fat (3 g sat fat), 35 mg
chol, 781 mg sod

12 oz spaghetti
2 Tbsp olive oil, preferably extra-virgin
1 Tbsp stick butter
1 cup chopped onion
1 Tbsp minced garlic
1 tsp fennel seeds
1 cup dry white wine or chicken broth
14.5-oz can petite diced tomatoes, drained
3 lb mussels (see *Mussels and Clams*, below)

TIP: Put a large empty bowl on the dinner table for discarded shells.

1 Cook pasta as pkg directs.

2 While water comes to a boil and pasta cooks, heat oil and butter in a 5- to 6-qt heavy Dutch oven or pot over medium-high heat. Add onion, garlic and fennel seeds; cook 4 to 5 minutes, stirring several times, until onion is golden. Add wine, reduce heat and simmer 3 to 4 minutes. Add tomatoes; increase heat to medium-high.

3 Add mussels to sauce (it won't cover them). Cover and cook, stirring once, 6 to 7 minutes until shells open. Discard any that do not open.

4 Drain pasta in a colander. Add to sauce, toss gently and serve.

## MUSSELS AND CLAMS
When buying mussels, clams and other bivalves in the shell, make sure the shells are closed tight (shows the bivalve is alive) and that most of the shells are whole, not broken nor chipped.
It is important that live mussels and clams have air; a good fish shop will never seal them tightly in a plastic bag but will always pierce a few holes in the bag so the bivalves don't suffocate. If you are not going to cook them right away, tip them into a dry bowl and cover them with damp paper towels for up to two day. Do not store on ice, in water, or, of course, in plastic.

# Caesar Spaghetti

WHY DOES ONE ALWAYS HAVE ONLY ROLLED ANCHOVIES ON HAND WHEN A RECIPE CALLS FOR FLAT? HERE IT WOULDN'T BE A PROBLEM; JUST UNROLL THEM. ALTHOUGH ANCHOVIES ARE STANDARD IN CAESAR SALAD, YOU CAN LEAVE THEM OUT.

12 oz spaghetti

2 Tbsp oil

½ cup plain dried bread crumbs

1 Tbsp minced garlic

1 chicken bouillon cube (for 1 cup broth)

1-lb head escarole, cut crosswise in strips (9 cups)

2-oz can flat anchovies, drained

¾ lb plum tomatoes, cut in 1-in. chunks (2½ cups)

⅓ cup grated Parmesan cheese

SERVES 4
TOTAL TIME: About 30 minutes

PER SERVING: 518 cal,
21 g pro, 81 g car, 6 g fiber,
12 g fat (3 g sat fat), 11 mg
chol, 1,078 mg sod

1 Cook pasta as pkg directs.

2 While pasta cooks, heat 1 Tbsp oil in a large nonstick skillet over medium-high heat. Add bread crumbs and, stirring often, cook 2 to 3 minutes until toasted. Pour into a small bowl. Wipe out skillet.

3 Heat remaining 1 Tbsp oil in skillet over medium heat. Add garlic and cook, stirring often, 1 minute or until fragrant. Add 1 cup water and the bouillon cube. Bring to a boil, stirring to dissolve cube.

4 Add escarole, cover and cook 3 minutes, stirring once or twice, until just wilted.

5 Drain pasta in a colander and return to pot. Add anchovies; toss with pasta until anchovies break up. Add escarole and tomatoes; toss to mix and coat. Pour into serving bowl(s). Stir cheese into bread crumbs; sprinkle over pasta.

# Orecchiette Alla Rustica

## VEGETARIAN · SKILLET

ORECCHIETTE MEANS "LITTLE EARS," BUT BEST NOT TELL THE KIDS THAT BEFORE DINNER.

**SERVES** 6
**TOTAL TIME:** 25 minutes

**PER SERVING:** 419 cal, 14 g pro, 70 g car, 5 g fiber, 9 g fat (2 g sat fat), 3 mg chol, 609 mg sod

1 lb orecchiette (tiny disk-shaped) pasta

SAUCE

2 Tbsp olive oil

3 large cloves garlic, thinly sliced

15-oz can cannellini beans, not drained

⅓ cup pitted kalamata olives, cut in half

½ cup diced, drained roasted red pepper (from a jar)

½ cup chopped fresh parsley

Freshly ground pepper, to taste

¼ cup grated Romano cheese

**1** Cook pasta as pkg directs.

**2** While water comes to a boil and pasta cooks, heat oil in a large, deep skillet over medium heat. Add garlic and stir about 1 minute, just until golden. Immediately add beans with their liquid, the olives, the roasted pepper and about half the parsley. Heat until hot, stirring often.

**3** Just before draining pasta scoop out ½ cup of the cooking water and add it to the skillet. Drain pasta in a colander; add to skillet along with remaining parsley and black pepper. Toss to mix and coat. Transfer to serving bowl or plates; sprinkle with cheese.

# Stovetop Ziti

## VEGETARIAN

**SERVES** 6
**TOTAL TIME:** 25 minutes

**PER SERVING:** 478 cal, 25 g pro, 74 g car, 5 g fiber, 10 g fat (3 g sat fat), 14 mg chol, 1,257 mg sod

1 lb ziti pasta

12 oz (6 cups) fresh broccoli florets

SAUCE

26-oz jar marinara sauce

1 cup (9 oz) skim ricotta cheese (see FYI, facing page)

¾ cup (4 oz) diced part-skim mozzarella cheese

⅓ cup chopped fresh parsley

¼ cup (1 oz) grated Parmesan cheese

**1** Cook pasta as pkg directs, adding broccoli 4 minutes before pasta is done.

**2** Shortly before pasta is cooked, put marinara sauce and about half the ricotta in a saucepan. Stir over medium-low heat until hot.

**3** Drain pasta and broccoli in a colander; return to pot. Add sauce mixture; toss to mix and coat. Immediately add mozzarella and about half the parsley and Parmesan. Toss until mozzarella melts.

**4** Transfer to serving bowl; sprinkle with remaining parsley and Parmesan. Top with spoonfuls of remaining ricotta.

> **FYI:** Ricotta's rich, slightly sweet taste makes it hard to believe that ricotta (the word means re-cooked) is a thrifty product made by heating the whey left over from making a different (but also cooked) cheese.

## Farfalle with Pesto, Goat Cheese & Grape Tomatoes

### VEGETARIAN · FOOD PROCESSOR OR BLENDER

IT'S EASY TO BUY PESTO BUT THERE'S NOTHING BETTER THAN YOUR OWN FRESH HOMEMADE. WHEN BASIL IS IN SEASON, MAKE SEVERAL BATCHES AND FREEZE THEM.

1 lb farfalle (bow-tie) pasta

PESTO
  ¼ cup chopped walnuts
  ¼ cup extra-virgin olive oil
  2 cups loosely packed fresh basil leaves
  2 small cloves garlic, smashed
  ½ tsp crushed red pepper
  ½ tsp salt

4 oz soft goat cheese, broken or cut in small pieces
1 pt grape, pear or cherry tomatoes, cut in half

> **SERVES 6**
> **TOTAL TIME:** 30 minutes
>
> **PER SERVING:** 477 cal, 16 g pro, 61 g car, 4 g fiber, 20 g fat (6 g sat fat), 15 mg chol, 559 mg sod

**1** Cook pasta as pkg directs.

**2** While water comes to a boil and pasta cooks, make Pesto: Put walnuts, oil, basil, garlic, crushed pepper and salt in a food processor or blender; process until a thick purée (if using blender you will need to push down leaves several times).

**3** Just before draining pasta, scoop out ¼ cup of the cooking water. Drain pasta in a colander; transfer to serving bowl. Add half the goat cheese and tomatoes. Toss to mix. Add Pesto and the ¼ cup cooking water; toss to coat. Sprinkle remaining goat cheese over top.

# Farfalle with Mushroom Ragout

## VEGETARIAN · SKILLET

HERE THE FRENCH WORD "RAGOUT," CLOSE KIN OF ITALIAN RAGU (SEE PAGE 25) MEANS
A STEW OF SOME KIND. THIS ONE, RICH WITH CREAM, IS A WONDERFUL INDULGENCE.

**SERVES** 4
**TOTAL TIME:** 30 minutes

**PER SERVING:** 761 cal, 16 g
pro, 76 g car, 4 g fiber, 45 g fat
(22 g sat fat), 122 mg chol,
626 mg sod

12 oz farfalle (bow-tie) pasta
3 Tbsp olive oil
1 cup finely chopped onion
2 tsp minced garlic
8 oz portobello mushrooms (see Tip, left), coarsely chopped
8 oz shiitake mushrooms (see Tip, left), coarsely chopped
½ cup dry white wine
1½ cups heavy (whipping) cream
½ tsp salt
¼ tsp freshly ground pepper
1 Tbsp thin strips fresh sage leaves or 1 tsp dried sage (see Tip, left)

**1** Cook pasta as pkg directs.

**2** While water comes to a boil and pasta cooks, heat 1 Tbsp oil in a
large skillet over medium heat. Add onion; cook about 6 minutes,
stirring often, until lightly browned. Stir in garlic and cook 30 seconds or until fragrant. Transfer to a large serving bowl.

**3** Add remaining 2 Tbsp oil to skillet, increase heat to medium-
high, add mushrooms and cook, stirring occasionally, 8 minutes or
until lightly browned and tender. Add wine; boil until about half has
evaporated. Stir in cream, salt and pepper. Bring to a boil; simmer
until slightly thickened.

**4** Drain pasta in a colander; add to serving bowl along with mushrooms and sage. Toss to mix.

TIP: Discard the tough
stems of shiitake mush-
rooms. To prepare portobel-
los, cut off end of the stems
but chop up and use the rest
of the tender stem. To shred
sage leaves, stack about six
on cutting board, then cut in
narrow strips.

## PASTA SHAPES

There are literally hundreds of pasta shapes and sizes available today and the confusion is increased by manufacturers who often use different names for the same shape. On most packages the name of the shape is given only in Italian. The following is a description of some of the more common pasta shapes and a literal translation of the name:

Agnolotti ("priest's caps"): Small crescent-shaped stuffed pasta

Anelli ("small rings"): Just what it says

Campanelle ("bellflower"): Flower-shaped pasta

Cannelloni ("large reeds"): Large round tubes often stuffed, covered with a sauce and baked

Capelli d'angelo ("angel hair"): Long, extremely fine strands of pasta

Capelletti ("little hats"): Small, hat-shaped stuffed pasta

Cavatappi ("corkscrew"): Short, thin, ridged spirals

Cavatelli ("little plugs"): Short, narrow, ripple-edged shells

Conchiglie ("conch shells"): Small, very short macaroni, often used in soup

Farfalle ("butterflies"): Bow-tie-shaped pasta

Fettuccine ("little ribbons"): Thin, flat ribbons about 1/4 in. wide

Fusilli ("little springs"): Short spirals

Linguine ("little tongues"): Flat, narrow ribbons about 1/8 in. wide

Linguini fini ("very narrow ribbons"): Very narrow ribbons

Lumache ("snails"): Large shells that are usually stuffed

Orecchiette ("little ears"): Small disk-shaped pasta

Orzo ("barley"): The size and shape of a grain of rice

Pastina ("little dough"): Tiny shapes used in soups

Penne ("pens" or "quills"): Diagonally-cut short tubes

Penne rigate: Penne with ridged sides

Radiatore ("little radiators"): Short, chunky pasta with rippled edges

Rigatoni ("with lines"): Small, curved grooved macaroni

Riso ("rice"): Rice-shaped pasta

Spaghetti ("little strings"): Long, thin, round strands

Stelline ("little stars"): Tiny star-shaped pasta with a hole in the middle; used in soups

Tagliatelle ("cut"): Long, flat ribbons about 1/4 in. wide

Vermicelli ("little worms"): Very thin strands of spaghetti

Ziti ("bridegrooms"): Long, straight-cut tubes that range in length from 2 to 12 in.

# Baked Macaroni & Cheese

VEGETARIAN · OVEN · SHALLOW 3-QT BAKING DISH

To dress up this family favorite at no extra cost,
ditch the elbows and try a new pasta shape.

**SERVES** 8
**PREP:** 20 minutes
**BAKE:** About 30 minutes

**PER SERVING:** 441 cal,
20 g pro, 54 g car, 2 g fiber,
16 g fat (9 g sat fat), 49 mg
chol, 736 mg sod

1 lb campanelle (bellflowers), radiatore (radiators) or fusilli
(little springs) pasta

2 tsp butter

1 cup fresh bread crumbs (from 2 slices white sandwich bread)
(see *Fresh Bread Crumbs*, page 66)

2 cups (8 oz) shredded extra-sharp Cheddar cheese

¼ cup (1 oz) grated Parmesan cheese

3½ cups whole milk

¼ cup flour

½ tsp minced garlic

1 tsp mustard

¾ tsp salt

**1** Cook pasta as pkg directs.

**2** While water comes to a boil and pasta cooks, heat oven to 350°F
and grease a shallow 3-qt baking dish.

**3** Melt butter in a large saucepan. Add bread crumbs and cook over
medium heat, stirring often, 3 minutes or until golden and crisp.
Scrape into a small bowl and stir in 2 Tbsp each Cheddar and Parmesan cheese.

**4** Wipe saucepan clean. Add milk, flour and garlic; whisk until
blended. Then, whisking frequently, bring to a boil over medium-
high heat. Reduce heat and simmer 2 to 3 minutes until thickened.
Remove from heat; stir in remaining cheeses, mustard and salt.

**5** As soon as pasta is cooked, drain it in a colander, rinse with cold
water and let drain.

**6** Pour pasta into baking dish. Stir in sauce. Sprinkle evenly with
crumb mixture.

**7** Bake 30 minutes or until hot and bubbly around edges.

## STORING PASTA

Dried pasta can be stored
in a cool dry place almost
indefinitely. However dried
whole-wheat pasta should
be used relatively quickly.
Tightly wrapped fresh pasta
can be refrigerated up to 5
days or double-wrapped
and frozen up to 4 months.
Frozen pasta does not have
to be thawed before
cooking.

# Baked Rigatoni with Mini Turkey Meatballs

## TURKEY MEATBALLS · OVEN · 2½-QT CASSEROLE

8 oz rigatoni (short, ridged tubes) pasta

32-oz jar fat-free marinara sauce

18 fully cooked, appetizer-size turkey meatballs (from a 24-oz pkg)

15-oz container part-skim ricotta cheese

½ cup (2 oz) grated Parmesan cheese

GARNISH: thin strips fresh basil leaves

**SERVES** 4
**PREP:** 20 minutes
**BAKE:** About 35 minutes

**PER SERVING:** 610 cal, 38 g pro, 77 g car, 6 g fiber, 18 g fat (9 g sat fat), 77 mg chol, 1,358 mg sod

**1** Cook pasta as pkg directs and drain in a colander. While pasta cooks, heat oven to 375°F. Have a 2½-qt casserole ready.

**2** Toss pasta, marinara sauce and meatballs in a large bowl to mix. Spread half in the casserole; top with spoonfuls of half the ricotta, then sprinkle with half the Parmesan cheese. Repeat layers once. Cover with lid or foil.

**3** Bake 35 minutes or until hot and edges bubble. Sprinkle with basil.

---

### PASTA: HOW MUCH TO COOK

The U.S. Department of Agriculture uses 1 cup cooked pasta as a serving. How many servings are right for you or other family members depends on size, age and calorie needs.

To get 1 cup cooked pasta (slightly more of egg noodles), cook:
· 2 oz spaghetti or other long pasta
· 2 oz (just over ½ cup) rigatoni or other short pasta
· 4 oz (1 cup) egg noodles

Most of the pasta recipes in this book call for 12 oz dry pasta. The approximate yield from 12 oz uncooked is:
· small to medium shapes, 4 cups cooked
· spaghetti or other long pasta, 4 cups cooked
· egg noodles, 3¾ cups cooked

The longer pasta cooks, the more it swells. Overcook a pound of pasta and you will end up with a big bowl of mushy, pasty pasta.

# Ham & Cheese Lasagna

**HAM · OVEN · 13 x 9-IN. BAKING DISH**

A COMPLETE MEAL IN ONE DISH.

**SERVES 8**
**PREP:** 25 minutes
**BAKE:** About 1 hour

**PER SERVING:** 543 cal,
34 g pro, 41 g car, 3 g fiber,
28 g fat (15 g sat fat), 148 mg
chol, 1,864 mg sod

**FYI:** Mustard powder is ground mustard seed. Find small tins of it near other spices.

**FYI:** Once opened, a jar of ground nutmeg loses much of its flavor after about a year. Whole nutmegs retain their flavor and aroma for years; grate what you need when you need it. Use a Microplane grater or other fine grater over a sheet of wax paper. Or just scrape the nutmeg with a small knife. You'll be surprised at how easy it is to grate your own.

CHEESE SAUCE
- Two 10.75-oz cans condensed Cheddar cheese soup
- 1 soup can 1% lowfat milk
- 14.5-oz can no-salt-added diced tomatoes, drained, large pieces cut up
- 1 Tbsp mustard powder (see FYI, left)
- 1 Tbsp instant minced onion
- ½ cup (2 oz) shredded Cheddar cheese
- ¼ cup (1 oz) grated Parmesan cheese
- 15-oz container ricotta cheese (1⅔ cups)
- 2 large eggs
- ¼ cup (1 oz) grated Parmesan cheese
- ¾ tsp grated or ground nutmeg (see FYI, left)
- 12 flat no-boil, oven-ready lasagna noodles (see FYI, facing page)
- 16-oz bag frozen chopped broccoli, thawed, pressed dry on paper towels
- 1½ cups (6 oz) shredded Cheddar cheese
- 8 oz thinly sliced baked Virginia ham (see *Specialty Hams*, page 135)
- 12-oz jar roasted red peppers, well drained, chopped

**1** Heat oven to 375°F. Lightly coat a 13 x 9-in. baking dish with cooking spray.

**2** CHEESE SAUCE: Put soup, milk, tomatoes, mustard, onion, Cheddar and Parmesan into a 2-qt saucepan; whisk until blended. Heat, stirring with whisk, until cheeses melt. Remove from heat.

**3** Put ricotta, eggs, Parmesan and nutmeg into a bowl. Stir until thoroughly combined.

**4** Layer lasagna in prepared baking dish as follows: Spread 1 cup Cheese Sauce over bottom, top with 4 overlapping noodles, half the ricotta mixture, the broccoli, 1½ cups Cheese Sauce and ½ cup Cheddar cheese.

**5** Add 4 more noodles, the remaining ricotta mixture, the ham, ½ cup Cheddar cheese, the chopped peppers and 1½ cups Cheese Sauce.

**6** Finish with rest of noodles, Cheese Sauce and Cheddar cheese. Cover tightly with foil.

**7** Bake 50 minutes or until sauce bubbles and noodles are tender. Uncover; bake 10 minutes longer. Let stand 15 minutes before cutting and serving.

**FYI:** Package directions for flat oven-ready lasagna noodles suggest overlapping them slightly while directions for the ridged kind say to leave space between each noodle and between noodles and edge of dish.

# Savory Noodle Pudding

### VEGETARIAN · OVEN · SHALLOW 2-QT BAKING DISH

A DELICIOUS SIDE DISH FOR MEAT OR POULTRY OR A VEGETARIAN MAIN DISH FOR 4.

8 oz medium egg noodles
2 Tbsp stick butter
2 cups chopped onions
8-oz brick ⅓-less-fat cream cheese (Neufchâtel), softened
2 large eggs
16-oz container reduced-fat sour cream
½ tsp salt
½ tsp freshly ground pepper

SERVES 9
PREP: 20 minutes
BAKE: 25 to 30 minutes

PER SERVING: 291 cal, 11 g pro, 24 g car, 1 g fiber, 17 g fat (9 g sat fat), 113 mg chol, 308 mg sod

**1** Cook noodles as pkg directs and drain in a colander.

**2** While water comes to a boil and pasta cooks, heat oven to 350°F. Have a shallow 2-qt baking dish ready.

**3** Melt butter in a large nonstick skillet over medium heat. Add onions and cook 8 to 10 minutes, stirring often, until golden brown and tender.

**4** Whisk cream cheese in a large bowl until smooth. Stir in eggs, sour cream, salt and pepper, then noodles and onions. Spread in ungreased baking dish.

**5** Bake uncovered 25 to 30 minutes until cream cheese mixture sets and noodles brown on top.

# Roasted-Vegetable Lasagna

**SERVES** 8
**PREP:** 35 to 40 minutes
**BAKE:** About 45 minutes

**PER SERVING:** 346 cal, 13 g pro, 36 g car, 3 g fiber, 18 g fat (8 g sat fat), 67 mg chol, 889 mg sod

**FYI:** Package directions for flat oven-ready lasagna noodles suggest overlapping them slightly while directions for the ridged kind say to leave space between each noodle and between noodles and edge of dish.

Garlic-flavor cooking spray
3 zucchini (about 6 oz each), sliced in ½-in.-thick rounds
3 yellow squash (about 6 oz each), sliced in ½-in.-thick rounds
3 red peppers, cut in long ½-in.-wide strips
16- or 17-oz jar Alfredo pasta sauce
9 no-boil, oven-ready lasagna noodles (see FYI, left)
1½ cups marinara sauce
1½ cups (6 oz) shredded mozzarella cheese
3 Tbsp grated Parmesan cheese

**1** Position racks to divide oven in thirds. Heat to 450°F. Coat 2 rimmed baking sheets and a 13 x 9-in. baking dish with garlic spray.

**2** Distribute vegetables evenly between the 2 prepared baking sheets, spreading them into a single layer. Coat vegetables with garlic spray.

**3** Roast 12 minutes, switch position of pans and roast 12 minutes longer or until vegetables are tender. Remove from oven; reduce temperature to 375°F.

**4** Spread ¾ cup Alfredo sauce in baking dish. Lay 3 noodles crosswise on sauce. Cover with ¾ cup marinara sauce; top with 2 cups roasted vegetables. Sprinkle with ½ cup shredded mozzarella and 1 Tbsp grated Parmesan cheese. Top with 3 more noodles, the remaining Alfredo sauce, another 2 cups vegetables, ½ cup mozzarella and 1 Tbsp grated Parmesan cheese. Finish with layers of remaining noodles, marinara sauce, vegetables and cheeses.

**5** Cover tightly with foil. Bake 45 minutes until tender all the way through when pierced with knife. Uncover; let stand 5 minutes before cutting.

# Fresh Tomato & Basil Sauce with Pasta

## VEGETARIAN

THIS SIMPLE (AND WONDERFUL) DISH NEEDS GOOD QUALITY OLIVE OIL, FLAVORFUL TOMATOES (USE ONES LABELED "VINE-RIPENED" WHEN LOCAL ONES ARE OUT OF SEASON), GARLIC, LOTS OF GOOD FRESH BASIL AND, IF YOU CAN, FRESHLY GRATED PARMESAN TO GO WITH IT.

12 oz spaghetti
¼ cup plus 1 Tbsp extra-virgin olive oil
5 cloves garlic, thinly sliced
2 lb tomatoes, chopped (3 cups)
¾ cup torn fresh basil leaves
½ tsp salt
Freshly ground pepper, to taste
SERVE WITH: grated Parmesan cheese

SERVES 4
TOTAL TIME: 20 minutes

PER SERVING: 514 cal, 13 g pro, 74 g car, 5 g fiber, 20 g fat (3 g sat fat), 0 mg chol, 604 mg sod

1  Cook pasta as pkg directs.

2  Meanwhile heat the ¼ cup oil in a small skillet. Add garlic; stir over low heat 1 minute or until it begins to change color. Immediately remove from heat and stir in the 1 Tbsp oil.

3  Drain pasta in a colander and return to pot. Add the garlic oil, tomatoes, basil, salt and pepper. Toss to mix and coat. Serve with Parmesan.

# Chicken & Turkey

Today, chicken appears on the dinner table at least once, if not twice, a week. And who can be surprised: It's available in so many forms, with or without skin or bones, it can be cooked quickly or slowly depending on your choice of recipe, it fits in well with the desire to eat less fat and fewer calories, and it's very easy on the wallet. But perhaps the top reason for enjoying chicken is that it is a great base for flavors and seasonings from all over the world. All the above holds true for turkey, too, which has graduated from a once-a-year festive appearance, whole, on the Thanksgiving table, to being a flavorful choice any night and available in many forms. This chapter offers a large and varied selection of recipes designed to please just about everyone. A quick glance under each recipe title will tell you which cut or form of chicken or turkey that recipe calls for and give you an idea of how it's prepared (skillet, oven, slow cooker, grill).

# Chicken Saltimbocca with Beans & Spinach

## BONELESS BREAST HALVES · SKILLET

Enjoy the smooth, rich flavor of prosciutto (Specialty hams, page 135) with the delicate chicken and you will understand why the Italians named this dish (often made with veal) "saltimbocca," or "jump in the mouth."

**SERVES 4**
**TOTAL TIME:** 15 to 20 minutes

**PER SERVING:** 435 cal, 47 g pro, 32 g car, 9 g fiber, 13 g fat (3 g sat fat), 99 mg chol, 896 mg sod

### TENDERS AND TENDONS

When you buy breast halves there is often a long, thicker piece on one side—the chicken **tender** (tenderloin). Many cooks like to pull it off so the breast is an equal thickness and cooks evenly. When you make breasts, wrap the tenders in plastic wrap and freeze them in a ziptop bag until you have enough to make a meal. From one end of some tenders a translucent silvery string—a **tendon**—extends. It can get tough when cooked. To remove it, lay the tender flat on a cutting board with the white tendon closest to you. Hold onto its end. Angle a sharp knife and slide it between meat and tendon, while gently pulling on the tendon.

⅓ cup flour
⅛ tsp salt
⅛ tsp freshly ground pepper
4 skinless, boneless chicken-breast halves (about 5 oz each), tenders removed (see *Tenders and Tendons*, left), trimmed of visible fat
1 Tbsp oil
1 Tbsp chopped fresh sage or 1 tsp dried
4 thin slices prosciutto (about ½ oz each)
½ cup chicken broth
1 Tbsp fresh lemon juice
2 tsp stick butter

BEANS
    19-oz can cannellini beans, drained and rinsed
    ¼ cup chopped roasted red peppers
    1 Tbsp oil
    ⅛ tsp salt
    ⅛ tsp freshly ground pepper

9 oz baby spinach in microwaveable bag
Garnish: **sage leaves**

**1** Mix flour, salt and pepper in a large plastic food bag. Add chicken and shake to coat. Remove chicken, shaking off excess flour.

**2** Heat oil in a large nonstick skillet over medium-high heat. Add chicken, cover and cook, turning once, 10 minutes or until golden and cooked. Put on plates, sprinkle with sage and top with prosciutto.

**3** Add broth and lemon juice to skillet. Increase heat to high and boil until about half the liquid has evaporated. Whisk in butter until melted. Drizzle sauce over chicken.

**4** Meanwhile, mix Bean ingredients in a bowl, cover and microwave until hot. Microwave spinach as bag directs. Serve with the chicken.

Chicken Saltimbocca with
Beans & Spinach *(page 48)*

Crunchy Chicken Fingers with Coleslaw *(page 54)*

Chicken with Olives *(page 57)*

Lemon-Garlic Roast Chicken *(page 64)*

# Thai Chicken Curry

SERVE OVER RICE. TRY BASMATI RICE IF YOU'RE NOT FAMILIAR WITH IT. IT'S A LONG-GRAIN RICE THAT'S A FAVORITE IN INDIA. TEXMATI IS A SIMILAR RICE THAT WAS BRED IN—SURPRISE—TEXAS.

1 lb skinless, boneless chicken breasts, cut in 1-in. chunks
2 tsp curry powder
2 tsp vegetable oil
1 large green or red pepper, sliced
1 cup finely chopped onion
2 tsp minced garlic
14-oz can coconut milk (not cream of coconut)
8-oz can pineapple chunks in juice, not drained
1 tsp salt
¼ tsp crushed red pepper
GARNISH: lime wedges, chopped fresh cilantro and peanuts

**SERVES** 4
**TOTAL TIME:** 25 minutes

**PER SERVING:** 408 cal, 30 g pro, 19 g car, 2 g fiber, 25 g fat (19 g sat fat), 66 mg chol, 673 mg sod

**1** Place chicken chunks on a sheet of wax paper and sprinkle with 1 tsp curry powder.

**2** Heat 1 tsp oil in a large nonstick skillet over medium-high heat. Add sliced pepper and chopped onion and cook 3 to 5 minutes, stirring several times, until crisp-tender. Add remaining 1 tsp oil and the chicken chunks; cook 2 minutes or until chicken is lightly browned.

**3** Stir in garlic; cook 1 minute or until fragrant. Add remaining 1 tsp curry powder, the coconut milk, pineapple and juice, salt and crushed red pepper. Bring to a boil, reduce heat and simmer uncovered 5 minutes or until vegetables are tender and chicken is cooked through.

# Grilled Chicken with Avocado, Tomato & Corn Salsa

## BONELESS BREAST HALVES · GRILL OR STOVETOP GRILL PAN OR BROILER

GRILL THE CHICKEN INDOORS OR OUT. THIS SALSA IS BEST SERVED
WITHIN 1 HOUR OF BEING MADE.

**SERVES** 4
**PREP:** 20 minutes
**GRILL:** 6 to 8 minutes

**PER SERVING:** 404 cal,
43 g pro, 22 g car, 3 g fiber,
17 g fat (3 g sat fat), 99 mg
chol, 561 mg sod

SALSA
    ¼ cup fresh lime juice
    2 Tbsp olive oil
    2 tsp sugar
    ½ tsp salt
    1 ripe avocado, diced
    1½ cups diced tomato (1 large)
    1 cup thawed frozen or canned corn kernels
    ¼ cup chopped red onion
    ¼ cup chopped fresh cilantro

4 skinless, boneless chicken-breast halves (about 5 oz each)
1 Tbsp olive oil
1 tsp dried oregano, crumbled
¼ tsp salt
¼ tsp freshly ground pepper
4 cups shredded lettuce

**1** SALSA: Mix lime juice, oil, sugar and salt in a medium bowl. Add remaining ingredients; toss gently to mix and coat.

**2** Heat outdoor grill, stovetop grill pan or broiler.

**3** Brush chicken with oil, then sprinkle with oregano, salt and pepper. Grill 3 to 4 minutes per side until cooked through.

**4** Divide lettuce among 4 plates; top each with chicken, then salsa.

# Chicken, Tomatoes & "Breadsticks" Italiano

## BONELESS BREAST HALVES · GRILL OR STOVETOP GRILL PAN

### MARINATE THE CHICKEN FOR AT LEAST 15 MINUTES, OR UP TO 2 HOURS.

5 Tbsp olive oil, preferably extra-virgin
2 Tbsp balsamic or red-wine vinegar
1 tsp minced garlic
1 tsp dried oregano
1 tsp dried basil
Salt
Freshly ground pepper
4 skinless, boneless chicken-breast halves (about 5 oz each)
2 large tomatoes, halved
8-oz loaf Italian bread
¼ cup shredded Italian Cheese Blend
GARNISH: chopped fresh parsley

**SERVES 4**
**TOTAL TIME:** 30 minutes

**PER SERVING:** 497 cal, 37 g pro, 35 g car, 3 g fiber, 23 g fat (4 g sat fat), 79 mg chol, 475 mg sod

**1** Heat grill or stovetop grill pan. Put into a large ziptop bag 3 Tbsp olive oil, the vinegar, garlic, oregano, basil and ½ tsp each salt and pepper. Add chicken, seal bag and turn to coat. Marinate a minimum of 15 minutes or up to 2 hours in the refrigerator.

**2** Brush tomatoes with 1½ tsp olive oil. Halve bread lengthwise; cut each half lengthwise in 4 sticks. Brush with remaining oil; sprinkle with ½ tsp each salt and pepper.

**3** Remove chicken from marinade, place on grill and drizzle with the marinade.

**4** Grill chicken 3 to 4 minutes per side, until cooked through; bread 4 to 6 minutes, turning until evenly toasted; and tomatoes, cut sides down, 1 minute.

**5** Turn tomatoes over, top with cheese and grill 3 minutes or until cheese melts. Sprinkle chicken and tomatoes with chopped parsley.

# Chicken Breasts with Fresh Orange Salsa

### BREASTS · SKILLET

GOOD WITH RICE AND STEAMED SPINACH.

**SERVES** 4
**TOTAL TIME:** About 27 minutes

**PER SERVING:** 264 cal,
35 g pro, 18 g car, 4 g fiber,
6 g fat (1 g sat fat), 82 mg chol,
447 mg sod

ORANGE SALSA

3 navel oranges

¾ cup chopped radishes

¼ cup chopped green olives

3 Tbsp finely chopped fresh cilantro

2 Tbsp minced red onion

2 Tbsp finely chopped jalapeño pepper (see *Handling Hot Peppers*, left)

2 Tbsp flour

2 tsp ground cumin

¼ tsp salt

⅛ tsp freshly ground pepper

4 skinless, boneless chicken-breast halves (about 5 oz each)

2 tsp oil

### HANDLING HOT PEPPERS

When cutting up jalapeños or other fiery peppers, be sure not to touch your face, eyes or other sensitive areas until you have thoroughly washed your hands. If you are working with a lot of hot peppers, slip on disposable gloves before you start.

**1** SALSA: On cutting board, slice skin off top and bottom of orange. Then stand orange on one end and cut off remaining skin from top to bottom, all around the orange. Working over a bowl, cut between membranes to release orange sections. Then squeeze (with your hand) any remaining juice from membrane into the bowl. Stir in remaining Salsa ingredients.

**2** Mix flour, cumin, salt and pepper in a large ziptop bag. Add chicken, close bag and shake until evenly coated.

**3** Heat oil in a large nonstick skillet over medium heat. Add chicken and cook 6 to 7 minutes, turning once, until golden outside and juices run clear when meat is pierced. Transfer to a serving platter; spoon on Salsa.

# Piquant Pecan Chicken Fingers

## TENDERS · SKILLET

THE TENDERS CAN BE COATED WITH EGG AND CRUMBS UP TO AN HOUR
BEFORE FRYING AND REFRIGERATED ON A WIRE RACK. COUSCOUS AND BROCCOLI OR
BROCCOLINI MAKE GOOD SIDE DISHES.

½ cup pecans, finely chopped

½ cup flour

½ tsp salt

½ tsp paprika

1 large egg

1 lb chicken tenders (about 8), cut in half lengthwise, white tendon
removed (see *Tenders and Tendons*, page 48)

1½ Tbsp oil

DIPPING SAUCE

½ cup orange marmalade

2 Tbsp prepared white horseradish

1 Tbsp Dijon mustard

2 Tbsp sliced scallions

**SERVES 4**
**TOTAL TIME:** 25 minutes

**PER SERVING:** 443 cal,
31 g pro, 42 g car, 2 g fiber,
17 g fat (2 g sat fat), 119 mg
chol, 516 mg sod

**1** Mix pecans, flour, salt and paprika on wax paper.

**2** Beat egg in a shallow bowl with a fork until frothy.

**3** Dip tenders in egg, then pecan mixture to coat.

**4** Heat oil in a large nonstick skillet. Add chicken; cook over
medium-low heat about 4 minutes, turning once or twice, until
golden and cooked through.

**5** Meanwhile stir Dipping Sauce ingredients together in a small
bowl. Serve with the chicken.

# Crunchy Chicken Fingers with Coleslaw

**SERVES 4**
**TOTAL TIME:** 20 to 25 minutes

**PER SERVING:** 388 cal, 33 g pro, 38 g car, 2 g fiber, 12 g fat (2 g sat fat), 133 mg chol, 953 mg sod

1 large egg

1 lb chicken tenders (see *Tenders and Tendons*, page 48)

4 oz baked potato chips, finely crushed (1 cup, see Tip, left)

¾ tsp paprika

¼ tsp salt

COLESLAW

  4 cups (about 8 oz) coleslaw mix

  ¾ cup seedless red grapes, halved if large

  3 Tbsp light mayonnaise

  3 Tbsp plain lowfat yogurt

  1 tsp sugar

  ¼ tsp salt

  ¼ tsp freshly ground pepper

½ cup reduced-fat ranch dressing

**1** Heat oven to 450°F. Line a rimmed baking sheet with foil (for easy cleanup). Lightly coat with cooking spray.

**2** Beat egg in a shallow bowl with a fork until frothy. Add tenders and toss to coat. In another bowl, mix crushed chips, paprika and salt. Add tenders, a few at a time, and toss with a fork to coat. Place on prepared baking sheet.

**3** Bake 10 minutes or until chicken is cooked through.

**4** Meanwhile put Coleslaw ingredients in a bowl; toss to mix and coat.

**5** Serve tenders with ranch dressing and the slaw.

TIP: Crush the potato chips in a food processor. Or seal them in a plastic food bag and crush them with a rolling pin.

# Fajita-Style Chicken Tenders with Corn & Black Beans

TENDERS · SKILLET

SERVE TENDERS WITH LIME WEDGES AND TORTILLA CHIPS
OR WARM CORN OR FLOUR TORTILLAS.

2 tsp olive oil
1 lb chicken tenders (see *Tenders and Tendons*, page 48)
1.12-oz pkt fajita seasoning mix
15-oz can black beans, drained and rinsed
11-oz can whole kernel corn
1 cup salsa
3 Tbsp chopped fresh cilantro

**SERVES 4**
**TOTAL TIME:** 10 minutes

**PER SERVING:** 295 cal,
32 g pro, 29 g car, 4 g fiber,
5 g fat (1 g sat fat), 66 mg chol,
1,535 mg sod

**1** Heat oil in a large nonstick skillet. Add tenders and cook over medium-high heat 3 minutes or until lightly colored, turning once. Sprinkle with fajita seasoning and 2 Tbsp water; toss over medium heat 1 minute until coated and chicken is cooked through.

**2** While tenders cook, combine beans, corn and salsa in a medium saucepan or microwave-safe dish. Heat until hot. Remove from heat and stir in cilantro. Serve with the tenders.

# Spicy Slow-Cooker Chicken

DRUMSTICKS AND THIGHS · SLOW COOKER

GOOD WITH RICE OR WITH CRUSTY BREAD FOR SOPPING UP THE SAUCE.

4 chicken drumsticks and 4 thighs (about 2½ lb)
Two 14.5-oz cans petite cut diced tomatoes with jalapeños
½ cup creamy peanut butter
GARNISH: chopped fresh cilantro

**SERVES 4**
**PREP:** 20 minutes
**COOK:** About 4 hours on high
or about 7 hours on low

**PER SERVING:** 451 cal, 48 g
pro, 14 g car, 7 g fiber, 24 g fat
(5 g sat fat), 154 mg chol,
1,141 mg sod

**1** Grasp chicken skin with paper towels and pull it off.

**2** Put chicken in a 3-qt or larger slow cooker. Add tomatoes and peanut butter; stir to mix. Cover and cook on high 4 to 5 hours or low 7 to 9 hours until chicken is tender.

**3** Carefully lift chicken (it's fall-off-the-bone tender) onto serving plates, spoon sauce over and garnish with chopped cilantro.

# Pesto Oven-Fried Chicken

### LEGS · RIMMED BAKING SHEET · WIRE RACK · OVEN

**SERVES** 4
**PREP:** 10 minutes
**BAKE:** About 50 minutes

**PER SERVING:** 528 cal,
45 g pro, 16 g car, 2 g fiber,
30 g fat (8 g sat fat), 150 mg
chol, 812 mg sod

TIP: Look for reduced-fat pesto in your market's fresh pasta or dairy section.

**FYI:** Pull off the chicken skin before cooking, if you like. See *Off with the Skin*, page 65.

½ cup reduced-fat basil pesto (see Tip, left)
4 chicken legs (about 3 lb, see FYI, left)
½ cup seasoned dried bread crumbs

**1** Heat oven to 400°F. Line a rimmed baking sheet with foil (for easy cleanup). Place a wire rack on foil.

**2** Spread pesto on chicken to cover. Put bread crumbs in a large plastic food bag, add 2 legs at a time and shake until chicken is coated. Place legs on rack.

**3** Bake 50 minutes or until coating is golden and chicken is cooked through.

# Tarragon Chicken

### DRUMSTICKS AND THIGHS · SLOW COOKER

HEAVY CREAM MAKES A RICH, VELVETY SAUCE. YOU NEED TO ALLOW 25 MINUTES AFTER THE CREAM IS ADDED FOR THE FLOUR TO COOK. GOOD WITH STEAMED CARROTS AND MASHED POTATOES.

**SERVES** 4
**PREP:** 20 minutes
**COOK:** About 4½ hours on high, 7½ hours on low

**PER SERVING:** 544 cal,
40 g pro, 12 g car, 1 g fiber,
36 g fat (14 g sat fat), 213 mg
chol, 706 mg sod

4 chicken drumsticks and 4 thighs (about 2½ lb)
1 cup very thinly sliced onion
4 cloves garlic, peeled and thinly sliced
1 cup diced plum tomatoes (6 oz)
⅓ cup tarragon vinegar
1½ Tbsp chopped fresh tarragon or 2 tsp dried
1 Tbsp Dijon mustard
¾ tsp salt
½ tsp freshly ground pepper
½ cup heavy (whipping) cream
2 Tbsp flour

**1** Grasp chicken skin with paper towels and pull it off. Put chicken in 4½-qt or larger slow cooker.

**2** Add onion, garlic, tomato, vinegar, tarragon, mustard, salt and pepper. Stir to mix.

**3** Cover and cook 4 hours on high or 7 hours on low, until chicken is cooked through and onion is soft.

**4** Whisk heavy cream and flour in a small bowl until smooth. Stir in some hot liquid from cooker; stir into liquid in cooker. Turn setting to high; cook 25 minutes until liquid thickens.

# Chicken with Olives

## DRUMSTICKS AND THIGHS · SLOW COOKER

GOOD WITH YELLOW RICE, WHICH YOU CAN MAKE FROM A MIX
(LOOK IN HISPANIC FOODS SECTION OF MARKET).

3 large all-purpose potatoes (1½ lb), cut bite-size (see Tip, right)
1 large green pepper, cut in thin strips
¾ cup chopped onion
15-oz can tomato sauce
½ cup dry white wine or chicken broth
½ cup pimiento-stuffed olives
1½ Tbsp minced garlic
1½ Tbsp olive oil
1 Tbsp tomato paste
½ tsp salt
½ tsp freshly ground pepper
1 bay leaf, broken in half
6 chicken drumsticks and 6 thighs (about 3 lb)

SERVES 6
PREP: 10 minutes
COOK: About 5 hours on high, 8 hours on low

PER SERVING: 340 cal, 35 g pro, 26 g car, 4 g fiber, 11 g fat (2 g sat fat), 123 mg chol, 1,056 mg sod

TIP: Just scrub the potatoes before cutting, no need to peel (see *To Peel or Not to Peel*, page 21).

**1** Mix all ingredients except chicken in a 4½-qt or larger slow cooker. Grasp chicken skin with paper towels and pull it off. Add chicken to cooker; stir until well mixed.

**2** Cover and cook on high 5 hours or low 8 hours until chicken is cooked through and tender and potatoes can be easily pierced. Discard bay leaf.

# Chicken Legs in Spicy Orange-Honey Sauce

LEGS · SKILLET

GOOD WITH RICE.

**SERVES 4**
**TOTAL TIME:** About 45 minutes

**PER SERVING:** 449 cal,
32 g pro, 25 g car, 4 g fiber,
24 g fat (6 g sat fat), 109 mg
chol, 790 mg sod

**FYI:** Pull off the chicken skin
before cooking, if you like. See
*Off with the Skin*, page 65.

4 chicken legs (about 3 lb, see FYI, left)
Salt
Freshly ground pepper
1 Tbsp oil
2 oranges
1½ cups chopped onion
1 Tbsp finely chopped garlic
½ tsp ground cinnamon
¼ to ½ tsp crushed red pepper
1 cup chicken broth
1 Tbsp honey
3 Tbsp raisins
2 Tbsp chopped fresh cilantro

**1** Season chicken with ¼ tsp each salt and pepper. Heat oil in a large nonstick skillet over medium heat. Add chicken, cover and cook, turning occasionally with tongs, 10 minutes or until browned. Transfer to a plate; pour off all but 2 Tbsp fat.

**2** While chicken is browning, peel and cut up oranges: On cutting board, slice skin off top and bottom of orange. Then stand orange on one end and cut off remaining skin from top to bottom, all around the orange. Working over a bowl, cut between membranes to release orange sections. Then squeeze (with your hand) any remaining juice from membrane into a cup measure. Add any juice which may have accumulated with the sections. You need ⅓ cup juice.

**3** Add onion, garlic, cinnamon and crushed pepper to skillet. Cook, stirring occasionally, 5 minutes or until onion is golden brown. Stir in broth, orange juice, honey, raisins and ½ tsp each salt and pepper. Return chicken to pan, cover, reduce heat and simmer 20 to 25 minutes until chicken is cooked through.

**4** Transfer chicken to plates. Stir orange sections into sauce and heat through. Spoon over chicken; sprinkle with cilantro.

# Creamy Succotash Chicken

FRESH-BAKED BISCUITS ARE A GREAT ACCOMPANIMENT.
BAKE EXTRA TO ENJOY WITH PRESERVES FOR DESSERT.

1 lb skinless, boneless chicken thighs, cut in 1½-in. chunks
1½ cups frozen corn
1½ cups frozen baby lima beans
10.75-oz can 30% less sodium condensed cream of chicken soup
½ cup diced ham
½ cup diced red pepper
½ cup milk
¼ cup sliced white part of scallions
½ tsp dried thyme
½ tsp ground red pepper (cayenne)

**SERVES** 4
**PREP:** 10 minutes
**COOK:** 4 to 7 hours on low

**PER SERVING:** 378 cal,
34 g pro, 39 g car, 6 g fiber,
10 g fat (3 g sat fat), 115 mg
chol, 673 mg sod

1  Put all ingredients in a 3-qt or larger slow cooker. Stir to mix well.

2  Cover and cook on low 4 to 7 hours until chicken and vegetables are tender.

## KEEPING CHICKEN AND TURKEY FRESH

Chicken and turkey may be kept in their original wrapping in the coldest part of the refrigerator up to 2 days.
If taking it elsewhere, transport it in an insulated container or ice chest.
For longer storage, wrap chicken and turkey in heavy-duty foil or freezer wrap, or seal in ziptop freezer bag and freeze up to 2 months. Thaw frozen chicken or turkey in the refrigerator. You can also thaw it in the microwave, but be sure to cook it immediately after thawing.
A slightly slower way is to put the package (in a sealed plastic bag) in cold water and change the water often until the poultry is thawed.
The only poultry it's OK to thaw at room temperature is very thin slices frozen in a very thin layer that are going to be cooked right away.

# Mediterranean Chicken

SERVE OVER COUSCOUS OR RICE.

**SERVES** 6
**PREP:** 8 minutes
**COOK:** 4 to 5 hours on high,
7 to 9 hours on low

**PER SERVING:** 234 cal,
19 g pro, 31 g car, 5 g fiber,
4 g fat (1 g sat fat), 63 mg chol,
594 mg sod

1½-lb butternut squash, peeled and cut in 1-in. chunks (about 4 cups)
1 lb skinless, boneless chicken thighs, cut in 1-in. chunks
1 large red pepper, cut in 1-in. pieces
½ cup salsa
14.5-oz can diced tomatoes in juice
¼ cup raisins
½ tsp cumin
½ tsp minced garlic
½ tsp salt
¼ tsp ground cinnamon
15-oz can chickpeas, drained and rinsed
¼ cup chopped fresh parsley

**1** Mix all ingredients except chickpeas and parsley in 3-qt or larger slow cooker.

**2** Cover and cook on high 4 to 5 hours or on low 7 to 9 hours until chicken and vegetables are tender.

**3** Stir in chickpeas and parsley.

# Curried Chicken, Couscous & Carrots

5.8-oz box roasted garlic and olive oil–flavored couscous mix
   (see *Couscous*, page 192)

3 tsp oil

1 lb skinless, boneless chicken thighs

Salt

Freshly ground pepper

1 Tbsp flour

1 Tbsp minced fresh ginger (see *Fresh Ginger*, below)

2 tsp curry powder

14-oz can lite coconut milk (not cream of coconut)

10-oz bag shredded carrots

1 cup dried fruit bits (from a 7-oz bag)

**SERVES 4**
**TOTAL TIME:** 20 minutes

**PER SERVING:** 533 cal,
31 g pro, 72 g car, 6 g fiber,
14 g fat (5 g sat fat), 94 mg
chol, 912 mg sod

**1** Put couscous, spices from packet and 2 tsp oil in a medium bowl. Add 1¼ cups boiling water, stir to mix, cover and let rest.

**2** Heat remaining oil in a large nonstick skillet over medium-high heat. Sprinkle chicken with ¼ tsp each salt and pepper. Cook 4 minutes on each side, or until golden.

**3** Meanwhile stir flour, ginger, curry powder and ¼ tsp salt into can of coconut milk. Add to skillet; top chicken with carrots and fruit bits. Bring to a simmer, cover and cook 5 to 6 minutes or until chicken is cooked through, sauce thickens slightly and carrots are crisp-tender. Serve with couscous.

## FRESH GINGER

One of the oldest and most important spices, ginger has been cultivated and used in Asia for more than 3,000 years. Fresh ginger is the hard, knobbly root (or rhizome) of the ginger plant. It has a lively, fresh aroma and a slightly hot and pungent flavor.

When buying fresh gingerroot, select roots with a smooth skin that are firm and heavy without any shriveled ends. Once home, you may want to store it in the refrigerator, although it will start to shrivel after a week or so. Wrap it in plastic to keep it firm.

To use, cut off small knobs. Peel some or all of the root with a vegetable peeler or small paring knife. Then cut slices to use as slices or to finely chop. You can also grate as much as you need with a box or Microplane grater. If you don't use ginger often slice the entire root and freeze the slices. Take out a few to chop as needed. Or freeze the peeled root, and grate off as much as you need when you need it (no need to thaw the root). Try simmering a few slices of fresh ginger in water before making tea or to use for a ginger lemonade. A few slices simmered in chicken broth imparts a fresh flavor.

# Roasted Drumsticks & Vegetables

DRUMSTICKS · 2 RIMMED BAKING SHEETS · OVEN

**SERVES** 4
**PREP:** 25 minutes
**ROAST:** About 45 minutes

**PER SERVING:** 649 cal,
41 g pro, 74 g car, 11 g fiber,
22 g fat (5 g sat fat), 139 mg
chol, 1,088 mg sod

8 chicken drumsticks (2¼ lb)

1½ lb all-purpose potatoes, scrubbed and quartered

1 lb carrots, cut in 2-in. lengths

2-lb butternut squash, cut in 1-in.-wide slices

2 medium onions, each cut in 8 wedges

5 cloves garlic, halved

2 Tbsp oil

1 Tbsp Italian seasoning

1½ tsp salt

1 tsp freshly ground pepper

**1** Position racks to divide oven in thirds. Heat to 425°F. Have 2 rimmed baking sheets ready.

**2** Put all ingredients in a large bowl; stir (or toss with hands) to mix and coat. Arrange in a single layer on the baking sheets.

**3** Roast, switching position of pans and turning vegetables halfway through roasting, 45 minutes or until chicken is cooked through and vegetables are tender.

# Brown Sugar-Baked Chicken & Oven Fries

DRUMSTICKS · 2 RIMMED BAKING SHEETS · WIRE RACK · OVEN

DINNER BAKES WITH LITTLE ATTENTION. ADD A SALAD TO MAKE A GREAT MEAL.

**SERVES** 4
**PREP:** 10 minutes
**BAKE:** About 40 minutes

**PER SERVING:** 470 cal,
36 g pro, 42 g car, 3 g fiber,
17 g fat (4 g sat fat), 109 mg
chol, 718 mg sod

3 large baking potatoes (1½ lb), cut lengthwise in ½-in.-thick sticks (see Tip, facing page)

1 Tbsp oil

3 Tbsp light-brown sugar

2 tsp chili powder

2 tsp freshly grated orange peel

Salt

8 chicken drumsticks (2¼ lb)

¼ tsp freshly ground pepper

**1** Position racks to divide oven in thirds. Heat to 450°F. Line 2 rimmed baking sheets with foil (for easy cleanup). Set a wire rack on 1 sheet; coat rack well with cooking spray.

**2** Put potatoes and oil in a large bowl; toss potatoes to coat. Spread out on prepared rack, overlapping if necessary. Bake on top oven rack 10 minutes.

**3** Meanwhile mix sugar, chili powder, orange peel and ½ tsp salt in a large plastic food bag. Add drumsticks and shake until chicken is coated. Arrange on second baking sheet.

**4** Place chicken on lower oven rack and bake 25 to 30 minutes or until potatoes are tinged golden brown and juices run clear when chicken is pierced with fork. Drizzle any juices in baking sheet over the chicken. Sprinkle potatoes with ½ tsp salt and the pepper.

> TIP: Leave the skins on the potatoes. Just give them a good scrubbing before you cut them up.

# Teriyaki-Orange Roast Chicken

## WHOLE BIRD · ROASTING PAN · WIRE RACK · OVEN

THE ORANGE MARMALADE IS BRUSHED ON ONLY FOR THE LAST 10 TO 15 MINUTES OF COOKING TIME SO THAT IT FORMS A GLAZE BUT DOESN'T SCORCH.

1 whole 4- to 4½-lb chicken (see *Giblets*, page 64)
⅓ cup Korean teriyaki stir-fry sauce
¼ cup orange marmalade

**1** Heat oven to 350°F. Line a roasting pan with foil (for easy cleanup). Place a wire rack on foil.

**2** Tuck wing tips under backbone of chicken; place breast side up on rack. Brush all over with some of the stir-fry sauce.

**3** Roast in upper third of oven, 1 hour 20 minutes, brushing with stir-fry sauce every 20 minutes.

**4** Stir marmalade; brush on chicken. Roast 10 to 15 minutes more or until an instant-read thermometer inserted in thigh, not touching bone, registers 170°F. Let chicken rest 10 minutes before carving (see *Resting Time*, right).

**SERVES** 4
**PREP:** 5 minutes
**ROAST:** About 1 hour 35 minutes

**PER SERVING:** 650 cal, 60 g pro, 20 g car, 0 g fiber, 35 g fat (9 g sat fat), 189 mg chol, 800 mg sod

**RESTING TIME**
Plan for grilled or roasted meat or poultry to rest at room temperature after cooking. This gives the juices a chance to redistribute and the meat to firm up for easier carving.

# Lemon-Garlic Roast Chicken

## WHOLE BIRD · DUTCH OVEN · OVEN

FOR EXTRA-JUICY MEAT, BAKE CHICKEN IN A COVERED CASSEROLE FOR THE FIRST HOUR, THEN UNCOVER FOR THE REMAINING 30 TO 45 MINUTES. JUST BETWEEN US CHICKENS, IF THE ROASTED BIRD IS NOT MAKING A PUBLIC APPEARANCE BEFORE IT IS CARVED, YOU CAN LEAVE THE LEGS UNTIED. WHILE TYING LEGS TAKES ONLY SECONDS, FINDING THE BUTCHER'S TWINE YOU KNOW YOU PUT SOMEWHERE CAN BE EXASPERATING.

**SERVES** 6
**PREP:** 20 minutes
**ROAST:** About 1¾ hours

**PER SERVING:** 583 cal, 57 g pro, 7 g car, 1 g fiber, 35 g fat (9 g sat fat), 178 mg chol, 367 mg sod

## GIBLETS

Giblets (the liver, heart and gizzard of a bird), along with the neck, should be found inside roasting chickens. Treat them as a valuable commodity. Chop up the liver, fry for a minute or two in butter, sprinkle with salt and pepper and enjoy as a snack. Or freeze until you have enough to share. Simmer the heart, gizzard and neck (along with a small onion, parsley stems, a small bay leaf and about 10 peppercorns) in water to cover for about 2 hours. Voila! Fresh chicken stock. Strain it into a freezer container. Chill. Spoon fat off the top. Then refrigerate or freeze until you need it.

1 roasting chicken (about 6 lb)
Salt
Freshly ground pepper
3 lemons, cut in half
2 heads garlic, broken into cloves but not peeled
1 bunch thyme sprigs (less than 1 oz)
1½ Tbsp olive oil

**1** Heat oven to 375°F. Have ready a 4-qt Dutch oven or casserole (see *Dutch Oven*, page 82), preferably oval, and 100% pure cotton string (such as butcher's twine).

**2** If there is a packet of giblets or the neck inside the bird, take them out, but don't throw them away (see *Giblets*, left). Rub body cavity of chicken with ⅛ tsp each salt and pepper. Then put into the cavity the juice of 1 lemon, the 2 squeezed lemon halves, 6 cloves of garlic and half the thyme. Tie legs together with the string. Tuck the wing tips under the backbone.

**3** Place chicken in casserole and brush the skin with the olive oil. Squeeze the juice from the 2 remaining lemons over the top of the chicken and sprinkle with ⅛ tsp salt and ⅛ tsp pepper. Scatter remaining garlic and thyme around bird.

**4** Cover and roast 1 hour in the upper third of the oven. Increase oven temperature to 450°F. Uncover casserole, add ¾ cup water and bake 30 to 45 minutes longer until a thermometer inserted in thickest part of thigh, not touching bone, registers 165°F. Transfer to a board or platter; cover loosely with foil to keep warm (internal temperature will continue to rise).

**5** Pour contents of casserole through a strainer into a small saucepan, pressing on solids with back of a spoon. Discard solids left in strainer. Let juices in saucepan settle, skim fat off surface, then season juices with ¼ tsp salt. Heat through. Carve chicken; serve with pan juices.

# Braised Chicken with Leeks

## CUT-UP BIRD · DUTCH OVEN · OVEN

THE CHICKEN BAKES IN A HEAVY POT WITH WINE, GARLIC, LEEKS, ROSEMARY AND THYME.

2 Tbsp flour

Salt

Freshly ground pepper

One chicken (about 4 lb), cut in 8 pieces, (see *Choose Your Chicken,* right) skin removed (see *Off with the Skin,* right)

2 Tbsp olive oil

1 Tbsp butter

2 lb leeks, white and pale green parts only, halved lengthwise, sliced crosswise

1 cup diced carrots

1 Tbsp minced garlic

1 cup chicken broth

½ cup dry white wine or chicken broth

1 tsp dried rosemary, crumbled

1 tsp dried thyme, crumbled

16 to 18 oz plum tomatoes cut in chunks (3 cups)

**1** Heat oven to 325°F. Have ready a 3-qt Dutch oven or casserole (see *Dutch Oven,* page 82).

**2** Mix flour and ¼ tsp each salt and pepper in a large ziptop bag. Add chicken, seal bag and shake to coat.

**3** Heat 1 Tbsp oil in casserole over medium heat. Add half the chicken; brown 4 minutes per side. Remove to a large plate. Repeat with remaining oil and chicken.

**4** Add butter and melt over medium heat. Add leeks, carrots and garlic; cook, stirring several times, 5 minutes or until softened.

**5** Add broth, wine, herbs, ¾ tsp salt and ¾ tsp pepper. Bring to a boil, stirring up bits on bottom. Add chicken.

**6** Cover and bake 25 minutes. Stir in tomatoes; bake 15 minutes more or until chicken is cooked through and vegetables are tender.

**SERVES** 4
**PREP:** 30 minutes
**BAKE:** 45 minutes

**PER SERVING:** 306 cal, 33 g pro, 17 g car, 2 g fiber, 11 g fat (3 g sat fat), 107 mg chol, 709 mg sod

## CHOOSE YOUR CHICKEN

Some of our recipes call for a whole chicken cut in 8 pieces, or for chicken legs (which are drumstick and thigh attached). If you prefer, you can buy chicken thighs and/or chicken drumsticks to use instead.

## OFF WITH THE SKIN

Chicken skin is slippery, but if you grab the skin with a paper towel in one hand and the drumstick or breast or other part with another paper towel in the other hand you will find you can easily pull off the skin.

# Chicken Meatball Stroganoff

**SERVES 4**
**TOTAL TIME:** 25 to 30 minutes

**PER SERVING:** 345 cal, 28 g pro, 17 g car, 2 g fiber, 19 g fat (6 g sat fat), 107 mg chol, 1,228 mg sod

## FRESH BREAD CRUMBS

To make fresh bread crumbs, tear two or three slices of firm white sandwich bread into small pieces, then process a few seconds in a food processor.

TIP: It's hard to make two meatballs the same size, let alone 32, so here's a trick that not only helps alleviate that problem but also speeds things up. Tear off a foot or so of wax paper and put it on a work surface. On it pat the chicken mixture into an even square, 10 to 11 in. Cut the square into 16 one way and 16 the other, then form the resulting small squares into balls.

MEATBALLS
   1 lb ground chicken
   1 cup fresh bread crumbs (see *Fresh Bread Crumbs*, left)
   ¼ cup sliced scallions
   1 tsp salt
   1 tsp freshly ground pepper
   1 tsp minced garlic

2 tsp oil
10-oz pkg sliced mushrooms
2 Tbsp dry sherry wine (optional)
12-oz jar beef gravy
½ cup reduced-fat sour cream
¼ cup sliced scallions

**1** MEATBALLS: Mix Meatball ingredients in a bowl; form into 32 meatballs (see Tip, left).

**2** Heat oil in a large nonstick skillet over medium-high heat. Add meatballs and cook 3 minutes or until golden. Remove to a plate. Add mushrooms to skillet; cook about 3 minutes, stirring often, until lightly browned.

**3** Stir in sherry (if using); cook 30 seconds. Stir in gravy and meatballs, cover and simmer 3 minutes, stirring occasionally, until cooked through. Off heat, stir in sour cream and scallions.

# Chicken Burgers Milanese

GROUND CHICKEN · SKILLET

Sᴇʀᴠᴇ ᴡɪᴛʜ ɢᴀʀʟɪᴄ ʙʀᴇᴀᴅ ᴀɴᴅ ɢʀᴇᴇɴ ʙᴇᴀɴs.

BURGERS

- 1 lb ground chicken
- ⅓ cup Italian-seasoned dried bread crumbs
- ⅓ cup grated Parmesan cheese
- ½ tsp salt
- ½ tsp freshly ground pepper

2 tsp olive oil
4 cups (2½ oz) baby arugula blend
1 cup diced plum tomatoes (6 oz)
¼ cup olive oil and vinegar dressing
¼ cup sliced red onion

**SERVES** 4
**TOTAL TIME:** 20 minutes

**PER SERVING:** 325 cal,
25 g pro, 13 g car, 1 g fiber,
19 g fat (5 g sat fat), 99 mg
chol, 952 mg sod

**1** BURGERS: Mix Burger ingredients in a bowl; form into four ½-in.-thick patties.

**2** Heat oil in large nonstick skillet over medium heat. Add burgers and cook 6 minutes, turning once, until cooked through.

**3** Put arugula, tomatoes, dressing and onion into a bowl; toss to mix. Put Burgers on plates; top with salad.

# Thai Chicken Salad

## COOKED CHICKEN

WHEN ROASTING OR GRILLING CHICKEN, IT'S ALWAYS WORTH COOKING EXTRA
FOR A DELICIOUS MAIN DISH SALAD SUCH AS THIS ONE.

**SERVES** 4
**TOTAL TIME:** 30 minutes

**PER SERVING:** 227 cal,
25 g pro, 13 g car, 5 g fiber,
8 g fat (2 g sat fat), 62 mg chol,
323 mg sod

PEANUT DRESSING
   ¼ cup Thai peanut stir-fry sauce
   3 Tbsp fresh lime juice
   2 tsp freshly grated ginger (see *Fresh Ginger*, page 61)
   ½ tsp minced garlic

8 cups loosely packed torn romaine lettuce
2 cups shredded cooked chicken
1½ cups thinly sliced seedless cucumber
¾ cup shredded carrots
⅓ cup chopped fresh cilantro
¼ cup chopped fresh mint leaves
GARNISH: chopped peanuts

**1** DRESSING: Whisk ingredients in a large serving bowl until well blended.

**2** Add remaining ingredients; toss to mix and coat. Sprinkle with peanuts.

# Cornish Hens with Potatoes & Greek-Style Asparagus

## CORNISH HENS · GRILL

*A WHOLE DINNER ON THE GRILL.*

2 Cornish hens (1½ lb each), halved and backbone removed
1 Tbsp Greek seasoning
4 medium (1½ lb) Yukon Gold potatoes (see Tip, right)
¾ cup diced onion
2 tsp minced garlic
5 Tbsp plus ¼ cup balsamic vinaigrette dressing
1½ lb medium-thick asparagus, woody ends snapped off
1⅓ cups diced tomato
¼ cup crumbled feta cheese

**SERVES** 4
**PREP:** 30 minutes
**GRILL:** About 30 minutes

**PER SERVING:** 693 cal, 41 g pro, 46 g car, 5 g fiber, 39 g fat (10 g sat fat), 195 mg chol, 614 mg sod

**1**  Heat outdoor grill. Have ready four 12-in. squares heavy-duty foil.

**2**  Loosen breast and leg skin from hens with fingers. Rub Greek seasoning under and over skin.

**3**  Thinly slice potatoes. Place one fourth of the potatoes, onion and garlic on lower third of each foil square. Drizzle each with 1 Tbsp vinaigrette. Fold foil over and double fold edges to seal packets.

**4**  Put asparagus and 1 Tbsp vinaigrette in a large bowl; toss to coat.

**5**  Grill packets and hens, turning both once, potato packets about 25 minutes until potatoes are fork tender, and hens 20 minutes or until an instant-read thermometer inserted in thickest part of thigh, not touching bone, registers 175°F. Remove to a platter. Cover hens loosely with foil. (Temperature will rise about 5 degrees while hens rest.)

**6**  Place asparagus on grill; grill 2 minutes per side or until lightly charred and tender. Transfer to a serving platter; drizzle with remaining ¼ cup vinaigrette. Top with tomato and feta.

**7**  Open packets carefully (beware of steam). Serve with hens and asparagus.

TIP: Yukon Gold potatoes do not need peeling, just a scrub with a vegetable brush.

# Sweet & Spicy Wings

**SERVES** 8
**PREP:** 10 minutes
**MARINATE:** 3 to 24 hours
**GRILL:** 25 to 30 minutes

**PER SERVING:** 498 cal,
37 g pro, 26 g car, 0 g fiber,
27 g fat (7 g sat fat), 109 mg
chol, 887 mg sod

SAUCE

   18-oz bottle spicy barbecue sauce

   18-oz bottle regular barbecue sauce

   ¾ cup (6 oz) beer

   ½ cup honey

6 lb chicken wings (about 24 to 30)

**1** SAUCE: Mix all ingredients in a bowl. Save half for a dipping sauce. Pour rest into a 2-gallon-size ziptop bag. Add wings, seal and turn to coat. Refrigerate 3 to 24 hours.

**2** Heat outdoor grill. Remove wings; discard marinade.

**3** Grill wings 20 to 25 minutes, turning often to prevent burning, until lightly charred and cooked through. Serve with reserved sauce for dipping.

---

**WING TIPS**

Trying to count the number of chicken wings in a package can be tricky, depending on how tightly they are packed and in how many layers. While they do vary in size, start with the thought that there are approximately 5 large wings (with tips) to the pound:

    5 lb: 22 to 26 wings

    6 lb: 26 to 30 wings

# Sicilian Eggplant Sauce

GROUND TURKEY · SKILLET

THE EGGPLANT SHOULD BE SO TENDER IT PRACTICALLY MELTS AND THICKENS THE SAUCE.
SERVE WITH A SHORT-CUT PASTA SUCH AS RIGATONI AND WITH PARMESAN CHEESE.

1 Tbsp olive oil
12 oz (1½ cups) lean ground turkey
1½ cups chopped onion
1 Tbsp minced garlic
1 lb eggplant, cut in ¾-in. chunks (6 cups)
16-oz can tomato sauce
⅓ cup raisins
1 Tbsp freshly grated lemon peel
2 tsp ground cumin
½ tsp Italian seasoning
½ tsp salt
¼ tsp ground cinnamon

SERVES 4
TOTAL TIME: About 40 minutes

PER SERVING: 282 cal,
19 g pro, 32 g car, 5 g fiber,
10 g fat (2 g sat fat), 62 mg
chol, 1,068 mg sod

**1** Heat oil in a large nonstick skillet over medium heat. Add turkey, onion and garlic and cook, breaking up clumps of meat with a wooden spoon, 2 to 3 minutes until meat is no longer pink.

**2** Stir in remaining ingredients and ⅔ cup water. Bring to a simmer, reduce heat, cover and cook about 25 minutes, stirring occasionally, until eggplant is very tender.

# Tex-Mex Turkey Tenders & Stuffing

TENDERLOINS USUALLY COME TWO TO THE PACKAGE, SO COOK BOTH THEN
SAVE ONE FOR ANOTHER MEAL.

**SERVES** 4 (with leftovers)
**PREP:** 15 minutes
**BAKE:** 1¼ hours

**PER SERVING:** 453 cal,
31 g pro, 43 g car, 4 g fiber,
18 g fat (3 g sat fat), 74 mg
chol, 1,231 mg sod

1 Tbsp oil

1½ cups diced zucchini (about 6 oz)

1 red pepper, chopped

½ cup chopped onion

¾ cup (3 oz) chopped chorizo sausage (see *Chorizo*, page 176)

1 tsp ground cumin

3 cups cornbread stuffing mix

2 turkey breast tenderloins (about 2 lb)

½ tsp chili powder

SERVE WITH: **turkey gravy**

**1** Heat oven to 350°F. Lightly coat a 2-qt shallow baking dish with cooking spray.

**2** Heat oil in a large nonstick skillet. Add zucchini, red pepper and onion; cook 5 to 6 minutes, stirring several time, until soft. Stir in chorizo, cumin and ¾ cup water. Simmer 1 minute. Add stuffing mix; toss to moisten evenly. Spoon into baking dish. Top with tenderloins; sprinkle turkey with chili powder. Cover dish tightly with foil.

**3** Bake 1¼ hours or until center of tenderloins register 165°F on a meat thermometer. Remove tenderloins to a cutting board. Let rest 5 minutes, then cut one in ⅓-in.-thick slices. Wrap the remaining tenderloin and refrigerate up to three days.

# Braised Turkey Thighs

## THIGHS · SLOW COOKER OR DUTCH OVEN AND OVEN

THE NICE THING ABOUT THIS RECIPE IS THAT THE TURKEY ACTUALLY MARINATES OVERNIGHT. IF USING A SLOW COOKER WITH A REMOVABLE STONEWARE INSERT, MIX INGREDIENTS IN INSERT, THEN COVER AND REFRIGERATE. TO COOK, DO NOT PREHEAT ELECTRICAL BASE. SET INSERT ON IT, THEN TURN COOKER ON.

2 turkey thighs (about 2 lb), skin removed (see *Off with the Skin*, page 65)

1 cup dry red wine, or 1 cup chicken broth plus 1 Tbsp red-wine vinegar

1 cup thinly sliced onions

2 tsp minced garlic

½ tsp dried rosemary

½ tsp dried sage

½ tsp dried thyme

½ tsp salt

2 or 3 Tbsp flour

**SERVES** 4
**PREP:** 5 minutes
**MARINATE:** 8 to 12 hours
**BAKE:** 1½ hours or
**SLOW COOKER:** 4 to 5 hours on high, 8 to 10 hours on low

**PER SERVING:** 200 cal, 27 g pro, 9 g car, 0 g fiber, 5 g fat (2 g sat fat), 97 mg chol, 398 mg sod

**1** Eight to 12 hours before cooking, put thighs, wine, onions, garlic, herbs and salt in a large ziptop bag. Seal, then turn to mix ingredients. Refrigerate.

**2** TO BAKE: Heat oven to 325°F. Empty bag into a 4- to 5-qt Dutch oven (see *Dutch Oven*, page 82). Cover tightly and bake 1½ hours or until turkey is tender. SLOW COOKER: Empty bag into a 3½-, 4- or 5-qt slow cooker. Cover and cook on high 4 to 5 hours or on low 8 to 10 hours until turkey is tender.

**3** Remove turkey thighs to cutting board and cover loosely with foil. TO THICKEN GRAVY ON STOVETOP: Heat cooking liquid over medium-high heat. Whisk 2 Tbsp flour and ¼ cup water in a small bowl until well blended. Whisk into liquid, bring to a boil and whisk 4 to 5 minutes until thickened. TO THICKEN GRAVY IN SLOW COOKER: Set slow cooker to high and cover. Whisk 3 Tbsp flour and ¼ cup water until well blended. Whisk into liquid in slow cooker. Cover and cook 15 minutes, stirring once, until thickened.

**4** TO SERVE: Cut meat in large pieces from both sides of each thigh bone. Arrange on serving plates; spoon on some gravy. Serve remaining gravy from a sauceboat.

# Turkey-Apple Patties

SERVE WITH MASHED SWEET POTATOES AND GREEN BEANS.

**SERVES** 4
**TOTAL TIME:** 25 minutes

**PER SERVING:** 280 cal,
22 g pro, 22 g car, 3 g fiber,
12 g fat (3 g sat fat), 83 mg
chol, 621 mg sod

1 lb lean ground turkey
2 slices whole-wheat bread, torn in pieces
1 medium apple, peeled and shredded (see Tip, left)
¾ tsp dried sage
Salt
Freshly ground pepper
2 tsp oil
1½ cups sliced onions
¾ cup apple juice

TIP: To shred the apple, peel but don't cut it. Shred it on the largest holes of a four-sided grater.

**1**  Put turkey, bread, apple, sage, ½ tsp salt and the pepper into a medium bowl. Mix well with hands or a wooden spoon. Shape into four ¾-in.-thick patties.

**2**  Heat 1 tsp oil in a large nonstick skillet over medium heat. Add onions and cook 4 to 5 minutes, stirring often, until tender and browned. Stir in ¼ tsp salt. Remove to a plate.

**3**  Heat another tsp oil in skillet. Add patties and cook 2½ minutes on each side until browned. Add apple juice and the onions. Reduce heat to low, cover and cook 2 to 3 minutes until an instant-read thermometer inserted from a side into centers of patties registers at least 165°F.

# Thai Turkey

GOOD WITH RICE AND SPRINKLED WITH CHOPPED FRESH CILANTRO.

**SERVES** 4
**TOTAL TIME:** About 25 minutes

**PER SERVING:** 258 cal,
19 g pro, 15 g car, 4 g fiber,
14 g fat (5 g sat fat), 62 mg
chol, 721 mg sod

2 tsp oil
12 oz (1½ cups) lean ground turkey
1 cup chopped onion
1 Tbsp minced garlic
14-oz can lite coconut milk (see Tip, facing page)
1 Tbsp curry powder
1 tsp salt
16-oz bag frozen Oriental vegetables

**1** Heat oil in a large nonstick skillet over medium heat. Add turkey, onion and garlic and cook, breaking up clumps of meat with a wooden spoon, 2 to 3 minutes until no longer pink.

**2** Stir in coconut milk, ½ cup water, the curry powder and salt. Bring to a boil, reduce heat and simmer, uncovered, about 5 minutes until slightly thickened.

**3** Stir in vegetables, cover and cook 3 to 5 minutes or until hot.

**TIP:** Be sure to buy coconut milk, found in the Asian food section of your market. Cream of coconut, used in mixed drinks, will turn dinner into dessert.

# Turkey Summer Chili

## GROUND TURKEY · SKILLET

RICE COOKS WITH THE BEANS AND TURKEY.

1 Tbsp olive oil
1 lb lean ground turkey
1 Tbsp minced garlic
2½ tsp ground cumin
½ tsp salt
½ tsp freshly ground pepper
2 cups chicken broth
19-oz can black beans, drained and rinsed
10-oz box frozen corn kernels
½ cup converted white rice
½ cup green salsa (salsa verde)
1 cup chopped sweet onion
½ cup chopped fresh cilantro
ACCOMPANIMENTS: reduced-fat sour cream, green salsa and
    chopped fresh cilantro

**SERVES 4**
**TOTAL TIME:** About 47 minutes

**PER SERVING:** 462 cal, 30 g pro, 54 g car, 7 g fiber, 14 g fat (3 g sat fat), 83 mg chol, 1,148 mg sod

**1** Heat oil in deep, large nonstick skillet over high heat. Add turkey and garlic and cook, stirring to break up meat, 3 to 4 minutes until browned. Add cumin, salt and pepper; cook, stirring, 30 seconds.

**2** Stir in broth, beans, corn, rice and salsa. Bring to a boil, reduce heat, cover and simmer, stirring occasionally, 20 minutes or until rice is tender.

**3** Remove from heat; stir in onion and cilantro.

# Pepperoni Pizza Turkey Meat Loaf

**SERVES** 4
**PREP:** 10 minutes
**COOK:** 4 to 6 hours on low

**PER SERVING:** 443 cal, 39 g pro, 22 g car, 2 g fiber, 22 g fat (8 g sat fat), 186 mg chol, 1,458 mg sod

TIP: Use regular ground turkey, not lean, to ensure a moist and flavorful meat loaf.

TIP: Instead of the 6-cheese blend you could use ¼ cup each Parmesan and Provolone, or mozzarella cheeses.

1¼ lb ground turkey (see Tip, left)
1 cup marinara sauce
½ cup roasted yellow or red peppers (from a jar), sliced
½ cup shredded Italian 6-cheese blend (see Tip, left)
½ cup Italian-seasoned dried bread crumbs
½ cup finely chopped onion
1 large egg
2 tsp minced garlic
¼ tsp salt
16 slices 70%-less-fat turkey pepperoni
GARNISH: sliced fresh basil leaves

**1** Put into a medium bowl the ground turkey, ½ cup of the marinara sauce, ¼ cup each peppers and cheese, all of the bread crumbs and onion, the egg, garlic and salt. Dice and add 8 slices pepperoni. Mix well, using your hands or a wooden spoon, then pat mixture over bottom of a 3½-qt slow cooker (if using a larger cooker, pat mixture into an 8-in. round). Spread top with ¼ cup marinara sauce.

**2** Cover and cook on low 4 to 6 hours or until a meat thermometer (preferably instant-read) inserted in center of loaf registers 165°F.

**3** Spread with remaining sauce, sprinkle with remaining cheese, then top with remaining pepperoni and peppers. Cover and cook 5 minutes or until cheese melts. Sprinkle with basil then cut in wedges and lift out.

# Unstuffed Cabbage

## GROUND TURKEY · SKILLET

USE A GREEN CABBAGE, NOT RED, FOR LOOKS. CRINKLY-LEAVED SAVOY, OR THE COMPACT HEADS THAT RANGE FROM CREAMY WHITE TO DARK GREEN, WORK WELL. FOR BEST QUALITY, A HEAD OF CABBAGE SHOULD FEEL HEAVY FOR ITS SIZE.

12 oz ground turkey or chicken

5 cups (about 1 lb) coarsely shredded cabbage

Two 14.5-oz cans diced tomatoes with garlic and onion

½ cup raisins

2 Tbsp lemon juice

1 Tbsp packed brown sugar

1 Tbsp chopped fresh dill or 1 tsp dried

½ tsp ground allspice

½ tsp freshly ground pepper

**SERVES 4**
**TOTAL TIME:** About 31 minutes

**PER SERVING:** 260 cal,
18 g pro, 33 g car, 5 g fiber,
6 g fat (2 g sat fat), 62 mg chol,
954 mg sod

**1** Coat a large nonstick skillet with cooking spray and heat over medium-high heat. Add turkey and cook about 4 minutes, breaking up meat with a wooden spoon, until no longer pink. Add cabbage; cover and cook 3 to 5 minutes, stirring once, or until wilted.

**2** Stir in remaining ingredients and bring to a boil. Reduce heat, cover and simmer 5 minutes to blend flavors.

TIP: Best eaten freshly made. Good with rice.

# Beef

You may be surprised to learn that a war started beef on the track to becoming Americans' favorite meat. There had been cattle in America since the 1500s, but before the Civil War (1861-1865) chicken and pork were preferred. Shortages of those meats created by the war turned attention to beef and our tastes have never looked back. For a while beef had a bad rap because of high fat content, but the good news for steak lovers is that today's cattle are raised to produce much leaner meat. And at the market, the meat is trimmed more thoroughly and leaner cuts are emphasized. Grilled steaks and burgers are favorites when pan-grilled or grilled outdoors winter or summer. Stir-fries are popular, too, quickly done in a skillet. As for stew, whether in a slow cooker or Dutch oven, nothing compares with the flavor of beef slowly cooked in a rich broth. The following pages include many delicious ways to prepare beef; check the line directly below the recipe title to see what cut of meat a recipe calls for and the primary cooking method.

# Home Again Pot Roast

## CHUCK POT ROAST · SLOW COOKER

**SERVES** 8 (with leftovers)
**PREP:** 15 minutes
**COOK:** 9 to 11 hours on low

**PER SERVING** (4 oz meat, vegetables and ¼ cup gravy): 385 cal, 51 g pro, 18 g car, 3 g fiber, 11 g fat (4 g sat fat), 137 mg chol, 818 mg sod

## WHY TIED?

Large cuts of meat for roast or pot roast often are tied in several places with butcher's twine. This helps to keep the meat firmly together so that it cooks more evenly, has a better shape and cuts a good slice. Even beef or pork tenderloins can benefit from tying.

Keep a ball of butcher's twine (100% cotton thread) on hand for those times when a chuck pot roast, for example, has not been tied before sale. Tie it firmly in three or four places.

2 beef bouillon cubes

14.5-oz can petite diced tomatoes

1 cup dry red wine or water

1.8-oz box leek soup mix

1 Tbsp Worcestershire sauce

1 Tbsp chopped garlic

1 tsp dried thyme

1 tsp dried marjoram

1 tsp dried rosemary

One 4-lb boneless beef chuck pot roast, tied (see *Why Tied?*, left)

12 oz carrots, cut in half

8 oz parsnips, cut in half

3 Tbsp flour

**1**  Dissolve bouillon cubes in ¼ cup boiling water. Pour into a 5-qt or larger slow cooker. Stir in tomatoes, wine, soup mix, Worcestershire sauce, garlic and herbs. Add meat; turn to coat with liquid. Cut thick pieces of carrot or parsnip in half or quarters lengthwise. Arrange vegetables around meat.

**2**  Cover and cook on low 9 to 11 hours until fork tender. Remove meat to cutting board and cover with foil. Leave liquid and vegetables in covered cooker. Set on high.

**3**  Whisk flour into ¼ cup cold water in a small bowl until blended. Stir into liquid, cover and cook 10 minutes until thickened.

**4**  Thinly slice beef; arrange on serving platter. Remove vegetables with a slotted spoon; arrange around beef. Spoon a little gravy on meat and serve rest at table.

Short Ribs with Sweet Potatoes *(page 82)*

Tex-Mex Beef Stew *(page 86)*

Blackened Skirt Steak with Cheddar-Sage Mashed Potatoes *(page 89)*

Neapolitan Meat Loaf *(page 95)*

# Rio Grande Pot Roast

1½ cups thick-and-chunky salsa

1 cup beer or water

6-oz can tomato paste

1.25-oz pkt taco seasoning

One 3-lb boneless beef bottom round roast

½ tsp salt

½ tsp freshly ground pepper

2 Tbsp peanut butter

⅓ cup chopped fresh cilantro

> **SERVES** 8
> **PREP:** 10 minutes
> **COOK:** 8 to 10 hours on low
>
> **PER SERVING:** 432 cal,
> 36 g pro, 11 g car, 1 g fiber,
> 25 g fat (9 g sat fat), 109 mg
> chol, 1,112 mg sod

**1** Put salsa, beer, tomato paste and taco seasoning in a 5-qt or larger slow cooker. Stir to mix. Rub beef with salt and pepper; add to cooker and spoon some of the sauce mixture over it.

**2** Cover and cook on low 8 to 10 hours or until beef is very tender when pierced. Remove to a cutting board. Stir peanut butter and cilantro into sauce. Slice meat across the grain(see *Across the Grain*, page 89); serve with the sauce.

---

## BEEF ROASTING CHART

Use this chart as a guide for roasting times. A meat thermometer (we like the instant-read kind) will register 145°F to 150°F for medium-rare, 160°F for medium. After taking the roast from the oven allow it to rest for 15 minutes before carving. During that time, the internal temperature will rise 5° to 10°F.

| CUT | WEIGHT | COOKING TIME |
| --- | --- | --- |
| Eye round | 2 to 3 lb | 20 to 22 minutes per lb at 325°F |
| Rib eye, boneless | 4 to 5 lb | 18 to 22 minutes per lb at 350°F |
| Rib, bone in | 4 to 6 lb | 25 to 30 minutes per lb at 325°F |
| Top round | 4 to 6 lb | 30 to 35 minutes per lb at 325°F |
| Tenderloin | 2 to 3 lb | 35 to 45 minutes total at 425°F |
| | 4 to 6 lb | 45 minutes to 1 hour total at 425°F |

# Short Ribs with Sweet Potatoes

SHORT RIBS · OVEN · DUTCH OVEN · RIMMED BAKING SHEET

THIS CAN BE MADE A FEW DAYS AHEAD, INCLUDING THE SWEET POTATOES.
STORE THE MASHED SWEETS IN A BOWL AND REHEAT THEM IN A MICROWAVE.

**SERVES** 6
**PREP:** 25 minutes
**BAKE:** About 2 hours

**PER SERVING:** 561 cal, 33 g pro, 54 g car, 6 g fiber, 23 g fat (10 g sat fat), 98 mg chol, 1,361 mg sod

## DUTCH OVEN

The pot known as a Dutch oven has a heavy bottom and is made of materials that distribute heat evenly. Those made of enameled iron and known as French ovens have thick walls as well. Two handles make it easy to lift the pot in and out of the oven, and a tight-fitting lid traps moisture inside.

A wide bottom allows plenty of surface for browning food and should be large enough to hold a whole chicken or a pot roast. If you are looking for a Dutch oven, check that it can be used stove-top as well as in the oven. These pots don't come cheap but are invaluable for cooking and should serve the cook well forever.

5 lb beef chuck short ribs, fat trimmed
Two 10.5-oz cans condensed French onion soup
1 Tbsp chopped garlic
Freshly ground pepper
1 Tbsp flour
⅓ cup prepared white horseradish

SWEET POTATOES
  3 lb sweet potatoes, scrubbed and pierced with a fork
  ½ cup orange juice
  2 Tbsp stick butter, softened
  1 tsp salt

GARNISH: **snipped chives**

**1** Adjust racks to middle and bottom of oven. Heat to 325°F. Have ready a 5-qt or larger Dutch oven (see *Dutch Oven*, left).

**2** Coat pot with cooking spray. Heat over medium heat. Add half the ribs (or all of them if there's plenty of space in bottom of pan) and brown on top and bottom, turning once, about 5 minutes. Brown remaining ribs. Pour off fat. Add onion soup, 1 soup can water, the garlic and ½ tsp pepper. Bring to a boil; cover and place on middle oven rack.

**3** SWEET POTATOES: Put potatoes on a rimmed baking sheet; place on bottom oven rack.

**4** Bake potatoes and short ribs 1½ hours or until ribs are tender and potatoes are soft when pierced. (Check sweet potatoes after 45 minutes.)

**5** Transfer ribs to a serving bowl. Skim fat off gravy then bring to a boil. Whisk flour and 2 Tbsp cold water in a small bowl. Whisk into gravy, add horseradish and boil 2 minutes until slightly thickened. Pour over ribs.

**6** When sweets are cool enough to handle cut them in half; scoop pulp into a medium bowl. Add orange juice, butter, salt and ½ tsp pepper; mash with a potato masher or handheld mixer. Serve with the ribs. Sprinkle servings with chives.

# Slow-Cooker Beef Short Ribs

SHORT RIBS · SLOW COOKER

1 cup dry red wine or water
⅓ cup tomato ketchup
1 pkt (from a box of 2) beefy onion soup mix
4 small garlic cloves, halved
½ tsp dried thyme
½ tsp dried rosemary
½ tsp freshly ground pepper
4 lb beef chuck short ribs, fat trimmed
Flour (optional)

SERVES 4
PREP: 10 minutes
COOK: 10 to 12 hours on low

PER SERVING: 1,124 cal, ·
50 g pro, 12 g car, 0 g fiber,
96 g fat (41 g sat fat), 213 mg
chol, 1,000 mg sod

**1** Put wine, ketchup, onion soup mix, garlic, thyme, rosemary and pepper in a 5-qt slow cooker. Stir to mix. Add short ribs; turn to coat.

**2** Cover and cook on low 10 to 12 hours, until tender. Remove ribs. Pour juices into a cup measure. Let rest a few minutes then skim off fat. To thicken juices for gravy, check amount then pour them into a small saucepan and bring to a boil. For each cup of juices, whisk 2 Tbsp flour and 3 Tbsp cool water in the cup measure or a small bowl. Whisk into boiling juices. Reduce heat and simmer 2 to 3 minutes until slightly thickened.

# Pepper-Coated Roast Beef with Red Pepper–Basil Butter

EYE-ROUND BEEF ROAST · OVEN · SHALLOW ROASTING PAN · WIRE RACK

THIS IS A WONDERFUL PARTY DISH, ESPECIALLY IF YOU CARVE IT
IN THE KITCHEN WITH GUESTS MILLING AROUND.

**SERVES** 12
**TOTAL TIME:** 1 hour 10 minutes

**PER SERVING:** 316 cal,
30 g pro, 1 g car, 0 g fiber,
20 g fat (9 g sat fat), 95 mg
chol, 288 mg sod

TIP: Look in the spice section for peppercorn medley (peppercorn and other spices) packed in a jar with its own grinder.

TIP: If you prefer, make the butter in the food processor. Don't mince the peppers, use ¼ cup each basil and parsley leaves and let the food processor do the chopping.

TIP: If you make the butter ahead, let it come to room temperature while the beef roasts.

BEEF

One 4-lb eye-round beef roast

⅓ cup Dijon mustard

3 Tbsp coarsely ground mixed peppercorns or black peppercorns (see Tip, left)

RED PEPPER BUTTER

6 Tbsp stick butter, softened

¼ cup bottled roasted red peppers, dried on paper towels, then minced

1½ Tbsp minced fresh basil or 1 tsp dried

1½ Tbsp minced fresh parsley

**1** BEEF: Heat oven to 425°F. Set a wire rack into a shallow roasting pan.

**2** Rub roast with mustard; sprinkle with pepper. Place on rack in pan.

**3** Roast 45 to 55 minutes or until a meat thermometer inserted in center registers 145°F. Remove roast to carving board, cover loosely with foil and let rest about 10 minutes. (Temperature will rise about 5 degrees to 150°F for medium rare.)

**4** MEANWHILE MAKE RED PEPPER BUTTER (see Tip, left): Beat butter in a small bowl with a wooden spoon until fluffy. Stir in remaining ingredients.

**5** TO SERVE: Thinly slice roast beef and arrange on a platter. Serve with the flavored butter to spread over the meat.

# Beef Stew

EVERY COOK NEEDS A GOOD, SIMPLE STEW LIKE THIS IN THEIR REPERTOIRE, WHICH CAN BE MADE AHEAD OR NOT. HERE SOME OF THE COOKED VEGETABLES ARE PURÉED TO THICKEN THE GRAVY.

¼ cup flour

2 lb lean beef chunks for stew (see *Cuts for Stew*, page 87)

2 Tbsp olive oil

2 medium onions, cut in 1-in. wedges

2 Tbsp minced garlic

2 tsp dried thyme

2 tsp dried rosemary

1 tsp salt

1 tsp freshly ground pepper

2½ cups beef broth

1 cup dry red wine or water

1½ lb turnips, cut in 1-in. wedges

1½ lb red-skinned potatoes, cut in 1-in. chunks

6 ribs celery, cut in 1½-in. lengths

4 cups (1 lb) baby carrots

**SERVES 8**
**PREP:** 20 to 25 minutes
**BAKE:** About 2 hours

**PER SERVING:** 355 cal, 27 g pro, 33 g car, 5 g fiber, 13 g fat (4 g sat fat), 75 mg chol, 747 mg sod

**1** Heat oven to 325°F. Put flour and beef in a large plastic food bag and shake until beef is well coated.

**2** Heat oil in a 5-qt or larger Dutch oven over medium-high heat (see *Dutch Oven*, page 82). Add half the beef and cook 4 to 5 minutes, turning pieces three or four times, until well-browned. Remove to a plate. Brown remaining meat in the same way, adding more oil if pan seems dry. Stir in onions, garlic, thyme, rosemary, salt and pepper. With all the meat in the pot, add broth and wine; bring to a boil.

**3** Cover and bake 30 minutes. Stir in vegetables. Cover and bake 1¼ hours longer, or until beef and vegetables are tender when pierced.

**4** Take out 1½ cups vegetables and 1 cup liquid; purée in food processor or blender. Stir into pot.

# Tex-Mex Beef Stew

GOOD SERVED WITH WARM CORNBREAD.

**SERVES** 4
**PREP:** 25 minutes
**COOK:** About 1¾ hours

**PER SERVING:** 651 cal,
35 g pro, 35 g car, 3 g fiber,
43 g fat (15 g sat fat), 124 mg
chol, 923 mg sod

TIP: Chuck is a lean and flavorful choice for stew, as is beef round.

3 ancho chiles (see FYI, left)
1½ lb lean beef chunks for stew (see *Cuts for Stew*, facing page)
¼ cup flour
2 Tbsp oil
14.5-oz can diced tomatoes in thick juice
2 cups beef broth
2 tsp ground cumin
½ tsp dried oregano
½ tsp salt
1-lb butternut squash, peeled and cut in ¾- to 1-in. chunks
   (3 cups)
1½ cups frozen corn kernels

**1** Cut chiles in half, remove stems and scoop out seeds (see *Handling Hot Peppers*, page 52). Soak chiles in 1½ cups hot water 20 minutes or until soft.

**2** While chiles soak, put beef and flour in a large plastic food bag and shake to coat.

**3** Heat 1 Tbsp oil in a 4-qt Dutch oven over medium-high heat (see *Dutch Oven*, page 82). Add half the beef and cook 4 to 5 minutes, turning pieces three or four times, until well-browned. Remove to a plate. Brown remaining meat in the same way. Put first batch back in pot.

**4** While beef browns, put chiles and soaking water in a blender or food processor; process until smooth. Add to beef. Stir in tomatoes, broth, cumin, oregano and salt.

**5** Bring to a boil, reduce heat, cover pot, leaving lid slightly ajar, and simmer 1 hour, stirring occasionally. Stir in squash and corn, return to a simmer, partially cover and cook 45 minutes longer, or until beef and squash are tender when pierced.

**FYI:** Anchos start life as poblanos, the dark-green chiles often stuffed for chiles rellenos. When dried, the 3- to 4-in.-long, not-too-incendiary chiles turn deep red and acquire a new name: anchos.

# Sweet & Sour Beef Stew

LEAN BEEF FOR STEW · OVEN · DUTCH OVEN

IN THIS RECIPE, THE BEEF IS NOT BROWNED BEFORE COOKING AND, LIKE MOST STEWS, THIS ONE CAN BE MADE AHEAD. GOOD WITH RICE, GREEN PEAS AND A GREEN SALAD.

1 Tbsp oil
1 cup chopped onion
3 Tbsp sugar
3 Tbsp Worcestershire sauce
1 Tbsp mustard powder (see FYI, right)
¼ cup distilled white vinegar
3 Tbsp flour
1 tsp salt
⅛ tsp freshly ground pepper
2 lb lean beef chunks for stew (see *Cuts for Stew*, below)

**SERVES** 4
**PREP:** 10 minutes
**BAKE:** 2½ hours

**PER SERVING:** 461 cal, 46 g pro, 21 g car, 1 g fiber, 21 g fat (7 g sat fat), 148 mg chol, 883 mg sod

**1** Heat oven to 350°F.

**2** Heat oil in a 1½- to 2-qt Dutch oven or other heavy stovetop-to-oven pot (see *Dutch Oven*, page 82). Add onion and cook 4 to 5 minutes, stirring a few times, until golden. Add sugar, Worcestershire, mustard powder, vinegar and 2 cups of water; stir until blended. Bring to a simmer.

**3** Meanwhile mix flour, salt and pepper in a large plastic food bag. Add beef; shake to coat. Add beef to pot; stir to coat.

**4** Cover and bake 2½ hours or until meat is tender when pierced.

**FYI:** Mustard powder is simply ground mustard seeds; find it in jars or small cans in the spice section. Sometimes in recipes it is called "dry mustard."

## CUTS FOR STEW

The long, slow, moist cooking that leads to a good stew also gives the toughest, less expensive cuts of meat a tender succulence and great flavor, so don't think that the more expensive cuts will give better results. Beef chuck has excellent flavor and is one of the best cuts for stew. Buy it already cut in chunks or cubes. If the chunks are very large, or if the size of the chunks varies greatly, take a minute and cut the chunks so they are more even in size.

If you are looking for ways to save money, check the price per pound of chunks for stew with the price per pound for boneless chuck steak. Often the chuck steak will be as much as a dollar less per pound, well worth the few minutes it will take you to cut it into stew-size chunks.

# Beef & Mushroom Ragout

## LEAN BEEF FOR STEW · SLOW COOKER

HERE'S THE SIMPLEST TAKE ON THE TRADITIONAL FRENCH BOEUF BOURGUIGNON.
SERVE OVER NOODLES, OR WITH MASHED OR BOILED POTATOES.

**SERVES 4**
**PREP:** 10 minutes
**COOK:** 4 hours on high, or
8 to 10 hours on low

**PER SERVING:** 478 cal,
47 g pro, 18 g car, 2 g fiber,
23 g fat (8 g sat fat), 148 mg
chol, 1,403 mg sod

**TIP:** If you use shiitake mushrooms discard the stems because they remain tough even after cooking.

10.75-oz can condensed cream of mushroom soup
½ cup dry red wine
1 pkt (from a box of 2) beefy onion soup mix
½ tsp dried thyme
2 lb lean beef chunks for stew (see *Cuts for Stew*, page 87)
2 cups (8 oz) baby carrots
8 oz shiitake or other mushrooms, sliced (see Tip, left)
GARNISH: **chopped parsley**

**1** Put mushroom soup, wine, soup mix and thyme in a 3-qt or larger slow cooker; whisk until well blended.

**2** Add beef, carrots and mushrooms; stir until coated. Cover and cook on high 4 hours or on low 8 to 10 hours or until meat is very tender. Sprinkle servings with parsley.

---

**GRADES: BEEF**
By law, the U.S. Department of Agriculture checks all meat sold in the United States for wholesomeness.
The USDA also grades beef, but it is an option paid for by wholesale meat packers. Only about 50% of American beef is graded.
The quality that determines grade is marbling (fat streaks) because the more fat the more tender, juicy and flavorful the beef is.
**USDA Prime** is the top grade, containing the highest degree of marbling. It is produced in limited quantities and sold at premium prices.
**Choice** is the grade generally sold at supermarkets. It is preferred by many customers because it contains some marbling but is a little leaner and less expensive than prime.
**Select** (or **Good**) is the lower-priced and leanest grade of meat. It is just as nutritious as the other grades but less juicy and flavorful.

# Blackened Skirt Steak with Cheddar-Sage Mashed Potatoes

SKIRT STEAK · SKILLET

FROZEN MASHED POTATOES ARE EASY TO MEASURE AND HAVE A VERY GOOD
FLAVOR THAT IS ENHANCED HERE BY INFUSING THE MILK WITH SAGE.
THE RUB BLACKENS AS THE STEAK COOKS, HENCE THE NAME.

SPICE RUB
   1 tsp freshly ground pepper
   1 tsp paprika
   1 tsp garlic powder
   ½ tsp dried thyme, crumbled
   ¼ tsp salt

One 1-lb beef skirt steak
1 Tbsp oil

CHEDDAR-SAGE MASHED POTATOES
   1⅓ cups milk
   1 tsp dried sage
   2⅔ cups frozen mashed potatoes
   ½ cup (4 oz) shredded Cheddar cheese

**SERVES** 4
**TOTAL TIME:** 15 minutes

**PER SERVING:** 475 cal,
31 g pro, 25 g car, 2 g fiber,
27 g fat (11 g sat fat), 94 mg
chol, 715 mg sod

**1** SPICE RUB: Mix ingredients in a small bowl. Rub half on each side of the skirt steak. Cut steak in 4 pieces. Heat oil in a large skillet over high heat. Add steak; cook 2 minutes each side for medium-rare. Remove to a platter or board and let rest 5 minutes before slicing across the grain (see *Across the Grain*, right).

**2** While steak cooks and rests crumble sage into milk in a medium saucepan. Heat over medium-high heat. Stir in frozen mashed potatoes and heat, stirring occasionally, about 4 minutes. When hot, remove from heat and stir in cheese.

## ACROSS THE GRAIN
Instructions to slice meat "against" or "across" the grain often confuse cooks. While "across" and "against" mean the same thing, we'll go with across. Look closely at a piece of flank steak, for example, and notice that the surface of the meat looks like long straight lines in one direction. Those lines are the grain of the meat. Cut parallel to the grain and you'll end up with long chewy fibers. Cut thin slices across the grain and you cut the meat fibers into fine, tender slices.
The way the grain runs in a steak or pot roast isn't always as simple and straightforward as with flank steak, but flank steak is a good cut to learn from.

# Panfried Steaks with Creamy Mustard or Mushroom Sauce

## BONELESS BLADE STEAKS · SKILLET

HERE'S A DIFFERENT APPROACH TO FLAVOR AND STEAK: INSTEAD OF USING A RUB OR MARINADE ON THE MEAT, MAKE IT DINNER-PARTY SPECIAL BY SERVING A DELICIOUS SAUCE WITH IT. YOU CAN MAKE THE SAUCE IN A SEPARATE PAN IF YOU PREFER.

**SERVES** 4
**TOTAL TIME:** 7 to 9 minutes

**PER SERVING WITHOUT SAUCE:** 337 cal, 26 g pro, 0 g car, 0 g fiber, 25 g fat (10 g sat fat), 100 mg chol, 351 mg sod

Four ¾-in.-thick boneless beef blade steaks (about 5 oz each)
½ tsp salt
¼ tsp freshly ground pepper
1 tsp olive oil
Mushroom Sauce or Creamy Mustard Sauce (recipes follow)

**1** Blot steaks dry with paper towels. Sprinkle salt and pepper on both sides, pressing to adhere.

**2** Heat oil in large nonstick skillet over medium-high heat. Add steaks and cook 2 minutes per side. Reduce heat to medium and cook another minute per side for medium-rare, 2 minutes per side for medium-well. Remove to dinner plates or a platter. Let rest 5 to 7 minutes before serving.

**3** Wipe or rinse skillet before preparing sauce (recipes follow).

## MUSHROOM SAUCE

**SERVES** 4
**PREP:** 5 minutes
**COOK:** 8 minutes

**PER SERVING:** 85 cal, 2 g pro, 5 g car, 1 g fiber, 3 g fat (2 g sat fat), 8 mg chol, 302 mg sod

12 oz mushrooms (see Tip, left)
½ cup dry Marsala wine
½ cup chicken broth
¼ tsp salt
¼ tsp freshly ground pepper
1 Tbsp stick butter

**1** Heat skillet over medium-high heat. Add mushrooms and cook, stirring often, until browned, about 5 minutes. Remove from skillet.

**2** Add Marsala, broth, salt and pepper to skillet and bring to a boil. Reduce heat and simmer 2 to 3 minutes until about half the liquid has evaporated.

**3** Remove from heat, add butter and stir until melted. Spoon over the steak. Top with sautéed mushrooms.

TIP: You choose the mushrooms. A mixture of white and cremini (sliced) with a few oyster mushrooms (cut in half if large) looks good and gives rich flavor.

## CREAMY MUSTARD SAUCE

⅓ cup reduced-fat sour cream

¼ cup chicken broth

¼ cup creamy mustard blend (such as Dijonnaise)

¼ tsp coarsely cracked peppercorns or freshly ground pepper (see Tip, right)

2 Tbsp sliced scallions

**1** While steaks cook, put sour cream, broth, creamy mustard blend and pepper in a small bowl. Whisk to blend.

**2** Pour into skillet, bring to a boil, reduce heat and simmer 1 minute, stirring often, until thickened. Remove from heat; stir in scallions. Serve with the steak.

SERVES 4
TOTAL TIME: 8 minutes

PER SERVING SAUCE: 44 cal, 1 g pro, 4 g car, 0 g fiber, 2 g fat (1 g sat fat), 8 mg chol, 280 mg sod

TIP: Wrap ¼ tsp peppercorns loosely in plastic wrap. Crush with flat side of knife to break them, then crush more with the bottom of a small dish.

# Korean Beef Bok Choy

## FLANK STEAK · SKILLET

THE "BABY" KIND OF BOK CHOY IS 6 TO 8 IN. LONG WHILE THE LARGER VARIETY IS ABOUT THE SIZE OF A HEAD OF CELERY. BOTH VARIETIES HAVE DARK GREEN LEAVES AND GLEAMING WHITE STEMS THAT WIDEN AT THE BOTTOM. THIS DISH IS GOOD WITH RICE.

1¼ lb baby bok choy

12-oz beef flank steak (see Tip, right)

4 tsp oil

⅓ cup Korean teriyaki stir-fry sauce

Crushed red pepper (optional)

**1** Pull off large outer leaves of bok choy; stack and quarter them. Cut the centers in 4 lengthwise. Cut steak diagonally across the grain in ¼-in.-thick slices.

**2** Heat 1 tsp oil in a large nonstick skillet over medium-high heat. Add half the meat; stir-fry 30 seconds until no longer pink. Remove to a bowl. Repeat with another tsp oil and rest of meat. Add to bowl; stir in 2 Tbsp stir-fry sauce.

**3** Add 2 more tsp oil to skillet, then bok choy. Stir-fry 30 seconds. Add 3 Tbsp water; cover and steam 1 minute. Uncover, add remaining stir-fry sauce and stir-fry 1 minute until bok choy is crisp-tender. Add meat and juices; stir-fry 30 seconds to heat through. Transfer to serving platter. Sprinkle with crushed red pepper.

SERVES 4
TOTAL TIME: 15 minutes

PER SERVING: 238 cal, 19 g pro, 11 g car, 1 g fiber, 10 g fat (4 g sat fat), 44 mg chol, 720 mg sod

TIP: Meat slices more quickly and evenly in a half-frozen state. Freeze the meat for close to an hour (set a timer if you're like me) then slice it. Cook it right away, or refrigerate or freeze the slices (wrap the slices so they are separate and they'll take only a short while to thaw).

# Italian Steak & Bread Salad

GRILLED SIRLOIN TURNS SALAD INTO A SUBSTANTIAL MAIN DISH.

SERVES 4
TOTAL TIME: 15 minutes

PER SERVING: 564 cal,
28 g pro, 41 g car, 4 g fiber,
32 g fat (10 g sat fat), 64 mg
chol, 1,120 mg sod

One 12-oz beef sirloin steak, ½ to ¾ in. thick
Half a 1-lb loaf French bread, split
Garlic cooking spray
½ tsp salt
½ tsp freshly ground pepper
2 cups tomato chunks
Two 6-oz bags baby spinach trio (baby spinach, arugula and
   carrots) or 6 oz baby spinach and 6 oz arugula
½ cup olive oil and vinegar dressing
½ cup sliced onion
½ cup (2 oz) crumbled blue cheese

1   Heat outdoor grill or stovetop grill pan. Coat steak and cut surfaces
of bread with garlic cooking spray; sprinkle with salt and pepper.

2   Grill steak, turning once, 6 minutes for medium-rare. Remove to
a board and let rest 3 minutes. Grill bread, cut sides down, 2 minutes
or until lightly toasted.

3   Cut bread in chunks; thinly slice steak. Put in a bowl with remaining ingredients; toss to mix.

## CUTTING AT AN ANGLE

In addition to cutting less tender steaks such as flank across the grain (see *Across the Grain*, page 89)
you will also get larger, nicer slices if you hold the knife at a 45° angle. Grill a flank steak and put the
cooked meat on a cutting board in front of you with the grain, or lines of the meat, parallel to your body.
Let rest a few minutes to make slicing easier (see *Resting Time*, page 63)

Right-handed person: Hold meat steady with fork in left hand. Hold thin, sharp knife in right hand and
turn hand slightly to the left, so top part of knife blade comes closer to the meat and knife blade is at
an approximately 45° angle to the meat. Keeping knife at this angle, slice meat.

Left-handed person: Hold meat steady with fork in right hand. Hold thin, sharp knife in left hand and
turn hand slightly to the right, so top part of knife blade is closer to the meat and knife blade is at an
approximately 45° angle to the meat. Keeping knife at this angle, slice meat. Slices should be higher
than if you just cut straight down.

# Beef Paprikash

GOOD WITH HOT COOKED NOODLES OR BOW-TIE PASTA TO CATCH THE SAUCE. RESIST ANY TEMPTATION TO COOK THE MEAT FURTHER IN THE SAUCE; IT IS GUARANTEED TO TOUGHEN.

1 lb boneless beef top sirloin strips (for stir-fry)
½ tsp salt
¼ tsp freshly ground pepper
4 tsp oil
1 cup thinly sliced onion
1 cup red pepper strips
1 Tbsp paprika
2 tsp minced garlic
1 cup chicken broth
1 cup reduced-fat sour cream
GARNISH: chopped parsley

**SERVES 4**
**TOTAL TIME:** 25 minutes

**PER SERVING:** 390 cal, 28 g pro, 19 g car, 1 g fiber, 22 g fat (7 g sat fat), 82 mg chol, 558 mg sod

**1** Season beef with salt and pepper.

**2** Heat 2 tsp oil in a large nonstick skillet over medium-high heat. Add half the beef and stir-fry 2 to 3 minutes, just until browned (don't overcook or meat will be tough). Remove to a plate. Brown remaining steak and add to plate.

**3** Reduce heat to medium and add remaining 2 tsp oil to pan drippings. Add onion and red pepper and cook about 4 minutes, stirring often, until soft. Stir in paprika, garlic and broth; simmer 5 minutes. Remove from heat; stir in sour cream, then beef. Pour into serving dish. Sprinkle with parsley.

# Bulgur Meatballs in Tomato Sauce

## LEAN GROUND BEEF · SKILLET

YOU CAN SHAPE THE MEATBALLS AHEAD AND COOK THEM SHORTLY BEFORE SERVING, OR YOU CAN MAKE THE ENTIRE DISH AHEAD AND REHEAT IT CAREFULLY.

**SERVES 4**
**TOTAL TIME:** 45 minutes

**PER SERVING:** 275 cal,
17 g pro, 33 g car, 7 g fiber,
10 g fat (3 g sat fat), 35 mg
chol, 807 mg sod

¾ cup bulgur (cracked wheat, see *Bulgur*, page 196)
8 oz lean ground beef
½ cup finely chopped onion
¾ tsp ground cinnamon
½ tsp ground allspice
Salt
Freshly ground pepper
3 tsp oil
1 Tbsp minced garlic
28-oz can crushed tomatoes
1 tsp sugar
½ cup chopped fresh cilantro

**1** Put bulgur, beef, onion, cinnamon, allspice, ½ tsp salt and ¼ tsp pepper into a bowl. Mix well with hands or a wooden spoon. Roll slightly rounded tablespoonfuls into balls (about 24).

**2** Heat 1 tsp oil in a large nonstick skillet over medium-low heat. Add meatballs; cook 8 minutes, shaking pan back and forth several times, until browned. Transfer to a plate.

**3** Heat remaining 2 tsp oil in skillet. Add garlic; cook 1 minute, until aromatic. Stir in tomatoes, sugar, ¼ tsp salt, ¼ tsp pepper then meatballs. Bring to a simmer, cover and cook 25 minutes or until bulgur is tender. Serve sprinkled with cilantro.

# Neapolitan Meat Loaf

LEAN GROUND BEEF · SKILLET · OVEN · 9 x 5-IN. LOAF PAN

A FESTIVE MEAT LOAF FOR FAMILY OR PARTY. GOOD TOPPED WITH MARINARA SAUCE
AND SERVED WITH GARLIC BREAD AND BROCCOLI RABE.

2 tsp oil
¾ cup finely chopped red pepper
½ cup finely chopped onion
2 tsp minced garlic
2 large eggs
3 slices firm white sandwich bread
1½ lb lean ground beef
¾ tsp salt
¾ tsp freshly ground pepper
10-oz box frozen chopped spinach, thawed and squeezed dry
1 cup (4 oz) shredded part-skim mozzarella cheese
4 oz (20 very thin slices) Genoa salami

**SERVES** 6 to 8
**PREP:** 25 minutes
**BAKE:** About 1¼ hours
**REST:** 10 minutes

**PER SERVING** (for 8): 376 cal,
25 g pro, 7 g car, 1 g fiber, 27 g
fat (11 g sat fat), 140 mg chol,
669 mg sod

**1** Heat oil in a large nonstick skillet over medium-high heat. Add
red pepper, onion and garlic and cook 4 to 5 minutes, stirring often,
until lightly browned and soft. Remove from heat.

**2** While onion and pepper cook, break eggs into a large bowl and
whisk to break up. Tear bread into small pieces and stir into egg.

**3** Heat oven to 350°F. Coat a 9 x 5-in. loaf pan with cooking spray.
Put a strip of foil or plastic wrap (about 20 in. long) on counter.

**4** Add beef, salt, pepper and onion mixture to bowl. Mix gently with
hands. Place on foil or plastic wrap and press into a 17 x 8-in. rectangle. Top with a layer of spinach, then cheese, then overlapping
slices salami. Roll up meat (but not the foil) from one short end; lift
seam side down into loaf pan.

**5** Bake 1 hour 10 minutes or until cooked through and a meat or
instant-read thermometer inserted in center of loaf registers 160°F.
Let rest 10 minutes before unmolding on cutting board or platter.

TIP: Because of the salami,
this is best sliced with a serrated knife.

# Spicy Glazed Meat Loaf

SLOW-COOKER MEAT LOAF IS INCREDIBLY MOIST AND JUICY, AND EVEN BETTER, IT IS READY WHEN YOU GET HOME. GOOD WITH MASHED POTATOES AND SAUTÉED ZUCCHINI.

**SERVES** 6
**PREP:** 10 minutes
**COOK:** 4 hours on high, or 8 to 10 hours on low

**PER SERVING:** 425 cal, 25 g pro, 21 g car, 1 g fiber, 26 g fat (10 g sat fat), 123 mg chol, 1,356 mg sod

TIP: If you can't find spicy ketchup, stir 1 tsp of hot-pepper sauce into plain.

¾ cup spicy tomato ketchup (see Tip, left)
1½ lb lean ground beef
¾ cup seasoned dried bread crumbs
¼ cup grated Parmesan cheese
½ cup finely chopped onion
1 large egg
1½ Tbsp Worcestershire sauce
2 tsp minced garlic
1 tsp salt
½ tsp freshly ground pepper

**1** Put ½ cup ketchup with the remaining ingredients into a large bowl and mix with hands or a wooden spoon until well blended. Form into a 7 x 4½ x 2-in. loaf. Place in 3-qt or larger slow cooker; spread top and sides of loaf with remaining ¼ cup ketchup.

**2** Cover and cook 4 hours on high or 8 to 10 hours on low, or until a meat or instant-read thermometer inserted in center of meat loaf registers 160°F. If your slow cooker is deep and narrow, cut loaf into halves or quarters before attempting to lift it out.

## WHERE'S THE BEEF?

Deciphering the label on a package of ground beef is a little like reading ancient Greek—backward. In simple terms, the names and numbers break down like this:

Ground beef: No more than 30% fat (or at least 70% lean)

Lean or extra-lean: No more than 22.5% fat (or at least 77.5% lean)

But that's it. Government regulations don't distinguish between lean and extra-lean. If your store uses these terms be sure the label spells out exactly what they mean. In the end, the difference between lean and extra-lean may be negligible, but the price may not be. In our recipes we call for "lean ground beef." The degree of lean is your call.

# Picadillo-Stuffed Peppers

### LEAN GROUND BEEF · SKILLET · OVEN

6 medium peppers, preferably red and yellow

26-oz jar green and black olive pasta sauce (Puttanesca)

1 lb lean ground beef

3 cups diced zucchini (12 oz)

1½ cups chopped onions

2 tsp minced garlic

½ tsp ground cinnamon

½ tsp ground cumin

½ tsp salt

½ tsp freshly ground pepper

⅓ cup raisins

1 Tbsp cider vinegar

1 Tbsp sugar

2 tsp olive oil

**SERVES** 6
**PREP:** 18 minutes
**BAKE:** About 30 minutes

**PER SERVING:** 392 cal, 17 g pro, 28 g car, 6 g fiber, 23 g fat (8 g sat fat), 57 mg chol, 960 mg sod

**1** Cut one quarter off stem end of each pepper and remove seeds. Stand peppers and tops in a microwave-safe baking dish. Add ½ cup water, cover with vented plastic wrap and microwave on high 5 minutes or until peppers are crisp-tender. Stir 1½ cups pasta sauce into water in dish.

**2** While peppers cook, heat a large nonstick skillet over medium-high heat. Add beef, zucchini and onion and cook 7 minutes, stirring to break up meat, or until beef is no longer pink and vegetables are almost tender.

**3** Stir in garlic, cinnamon, cumin, salt and pepper; cook 1 minute until fragrant. Remove from heat; stir in raisins, vinegar, sugar and remaining pasta sauce. Spoon filling into peppers; replace tops.

**4** TO BAKE (see Tip, right): Heat oven to 400°F. Brush peppers with the oil. Bake uncovered 30 minutes or until sauce bubbles and pepper tops are lightly charred.

TIP: You can fill the peppers up to 2 days before baking them. Cover the dish tightly and refrigerate.

# Stuffed Cabbage with Cranberry-Tomato Sauce

## LEAN GROUND BEEF · SLOW COOKER

RAISINS, BROWN SUGAR, CRANBERRY SAUCE AND TOMATOES COOK INTO A MELLOW, RICH SAUCE.

**SERVES** 6
**PREP:** 35 minutes
**COOK:** 7 to 9 hours on low

**PER SERVING:** 584 cal,
24 g pro, 67 g car, 2 g fiber,
24 g fat (10 g sat fat), 121 mg
chol, 821 mg sod

**FYI:** The crinkled leaves of savoy cabbage are quite soft and pliable so the usual parboiling is unnecessary. Just cut the hard rib from each leaf.

12 savoy cabbage leaves (see FYI, left)
1½ lb lean ground beef
⅓ cup converted white rice
1 large egg
¾ tsp ground allspice
1 tsp salt
½ tsp freshly ground pepper
16-oz can whole-berry cranberry sauce
14.5-oz can diced tomatoes with onion and garlic
½ cup raisins, preferably golden
⅓ cup packed light-brown sugar
¼ cup fresh lemon juice

**1** Have ready a 5-qt or larger slow cooker. Cut the hard rib from each cabbage leaf and set leaves out on work surface. Put beef, rice, egg, allspice, salt and pepper into a large bowl. Mix with hands or a wooden spoon.

**2** Spoon a slightly rounded ¼ cup beef mixture on bottom center of each cabbage leaf. Fold over the sides and roll each leaf up. Stack in cooker seam sides down.

**3** Top with remaining ingredients. Cover and cook on low 7 hours until cabbage is soft and meat mixture cooked through.

# Beef Salpicón

LEFTOVER ROAST BEEF OR STEAK WOULD ALSO WORK WELL IN THIS MAIN-DISH SALAD.

DRESSING
- ⅓ cup fresh lime juice
- 3 Tbsp olive oil
- ½ tsp minced garlic
- ½ tsp ground cumin
- ½ tsp salt
- ¼ tsp freshly ground pepper

SALAD
- 4 cups shredded romaine lettuce
- 12 oz sliced deli roast beef, cut in strips
- 2 Kirby (pickling) cucumbers, quartered lengthwise, sliced
- 1 Hass avocado (dark, pebbly-skin variety), diced
- 1 cup diced jicama
- 1 cup grape, cherry or pear tomatoes, halved
- ¾ cup coarsely chopped fresh cilantro
- ½ cup thin slivers sweet onion

GARNISH: toasted pumpkin seeds

**1** DRESSING: Put ingredients and 3 Tbsp water in a large bowl. Whisk to blend.

**2** Add Salad ingredients. Toss to mix and coat. Mound on platter; sprinkle with pumpkin seeds.

**SERVES** 4
**TOTAL TIME:** 20 minutes

**PER SERVING:** 319 cal, 20 g pro, 16 g car, 5 g fiber, 21 g fat (4 g sat fat), 37 mg chol, 1,176 mg sod

**FYI:** In Mexico, salpicón (sal-p-kon) means a salad of shredded cooked meat or fish ("salpicón de marisco," seafood cocktail). In the French kitchen, where the expression originated, the meaning is "mixed," but usually the mixture (of cooked, cut up meat, fish or vegetables) is bound with a sauce or dressing and stuffed into a tart shell or bread case. It can also be stuffed into eggs, or formed into rissoles and fried.

# Fish & Seafood

Farming of fish and shellfish, plus improved methods of freezing and transportation, have made good fish an option for all of us, often at a very reasonable cost. Even people who don't live near water can enjoy fresh fish whenever they want. Fish farming, or aquaculture, is now practiced on a global scale. In our markets we may find farmed salmon from Norway, Scotland, Canada, the U.S. and Chile to name but three or four countries, and wild salmon from Alaska or the Pacific Coast. We may find mussels from New Zealand, or from Canada's Prince Edward Island; trout and tilapia from Chile or our own Idaho (although trout are pond-raised in at least five other states). Shrimp are farmed in many countries and flash-freezing means they get to us in good condition. Fish is gaining popularity and for good reason: It's easy to prepare, it's light on fat and calories, the fats are good-for-us fats and it tastes good prepared in so many different ways.

# Cajun Shrimp with Creamy Grits & Greens

A COMPLETE MEAL IN AN INCREDIBLY SHORT TIME.

**SERVES** 4
**TOTAL TIME:** 20 minutes

**PER SERVING:** 317 cal,
30 g pro, 26 g car, 3 g fiber,
10 g fat (4 g sat fat), 189 mg
chol, 813 mg sod

**FYI:** Either Boursin, Alouette
or Rondelé cheese works
well here.

## THAWING SHRIMP

Almost all shrimp sold in
our markets has been
frozen, whether it is sold
frozen or not. This is a good
thing since shrimp is highly
perishable. High-tech flash-
freezing preserves flavor
and texture of shrimp
whether they are frozen
shell on or peeled.
Most shrimp are
individually quick frozen
(IQF), so you can easily
take just as many as you
need from a package. To
quickly thaw, put them in a
strainer or colander and
rinse under cold running
water for a few minutes.

**CREAMY GRITS**
> ¾ cup quick-cooking grits
> ¼ tsp salt
> 3 cups water
> 4.4-oz container spreadable light garlic and herb cheese
>     (see FYI, left)

**GREENS**
> 9 oz leafy greens blend
> 1 tsp olive oil
> ⅛ tsp salt
> ⅛ tsp crushed red pepper

**CAJUN SHRIMP**
> 2 tsp olive oil
> 1 lb raw, peeled and deveined large shrimp, thawed if frozen
>     (see *Thawing Shrimp*, left; see *Deveining Shrimp*, facing page)
> 1 tsp Cajun seasoning

**1** CREAMY GRITS: Cook grits in salted water as pkg directs.
Remove from heat, stir in cheese, cover and set aside.

**2** GREENS: Place ingredients in a large bowl. Cover with vented
plastic wrap and microwave on high 3 minutes or until greens are
tender. Toss; cover and set aside.

**3** CAJUN SHRIMP: While grits and greens cook, heat oil in a large
nonstick skillet over medium-high heat. Add shrimp, sprinkle with
Cajun seasoning and cook 2 to 3 minutes, stirring frequently, until
cooked through. Serve with the grits and greens.

# Spanish Garlic Shrimp

## RAW SHRIMP · SKILLET

Sᴇʀᴠᴇ ᴡɪᴛʜ ʟᴇᴍᴏɴ ᴡᴇᴅɢᴇs ᴏᴠᴇʀ ϙᴜɪᴄᴋ-ᴄᴏᴏᴋɪɴɢ sᴀꜰꜰʀᴏɴ ʀɪsᴏᴛᴛᴏ ᴏʀ ʏᴇʟʟᴏᴡ ʀɪᴄᴇ.

2 tsp olive oil
1 cup chopped onion
1 cup chopped red or green pepper
2 tsp flour
3 Tbsp dry sherry wine or water
1½ cups chicken broth
2 Tbsp minced garlic
2 Tbsp lemon juice
¼ tsp paprika
¼ tsp salt
¼ tsp freshly ground pepper
1½ lb raw, peeled and deveined large shrimp, thawed if frozen
(see *Thawing Shrimp*, facing page; see *Deveining Shrimp*, below)

**SERVES** 4
**TOTAL TIME:** 20 minutes

**PER SERVING:** 265 cal,
36 g pro, 12 g car, 1 g fiber,
6 g fat (1 g sat fat), 259 mg
chol, 775 mg sod

**1** Heat oil in large nonstick skillet. Add onion and red pepper; cook about 4 minutes, stirring often, until tender. Whisk or stir flour and sherry in a small bowl. Add to skillet with remaining ingredients except shrimp. Stir until simmering, then cook 2 minutes.

**2** Add shrimp and, stirring often, cook 2 minutes or until cooked through.

---

### DEVEINING SHRIMP

The most efficient way to do this is to first remove the shells from all the shrimp. Next, take a small sharp knife and cut a shallow incision along the center of each outside curve, following the dark line of the vein. Then, quickly rinse each shrimp under running cold water as you pull or push out the dark vein.

Shrimp are sold shelled, but usually not deveined except for easy-peel shrimp, which have the shell on, but a slit has been made down the back and the vein removed.

Tiny salad shrimp do not require deveining.

# Easy Paella

RAW SHRIMP · SKILLET

PAELLA, A SPANISH DISH OF RICE COOKED WITH SAUSAGE, SHRIMP AND OFTEN CHICKEN, TOO, IS SIMILAR TO CREOLE JAMBALAYA (FACING PAGE) BUT HAS DIFFERENT SEASONING.

**SERVES** 4
**TOTAL TIME:** 35 minutes

**PER SERVING:** 443 cal, 29 g pro, 57 g car, 4 g fiber, 10 g fat (3 g sat fat), 135 mg chol, 1,462 mg sod

**FYI:** Kielbasa is a garlicky smoked sausage of Polish origin.

**FYI:** Look for jars of sofrito, a seasoning sauce that includes tomato, green pepper, cilantro, onion and garlic in the Hispanic-food section of your supermarket.

2 tsp olive oil
8-oz turkey kielbasa sausage, sliced (see FYI, left)
1 cup chopped onion
1 cup converted long-grain rice
2 cups chicken broth
12 oz raw, peeled and deveined large shrimp, thawed if frozen
(see *Thawing Shrimp*, page 102; see *Deveining Shrimp*, page 103)
6-oz jar sofrito (see FYI, left)
1 cup frozen petite green peas, thawed
¼ cup chopped fresh parsley

**1** Heat oil in a large nonstick skillet over high heat. Add kielbasa and onion and cook, stirring often, about 3 minutes or until onion is golden.

**2** Add rice, broth and ½ cup water; bring to a boil. Reduce heat, cover and simmer 17 minutes until rice is almost tender.

**3** Add shrimp; cover and cook 2 minutes. Stir in sofrito and peas; cook, stirring, 1 minute or until rice is tender and shrimp are cooked. Remove from heat; stir in parsley.

# Skillet Enchiladas Suizas

RAW SHRIMP · SKILLET

AN EASY SKILLET VERSION OF SWISS-STYLE ENCHILADAS (PAGE 208) THAT NEATLY BYPASSES THE FILLING, ROLLING AND BAKING. THE SAUCE IS WONDERFULLY RICH AND CREAMY.

**SERVES** 4
**TOTAL TIME:** 10 minutes

**PER SERVING:** 275 cal, 29 g pro, 22 g car, 2 g fiber, 9 g fat (4 g sat fat), 192 mg chol, 929 mg sod

1½ cups mild green salsa (salsa verde)
5 corn tortillas, torn in quarters
1 lb raw, peeled and deveined medium shrimp, thawed if frozen
(see *Thawing Shrimp*, page 102; see *Deveining Shrimp*, page 103)
2 oz ⅓-less-fat cream cheese (Neufchâtel), softened
⅓ cup shredded Jack cheese
⅓ cup chopped fresh cilantro

**1** Bring ½ cup water, the salsa and the torn tortillas to a simmer in large nonstick skillet over medium heat. Cover and simmer 1 minute.

**2** Add shrimp, cover and cook 1 minute. Over low heat, stir in cream cheese until melted. Sprinkle with Jack cheese and cilantro; cover and cook 1 minute until cheese melts and shrimp are cooked.

# Jambalaya

## RAW SHRIMP · SLOW COOKER

HOLD THE SHRIMP! UNLIKE MOST OF OUR SLOW COOKER RECIPES, WHERE MOST INGREDIENTS GO IN AT THE BEGINNING, HERE THE SHRIMP ARE ADDED FOR 20 MINUTES AT THE END. SERVE WITH RICE (COOK IT WHILE THE SHRIMP ARE COOKING) AND HOT PEPPER SAUCE.

1½ cups chopped onions
1 medium green pepper, chopped
1 cup chopped celery
8 oz smoked sausage, sliced
28-oz can diced tomatoes in thick juice
1½ Tbsp chopped garlic
1 tsp dried thyme
½ tsp salt
½ tsp freshly ground pepper
½ tsp hot pepper sauce
12 oz raw, peeled and deveined medium shrimp, thawed if frozen
  (see *Thawing Shrimp*, page 102; see *Deveining Shrimp*, page 103)
2 Tbsp chopped fresh parsley

**SERVES** 4
**PREP:** 10 minutes
**COOK:** 6 to 8 hours on low

**PER SERVING:** 355 cal, 28 g pro, 23 g car, 3 g fiber, 17 g fat (6 g sat fat), 167 mg chol, 1,386 mg sod

**SHRIMP COUNT**
The number of shrimp you get per pound varies with their size. While there are no hard and fast rules and the number may vary with the packer, on average:
Small      36 to 45 shrimp
              per lb
Medium   31 to 35 shrimp
              per lb
Large      21 to 30 shrimp
              per lb
Jumbo     11 to 15 shrimp
              per lb

**1** Mix all ingredients except shrimp and parsley in a 3½-qt or larger slow cooker. Cover and cook on low 6 to 8 hours or until vegetables are tender.

**2** Stir in shrimp, cover and cook 20 minutes or until cooked through. Stir in parsley.

# Scallops with Creamy Pesto

## SEA SCALLOPS · SKILLET

SERVE WITH LEMON COUSCOUS SPRINKLED WITH TOASTED PINE NUTS, AND WITH ASPARAGUS.

**SERVES** 4
**TOTAL TIME:** 10 minutes

**PER SERVING:** 268 cal,
31 g pro, 7 g car, 1 g fiber,
12 g fat (4 g sat fat), 73 mg
chol, 452 mg sod

**TIP:** Look for pesto in your market's fresh pasta or dairy section.

1½ lb sea scallops
1½ Tbsp flour
1½ tsp olive oil
⅓ cup refrigerated basil pesto
2 Tbsp heavy (whipping) cream

**1** Blot scallops dry with paper towels and toss with the flour to coat.

**2** Heat ¾ tsp oil in a large nonstick skillet over medium-high heat. Add half the scallops and cook 4 minutes, turning once, until golden and just barely opaque at centers. Remove to a plate. Repeat with remaining scallops.

**3** Off heat, add pesto and cream to skillet; stir to blend.

**4** Spoon pesto-cream sauce onto serving plates and top with scallops.

### BUYING AND STORING SCALLOPS

Look for firm, moist scallops with a creamy white color and fresh scent. Those that are not fresh have an unmistakable sulfurous odor. The best scallops are also "dry," that is, not oozing liquid into the package, and have a pearly look. Cook scallops within a day of buying them, or freeze them. To freeze large scallops cut them into thinner disks. Spread them out between plastic wrap on a baking sheet and freeze. When hard pack them, still in plastic, into a container or ziptop bag. The thinner pieces of scallop will thaw quickly. Cook them as soon as possible to maintain flavor and texture.

# Crunchy Fish Sticks

EVERY KID'S FAVORITE AND, ACCORDING TO ONE 10-YEAR-OLD, HOMEMADE ARE BEST.
IF YOU'D LIKE TO MAKE CHICKEN TENDERS THE SAME WAY, SEE PAGE 54.

SAUCE
  ½ cup tartar sauce
  ¾ cup grape, cherry or pear tomatoes, cut up

FISH STICKS
  1 large egg
  5 oz baked potato chips, finely crushed (1¼ cups, see Tip, right)
  ¾ tsp paprika
  ¾ tsp salt
  1 lb skinless flounder, sole or red snapper fillets, cut in 1-in.-
    wide strips (see Tip, right)

> **SERVES** 4
> **PREP:** 15 minutes
> **BAKE:** About 20 minutes
>
> **PER SERVING:** 421 cal, 26 g pro, 32 g car, 3 g fiber, 21 g fat (4 g sat fat), 122 mg chol, 938 mg sod

**1** Heat oven to 450°F. Line a rimmed baking sheet with foil (for easy cleanup). Set a wire rack on foil; coat rack well with cooking spray.

**2** Mix Sauce ingredients in a small bowl.

**3** Beat egg with a fork in a medium bowl until foamy. In another bowl, mix crushed chips, paprika and salt. Add fish strips to egg; toss to coat. Drop a few fish strips into chip mixture. Toss with a fork to coat. Place on prepared rack. Repeat until all fish strips are coated.

**4** Bake 10 minutes or until coating is crisp and fish is cooked through. Using a broad spatula, lift fish sticks from rack to serving platter. Serve with Sauce.

> **TIP:** Seal potato chips in a plastic food bag and crush with a rolling pin, or use a food processor.

> **TIP:** For long fish sticks, cut the fillets lengthwise; for shorter sticks, cut crosswise.

# Roasted Halibut with Orange Salsa

## HALIBUT FILLET · RIMMED BAKING SHEET · OVEN

GOOD, FAST AND EASY. MAKE THE SALSA FIRST BECAUSE THE ONION NEEDS HALF AN HOUR (LONGER IS OK) TO MELLOW. SERVE FISH WITH COUSCOUS AND A GREEN VEGETABLE.

**SERVES 4**
**TOTAL TIME:** 25 minutes (plus about 30 minutes standing time for the salsa)

**PER SERVING:** 275 cal, 43 g pro, 13 g car, 2 g fiber, 6 g fat (1 g sat fat), 64 mg chol, 511 mg sod

**TIP:** You can use fresh jalapeños instead of pickled, but the pickled are far more fiery, so use at least 2½ fresh ones to achieve the same effect.

ORANGE SALSA
    ½ cup chopped red onion
    ¼ cup fresh lemon juice
    2 navel oranges, peeled and diced
    2 pickled jalapeño peppers, chopped (see Tip, left; see *Handling Hot Peppers*, page 52)
    ½ cup fresh chopped cilantro

Four ¾-in.-thick pieces halibut fillet (6 to 8 oz each)
½ tsp salt
¼ tsp freshly ground pepper
Olive oil cooking spray

**1** ORANGE SALSA: Toss onion with lemon juice in a medium bowl. Let stand at least 30 minutes, then stir in remaining ingredients.

**2** Heat oven to 500°F. Line a rimmed baking sheet with foil (for easy cleanup). Place pieces of fish on sheet; sprinkle with salt and pepper. Coat tops with cooking spray.

**3** Roast 10 minutes, or until still slightly opaque in the center. Serve with Orange Salsa.

# Quick French Fish & Potato Stew

## COD OR SCROD FILLET · 4- TO 5-QT POT

SERVE WITH FRENCH BREAD TO DIP IN THE SOUP.

2 large cloves garlic, peeled
2 tsp fennel seeds
½ tsp dried thyme
½ tsp salt
2 tsp olive oil, preferably extra-virgin
1½ cups chopped onions
1½ cups thinly sliced carrots
4 cups chicken broth
2 lb (about 4 medium) baking potatoes, peeled and cut in
    1-in. chunks
14-oz can diced tomatoes
1½ lb cod or scrod fillets, cut in 1-in. chunks
½ to 1 tsp freshly ground pepper

**MAKES** 6 two-cup servings
**TOTAL TIME:** About 50 minutes

**PER SERVING:** 265 cal, 26 g pro, 32 g car, 4 g fiber, 4 g fat (1 g sat fat), 49 mg chol, 1,050 mg sod

**1** Put garlic, fennel seeds, thyme and salt on a cutting board. Chop, then mash to a fairly smooth paste with the side of a large, heavy knife.

**2** Heat oil in a 4- to 5-qt pot over medium heat. Add garlic mixture and cook, stirring, 1 minute or until fragrant. Stir in onions and carrots. Cook, stirring often, 5 minutes or until onions are translucent.

**3** Stir in chicken broth and potatoes. Bring to a boil, reduce heat, cover and simmer 15 to 20 minutes until potatoes are tender. Stir in tomatoes, increase heat to medium and gently boil 2 to 3 minutes.

**4** Stir in fish. Cover and simmer 5 minutes or until fish is opaque at center. Stir in pepper. Ladle into serving bowl(s).

# Roasted Red Snapper with Coconut-Ginger Sauce

## RED SNAPPER FILLETS · RIMMED BAKING SHEET · OVEN

**SERVES 4**
**TOTAL TIME:** 38 minutes

**PER SERVING:** 449 cal, 45 g pro, 17 g car, 5 g fiber, 24 g fat (19 g sat fat), 73 mg chol, 541 mg sod

**FYI:** Look for coconut milk near Thai foods in the supermarket. (Heavily-sweetened cream of coconut, which would be totally wrong here, is with cocktail mixes.)

**SHREDDING CARROTS**
When a recipe calls for shredded carrots you can use the kind you buy in the produce section of the supermarket. Or shred them yourself using a food processor and the shredding disk or the largest holes on a box (four-sided) grater.

2 tsp dry Caribbean jerk seasoning
½ tsp salt
14-oz can coconut milk (not cream of coconut, see FYI, left)
⅓ cup sliced scallions
1 Tbsp minced garlic
1 Tbsp minced or grated fresh ginger (see *Fresh Ginger*, page 61)
4 red snapper fillets (about 8 oz each), each cut in 3 pieces
Cooking spray
2 cups shredded carrots (see *Shredding Carrots*, left)
1 red pepper, cut in thin strips
6 oz baby spinach
GARNISH: chopped fresh cilantro or parsley

**1** Heat oven to 400°F. Lightly coat a rimmed baking sheet with cooking spray. Mix jerk seasoning and salt in a small bowl.

**2** Put coconut milk, scallions, garlic, ginger and ¾ tsp jerk seasoning mixture in a large nonstick skillet. Bring to a boil, reduce heat and gently boil 3 minutes to thicken slightly.

**3** Meanwhile sprinkle both sides of fish with remaining seasoning mixture. Arrange skin side up on baking sheet; coat skin with cooking spray. Bake 8 to 10 minutes until cooked through.

**4** Add carrots and pepper strips to skillet, cover and cook 5 minutes. Stir in spinach; cook until it wilts.

**5** Place snapper on serving plates. Spoon vegetables and sauce over fish. Garnish with cilantro.

# Cod Veracruz-Style

## COD FILLET · SKILLET

GOOD WITH RICE, OR WITH NEW POTATOES. COOKS AROUND THE MEXICAN CITY OF VERACRUZ, ON THE GULF OF MEXICO, ARE FAMOUS FOR THE FLAVOR AND VARIETY OF THEIR FISH DISHES.

2 Tbsp flour

¼ tsp salt

¼ tsp freshly ground pepper

Four ¾-in.-thick pieces cod fillet (about 6 oz each)

1½ Tbsp olive oil, preferably extra-virgin

1 cup sliced onion

1 tsp minced garlic

14.5-oz can diced tomatoes (preferably fire-roasted) with green chiles

⅓ cup pimiento-stuffed green olives, halved

1 Tbsp capers, rinsed (see FYI, right)

½ tsp dried oregano

GARNISH: chopped parsley

**SERVES** 4
**TOTAL TIME:** 25 minutes

**PER SERVING:** 247 cal, 32 g pro, 11 g car, 3 g fiber, 8 g fat (1 g sat fat), 73 mg chol, 1,000 mg sod

**1** Mix flour, salt and pepper on sheet of wax paper; add fish and turn to coat.

**2** Heat 1 Tbsp oil in a large nonstick skillet over medium-high heat. Add cod skin side up and cook 5 to 7 minutes, turning once, until golden and barely opaque in the center. Remove to a platter; cover to keep warm.

**3** Heat remaining ½ Tbsp oil in skillet. Add onion and cook over medium-high heat about 3 minutes, stirring once or twice, until golden. Add garlic; cook 1 minute until fragrant. Stir in the tomatoes, olives, capers, oregano and ½ cup water. Bring to a boil, reduce heat and simmer 2 minutes to develop flavors. Spoon over fish.

**FYI:** Capers are the buds of the caper bush, which grows wild in the South of France, Italy, Algeria, Turkey and parts of Asia. The French ones, called "nonpareils," are smaller than a green pea and are sold pickled in a vinegar brine. The largest ones, favored in Italy, are about the size of a small olive and are often packed in salt and sold by the ounce. Capers are used as a garnish, or to give a tiny sharp bite to a sauce or salad. For this recipe use the very tiny capers. All sizes, however, need to be rinsed before using to get rid of excess salt or vinegar.

# Grilled Cod with Caponata

## COD STEAKS · SKILLET · GRILL OR STOVETOP GRILL PAN

CAPONATA IS A POPULAR SALAD OR SIDE DISH IN SOUTHERN ITALY. ALTHOUGH SMALL CANS OF IT CAN BE FOUND IN U.S. SUPERMARKETS AND ARE GOOD TO KEEP ON HAND FOR AN APPETIZER, THIS "FROM SCRATCH" CAPONATA HAS MORE TEXTURE AND COLOR AND MAKES A FLAVORFUL SAUCE FOR COD.

**SERVES** 4
**TOTAL TIME:** 1 hour (includes 30 minutes to marinate)

**PER SERVING:** 369 cal, 35 g pro, 34 g car, 5 g fiber, 12 g fat (2 g sat fat), 75 mg chol, 927 mg sod

TIP: Halibut steaks or fillets of other firm white fish such as red snapper or tilapia are also great cooked this way.

### COD MARINADE
- 2 Tbsp olive oil, preferably extra-virgin
- 2 Tbsp fresh lemon juice
- 1 tsp minced garlic
- 1 tsp dried oregano
- 1 tsp salt

4 cod steaks, each a scant 1 in. thick (about 1¾ lb)

### CAPONATA
- 2 Tbsp olive oil, preferably extra-virgin
- ½ cup chopped onion
- 1 Italian frying pepper, cut in thin strips
- 1 orange pepper, cut in thin strips
- 1 yellow pepper, cut in thin strips
- 2 tsp minced garlic
- 1½ lb striped or purple eggplant, unpeeled, cut in ¾-in. pieces (about 6 cups)
- 8-oz can (1 cup) tomato sauce
- ½ cup golden raisins
- 2 Tbsp red-wine vinegar
- 2 Tbsp rinsed capers

GARNISH: lemon wedges, chopped parsley

**1** COD MARINADE: Mix marinade ingredients in a large ziptop bag. Add cod, seal, then turn bag to distribute marinade. Leave at room temperature 30 minutes while preparing Caponata.

**2** CAPONATA: Heat oil in a large nonstick skillet over medium heat. Add onion and peppers; cook 2 to 3 minutes or until vegetables are just starting to soften.

**3** Add garlic; stir 30 seconds until aromatic. Stir in eggplant and cook, stirring often, 2 to 3 minutes. Stir in tomato sauce, cover, reduce heat and simmer, stirring once or twice, 12 minutes or until eggplant is very tender.

Easy Paella *(page 104)*

Scallops with Creamy Pesto *(page 106)*

Cod Veracruz-Style *(page 111)*

Swordfish with Cucumber Sauce & Tabbouleh *(page 120)*

**4** Meanwhile heat outdoor grill or stovetop grill pan. Remove fish from marinade; discard marinade.

**5** Grill fish (4 to 6 in. from heat source on outdoor grill) 8 to 10 minutes, turning once, until opaque at center.

**6** Add raisins, vinegar and capers to Caponata. Cover and simmer 5 minutes to develop flavors.

**7** Serve fish with Caponata on the side. Garnish with lemon and parsley.

# Baked Tilapia with Avocado & Tomato

### TILAPIA FILLETS · RIMMED BAKING SHEET · OVEN

TILAPIA (ALSO KNOWN AS ST PETER'S FISH) IS A LEAN FISH WITH A MILD FLAVOR THAT IS FARMED IN MANY PARTS OF THE WORLD. BROCCOLI, AND COUSCOUS OR RICE, MAKE NICE ACCOMPANIMENTS.

4 tilapia fillets (about 5 oz each)
2 Tbsp olive oil, preferably extra-virgin
¼ tsp garlic powder
¼ tsp dried basil
¼ tsp dried marjoram
Salt
Freshly ground pepper
2 cups diced tomatoes (12 oz)
1 ripe avocado (preferably Hass), diced

**SERVES 4**
**TOTAL TIME:** 20 minutes

**PER SERVING:** 294 cal, 28 g pro, 7 g car, 2 g fiber, 18 g fat (2 g sat fat), 0 mg chol, 374 mg sod

**1** Heat oven to 350°F. Line a rimmed baking sheet with foil (for easy cleanup).

**2** Brush both sides of fish with 1 Tbsp oil; place on lined pan. Sprinkle fish with the garlic powder, basil, marjoram, ¼ tsp salt and ⅛ tsp pepper.

**3** Bake 7 to 10 minutes or until fish is just barely opaque at center.

**4** Meanwhile put tomato and avocado into a medium bowl. Add remaining 1 Tbsp oil, ¼ tsp salt and ⅛ tsp pepper. Toss to mix and coat. Serve over the fish.

# Cajun Catfish

CATFISH FILLET · SKILLET

SERVE WITH COLESLAW, HOMEMADE OR FROM THE DELI.

**SERVES 4**
**TOTAL TIME:** 32 minutes

**PER SERVING:** 386 cal, 27 g pro, 42 g car, 2 g fiber, 11 g fat (2 g sat fat), 48 mg chol, 1,015 mg sod

**TIP:** Already-seasoned cat-fish fillets can be found at the seafood counter of many supermarkets.

10-oz box frozen chopped spinach
2 cups chicken broth
1 cup converted long-grain rice
1 tsp ground cumin
½ tsp dried thyme
4 catfish fillets (about 5 oz each)
2 tsp Cajun or Cajun Creole seasoning

**1** Put frozen spinach and ½ cup water in a 12-in. skillet. Bring to a boil, cover and cook 3 minutes, breaking up greens, until almost thawed. Stir in broth, rice, cumin and thyme. Bring to a boil, reduce heat, cover and simmer 12 minutes, stirring once.

**2** Sprinkle fish fillets with seasoning, place on rice, cover and cook 10 minutes, or until fish is barely opaque in thickest part and rice is tender.

# Poached Salmon with Dill Sauce

SALMON FILLET · SKILLET · FOOD PROCESSOR

**SERVES 4**
**TOTAL TIME:** 15 minutes

**PER SERVING:** 490 cal, 35 g pro, 5 g car, 0 g fiber, 35 g fat (8 g sat fat), 120 mg chol, 457 mg sod

1 Tbsp distilled white vinegar
4 pieces (5 to 6 oz each) salmon fillet

DILL SAUCE
   1 cup packed fresh dill (see Tip, facing page)
   1 small scallion, cut up
   ¾ cup light mayonnaise
   ¼ cup reduced-fat sour cream
   1 Tbsp distilled white vinegar

**1** Bring vinegar and 1 in. water to boil in a wide, deep skillet. Add salmon, reduce heat until water barely simmers, cover and cook 10 minutes or until fish is barely opaque in the center.

**2** Meanwhile put Dill Sauce ingredients in a food processor; process until dill and scallions are finely chopped.

**3** Using a broad, slotted spatula, remove fish to a serving platter or plates. Serve with the sauce.

> **TIP:** Grasp dill fronds by the handful, twist them off stems, rinse, shake off water, then measure. The food processor will do the rest. The sauce can be made a day ahead and is also delicious with asparagus. The salmon is good warm or cold.

# Moroccan Salmon

## SALMON FILLET · OVEN

GOOD WITH WHOLE-WHEAT COUSCOUS.

2 tsp olive oil
2 cups thinly sliced onions
2 tsp minced garlic
¾ tsp ground cumin
¾ tsp ground turmeric
¾ tsp salt
⅛ tsp ground cinnamon
3 plum tomatoes, cut in thin wedges
¼ cup raisins, preferably golden
1 bay leaf
Four 1-in.-thick pieces (6 to 7 oz each) salmon fillet

> **SERVES 4**
> **TOTAL TIME:** 1 hour
>
> **PER SERVING:** 428 cal, 38 g pro, 17 g car, 2 g fiber, 23 g fat (4 g sat fat), 109 mg chol, 552 mg sod

**1** Heat oven to 425°F. Have ready a large baking dish.

**2** Heat oil in a large nonstick skillet over medium-low heat. Add onions, garlic, cumin, turmeric, salt and cinnamon. Cover and cook 10 minutes, stirring occasionally, until onions start to soften. Stir in tomatoes, raisins and bay leaf; cover and cook 3 minutes or until tomatoes begin to soften.

**3** Place salmon in one layer in baking dish; top with onion mixture. Cover tightly and bake 20 to 30 minutes until fish is opaque at thickest part. Discard bay leaf.

# Salmon with Cilantro Pesto & a Riot of Peppers

SALMON FILLET · SKILLET · BROILER · FOOD PROCESSOR

THIS IS A WONDERFUL DISH TO MAKE WHEN FARMER'S MARKETS ARE OVERFLOWING
WITH BRILLIANTLY COLORED PEPPERS RANGING FROM SWEET TO INCENDIARY.
THE PEPPERS ARE BEST DONE IN A SKILLET, BUT YOU COULD COOK THE SALMON ON AN
OUTDOOR GRILL OR STOVETOP GRILL PAN.

**SERVES** 6
**PREP:** 25 minutes
**COOK & BROIL:** About 15 minutes

**PER SERVING:** 442 cal, 30 g pro, 10 g car, 3 g fiber, 31 g fat (5 g sat fat), 84 mg chol, 287 mg sod

CILANTRO PESTO
   ¼ cup plus 2 Tbsp olive oil
   4 cups packed fresh cilantro
   2 Tbsp fresh lime juice
   1 medium jalapeño pepper, cut up (see *Handling Hot Peppers*, page 52)
   1 small clove garlic, peeled and halved
   ½ tsp ground cumin
   ½ tsp salt
   1 Tbsp olive oil

1 Tbsp olive oil
1 cup thinly sliced onion
3 peppers, preferably 1 purple, 1 red and 1 orange, halved and thinly sliced
2 poblano peppers, quartered
2 Hungarian cherry peppers, quartered
2 yellow banana peppers, quartered
¾ tsp salt
6 pieces (5 to 6 oz each) salmon fillet

**1** CILANTRO PESTO: Process ingredients in a food processor until smooth, scraping down sides of bowl as needed (makes about ¾ cup).

**2** Remove broiler pan from oven; heat broiler.

**3** Heat oil in a large nonstick skillet over medium heat. Add onion, peppers and salt and, stirring occasionally, cook 10 to 15 minutes until peppers are soft and lightly browned.

**4** Meanwhile coat broiler-pan rack with cooking spray. Place salmon on rack. Broil about 4 in. from heat source 5 to 8 minutes until opaque in center. Serve salmon topped with peppers.

# Salmon-Potato Skillet

### SALMON FILLET · SKILLET

2 cups chicken broth

1 Tbsp fresh lemon juice

⅛ tsp dried thyme, crumbled

1 lb red-skinned potatoes, thinly sliced

Four 1-in.-thick pieces (5 to 6 oz each) salmon fillet, skin removed (see Tip, right)

1 red pepper, halved and thinly sliced

⅓ cup thinly sliced white part of scallions

2 Tbsp creamy mustard spread (such as Dijonnaise)

⅓ cup thinly sliced green part of scallions

**SERVES** 4
**TOTAL TIME:** 25 minutes

**PER SERVING:** 407 cal, 34 g pro, 25 g car, 3 g fiber, 19 g fat (3 g sat fat), 92 mg chol, 584 mg sod

TIP: Buy salmon with skin already removed.

**1** Bring broth, lemon juice and thyme to a boil in a large deep non-stick skillet. Add potatoes, bring to a gentle boil, cover and cook 10 minutes.

**2** Arrange salmon on potatoes; top with pepper strips and white part of scallion. Bring to a simmer, cover and cook 10 minutes or until salmon is still slightly opaque in the center and potatoes are tender. Remove skillet from heat.

**3** Using a slotted spoon, transfer salmon, vegetables and potatoes to dinner plates. Stir mustard and green part of scallion into liquid in skillet. Spoon over the salmon.

---

### THE 10-MINUTE RULE

Overcooking fish makes it tough and dry. To avoid this, follow the guide professional chefs use: Measure fish at its thickest part and cook for 10 minutes for each inch of thickness, 15 minutes if it is enclosed in foil or baked in a sauce. When the fish goes on the fire, set a timer to go off about 2 minutes before the estimated end of cooking time. When that time is up, cut a slit in the thickest part of the fish and take a look. If the flesh in the center is just slightly opaque (looks not quite cooked), remove the fish from the heat source. There will be enough internal heat to continue to cook the fish for the next few minutes.

# Salmon Cakes with Lemon Sauce

A CAN OF SALMON ON THE PANTRY SHELF CAN QUICKLY RESOLVE "THERE'S NOTHING IN THE HOUSE TO EAT." SERVE WITH RICE PILAF OR MASHED POTATOES, AND A CRUNCHY SALAD OR BUTTERED GREEN PEAS.

**SERVES 4**
**TOTAL TIME:** 15 to 20 minutes

**PER SERVING:** 417 cal, 26 g pro, 25 g car, 2 g fiber, 23 g fat (5 g sat fat), 120 mg chol, 1,040 mg sod

**TIP:** Shred onion on the coarse side of a four-sided grater. Essentially you'll get onion juice, but that's just what you want in this recipe.

LEMON SAUCE
- ⅓ cup light mayonnaise
- 2 tsp freshly grated lemon peel
- 1 Tbsp fresh lemon juice
- 1 Tbsp milk
- ½ tsp dried dill weed

- 14.75-oz can pink salmon, not drained
- 1 large egg
- 1 small onion, shredded (see Tip, left)
- 2 Tbsp light mayonnaise
- 1 cup plain dried bread crumbs
- 4 tsp oil

**1** LEMON SAUCE: Mix mayonnaise, lemon peel, lemon juice, milk and dill in a small bowl.

**2** Mash the salmon, including the skin and bones, in a medium bowl. Add egg, onion, mayonnaise and ½ cup bread crumbs. Stir to mix well.

**3** Spread remaining ½ cup crumbs on wax paper. Form salmon mixture into 8 patties. Lightly press in crumbs to coat.

**4** Heat oil in a large nonstick skillet over medium-high heat. Add patties; fry 2 to 3 minutes per side until heated through and browned. Serve with sauce.

# Saucy Salmon Grill

SALMON FILLET · GRILL

BASTING SAUCE
   ¼ cup mayonnaise
   2 Tbsp packed brown sugar
   ½ tsp liquid smoke (look near barbecue sauce in your market)

2-lb salmon fillet
Cooking spray

> SERVES 6
> TOTAL TIME: 18 minutes
>
> PER SERVING: 277 cal,
> 27 g pro, 5 g car, 0 g fiber,
> 16 g fat (2 g sat fat), 80 mg
> chol, 114 mg sod

**1** BASTING SAUCE: Mix mayonnaise, brown sugar and liquid smoke in a small bowl.

**2** Heat outdoor grill. Lightly coat skin side of salmon with cooking spray.

**3** Grill skin side down, brushing top with half the sauce, 6 minutes or until skin is blackened. Turn fish over, remove skin and brush with rest of sauce. Grill 6 minutes. Turn; grill 3 minutes to sear skinned side. Cut crosswise in 4 pieces to serve.

# Swordfish with Olive Tapenade

SWORDFISH STEAKS · GRILL OR STOVETOP GRILL PAN

Four 1-in.-thick swordfish steaks (6 to 8 oz each)
2 tsp olive oil
½ tsp salt
½ tsp freshly ground pepper
4 cups arugula or baby spinach
¼ cup prepared olive spread (tapenade, see FYI, right)
1 pt grape, cherry or pear tomatoes, halved
GARNISH: chopped parsley

> SERVES 4
> TOTAL TIME: 25 to 30 minutes
>
> PER SERVING: 274 cal,
> 32 g pro, 5 g car, 1 g fiber,
> 13 g fat (2 g sat fat), 59 mg
> chol, 831 mg sod

**1** Heat outdoor grill or stovetop grill pan.

**2** Brush fish with oil; sprinkle with salt and pepper.

**3** Grill, turning once, 8 to 10 minutes until just cooked through.

**4** Place arugula on 4 serving plates. Top with swordfish; top each piece of fish with 1 Tbsp olive spread. Scatter tomatoes on top. Sprinkle with parsley.

> **FYI:** Tapenade is a flavorful spread made of ripe olives, often with capers and anchovies added. It is delicious as a sauce with pasta, as a dip, and as a topping for a rich fish. Look for tapenade in the refrigerated pasta section of your market.

# Swordfish with Cucumber Sauce & Tabbouleh

**SERVES 4**
**PREP:** 20 minutes
**REST:** 30 minutes
**GRILL:** 10 minutes

**PER SERVING:** 379 cal,
43 g pro, 35 g car, 7 g fiber,
9 g fat (3 g sat fat), 72 mg chol,
978 mg sod

**FYI:** Tabbouleh (also seen as taboule and tabbouli) is a Middle-Eastern salad made from bulgur wheat, tomato and cucumber and often with as much—or more—chopped parsley as grain.

TABBOULEH
  5.25-oz box tabbouleh (tabouli) mix (see FYI, left)
  1 tsp freshly grated lemon peel
  ¼ cup fresh lemon juice
  1 cup diced tomato (6 oz)
  1 large cucumber

CUCUMBER SAUCE
  1 cup plain lowfat yogurt
  3 Tbsp chopped fresh dill
  2 tsp minced garlic
  ¼ tsp salt

Four ¾-in.-thick swordfish steaks (6 to 8 oz each)
Olive oil cooking spray
½ tsp salt
¼ tsp freshly ground pepper

**1** TABBOULEH: Cook mix as pkg directs. Meanwhile, peel half the cucumber, then cut the cucumber in half lengthwise and scoop out the seeds. Dice or chop the peeled half for the Cucumber sauce, the unpeeled half for the Tabbouleh. When Tabbouleh mix is cool, add the lemon peel, lemon juice, tomato and the diced unpeeled cucumber. Stir to mix. Let stand at least 30 minutes to blend flavors.

**2.** CUCUMBER SAUCE: Put yogurt, dill, garlic, salt and peeled diced cucumber in a bowl. Stir to mix.

**3** Heat outdoor grill, stovetop grill pan or broiler.

**4** Coat fish with cooking spray; season with salt and pepper.

**5** Grill fish, turning over once, about 8 minutes until barely opaque when pierced in thickest part. Serve fish with the sauce and tabbouleh alongside.

# Swordfish with Chili-Lime Dressing & Tortillas

DRESSING

 2 Tbsp olive oil and vinegar or white-wine vinaigrette dressing

 2 Tbsp fresh lime juice

 1 tsp Mexican-style hot chili powder

 1 tsp ground cumin

2 Tbsp light mayonnaise

Four 1-in.-thick swordfish steaks (6 to 8 oz each)

8 fajita-size flour tortillas

> **SERVES** 4
> **PREP:** 8 minutes
> **GRILL:** 8 to 10 minutes
>
> **PER SERVING:** 412 cal,
> 39 g pro, 24 g car, 2 g fiber,
> 17 g fat (4 g sat fat), 71 mg
> chol, 452 mg sod

**1** Heat outdoor grill or stovetop grill pan.

**2** Whisk Dressing ingredients in a small bowl. Spoon 2 Tbsp into another bowl, add mayonnaise and whisk until blended. Set aside to serve with the fish.

**3** Brush half the Dressing on 1 side of the swordfish. Place brushed side down on grill; brush tops of the fish with the remaining dressing.

**4** Grill 4 to 5 minutes per side or until barely opaque in center. Transfer to a serving platter.

**5** Grill tortillas about 1 minute per side until warm but not crisp. Fold each in half. Serve fish with the reserved mayonnaise mixture and tortillas.

# Pork & Ham

Americans have renewed their love affair with pork in part because today's fresh pork is lower in fat and calories and higher in protein than it used to be. Markets carry a wide variety of lean, well-trimmed, easy-to-prepare cuts that can be quickly cooked for a fast dinner or that will roast well for special occasions. Pork can also emerge moist and flavorful from a slow cooker; try the Cranberry Pork Roast, in which pork loin cooks in a sweet-sour sauce of cranberry sauce and apricots, or Pork Pozole, with flavorings of garlic, enchilada sauce and cumin. Pork sells in the marketplace as either fresh, including chops, cutlets, loin and tenderloin, or smoked and cured like ham, bacon and smoked pork butt. If you like the smoked flavor, be sure to try the Smoked Pork Butt with Onions & Cider and the Smoked Pork Chops with Red Cabbage. Check the line underneath each recipe title for the cut of meat used in the recipe and the main form of cooking.

# Italian Roast Pork & Vegetables

## BONELESS LOIN · OVEN · RIMMED BAKING SHEET

**SERVES** 4 (with leftover meat)
**PREP:** 25 minutes
**ROAST:** 1 hour 5 minutes

**PER SERVING** (4 oz meat and ¼ the vegetables): 521 cal, 36 g pro, 43 g car, 6 g fiber, 23 g fat (7 g sat fat), 93 mg chol, 1,166 mg sod

TIP: Fennel seeds tend to fly off the chopping board when a knife blade hits them. Make a tent with your hand to confine them. Hold knife in right hand (if right handed), put your left hand on top of the knife blade with the fingertips touching the chopping board in front and the heel of your hand resting on the board in the back. Chop slowly at first, lifting the knife only a very short distance from the board. The seeds will break up quickly and those that fly will be restrained by the tent of your hand.

TIP: To crumble or crush dried rosemary, which will help release the flavor, rub it between your thumb and fingers. It's a good trick for all "hard" dried herbs, including thyme, sage and oregano.

PORK
  1 Tbsp fennel seeds (see Tip, left)
  1 Tbsp chopped garlic
  1½ tsp salt
  1 tsp dried rosemary, crumbled
  1 tsp freshly ground pepper
  One 2½-lb boneless pork loin roast

VEGETABLES
  3 red, yellow or green peppers, quartered
  1½ lb small red-skinned potatoes, halved
  2 medium red onions, cut in 1-in. wedges
  1½ Tbsp olive oil
  1 tsp salt
  1 tsp dried rosemary, crumbled (see Tip, left)

**1** Heat oven to 350°F. Lightly coat a rimmed baking sheet with cooking spray.

**2** PORK: Put fennel seeds, garlic, salt, rosemary and pepper on a cutting board. Chop with a sharp knife until mixture forms a paste. Rub all over pork. Place in center of baking sheet.

**3** VEGETABLES: Toss all ingredients in a large bowl to mix. Scatter around meat.

**4** Roast 50 minutes, or until an instant-read thermometer inserted in the center of the meat registers 155°F to 160°F and the vegetables are nearly tender.

**5** Remove pork to a cutting board and cover loosely with foil (the internal temperature will continue to rise).

**6** Return vegetables to oven. Increase heat to 450°F and roast 15 minutes more or until tender. Cut roast in ½-in.-thick slices. Serve with vegetables and pan juices.

# Tex-Mex Pulled Pork

GOOD WITH WARMED BURRITO-SIZE FLOUR TORTILLAS, OR SERVE IN TACO SHELLS OR ON BURGER BUNS. SHREDDED LETTUCE, DICED RED ONION AND SOUR CREAM MAKE GREAT TOPPINGS.

SAUCE

    8-oz can (1 cup) tomato sauce

    1 cup barbecue sauce

    1 cup thinly sliced onion

    Two 4.5-oz cans diced green chiles

    ¼ cup chili powder

    1 tsp ground cumin

    1 tsp dried oregano, crumbled

    ¼ tsp ground cinnamon

One 2½-lb boneless pork loin roast

½ cup chopped fresh cilantro

**SERVES** 6
**TOTAL TIME:** About 3½ hours on high; 8 to 10 hours on low

**PER SERVING:** 265 cal, 32 g pro, 12 g car, 2 g fiber, 9 g fat (3 g sat fat), 84 mg chol, 734 mg sod

**1** Put Sauce ingredients in a 3-qt or larger slow cooker and stir to mix. Add pork and spoon sauce over it.

**2** Cover cooker and cook on high 3½ hours or on low 8 to 10 hours, until pork is fork-tender. Remove pork to a cutting board. Using 2 forks, pull meat into shreds. Put shreds into a serving bowl.

**3** Spoon any fat off sauce. Pour sauce over meat; stir in the cilantro.

# Cranberry Pork Roast

## BONELESS LOIN · SLOW COOKER

**SERVES** 6
**PREP:** 6 minutes
**COOK:** 6 to 8 hours on low

PER SERVING: 497 cal,
41 g pro, 57 g car, 3 g fiber,
11 g fat (4 g sat fat), 112 mg
chol, 527 mg sod

16-oz can whole-berry cranberry sauce
1 cup chopped onion
6-oz can apricot nectar
½ cup sugar
½ cup coarsely chopped dried apricots
2 tsp cider or distilled white vinegar
1 tsp dry mustard
1 tsp salt
¼ tsp crushed red pepper
One 2½-lb boneless pork loin roast

**1** Mix all ingredients except pork in a 3-qt or larger slow cooker. Add pork and spoon some of the cranberry mixture over it.

**2** Cover and cook on low 6 to 8 hours or until pork is tender.

**3** Remove pork to cutting board. Spoon any fat off sauce. Slice pork and serve with sauce.

# Pork Goulash

## BONELESS SHOULDER · SLOW COOKER

**SERVES** 6
**TOTAL TIME:** 7 to 9 hours on low

PER SERVING: 300 cal,
20 g pro, 11 g car, 1 g fiber,
20 g fat (7 g sat fat), 77 mg
chol, 61 mg sod

1¼-lb boneless pork shoulder (Boston butt), visible fat trimmed, cut in 1-in. chunks (see *When a Butt Is a Shoulder*, facing page)
14-oz can crushed tomatoes in purée
1 pkt beefy-onion soup mix
2 Tbsp sweet paprika
2 tsp minced garlic
1 tsp caraway seeds
¾ cup reduced-fat sour cream
3 Tbsp snipped fresh dill

**1** Mix first 6 ingredients in a 3-qt or larger slow cooker.

**2** Cover and cook on low 7 to 9 hours until pork is tender. Stir in sour cream and dill.

# Pork Pozole

SERVE IN SOUP BOWLS WITH WARM FLOUR TORTILLAS AND SALSA.

Two 15- to 16-oz cans hominy, drained
Three 10-oz cans green enchilada sauce
1½ cups chopped onion
1 Tbsp chopped garlic
2 tsp ground cumin
1 tsp salt
½ tsp freshly ground pepper
One 2½-lb boneless pork loin roast
1 cup chopped fresh cilantro
2 Tbsp fresh lime juice

**SERVES** 6
**PREP:** 8 minutes
**COOK:** 7 to 9 hours on low

**PER SERVING:** 448 cal, 44 g pro, 30 g car, 5 g fiber, 15 g fat (5 g sat fat), 115 mg chol, 773 mg sod

**1** Put hominy, enchilada sauce, onion, garlic, cumin, salt and pepper in a 4-qt or larger slow cooker. Add pork; spoon hominy mixture over it. Cover and cook on low 7 to 9 hours or until pork is tender.

**2** Remove pork to a cutting board. Spoon any fat off sauce. Stir in cilantro and lime juice. Using 2 forks, tear meat into bite-size shreds. Put meat back in cooker for a few minutes to warm through. Ladle into soup bowls.

## WHEN A BUTT IS A SHOULDER
According to the National Pork Board, in pre-revolutionary times and into the Revolutionary War, some pork cuts (not those highly valued, or "high on the hog") were packed into casks or barrels—also known as "butts"—for storage and shipment. The way the shoulder was cut in the Boston area became known in other regions as "Boston butt." This name stuck and today Boston butt is called that almost everywhere in the U.S., except in Boston.

# Smoked Pork Butt with Onions & Cider

### BONELESS SMOKED BUTT · SLOW COOKER

GOOD SERVED OVER NOODLES.

**SERVES 6**
**TOTAL TIME:** 7 to 8 hours
on low

PER SERVING: 491 cal,
27 g pro, 21 g car, 3 g fiber,
33 g fat (12 g sat fat), 80 mg
chol, 1,901 mg sod

2-lb boneless smoked pork butt, cut in 1-in. chunks
(see *When a Butt Is a Shoulder*, page 127)
2-lb butternut squash, peeled and cut in ¾-in. chunks (about 6 cups)
1½ cups chopped onion
½ cup apple cider
½ tsp dried thyme
½ tsp dried rosemary
½ tsp freshly ground pepper
½ cup chopped fresh parsley

**1** Mix all ingredients except parsley in a 3-qt or larger slow cooker.

**2** Cover and cook on low 7 to 8 hours or until vegetables are tender.
Stir in parsley.

# Pork, Black Bean & Corn Chili

### BONELESS SHOULDER · DUTCH OVEN

GOOD TOPPED WITH SOUR CREAM AND CHOPPED ONION AND TOMATO. SERVE WITH TORTILLA CHIPS.

**SERVES 6**
**SOAK** (beans): At least 1 hour
**PREP:** 45 minutes
**COOK:** About 1¾ hour

PER SERVING: 408 cal,
33 g pro, 41 g car, 9 g fiber,
14 g fat (4 g sat fat), 75 mg
chol, 731 mg sod

¾ cup dried black beans (see FYI, facing page), rinsed and drained
(see *Searching for Stones*, page 162)
1 Tbsp oil
4 poblano chile peppers, cut in half, seeded and diced (see *Handling
Hot Peppers*, page 52)
1½ cups diced onion
2 Tbsp chili powder
1 Tbsp chopped garlic
1½-lb boneless pork shoulder, visible fat trimmed, cut in
¾-in. cubes (see *When a Butt Is a Shoulder*, page 127)
2 lb tomatillos, husked, rinsed and diced
4 cups chicken broth
½ tsp salt
11-oz can corn kernels, drained
½ cup finely chopped cilantro

Italian Roast Pork & Vegetables *(page 124)*

Tex-Mex Pulled Pork *(page 125)*

Smoked Pork Chops with Red Cabbage
*(page 131)*

Ham with Pineapple Salsa & Sweet Potatoes *(page 134)*

**1** Put beans in a saucepan, add water to cover by 3 in. and bring to a boil. Remove from heat, cover and let soak 1 to 2 hours. Or, if time permits, put beans in a bowl, add water to cover by 3 in. and let soak 6 to 12 hours. Drain well.

**2** Heat oil in a 5-qt or larger Dutch oven or heavy-bottomed pot over medium heat. Stir in chiles and onion and cook, stirring occasionally, 8 minutes or until soft. Stir in chili powder and garlic and cook 1 minute until fragrant.

**3** Stir in pork, beans, tomatillos, broth and salt. Bring to a boil, reduce heat, cover and simmer 1½ hours or until pork and beans are tender. Stir in corn and cilantro; heat through.

> **FYI:** You can use a 15- to 19-oz can of black beans instead of the dried. Drain and rinse the beans, then add them to the pot along with the corn and cilantro.

# Pork with Mushroom Gravy

## BONELESS TENDERLOIN · SKILLET

This dish, too, is good with noodles or with rice.

1 Tbsp oil
One 12-oz pork tenderloin, cut in ½-in.-thick slices
8-oz pkg assorted wild mushrooms (such as crimini, oyster or shiitake), mushrooms sliced, or 8 oz sliced white mushrooms
1.3-oz pkt roasted pork gravy mix
Garnish: chopped parsley

> SERVES 4
> TOTAL TIME: 25 minutes
>
> PER SERVING: 190 cal, 19 g pro, 7 g car, 1 g fiber, 8 g fat (2 g sat fat), 56 mg chol, 331 mg sod

**1** Heat oil in a large nonstick skillet over medium-high heat. Add pork and cook 2 to 3 minutes per side until lightly browned and just barely pink in center. Remove to plates; cover loosely with foil to keep warm.

**2** Reduce heat to medium, add mushrooms to pan and cook, stirring occasionally, 5 minutes or until lightly browned and soft. Stir in 1¼ cups water and gravy mix; cook, stirring occasionally, 3 minutes or until gravy thickens. Spoon over pork; garnish with parsley, if desired.

# Spice-Rubbed Pork with Black Bean Citrus Salad

**SERVES** 4
**TOTAL TIME:** 10 minutes

**PER SERVING:** 581 cal, 27 g pro, 42 g car, 4 g fiber, 34 g fat (8 g sat fat), 70 mg chol, 561 mg sod

4 thin pork loin chops (about 1¼ lb)
1½ tsp mild Mexican seasoning or chili powder
1 tsp oil
24-oz jar refrigerated citrus salad, drained
15-oz can black beans, drained and rinsed
1 ripe Hass avocado, diced
½ cup chopped fresh cilantro
⅓ cup olive oil and vinegar dressing
¼ cup sliced red onion

**1** Sprinkle pork with Mexican seasoning. Heat oil in large nonstick skillet. Add pork and cook over medium-high heat, turning once, 4 minutes or until cooked through.

**2** Meanwhile put remaining ingredients in a bowl; toss gently to mix and coat. Serve with pork.

# Pork Chops with Tomato Sauce

**SERVES** 4
**TOTAL TIME:** 15 minutes

**PER SERVING:** 413 cal, 28 g pro, 17 g car, 3 g fiber, 26 g fat (7 g sat fat), 84 mg chol, 1,054 mg sod

3 Tbsp olive oil
4 thin pork loin chops (about 1¼ lb)
2 cups halved and sliced onion
1 Tbsp minced garlic
16-oz can tomato sauce
½ tsp salt
¼ tsp freshly ground pepper

**1** Heat oil in a large nonstick skillet. Add pork chops and brown well on each side. Remove to a plate. Add onions and garlic to skillet; cover and cook about 5 minutes, stirring often, until onions are almost soft.

**2** Stir in tomato sauce, salt, pepper and ½ cup water. Bring to a boil, reduce heat to low, add chops, cover and simmer 10 to 15 minutes, turning pork and stirring sauce 2 or 3 times, until pork is cooked through and flavor of sauce has developed.

# Smoked Pork Chops with Red Cabbage

SERVE WITH MASHED POTATOES AND DILLED CARROTS.

2 tsp oil

Four 1-in.-thick, smoked, bone-in pork chops (about 2 lb)

¾ tsp dried sage

¾ tsp dried thyme

6 cups coarsely shredded red cabbage

1½ cups thinly sliced red onion

½ cup cider vinegar

½ cup water

3 Tbsp packed brown sugar

¼ cup red currant jelly

**SERVES** 4
**TOTAL TIME:** 37 minutes

**PER SERVING:** 439 cal, 31 g pro, 42 g car, 3 g fiber, 19 g fat (6 g sat fat), 167 mg chol, 1,885 mg sod

**1**  Heat oil in a large nonstick skillet over medium-high heat. Season chops on both sides with ½ tsp each sage and thyme. Brown in skillet 5 minutes, turning once. Remove chops; cover loosely with foil to keep warm.

**2**  Add remaining ¼ tsp each sage and thyme, and rest of ingredients to skillet; stir to combine. Bring to a boil, reduce heat to medium-low, cover and simmer 15 minutes or until cabbage is tender. Place chops on cabbage, cover and cook 5 to 7 minutes or until an instant-read thermometer inserted from side to middle of a chop registers 160°F.

## CHOPS

Chops are the most popular cut from the pork loin, which is the strip of meat that runs from the pig's hip to shoulder. Depending on which part they were cut from, pork chops can be found under a variety of names including loin, rib and blade chops. Loin chops are from the lower back and usually include some back and rib bone. Top loin chops are located closer to the head; they are T-bone chops and are often sold boneless. Blade chops are cut from where the loin starts in the shoulder area. They may contain some blade bone as well as back rib bone. Blade chops are usually thicker and marbled. They are often butterflied and sold as country-style ribs.

Whichever part they are cut from, all pork chops cook the same way, the length of cooking time depending primarily on the thickness.

# Pork Albondigas

SERVE THESE MEATBALLS WITH RICE.

**SERVES 4**
**TOTAL TIME:** 22 minutes

**PER SERVING:** 330 cal,
17 g pro, 11 g car, 1 g fiber,
24 g fat (7 g sat fat), 114 mg
chol, 618 mg sod

**TIP:** Crush tortilla chips in a
food processor or seal in
ziptop bag and crush with a
rolling pin.

MEATBALLS
- 12 oz lean ground pork
- ½ cup grated zucchini
- ½ cup (2 oz) crushed unsalted tortilla chips (see Tip, left)
- ¼ cup sliced scallions
- 2 Tbsp chopped fresh cilantro or mint leaves
- 1 large egg
- 1½ tsp minced garlic
- ½ tsp salt
- ½ tsp ground cumin
- ½ tsp dried oregano, crumbled
- 10-oz can mild enchilada sauce

**1** MEATBALLS: Put all Meatball ingredients into a large bowl. Mix with hands or a spoon until blended. With moistened hands, roll into twenty 1½-in. meatballs.

**2** Coat a large nonstick skillet with cooking spray and heat over medium heat. Add Meatballs, increase heat to medium-high and cook about 5 minutes, shaking pan to turn Meatballs, until brown all over.

**3** Add enchilada sauce and ½ cup water to skillet. Bring to a boil, reduce heat, cover and simmer, stirring occasionally, 5 minutes or until meatballs are cooked through.

# Barbecue Spareribs

## SPARERIBS · GRILL

FOR EXTRA FLAVOR, PREPARE SPARERIBS THROUGH STEP 2, BUT BRUSH THE RIBS
WITH ONLY HALF THE SAUCE, COVER AND REFRIGERATE OVERNIGHT.
BRUSH WITH REMAINING SAUCE BEFORE GRILLING.

1 whole rack (about 4 lb) pork spareribs
1 large onion, cut in chunks
1 tsp salt
1 tsp freshly ground pepper

BARBECUE SAUCE
  2 tsp olive oil
  1 Tbsp minced garlic
  ¾ cup tomato ketchup
  ¾ cup chili sauce
  ¼ cup packed brown sugar
  ¼ cup orange juice (see Tip, right)
  ¼ cup cider vinegar
  2 tsp grated orange peel

**SERVES 4**
**TOTAL TIME:** About 1½ hours

**PER SERVING:** 889 cal,
54 g pro, 42 g car, 1 g fiber,
56 g fat (20 g sat fat), 214 mg
chol, 1,679 mg sod

TIP: Grate orange peel
before cutting orange to
squeeze juice.

**1** Place spareribs (rack cut in half to fit if necessary), onion, salt and pepper in a large pot. Add water to cover. Bring to a boil, reduce heat, cover and simmer 1 hour or until meat is tender.

**2** MEANWHILE PREPARE BARBECUE SAUCE: Heat oil in a 2- to 3-qt saucepan. Add garlic; cook a few seconds until fragrant. Add remaining ingredients, bring to a boil, reduce heat, partially cover and simmer 15 to 20 minutes, stirring often to prevent sticking. Let cool. Brush spareribs with sauce.

**3** Heat outdoor grill or broiler (line broiler pan with foil and coat broiler-pan rack with cooking spray for easy cleanup).

**4** Grill ribs (or broil 4 to 6 in. from heat source) 12 to 14 minutes, basting with sauce a few times and turning ribs over occasionally to prevent burning, until lightly charred.

**5** TO SERVE: Cut rack(s) in 1-rib portions.

# Ham with Pineapple Salsa & Sweet Potatoes

HAM STEAK · GRILL OR STOVETOP GRILL PAN

**SERVES** 4
**TOTAL TIME:** 50 minutes

**PER SERVING:** 416 cal,
20 g pro, 44 g car, 5 g fiber,
18 g fat (4 g sat fat), 58 mg
chol, 1,791 mg sod

## STORING HAM

Fully cooked, brine-cured
hams, either smoked or
non-smoked, may be stored
in their original packaging
for at least 7 days in the
coldest part of the
refrigerator. Use packaged
ham slices within 3 to 4
days. Leftovers may be
refrigerated, tightly wrapped
in plastic, for 7 to 10 days.
If you must freeze ham, do
it in large chunks, tightly
wrapped, for up to 2
months. Thaw before using.

SALSA
   2 cups finely diced fresh pineapple
   ½ cup chopped red onion
   2 Tbsp chopped fresh cilantro
   2 tsp freshly grated lime peel
   1 Tbsp fresh lime juice
   ¼ tsp crushed red pepper
   ¼ tsp salt

SWEET POTATOES
   2 Tbsp oil
   ½ tsp salt
   ¼ tsp freshly ground pepper
   2 large sweet potatoes (about 12 oz each), each cut in
      8 long wedges

HAM
   1½ tsp honey
   One 1-lb fully cooked ham steak

**1** SALSA: Gently mix ingredients in a serving bowl.

**2** Heat outdoor grill or stovetop grill pan.

**3** SWEET POTATOES: Mix oil, salt and pepper in a large bowl. Add potatoes; stir to coat. Grill 30 minutes, turning wedges occasionally, until slightly charred and tender when pierced.

**4** HAM: Mix honey with 1 tsp water. Brush on ham. About 3 minutes before potatoes are done, add ham to grill. Grill, turning once, until hot and marked with grill lines. Serve with the salsa and sweet potatoes.

## SPECIALTY HAMS

COUNTRY HAMS It has been said that "city ham," found in most supermarkets, is usually boneless, moist and mild-tasting. The salt and cure are dissolved in water and injected into the meat, a process that takes about 24 hours and allows for more even distribution of the cure. "Country hams" are dry cured, that is the fresh ham is packed in salt mixed with other curing ingredients and slowly cured, up to 40 days, sometimes smoked and always aged. In the dry-cure technique, the salt draws out the natural moisture from the meat, yielding a very flavorful finished product with firmer texture. Traditional hams—the custom of curing began in the state of Virginia during the mid-1700s—are still being produced today, in states from Georgia to Missouri and points in between. Each region, indeed each producer, has an individual style of curing, all similar. Some are slow-smoked with hickory wood, others might have a little sugar in the cure and be smoked over apple wood.

SMITHFIELD HAM Perhaps the most widely known country hams, even by those who have yet to taste one, Smithfield hams are produced in Smithfield, Virginia, by a unique process where the ham is hand-rubbed with salt, smoked and dried. The result is a very dry, salty ham. The hams require extensive soaking and simmering in liquid but just a sliver or two between bread or a biscuit provides a jolt of wonderful flavor.

PROSCIUTTO Prosciutto is the dry country ham of Italy, the standard bearer of which is prosciutto di Parma. (Of course they have had practice: 100 years BC an author mentioned the wonderful air-and-salt-cured hams produced around the town of Parma, in Italy.) Aged for more than a year, prosciutto di Parma has a silky texture and delicate flavor. It is served wafer thin, sometimes wrapped around a piece of melon. Prosciutto is also produced in Germany and the U.S., among other countries, while Spain has its "jamon de Serrano" and France its "jambon." Prosciutto is sold prepackaged, or you can have it sliced for you at the deli counter.

# Glazed Ham Steaks with Pears & Cornbread Stuffing

## HAM STEAK FILLETS · SKILLET

**SERVES** 4
**TOTAL TIME:** 8 minutes

**PER SERVING:** 549 cal,
22 g pro, 63 g car, 4 g fiber,
25 g fat (8 g sat fat), 61 mg
chol, 1,958 mg sod

2 Tbsp butter or margarine
6-oz box one-step cornbread stuffing mix
¼ cup pecans, chopped
¼ cup dried sweetened cranberries
Four 3-oz ham steak fillets
2 Tbsp maple syrup or maple-flavored pancake syrup
1½ tsp Dijon mustard
15-oz can chunky Bartlett pears in light syrup, drained

**1** Bring 1 cup water and the butter to boil in a small saucepan. Stir in stuffing mix, nuts and cranberries. Remove from heat; cover and let rest 5 minutes.

**2** Meanwhile, heat a large nonstick skillet over medium-high heat. Add ham; cook 3 minutes, turning once, until lightly browned.

**3** Mix syrup and mustard. Brush on top of ham then turn steaks over; cook 30 seconds until glazed. Brush steaks again, turn over and cook 30 seconds until other side is glazed. Remove to a plate.

**4** Add pears to skillet; stir gently, until hot. Spoon over ham. Fluff stuffing with a fork; serve alongside.

**TIP:** Serve with a crisp green salad.

## HEATING HAM

Most fully cooked hams have heating instructions on the label but if there are none, follow these general rules.

Baking: Check the weight on the wrapper and figure the total cooking time. Allow 15 to 20 minutes per pound of fully cooked ham, 18 to 22 minutes per pound for cook-before-eating hams. (To avoid last-minute panic, do these calculations the day before you plan to cook the ham, so you can estimate when it needs to go in the oven.) Heat the oven to 325°F. Put the ham, fat side up, in a foil-lined pan and bake until a meat thermometer registers 130° to 140°F (fully cooked ham) or 160°F for a cook-before-eating ham. Allow time for the baked ham to rest at room temperature for 10 to 20 minutes before carving.

Skillet or stovetop grill pan: Either pan is great for heating up steaks and slices. Cut several slashes in the fat around the edge to prevent curling. You can spray either pan with cooking spray before adding the ham, or heat a very small amount of butter or oil in the skillet. Cook the ham slices or steaks as short a time as possible to heat and brown them. Overcooked ham tends to dry out.

Microwave: Because of the variation in wattage between one microwave oven and another it is not possible to give general directions. Check the cookbook or web site of your oven's manufacturer.

# Ham, Corn & Potato Patties

1 tsp minced garlic

1½ cups instant mashed potato flakes

2 cups (12 oz) diced ham

⅔ cup shredded pepperjack cheese

1 cup frozen corn kernels, thawed

1 large egg

3 Tbsp chopped fresh cilantro or parsley

¼ cup plain dried bread crumbs

2 tsp oil

**SERVES 4**
**TOTAL TIME:** 23 minutes

**PER SERVING:** 342 cal, 24 g pro, 28 g car, 1 g fiber, 15 g fat (6 g sat fat), 61 mg chol, 1,255 mg sod

Tɪᴘ: Serve with salsa.

**1** Put the garlic and 1¼ cups water in a large bowl. Bring to a boil in a microwave oven. Stir in instant potatoes. When blended, stir in ham, cheese, corn, egg and cilantro.

**2** Spread crumbs on a plate. Shape ham mixture into eight ½-in.-thick patties; turn in crumbs to coat.

**3** Heat 1 tsp oil in a large nonstick skillet. Add 4 patties and cook over medium-high heat 5 minutes per side until golden. Remove to a plate; cover to keep warm. Repeat with remaining oil and patties.

## THE LOWDOWN ON HAM

Ham is meat from the hind leg of a hog, usually sold cured. (Sometimes this cut of meat, when it is fresh pork, is confusingly called "fresh ham.") Turning fresh meat into cured involves a number of different steps, depending of the kind of ham.
Brine-curing: Meat is injected with a solution of water, salt, sodium nitrate and nitrites, plus sugar or honey. This is the largest-selling form of ham in the U.S. and it is usually sold cooked.
Dry-curing: Salt, sugar, sodium nitrate and nitrites and sometimes other ingredients such as smoke flavoring are mixed together and rubbed on the meat's surface. This process, which is used for most specialty hams, draws out the moisture and deepens the flavor and color.
Smoking: After curing, some hams are hung in a smokehouse over smoldering fires. Smoking imparts a distinctive flavor, which can vary according to the type of wood used, and continues the aging and drying process.

# Lamb & Veal

L amb and veal, prized by European and Middle Eastern cooks for centuries, are coming into their own in American kitchens. Perhaps one of the reasons is that these meats are not only tender and flavorful, but also extremely adaptable. There's lots of wonderful American lamb, and lamb also comes to the United States from New Zealand, and, in small amounts, from Iceland. Roast leg of lamb can be a star for special occasions while a leg that's been butterflied (boned and opened out flat) grills quickly and easily. For quick weeknight meals try the Quick Lamb Stew (made with ground lamb) or the Lamb Patties Piccata, a take on an Italian favorite usually made with veal cutlets. Try the Moroccan Lamb Shanks, where the meaty shanks do time in a slow cooker along with dried fruits and spices. Or simmer veal shanks in a Dutch oven for the famous Osso Buco Milanese. Look at the line directly below each recipe title for a quick fix on the cut of meat called for.

# Greek Lamb Casserole

GOOD ACCOMPANIMENTS ARE COUSCOUS AND YELLOW SQUASH SAUTÉED WITH MINCED GARLIC.

**SERVES** 6
**PREP:** 20 minutes
**COOK:** 12 minutes
**BAKE:** 1½ hours

**PER SERVING:** 469 cal, 44 g pro, 26 g car, 6 g fiber, 20 g fat (5 g sat fat), 125 mg chol, 1,379 mg sod

1 lemon
¼ cup flour
Salt
Freshly ground pepper
2½-lb boneless lamb shoulder, cut in 1½-in. chunks
1 Tbsp olive oil
2 cups chopped onion
1 Tbsp minced garlic
2 cups chicken broth
2 tsp dried oregano
1 tsp ground cinnamon
1 tsp ground ginger
Two 15.5-oz cans chickpeas, drained and rinsed
¾ cup mixed country olives (from a 7-oz jar), pitted
About 3 Tbsp chopped fresh parsley or mint

**1** Heat oven to 325°F. Have a deep 2½- to 3-qt baking dish ready.

**2** With a vegetable peeler, peel yellow part of lemon peel in strips; wrap tightly in plastic and set aside. Halve and juice lemon.

**3** Mix flour and ½ tsp each salt and pepper in a large plastic food bag. Add lamb; shake to coat.

**4** Heat oil in a large, deep skillet over medium-high heat. Add some of the lamb and brown on all sides. Remove with slotted spoon to baking dish. Brown and add remaining lamb. Add onion and garlic to skillet; cook about 3 minutes, stirring often, until soft. Add broth, lemon juice, oregano, cinnamon, ginger, chickpeas and ½ tsp each salt and pepper. Bring to a boil, stir in olives, then pour over lamb. Cover tightly with a lid or foil.

**5** Bake 1½ hours or until lamb is tender.

**6** Meanwhile cut lemon peel in long narrow strips, then cut crosswise in small pieces; mix peel and parsley in a small serving bowl. Cover and refrigerate until ready to use. Serve at table to sprinkle on individual portions.

# Moroccan Lamb Shanks

LAMB SHANKS · SLOW COOKER

SERVE WITH COUSCOUS.

Two 15.5-oz cans chickpeas, drained and rinsed
1 cup pitted dried plums (prunes)
1 cup dried apricot halves
1 cup finely chopped onion
1 Tbsp minced garlic
1 cup chicken broth
¼ cup fresh orange juice (see Tip, right)
1 Tbsp freshly grated orange peel
½ tsp salt
½ tsp ground cinnamon
½ tsp ground cumin
½ tsp ground ginger
4 lamb shanks (¾ to 1 lb each)
GARNISH: **toasted sliced almonds and chopped fresh parsley**

**SERVES** 4
**TOTAL TIME:** 10 to 12 hours on low

**PER SERVING:** 850 cal, 69 g pro, 74 g car, 12 g fiber, 31 g fat (11 g sat fat), 196 mg chol, 931 mg sod

TIP: Grate orange peel before cutting the orange for juicing.

**1** Put all ingredients except lamb in an oval 5½-qt or larger slow cooker. Stir to mix. Add lamb and spoon some mixture over the shanks.

**2** Cover cooker and cook on low 10 to 12 hours until lamb is very tender.

**3** Remove lamb to serving plates; spoon out chickpeas and fruit with a slotted spoon and add to plates. Pour pan juices into a bowl, skim off fat and pour juices into a gravy boat. Garnish lamb with almonds and parsley. Serve with the pan juices.

# Greek Lamb, Artichoke & Onion Stew

**SERVES** 6
**TOTAL TIME:** 8 to 10 hours
on low

**PER SERVING:** 320 cal,
34 g pro, 23 g car, 4 g fiber,
11 g fat (4 g sat fat), 100 mg
chol, 639 mg sod

**FYI:** Boiling onions are larger than pearl onions and are harvested when the plant has formed 1- to 2-in. bulbs. You can find white, yellow or red boiling (or boiler) onions. They are often cooked whole in stews or casseroles, or they may be roasted. To peel quickly, immerse them in boiling water for 2 to 3 minutes, then in cold water for 2 to 3 minutes more. Cut off the root portion of the bulb and squeeze gently. The onion should pop out of its skin.

2-lb boneless lamb shoulder, cut in 1-in. chunks

12 boiling onions (about 1½ lb), halved lengthwise (see FYI, left)

2 cups canned tomato purée

1 cup dry red wine

3 Tbsp red-wine vinegar

2 Tbsp minced garlic

1 cinnamon stick (about 3 in.)

½ tsp salt

½ tsp freshly ground pepper

½ tsp sugar

¼ tsp ground allspice

¼ tsp ground cumin

¼ tsp dried oregano

14-oz can artichoke hearts, drained and quartered

½ cup chopped fresh parsley

TOPPINGS: chopped walnuts and crumbled feta cheese (optional)

**1** Put all ingredients except artichoke hearts and parsley in a 4-qt or larger slow cooker. Stir to mix. Cover and cook on low 8 to 10 hours or until lamb and onions are tender.

**2** Stir in artichoke hearts and parsley. Cover and let stand 2 minutes or until artichokes are hot. Remove cinnamon stick. Serve sprinkled with walnuts and feta cheese.

# Lancashire Lamb Stew

2½ lb meaty lamb neck bones for stew

3 Tbsp flour

2 Tbsp oil

1½ cups chopped onions

1 Tbsp minced garlic

5 cups chicken broth

½ tsp dried thyme, crumbled

½ tsp dried rosemary, crumbled

1½ lb red-skinned potatoes (see Tip, right), cut in 1½-in. chunks (about 4½ cups)

2 cups thickly sliced carrots

2 cups ½-in. chunks of turnips (see Tip, right)

2 cups chopped onions

1 cup frozen green peas

**SERVES** 5 (makes 10 cups)
**PREP:** 30 minutes
**BAKE:** 3½ to 4 hours

**PER SERVING:** 405 cal, 22 g pro, 55 g car, 9 g fiber, 11 g fat (2 g sat fat), 45 mg chol, 583 mg sod

TIP: Red-skinned potatoes and white turnips don't need peeling, just washing.

**1** Heat oven to 325°F. Have ready a 5- to 6-qt Dutch oven (see *Dutch Oven*, page 82) or ovenproof pot with a tight-fitting lid.

**2** On a sheet of wax paper, coat meat in flour; shake off excess. Heat 1 Tbsp oil in pot over medium heat. Add some of the meat (don't crowd it in the pan) and brown, turning pieces over with tongs. Remove browned pieces to a bowl or plate and brown remaining meat using remaining 1 Tbsp of oil. When all the meat is browned and out of the pot, add onions and garlic and cook 5 to 6 minutes, stirring often, until onions just begin to brown.

**3** Stir in broth and herbs, scraping up any browned bits on bottom of pot. Return meat to pot. Cover tightly and bake 2½ to 3 hours until just tender, stirring once or twice during baking.

**4** Skim off fat and discard. Stir in vegetables. Cover and bake 1 hour longer or until meat falls off the bones and vegetables are tender. If you wish, remove large bones before serving.

# Onion & Mustard-Coated Leg of Lamb with Ginger-Rosemary Gravy

## BONE-IN LEG · OVEN · ROASTING PAN WITH RACK

**SERVES 8** (with leftovers)
**PREP:** 15 minutes plus
20 minutes
**COOK:** 2 to 3 hours

**PER SERVING** (4 oz meat with
3 Tbsp gravy): 267 cal, 33 g pro,
5 g car, 1 g fiber, 10 g fat
(4 g sat fat), 102 mg chol,
583 mg sod

One 7-lb bone-in leg of lamb, trimmed of excess fat
3 cloves garlic, cut in 12 thin slices
Salt
Freshly ground pepper
1⅔ cups finely chopped onion
½ cup grainy mustard
3 Tbsp chopped fresh rosemary or 1 Tbsp dried
¾ cup dry red wine
2 Tbsp minced fresh ginger (see *Fresh Ginger*, page 61)
3 Tbsp flour
3 cups chicken broth
GARNISH: **rosemary sprigs and lemon slices**

TIP: You can do Step 1 up
to 1 day ahead. Cover the
meat with plastic wrap and
refrigerate. Unwrap before
roasting.

**1** Have ready a large roasting pan with rack (see Tip, bottom of facing page). Place lamb on rack. With tip of a knife, cut 12 deep slits all over lamb. Insert a slice of garlic into each slit. Sprinkle lamb with ½ tsp salt and ½ pepper. In a small bowl mix onion, mustard and 2 Tbsp rosemary. Spread all over lamb. (See Tip, left.)

**2** Heat oven to 325°F. Roast lamb 2 to 3 hours or until meat thermometer inserted in thickest part of meat registers 135°F for rare, 145°F for medium and 150°F for medium-well. (See Tip, bottom left.)

**3** Remove to serving platter, cover loosely with foil to keep warm and let rest while preparing gravy. (As meat rests, juices redistribute and internal temperature should rise 5 to 10 degrees.)

TIP: When inserting the
meat thermometer, be sure
it's in the thickest part of the
meat, not touching fat or
bone.

**4** Pour wine into roasting pan and stir to scrape up browned bits on bottom. Pour into a small bowl or 1-cup glass measure. Let rest while fat rises to surface. Spoon 2 Tbsp fat into roasting pan (see Tip, bottom of facing page); discard any remaining fat.

**5** Place pan over medium-high heat. Add ginger and stir 1 minute until fragrant. Whisk in flour and cook 1 minute. Whisk in wine mixture, chicken broth and remaining 1 Tbsp rosemary. Bring to a boil (mixture will thicken), reduce heat to low and simmer about 5 minutes to get rid of floury taste. Stir in ¼ tsp each salt and pepper. Pour gravy into a sauceboat. (Makes 2½ cups.)

**6** Garnish platter with rosemary sprigs and lemon slices. Serve lamb with gravy.

Onion & Mustard–Coated Leg of Lamb with Ginger-Rosemary Gravy *(page 144)*

Greek Lamb Casserole
*(page 140)*

Lamb Chops with Spicy Yogurt Marinade
*(page 148)*

Osso Buco Milanese *(page 152)*

# Garlic-Ginger Roast Leg of Lamb

One 8-lb bone-in leg of lamb, trimmed of excess fat

CRUST

    1 Tbsp olive oil

    1 Tbsp chopped fresh mint (optional)

    2 tsp minced garlic

    2 tsp minced fresh ginger (see *Fresh Ginger*, page 61)

    ½ tsp salt

    ½ tsp freshly ground pepper

    2 Tbsp flour

1 cup beef broth

2 tsp lemon juice

⅛ tsp freshly ground pepper

**1** Have ready a large roasting pan with a rack (see Tip, bottom right). Place lamb on rack.

**2** To make Crust, mix oil, mint, garlic, ginger, salt and pepper in a small bowl. Add flour and stir until blended. Spread over top and sides of lamb. (See Tip, right)

**3** Heat oven to 450°F. Roast lamb 30 minutes, then reduce temperature to 325°F and roast 45 to 60 minutes longer or until meat thermometer inserted in thickest part of meat registers 135°F for rare, 145°F for medium and 150°F for medium-well done (see Tip, bottom left, facing page).

**4** Remove to a serving platter, cover loosely with foil to keep warm and let rest 15 minutes. (As meat rests, juices redistribute and internal temperature should rise 5 to 10 degrees.)

**5** Meanwhile spoon off and discard fat from roasting pan. Place pan over medium-high heat (see Tip, right, if using a disposable foil pan), add beef broth and bring to a boil, scraping up browned bits from bottom of pan. Boil 2 minutes to reduce liquid slightly. Pour into a sauceboat and stir in lemon juice and pepper. (Makes ⅔ cup.) Drizzle over sliced lamb.

---

**SERVES** 12 (with leftovers)
**PREP:** 15 minutes plus 10 minutes
**ROAST:** 1½ hours

**PER SERVING** (4 oz meat with sauce): 234 cal, 0 g fiber, 32 g pro, 1 g car, 10 g fat (3 g sat fat), 101 mg chol, 242 mg sod

**TIP:** The Crust mixture can be spread on the lamb up to 1 day ahead. Cover loosely with foil and refrigerate.

**FYI:** This lamb starts roasting at a higher temperature than the Onion & Mustard-Coated Leg of Lamb in order to get a crustier outside.

**TIP:** Lamb is heavy; if using a foil pan, use two pans, one inside the other, for safety. When making gravy, pour liquid into pan to help dissolve brown bits, but do not set foil pan over burners; make gravy in saucepan.

# Butterflied Leg of Lamb with Minted Cucumber Salad

BUTTERFLIED LEG · GRILL OR STOVETOP GRILL PAN

**SERVES** 4 (with leftover lamb)
**TOTAL TIME:** 1 hour (plus
at least 30 minutes marinating
lamb)

**PER SERVING** (4 oz lamb):
286 cal, 35 g pro, 7 g car,
2 g fiber, 13 g fat (4 g sat fat),
106 mg chol, 394 mg sod

## WHY BUTTERFLY?

To butterfly leg of lamb the leg is first boned, then cut once so that it can be opened out flat. The resulting piece of meat grills quickly (compared to a whole leg). It is easy to carve, and because it is unevenly thick, you get rare, medium and well-done meat at the same time. Beef flank steak is sometimes butterflied, then stuffed and rolled up. With flank steak the butterfly analogy is clearer: The steak, normally about 1 in. thick, is cut in half horizontally, but not quite all the way through. The top portion is then lifted up and folded back. Since the portions are the same shape but still joined in the middle, the piece of meat roughly resembles a butterfly with two wings.

LAMB

One butterflied leg of lamb (about 3¾ lb), excess fat trimmed

4 medium cloves garlic, cut in 16 slices

¼ cup Dijon mustard

2 Tbsp olive oil

½ tsp salt

¼ tsp freshly ground pepper

MINTED CUCUMBER SALAD

¼ cup reduced-fat sour cream

2 tsp sugar

2 Tbsp chopped fresh mint

¼ tsp salt

⅛ tsp freshly ground pepper

1 long seedless cucumber, halved lengthwise and sliced

6 red radishes, sliced

4 pitas

1 Tbsp olive oil

1 LAMB: With tip of a knife, cut 8 deep slits in each side of lamb. Insert a garlic slice in each. Mix mustard, oil, salt and pepper in a large ziptop bag. Add lamb; turn to coat. Refrigerate 30 minutes or overnight.

2 Heat outdoor grill or stovetop grill pan. Remove meat from bag; place on grill (discard bag with marinade).

3 Grill, turning as needed, 45 minutes or until a meat thermometer inserted in thickest part registers 140°F for medium-rare. Transfer to cutting board, cover loosely with foil and let rest 5 to 10 minutes (internal temperature will rise about 5 degrees while resting).

4 WHILE LAMB COOKS, PREPARE MINTED CUCUMBER SALAD: Put sour cream, sugar, mint, salt and pepper in a serving bowl. Add cucumber and radishes; stir to mix and coat.

5 While lamb rests, brush pitas with olive oil. Grill, turning pitas once, 1 minute until hot and marked with grill lines. Cut in wedges. Thinly slice meat; serve with pitas and the salad.

# Balsamic Lamb Steaks with Spinach & Couscous

⅓ cup balsamic vinaigrette dressing

Two lamb center-cut leg steaks (about 12 oz each)

2 tsp olive oil

5.6-oz box toasted pine nut couscous mix (see *Couscous*, page 192)

2-oz jar sliced pimientos

2 Tbsp chopped fresh mint or parsley

10 oz fresh spinach

¼ cup sliced scallions

> **SERVES** 4
> **TOTAL TIME:** 22 minutes
>
> **PER SERVING:** 550 cal, 31 g pro, 34 g car, 4 g fiber, 33 g fat (11 g sat fat), 93 mg chol, 681 mg sod

**1** Put dressing in shallow dish, add lamb steaks and turn to coat. Let marinate at room temperature 5 minutes.

**2** While lamb marinates, bring oil, spice packet from couscous mix and 1¼ cups water to a boil in a medium saucepan. Remove from heat, add couscous, cover and let stand 5 minutes or until water is absorbed.

**3** Meanwhile heat a large nonstick skillet over medium heat. Add lamb, increase heat to medium-high and cook 5 minutes, turning steaks over once, until browned on the outside but still slightly pink at center. Remove to a cutting board.

**4** Fluff couscous with a fork; stir in pimientos and chopped mint. Cover until serving.

**5** Add some of the spinach to the skillet; toss over high heat 2 minutes, adding the rest of the spinach as the first wilts.

**6** Slice lamb; sprinkle with scallions. Serve with the couscous and spinach.

# Lamb Chops with Spicy Yogurt Marinade

SHOULDER CHOPS · GRILL OR STOVETOP GRILL PAN

GOOD WITH GRILLED RED PEPPERS, PITAS, OLIVES AND HUMMUS.

**SERVES** 4
**PREP:** 5 minutes
**MARINATE:** 30 minutes to 24 hours
**GRILL:** About 12 minutes

**PER SERVING:** 231 cal, 29 g pro, 2 g car, 0 g fiber, 11 g fat (4 g sat fat), 95 mg chol, 322 mg sod

MARINADE
½ cup plain nonfat yogurt
2 tsp ground cumin
1 tsp ground ginger
½ tsp salt
¼ tsp ground cinnamon
¼ tsp ground red pepper (cayenne)

Four ¾-in.-thick shoulder lamb chops (about 2 lb)

**1** MARINADE: Mix ingredients in a large ziptop bag. Add chops and turn to coat. Refrigerate at least ½ hour or up to 1 day.

**2** Heat outdoor grill or stovetop grill pan. Remove chops from bag; shake off excess Marinade. Discard bag with Marinade.

**3** Grill the chops 5 to 6 minutes per side turning once, for medium.

## STORING LAMB

Follow these guidelines to help maintain optimum quality.
Refrigerate 32° to 40°F.

| CUT | NO LONGER THAN | WRAPPING |
|---|---|---|
| Ground lamb | 24 hours | In original packaging |
| All other cuts | 1 to 2 days | In original packaging |
|  | 2 to 4 days | Remove the original wrapping and cover lamb loosely with plastic wrap or aluminum foil |
| Cooked lamb | 3 to 4 days | For best quality, wrap and refrigerate leftover roast or grilled lamb an hour after carving. Refrigerate lamb stews in a covered bowl or plastic container. |

Freeze 0°F or colder.

| CUT | NO LONGER THAN | WRAPPING |
|---|---|---|
| Ground lamb | 3 to 4 months | Wrap all cuts in freezer wrap, aluminum foil or plastic freezer bags. Individually wrap patties and chops so they thaw more quickly and it is easy to take out a few at a time. |
| All other cuts | 6 to 9 months |  |

# Lamb Patties Piccata

## GROUND LAMB · SKILLET

SERVE WITH COOKED BABY BEET OR OTHER GREENS AND COUSCOUS MADE FROM A MIX.

1 lb lean ground lamb
¼ cup plus 2 Tbsp minced fresh parsley
¼ cup plain dried bread crumbs
1 Tbsp freshly grated lemon peel
2 tsp minced garlic
¾ tsp salt
3 Tbsp fresh lemon juice
2 tsp butter

**SERVES 4**
**TOTAL TIME:** 20 minutes

**PER SERVING:** 275 cal,
21 g pro, 7 g car, 1 g fiber,
18 g fat (8 g sat fat), 81 mg
chol, 580 mg sod

**1** Put lamb, ¼ cup parsley, the bread crumbs, lemon peel, garlic, salt and ¼ cup cold water into a bowl. Mix with hands or a wooden spoon until well blended. Shape into four 4-in. patties.

**2** Lightly coat a large nonstick skillet with cooking spray and heat over medium heat. Add patties and cook 5 to 6 minutes per side until an instant-read thermometer inserted from side to center registers 160°F. Remove to serving plate; cover loosely with foil.

**3** Drain fat from skillet. Stir in lemon juice and 1 Tbsp water; bring to a boil. Add butter and stir to melt and blend. Remove from heat, stir in 2 Tbsp parsley and pour over patties.

# Quick Lamb Stew with Rice

GROUND LAMB · SKILLET

SERVES 4
TOTAL TIME: 15 minutes

PER SERVING: 507 cal,
22 g pro, 59 g car, 5 g fiber,
21 g fat (9 g sat fat), 62 mg
chol, 1,386 mg sod

TIP: You can use ground beef, chicken or turkey instead of lamb.

TIP: You can use a mixture of zucchini and yellow summer squash.

12 oz lean ground lamb (see Tip, left)
1 Tbsp minced garlic
1 tsp ground cumin
½ tsp dried oregano, crumbled
½ tsp ground cinnamon
½ tsp salt
15-oz can tomato sauce
4 zucchini or yellow summer squash (about 6 oz each), cut in half lengthwise then in ½-in. slices (see Tip, left)
15-oz jar whole small onions, drained
2 cups 5-minute rice

1  Put lamb, garlic, cumin, oregano, cinnamon and salt into a large nonstick skillet and cook 3 to 4 minutes over medium-high heat, breaking up clumps of meat with a spoon, until meat is no longer pink.

2  Stir in tomato sauce, ⅓ cup water, the squash and onions. Cover, bring to a boil, reduce heat and simmer 10 minutes or until squash is tender.

3  Meanwhile cook rice as pkg directs. Serve stew over rice.

## BUYING AND STORING LAMB

Choose meat that is pinkish-red and has a velvety texture. Since lamb is from young animals that have little time to store fat, there is little marbling and only a thin layer of fat around the outside of the meat. Bones should be porous and reddish.

As with all meats, store lamb in the coldest part of the refrigerator as soon as you get home from the market. Lamb can be left in its original wrapping. Cuts not prepackaged can be stored in the butcher paper. All lamb cuts (but not ground lamb) can be refrigerated for 3 to 4 days. Keep ground lamb no longer than 24 hours.

Rewrap or tightly overwrap lamb with foil or plastic wrap if you freeze it. Fresh lamb can be frozen up to 9 months, but ground lamb is best used within 4 months.

Thaw frozen lamb, still it its wrapping, in the refrigerator or in the microwave. Thawing any meat or poultry at room temperature is not recommended as it can promote bacterial growth. When you thaw any meat in the microwave, cook it right after thawing.

# Veal Milanese Insalata

## VEAL CUTLETS · SKILLET

2 large eggs

⅔ cup plain dry bread crumbs

¼ cup grated Parmesan cheese

Four 4-oz veal cutlets

3 Tbsp olive oil

4 packed cups (3 oz) mesclun, or other mixed salad greens

½ a medium bulb fennel, thinly sliced lengthwise

12 grape, cherry or pear tomatoes, cut in half

¼ cup thinly sliced red onion

¼ cup balsamic vinaigrette dressing

Parmesan shavings (see FYI, right)

**SERVES** 4
**TOTAL TIME:** 21 minutes

**PER SERVING:** 425 cal, 32 g pro, 21 g car, 3 g fiber, 23 g fat (5 g sat fat), 199 mg chol, 555 mg sod

**FYI:** For Parmesan shavings, pull a vegetable peeler across a chunk of (preferably) room-temperature Parmesan cheese.

**1** Break eggs into a rimmed plate and beat with a fork to break up. Mix crumbs and cheese in another plate. Coat 1 cutlet at a time with egg then crumb mixture.

**2** Heat 1½ Tbsp oil in a large nonstick skillet over medium heat. Add 2 cutlets; cook 1 to 1½ minutes per side until golden and just cooked through. Repeat with remaining oil and cutlets.

**3** Meanwhile put salad greens, fennel, tomatoes and red onion in a large bowl.

**4** Just before serving, add vinaigrette to salad; toss to coat. Top cutlets with salad and scatter Parmesan shavings over the salad.

---

## BUYING AND STORING VEAL

Look for veal with a fine grain and creamy pink color; any fat should be milky white.

As with all prepackaged meat the packages should feel cold to the touch and be securely wrapped without any tears or punctures where air could get in. Checking the sell-by date is always a good idea. Store veal in the coldest part of the refrigerator as soon as you get home.

Unopened packages of veal can be refrigerated up to 2 days after purchase although ground veal, like any ground meat, is best used or frozen within 24 hours.

Veal can be frozen in its original wrapping up to 2 weeks. For longer freezer storage (up to 9 months) rewrap or overwrap the package in foil or plastic wrap, or place in a freezer bag and squeeze out the air before sealing.

Thaw frozen veal in the refrigerator. Allow 4 to 7 hours per pound to thaw large roasts, 3 to 5 hours per pound for small roasts, and 12 hours for 1-in. chops. Defrosting at room temperature is not recommended.

# Osso Buco Milanese

## CROSSCUT VEAL SHANKS · DUTCH OVEN

SERVES 4
PREP: 25 minutes
BAKE: 1 hour 35 minutes to
2 hours 5 minutes

PER SERVING: 429 cal,
49 g pro, 11 g car, 1 g fiber,
20 g fat (7 g sat fat), 191 mg
chol, 620 mg sod

**FYI:** This dish uses crosscut veal shanks. The soft, fatty marrow in the hollow of the bone is considered a delicacy and is eaten after the meat. Gremolata—a mixture of lemon peel, garlic and parsley—is the traditional accompaniment.

## MILK-FED AND GRAIN-FED VEAL

The most expensive veal is called milk-fed veal and comes from animals that have been raised on milk or special formulas.

The delicate meat has a fine grain with a creamy pink, almost white, appearance. Veal animals that have grain in their diet—grain-fed veal—will have meat with a rosier color, coarser texture and slightly stronger flavor.

Four 2- to 2½-in.-thick meaty pieces veal shank (about 12 oz each)
¼ cup flour
2 Tbsp stick butter
2 Tbsp olive oil
1 cup finely chopped onion
2 tsp minced garlic
1 cup dry white wine or dry vermouth
½ cup chicken broth
2 tsp chopped fresh rosemary or ¼ tsp dried
½ tsp salt
¼ tsp freshly ground pepper

GREMOLATA
    2 Tbsp minced fresh parsley
    1 Tbsp freshly grated lemon peel
    1 tsp minced garlic

GARNISH: fresh rosemary sprigs

**1** Heat oven to 325°F. Have ready a Dutch oven (see *Dutch Oven*, page 82) or stovetop-to-oven casserole (with lid) large enough to hold meat in one layer.

**2** Coat veal shanks with flour; tap off excess. Heat butter and oil in Dutch oven over medium heat. Add shanks and brown 3 to 4 minutes per side. Remove to a plate.

**3** Add onion and garlic to pot and cook 4 to 5 minutes, stirring often, until onion is translucent. Add wine and bring to a gentle boil, scraping up browned bits on bottom. Boil 5 to 6 minutes until about half the wine has evaporated. Add broth, rosemary, salt and pepper then remove from heat.

**4** Arrange shanks side by side in pot with large marrow surface up. Spoon a little liquid over meat and cover with a tight-fitting lid or with foil, then the lid.

**5** Bake 1½ to 2 hours until meat is fork-tender. Meanwhile mix Gremolata ingredients. Spoon over meat and bake, uncovered, 5 minutes. Remove shanks to a serving platter, and garnish with rosemary. Cover loosely with foil.

**6** Skim off and discard fat from liquid in pot. Boil gently until slightly thickened and only about 2 cups remain. Serve with meat.

# Sweet & Spicy Meatball Kabobs

GROUND VEAL, PORK, BEEF · 2 RIMMED BAKING SHEETS · OVEN

HIGHLY POPULAR AS AN HORS D'OEUVRE, THESE MEATBALLS ALSO MAKE A GREAT DINNER.
SKIP THE SKEWERING AND THE PEPPERS; INSTEAD, SERVE THE MEATBALLS AND GRAVY WITH RICE
OR MASHED POTATOES AND A GREEN VEGETABLE.

1 medium green pepper

1 medium red pepper

MEATBALLS

    2 slices firm white bread, torn in small pieces

    ⅓ cup 1% lowfat milk

    8 oz each lean ground veal, pork and beef, or 1½ lb lean ground beef

    ½ cup finely chopped onion

    1 large egg

    ¾ tsp ground allspice

    ¾ tsp salt

    ½ tsp freshly ground pepper

12-oz jar beef gravy

3 Tbsp grape jelly

**MAKES** 36
**PREP:** 20 minutes
**BAKE & COOK:** 15 minutes

**PER 3 KABOBS:** 160 cal, 13 pro, 9 g car, 1 g fiber, 8 g fat (3 g sat fat), 58 mg chol, 231 mg sod

TIP: Can be prepared 1 day ahead and refrigerated. To serve, cover with foil and reheat in a 400°F oven 20 minutes.

**1** Heat oven to 400°F. Line 2 rimmed baking sheets pans with foil (for easy cleanup).

**2** Halve peppers lengthwise; remove core and seeds. Cut each half in 3 long strips. Cut each strip crosswise in thirds.

**3** MEATBALLS: Mix bread and milk in a large bowl. Add remaining Meatball ingredients; mix well. Roll into 36 balls.

**4** Using sturdy round wooden toothpicks, skewer 1 pepper chunk and 1 meatball on each. Place in lined pans. Bake 15 minutes or until meatballs are cooked through.

**5** Meanwhile bring gravy and jelly to a boil, stirring in some water if too thick. Place kabobs in a shallow serving platter or bowl; pour gravy over kabobs.

# Sausages

A virtual explosion has occurred in supermarket sausage departments. Wurstmachers have turned their skills to reworking many old favorites, including salami, kielbasa, bratwurst, Italian sausage and andouille, and come up with delicious, lower-fat versions made with turkey instead of traditional pork or beef. Other creative sausage makers have come up with new flavors for chicken sausage, including tequila chicken sausages with jalapenos, corn and fresh lime; artichoke and garlic sausage; portobello mushroom; apple; cilantro; and Moroccan with pistachios. Most of these sausages are sold fully cooked, requiring only a few minutes on the grill or in a skillet to heat them. Sausage is perfect for today's time-pressed cook; it supplies lots of flavor with minimum effort. In the *Woman's Day* test kitchens kielbasa and Italian sausage are favorites, both as a flavoring; check out "Big Easy" Gumbo, Hungarian Sausage Soup or Warm Lentil-Sausage Salad, and as the main event see Glazed Sausages & Onions with Corn. In this chapter you will find lots of recipes that celebrate the new role of sausage on American menus.

# Sausage-Potato Lasagna

## ITALIAN TURKEY SAUSAGE · OVEN · 13 X 9-IN. BAKING DISH

**SERVES 8**
**PREP:** 30 minutes
**BAKE:** About 1½ hours
**STAND:** 10 minutes

**PER SERVING:** 464 cal, 29 g pro, 39 g car, 4 g fiber, 23 g fat (10 g sat fat), 99 mg chol, 1,257 mg sod

TIP: Peel the potatoes, then submerge them in a bowl of cold water to prevent browning. Slice only 2 at a time for the same reason. The slicing disk on a food processor makes quick work of it.

SAUCE
- 1 tsp olive oil
- 1 lb sweet or hot Italian turkey sausage, removed from casings
- 1 cup chopped onion
- 26-oz jar marinara sauce

- 15-oz tub (1¾ cups) part-skim ricotta cheese
- ¼ cup plus 2 Tbsp grated Parmesan cheese
- 1 large egg
- 3 lb (about 6 medium) baking potatoes, peeled (see Tip, left)
- 1 cup (4 oz) shredded Cheddar cheese mixed with 1 cup (4 oz) shredded part-skim mozzarella cheese

**1** Heat oven to 350°F. Have a 13 x 9-in. baking dish ready.

**2** SAUCE: Heat oil in a large nonstick skillet over medium-high heat. Add sausage and onion. Cook 5 to 6 minutes, breaking up chunks of sausage with a spoon, until sausage is browned and onion is translucent. Stir in marinara sauce. Reduce heat and simmer 8 to 10 minutes until slightly thickened.

**3** Meanwhile, mix ricotta, the ¼ cup Parmesan and the egg in a medium bowl.

**4** Spread 1 cup Sauce over bottom of ungreased baking dish.

**5** Dry 2 of the potatoes with a paper towel and thinly slice by hand or with slicing disk of food processor. Place a layer, overlapping fairly evenly, in baking dish. Spread with 1 cup Sauce. Spoon on half the ricotta mixture, then sprinkle with one-third the Cheddar mixture. Repeat layers once, starting with 2 potatoes and ending with half the remaining Cheddar mixture.

**6** Top with final layers of 2 sliced potatoes, the remaining sauce, Cheddar mixture and the 2 Tbsp Parmesan cheese.

**7** Lightly coat a sheet of foil with cooking spray (or use nonstick foil). Place coated side down on lasagna; press edges to cover tightly.

**8** Bake 1¼ hours or until potatoes feel tender when pierced through the foil with the tip of a knife. Remove foil; bake 15 minutes longer. Let stand at room temperature 10 minutes before serving.

# Two-Timing Turkey Burgers

ITALIAN TURKEY SAUSAGE, GROUND TURKEY · GRILL OR STOVETOP GRILL PAN

SERVE WITH CHIPS AND PICKLES.

¼ cup tomato ketchup
¼ cup light mayonnaise
1 lb lean ground turkey
1 lb sweet or hot Italian turkey sausage, removed from casings
¼ cup minced or shredded onion
2 tsp minced garlic
¾ tsp freshly ground pepper
Cooking spray
6 hamburger buns
2 medium tomatoes, sliced
6 thin slices sweet onion

**SERVES** 6
**PREP:** 20 minutes
**GRILL:** About 12 minutes

**PER SERVING:** 425 cal, 31 g pro, 31 g car, 2 g fiber, 20 g fat (5 g sat fat), 99 mg chol, 954 mg sod

**1** Heat outdoor grill or stovetop grill pan. Line a baking sheet or tray with wax paper or foil. Coat with cooking spray. Mix ketchup and mayonnaise in a small bowl.

**2** In a large bowl mix ground turkey, sausage, onion, garlic and pepper. Divide mixture in six ⅔-cup portions. Gently form each into a ¾-in.-thick burger and put on the lined baking sheet. Coat tops with cooking spray.

**3** Grill burgers, turning once, 10 minutes or until an instant-read thermometer inserted through side of burgers to center registers 165°F and juices run clear when burgers are pierced. About 2 minutes before burgers are done, place buns cut side down on grill to toast.

**4** Serve burgers, topped with ketchup mixture, tomato and onion, in toasted buns.

# Sausage-Topped Polenta

**SERVES** 4
**TOTAL TIME:** 15 minutes

PER SERVING: 629 cal,
25 g pro, 36 g car, 8 g fiber,
42 g fat (13 g sat fat), 86 mg
chol, 1,299 mg sod

Tɪᴘ: Cutting thin strips of basil leaves is at least as easy as chopping them. Stack six or more leaves, fold the stack lengthwise (over the veins), hold firmly and cut thin slices from tip to stem.

16- to 20-oz tube polenta, cut in twelve ½-in.-thick slices
Cooking spray
1 Tbsp olive oil
1 lb sweet Italian sausage, removed from casings
½ cup chopped onion
15-oz can cannellini beans, drained and rinsed
14.5-oz can diced tomatoes
2 Tbsp thin strips fresh basil leaves (see Tip, left)

**1** Coat both sides of polenta slices with cooking spray. Heat a large nonstick skillet or a stovetop grill pan. Cook polenta 2 minutes each side until slightly browned and hot.

**2** Meanwhile, heat oil in large nonstick skillet over medium-high heat. Add sausage and onion and cook about 3 minutes, breaking up sausage with a spoon, until no longer pink. Stir in beans, tomatoes and basil. Bring to a simmer and cook about 2 minutes more until sausage is cooked.

**3** To serve, spoon sausage mixture over polenta.

**WHAT'S POLENTA?**

Polenta means cooked cornmeal or cornmeal mush. But you will also find the name on bags of ground cornmeal. (Look near rice and other grains in the supermarket.) Freshly made, polenta is thick and creamy, delicious plain or with cheese stirred in, alone or with a meat sauce. Polenta firms up when cold and can then be sliced and fried or grilled.

Polenta is also sold cooked, packaged in a clear plastic cylinder. It may be sold on an open shelf or refrigerated. Either way, it will keep for months and is a great staple to have on hand. Open the package, slide out the polenta and cut it into slices about ¹/₂ in. thick. You can fry the slices in olive oil or butter in a nonstick skillet, or brush with a little oil and grill. Serve plain or with cheese sprinkled on top. Good with a tomato-based sauce or a mushroom one. Great for breakfast, alone or with bacon and eggs. An added bonus: It is made with whole-grain cornmeal.

# Slow-Cooker Sausage Lasagna

## CHICKEN SAUSAGE · SLOW COOKER

SERVE WITH EXTRA MARINARA SAUCE, IF DESIRED.

26-oz jar marinara sauce

12 oz fully cooked Italian-style chicken sausages, diced

32-oz container part-skim ricotta cheese

2 cups (8 oz) shredded part-skim mozzarella cheese

¾ cup (3 oz) grated Parmesan cheese

2 tsp minced garlic

1 tsp Italian seasoning

8-oz box no-boil, oven-ready lasagna noodles

**SERVES** 8
**PREP TIME:** 20 minutes
**COOK:** About 5½ hours on low

**PER SERVING:** 523 cal, 35 g pro, 38 g car, 2 g fiber, 27 g fat (13 g sat fat), 96 mg chol, 1,411 mg sod

**1** Have ready a 5-qt or larger slow cooker. Mix marinara sauce, sausage and ½ cup water in a bowl. In another bowl, mix ricotta, 1½ cups mozzarella, ½ cup Parmesan, the garlic and Italian seasoning.

**2** Spread one-quarter the sauce mixture over bottom of cooker. Top with one-third the noodles, breaking noodles and overlapping as needed. Spread with one-third the ricotta mixture, covering noodles completely. Repeat sauce, noodle and cheese layers twice. Spread with remaining sauce mixture.

**3** Cover and cook on low 5 hours or until noodles are tender.

**4** Sprinkle with remaining ½ cup mozzarella and ¼ cup Parmesan. Cover and let stand 10 minutes to melt cheese.

# "Big Easy" Gumbo

SERVES 5
TOTAL TIME: 35 minutes

PER SERVING: 294 cal,
13 g pro, 52 g car, 8 g fiber,
4 g fat (1 g sat fat), 20 mg chol,
1,127 mg sod

2 tsp oil

2 green peppers, chopped

1 cup chopped onion

1 cup long grain white rice

1 tsp dried thyme

1 tsp salt

10-oz box frozen chopped kale, thawed (see Tip, left)

2¼ cups frozen cut okra, thawed

14-oz can stewed tomatoes, broken up

8-oz kielbasa sausage, cut in half and thinly sliced (see *Kielbasa*, page 163)

TIP: Thaw frozen vegetables quickly in your microwave. If you prefer use fresh okra and kale. Slice the okra. Pull the kale leaves off the stems then slice the leaves.

**1** Heat oil in a large nonstick skillet over medium-high heat. Add green peppers and onion and cook about 5 minutes, stirring often, until lightly browned. Stir in 1½ cups water, the rice, thyme and salt. Bring to a boil, reduce heat, cover and simmer 10 minutes.

**2** Stir in kale, okra, tomatoes and kielbasa. Return to a simmer, cover and cook 10 minutes longer or until rice is tender.

# New England Pierogi Dinner

PIEROGIES ARE DUMPLINGS OF POLISH ORIGIN THAT CAN BE BOILED, BAKED OR BROWNED IN A SKILLET AND SERVED IN A VARIETY OF WAYS, AS A SIDE OR MAIN DISH. THE FILLING MAY CONSIST OF POTATO OR OTHER VEGETABLE, OFTEN MIXED WITH CHEESE.

SERVES 4
TOTAL TIME: 20 minutes

PER SERVING: 304 cal,
16 g pro, 43 g car, 5 g fiber,
8 g fat (2 g sat fat), 46 mg chol,
1,137 mg sod

12-oz box frozen potato and Cheddar mini pierogies

1 tsp Old Bay Seasoning

½ medium head green cabbage, quartered (1¼ lb)

2 ears of corn, each cut in thirds

8-oz kielbasa sausage, sliced

1½ Tbsp butter

"Big Easy" Gumbo *(page 160)*

Sausage-Topped Polenta *(page 158)*

Kielbasa & Cabbage *(page 164)*

Broccoli Rabe & Sausage with Pasta *(page 167)*

**1** Start cooking pierogies as pkg directs.

**2** Meanwhile, bring 1 cup water and the seasoning to a boil in a 4- to 5-qt pot. Add cabbage, corn, kielbasa and ½ Tbsp butter. Cover and cook 10 minutes, turning cabbage and corn once or twice, until tender.

**3** Add cooked pierogies to cabbage and corn along with remaining Tbsp butter. Toss to mix.

# Hungarian Sausage Soup

### KIELBASA · 4- TO 5-QT POT

GREAT WITH TOASTED RYE OR PUMPERNICKEL BREAD.

6 cups chicken broth
2 cups chopped onion
2 Tbsp paprika
1 tsp caraway seeds (optional)
5 cups diced, peeled all-purpose potatoes (about 4)
8 cups (1 lb) coarsely shredded green cabbage
8 oz kielbasa sausage, coarsely chopped (see *Kielbasa*, page 163)
8-oz can stewed tomatoes
½ cup reduced-fat sour cream

**SERVES** 6 (makes 14 cups)
**TOTAL TIME:** About 40 minutes

**PER SERVING:** 280 cal, 11 g pro, 31 g car, 4 g fiber, 14 g fat (5 g sat fat), 32 mg chol, 922 mg sod

**1** Pour chicken broth and 1 cup water into a 4- to 5-qt pot. Add onion, paprika and caraway seeds and bring to a boil over high heat. Add potatoes and cabbage, and when boiling reduce heat and simmer 20 minutes or until vegetables are tender.

**2** Stir in kielbasa and tomatoes. Increase heat to medium and boil gently 5 to 10 minutes to let flavors develop. Remove from heat; stir in sour cream.

# Warm Lentil-Sausage Salad

TURKEY KIELBASA · SKILLET

UNLIKE MOST DRIED BEANS AND PEAS, LENTILS REQUIRE NO SOAKING
AND COOK IN LESS THAN HALF AN HOUR.

**SERVES 4**
**TOTAL TIME:** About 35 minutes

**PER SERVING:** 371 cal,
27 g pro, 44 g car, 8 g fiber,
9 g fat (3 g sat fat), 30 g chol,
1,462 mg sod

1 cup brown lentils, picked over and rinsed
  (see *Searching for Stones*, below)
3 cups chicken broth
1 Tbsp minced garlic
8-oz turkey kielbasa sausage, sliced (see *Kielbasa*, facing page)
10 oz baby spinach
1 pt grape, cherry or pear tomatoes, halved
½ cup thinly sliced red onion
⅓ cup lite honey-mustard dressing
¼ cup whole-grain mustard

**1.** In a 2-qt saucepan, bring lentils, broth and garlic to a boil. Reduce heat, partly cover the pan and simmer 20 to 25 minutes until lentils are tender.

**2** While lentils cook, heat a large nonstick skillet over medium heat. Add kielbasa; cook 3 to 5 minutes, stirring often, until browned. Place in a large bowl; add spinach, tomatoes and onion.

**3** Add dressing, mustard and ¼ cup water to skillet. Heat, scraping to incorporate brown bits from bottom. Pour over spinach mixture; toss to mix. Drain lentils (if necessary); add to salad and toss again.

### SEARCHING FOR STONES
Check dried beans and lentils before cooking for any small stones or tiny clumps of mud that may have evaded detection during the mechanical cleaning process and need to be removed. Although unlikely to be a sanitary problem, a small stone could be unpleasant to crunch down on.
Spread the beans or lentils out on a surface in good light and quickly move them around with your fingers, keeping an eagle-eye out for stones or other foreign objects (this is called picking over). Then put the beans into a strainer and rinse briefly under cool running water. This inspection is more important when you buy beans loose by the pound from an open bag than when you buy them prepackaged.

# Glazed Sausages & Onions with Corn

## KIELBASA AND CHICKEN SAUSAGES · GRILL

4 ears corn

¼ cup honey mustard

2 Tbsp orange juice

1 Tbsp olive oil

4 fully cooked chicken sausages (8 oz)

8-oz kielbasa sausage, cut in 4 pieces (see *Kielbasa*, right)

2 cups ½-in.-thick slices red onions

4 to 5 oz arugula or other salad greens

**SERVES** 4
**TOTAL TIME:** 20 minutes

**PER SERVING:** 338 cal, 23 g pro, 39 g car, 6 g fiber, 11 g fat (3 g sat fat), 65 mg chol, 1,125 mg sod

**1** Heat outdoor grill. Pull corn husks back but leave attached. Remove silks; place husks back up and wet ears under running water.

**2** Put mustard, orange juice and oil in a small bowl; stir until blended. Brush on the sausages and onions.

**3** Grill sausages, onions and corn 10 to 12 minutes, turning sausages and corn often and onions once, until sausages are lightly charred and onions and corn are tender.

**4** Arrange sausages on greens; top with onions and remaining mustard mixture. Serve with corn.

### KIELBASA
Kielbasa, also known as Polish sausage, is a smoked sausage seasoned with liberal amounts of garlic. Kielbasa was originally a Polish word for all sausage.

# Kielbasa & Cabbage

TURKEY KIELBASA · SKILLET

**SERVES 5**
**TOTAL TIME:** 20 minutes

**PER SERVING:** 296 cal,
17 g pro, 41 g car, 6 g fiber,
9 g fat (4 g sat fat), 48 mg chol,
928 mg sod

TIP: Good with rye bread.

1-lb turkey kielbasa sausage, cut in 2-in. pieces (see *Kielbasa*,
   page 163)
1½ cups thinly sliced red onion
2 Tbsp sugar
8 cups (about 1½ lb) thinly sliced green cabbage
2 apples, cored and cut in ½-in. chunks
½ cup raisins
½ cup cider vinegar
¼ tsp freshly ground pepper

**1** Coat a large nonstick skillet with cooking spray and heat over medium heat. Add kielbasa and cook 3 to 4 minutes, stirring once or twice, until browned. Remove to a plate.

**2** Add onion and sugar to skillet; cook, stirring often, about 3 minutes until golden. Stir in sausage, cabbage, apples, raisins, vinegar and pepper. Cover and cook 10 minutes or until cabbage wilts.

# White Beans, Sausage & Arugula with Pasta

ITALIAN SAUSAGE · SKILLET

SERVE WITH GRATED PARMESAN CHEESE.

**SERVES 4**
**TOTAL TIME:** 20 minutes

**PER SERVING:** 748 cal,
31 g pro, 89 g car, 10 g fiber,
29 g fat (10 g sat fat), 66 mg
chol, 1,256 mg sod

12 oz spaghettini
12 oz hot or sweet Italian sausage, removed from casings
1 cup thinly sliced quartered onion
14-oz can roasted garlic–flavored chicken broth
19-oz can cannellini beans, drained and rinsed
4 oz baby arugula or 5 oz baby spinach

**1** Cook pasta as pkg directs. Drain; return to pot.

**2** While water comes to a boil and pasta cooks, heat a large nonstick skillet over medium-high heat. Add sausage and onion and cook about 6 minutes, breaking up sausage with a wooden spoon, until no longer pink. Add broth and beans; bring to a boil. Reduce heat; simmer 3 to 4 minutes to blend flavors.

**3** Pour over pasta, add arugula and toss to mix and coat.

# Umbrian Meat Sauce

FETTUCINE, WITH ITS FLAT, SAUCE-CATCHING SURFACE, IS THE PERFECT PASTA TO SERVE WITH THIS RICHLY FLAVORED SAUCE.

2 tsp olive oil
1 cup chopped onion
½ cup chopped celery
½ cup chopped carrot
12-oz tube pork sausage, thawed if frozen
8 oz ground veal
4 oz chicken livers, diced (½ cup)
1 tsp dried sage
1 tsp dried basil
½ tsp salt
½ tsp freshly ground pepper
¾ cup dry red wine
1 cup chicken broth
14.5-oz can diced tomatoes, drained
12 oz fettuccine
½ cup heavy (whipping) cream
SERVE WITH: shredded Parmesan or Asiago cheese

SERVES 4
TOTAL TIME: 35 minutes

PER SERVING: 862 cal, 39 g pro, 78 g car, 4 g fiber, 43 g fat (18 g sat fat), 257 mg chol, 1,550 mg sod

TIP: You can make the sauce ahead and reheat it. You can also use sweet Italian sausage instead of plain sausage.

1  Bring a large pot of lightly salted water to a boil.

2  Meanwhile, heat oil in a large nonstick skillet over medium-high heat. Add onion, celery and carrot. Cook about 3 minutes, stirring occasionally until crisp-tender.

3  Add sausage, veal, chicken livers, sage, basil, salt and pepper. Cook 5 to 6 minutes, breaking up meat with a wooden spoon, until meat is no longer pink. Drain off fat. Increase heat to high, add wine and cook 3 minutes or until about half the wine has evaporated. Add broth and tomatoes, bring to a boil, reduce heat and simmer uncovered 10 to 15 minutes to develop flavor.

4  Meanwhile, stir fettuccine into boiling water; cook as pkg directs. Drain and return to pot.

5  Stir cream into the sauce. Pour over pasta and toss to mix and coat.

# Sausage & Peppers with Pasta

## ITALIAN TURKEY SAUSAGE · SKILLET

ANY RIDGED SHORT-CUT PASTA WILL WORK WELL HERE.

**SERVES** 6
**TOTAL TIME:** 25 minutes

**PER SERVING:** 432 cal,
22 g pro, 58 g car, 4 g fiber,
13 g fat (3 g sat fat), 40 mg
chol, 1,253 mg sod

**FYI:** Fennel seed has a mild
licorice taste. You can leave
it out if you don't care for
that flavor.

12 oz penne rigate
1 tsp olive oil
2 small red or green peppers, cut in narrow strips
1 lb Italian turkey sausage, removed from casings
½ tsp fennel seeds (see FYI, left)
3 cups marinara sauce
¼ cup dry white wine (optional)
GARNISH: chopped fresh parsley

**1** Cook pasta as pkg directs.

**2** While water comes to a boil and pasta cooks, heat oil in large nonstick skillet over medium-high heat. Add peppers and cook 3 to 4 minutes, stirring often, until lightly charred in a few places and crisp-tender.

**3** Reduce heat to medium-high. Add sausage and fennel seeds (if using) to skillet. Cook about 3 minutes, breaking sausage into small chunks with a wooden spoon. When lightly browned, stir in marinara sauce and wine; bring to a simmer and cook 3 to 5 minutes to blend flavors.

**4** Drain pasta; return to pot. Add Sauce; toss to mix. Sprinkle with parsley.

# Broccoli Rabe & Sausage with Pasta

## ITALIAN SAUSAGE · SKILLET

THIS IS AN ITALIAN WAY OF ENJOYING PASTA; NOT WITH A RED SAUCE, BUT WITH A VEGETABLE AND A FLAVORING MEAT. PASTA WATER PROVIDES MOISTURE. IN ADDITION TO PARMESAN, HAVE A SMALL BOWL OF CRUSHED RED PEPPER ON THE TABLE FOR THOSE WHO LIKE TO ADD A SPICY TOUCH.

12 oz mini rigatoni pasta

1 lb broccoli rabe, ends trimmed, stacked and cut in 1-in.-wide strips

1 lb hot Italian sausage, removed from casings

SERVE WITH: grated Parmesan cheese and crushed red pepper

**SERVES** 4
**TOTAL TIME:** 30 minutes

**PER SERVING:** 724 cal, 29 g pro, 67 g car, 2 g fiber, 37 g fat (13 g sat fat), 86 mg chol, 1,239 mg sod

**1** Bring a large pot of lightly salted water to a boil. Add pasta and cook as pkg directs, adding broccoli rabe 3 minutes before pasta will be done. Scoop out 1 cup of the pasta cooking water; drain pasta and broccoli rabe in a colander then put them back in the pot.

**2** While pasta cooks, heat a large nonstick skillet over medium-high heat. Add sausage and cook, breaking up large chunks with a spoon, 5 to 7 minutes until browned and cooked through.

**3** Add the 1 cup cooking water and cook 1 minute, stirring to loosen brown bits on bottom of pan. Pour over pasta in pot and stir over heat about 1 minute.

## BROCCOLI RABE

Fresh broccoli rabe, as long as the leaves are dry, will keep a few days in a plastic bag in the refrigerator. Wet leaves quickly turn yellow; either wrap them in paper towels before storing or trim, wash and dry in a salad spinner.

To prepare broccoli rabe (also known as broccoli rape [rah-pay]), cut off the stems just below the tie. Untie the bunch and pluck off any yellow leaves. Hold the bunch together and cut in 1-in. pieces. Wash thoroughly in cold water and drain.

# Eggs & Cheese

Eggs and cheese are two of the most useful and nutritious foods available to the cook. They are delicious in their own right, and make a great couple! In the past, we tended to relegate eggs to breakfast, but research shows that now we also see eggs as dinner. This is partly because although Americans love a breakfast of eggs, we don't have the time to cook it. But eggs for dinner appeal to everyone. With the large variety of packaged shredded cheeses, cooking with cheese has become easier than ever. There are also many lowfat cheeses available. Some are naturally low in fat; others are made with part-skim milk. When adding cheese to a sauce, keep in mind that if you use a more highly flavored cheese you will need less to achieve a rich cheese flavor. So even if you prefer mild Cheddar for eating, try sharp or extra-sharp in a sauce. Keep fresh eggs and cheese on hand and you will never be at a loss for a quick and tasty meal.

# Chiles Rellenos Casserole

## EGGS & CHEESE · OVEN · SHALLOW 2-QT BAKING DISH

SERVE WITH WARM CORN OR FLOUR TORTILLAS.

SERVES 8
PREP: 15 minutes
BAKE: About 35 minutes

PER SERVING: 262 cal,
16 g pro, 13 g car, 1 g fiber,
17 g fat (9 g sat fat), 203 mg
chol, 357 mg sod

TIP: Instead of preparing the egg mixture in a bowl, use a blender. First put in the milk and eggs, then the flour and seasoning. Start on a low speed.

FYI: Rellenos means stuffed, but in this easy version of a Tex-Mex favorite we've side-stepped stuffing the peppers, but not the flavor.

16-oz can (or four 4-oz cans) whole mild green chiles, rinsed and drained

1 cup (4 oz) shredded Cheddar cheese

1 cup (4 oz) shredded Monterey Jack cheese

2 Tbsp flour

12-oz can evaporated milk (not sweetened condensed)

6 large eggs

½ tsp ground cumin

½ tsp garlic powder

½ tsp salt

¼ tsp freshly ground pepper

**1** Heat oven to 350°F. Lightly grease a shallow 2-qt baking dish.

**2** Cut chiles in half lengthwise; pat dry between paper towels. Cover bottom of prepared baking dish with half the chiles; sprinkle with half the cheeses. Repeat with remaining chiles and cheeses.

**3** In a medium bowl (see Tip, left), whisk flour into about ¼ cup evaporated milk until well blended, then whisk in remaining milk, the eggs, cumin, garlic powder, salt and pepper until smooth. Pour over chiles and cheese.

**4** Bake 30 to 35 minutes or until a knife inserted near center comes out clean (see *Clean Knife Test*, page 183) and edges just begin to brown.

# Ham & Egg Hash Brown Pie

CHEESE, EGGS, HAM · TWO 9-IN. PIE PLATES · OVEN

3 lb all-purpose potatoes

4 tsp oil

Salt

1½ cups (8 oz) diced ham

1½ cups (6 oz) shredded Cheddar cheese

1 red pepper, finely chopped

½ cup thinly sliced scallions

6 large eggs

1½ cups whole milk

2 tsp dry mustard powder (see FYI, page 42)

**MAKES** 2 pies (6 servings each)
**PREP:** 30 minutes
**BAKE:** About 40 minutes

PER SERVING: 231 cal, 13 g pro, 18 g car, 2 g fiber, 12 g fat (5 g sat fat), 135 mg chol, 615 mg sod

**1** Lightly coat two 9-in. pie plates with cooking spray.

**2** Coarsely shred potatoes (see Tip, right), then put them into a large bowl of cold water to keep them from discoloring and to rinse off excess starch.

**3** Drain half the potatoes very well. Heat 2 tsp oil in a large nonstick skillet over medium-high heat. Add the drained potatoes and sprinkle with ½ tsp salt. Cook about 8 minutes, stirring often, until potatoes are soft and pale golden.

**4** Press potatoes evenly over bottom and up sides of one pie plate. Repeat with rest of potatoes. Cover and refrigerate up to 1 day.

**5** About 50 minutes before serving: Heat oven to 350°F. Sprinkle ham, cheese, red pepper and scallions over potato crusts. Whisk eggs, milk, dry mustard and ¼ tsp salt in a large bowl to blend. Pour half into each pie plate.

**6** Bake 35 to 40 minutes until a knife inserted near center of pies comes out clean (see *Clean Knife Test*, page 183).

Tɪᴘ: Shred potatoes in seconds in a food processor fitted with a shredding blade. Or use the large holes on a box grater.

FYI: Up to a day ahead the crusts can be made through Step 4, the ham diced, cheese shredded and scallions sliced. Wrap and refrigerate all.

# Tomato & Cheese Casserole

EGGS, CHEESE · OVEN · 8-IN. SQUARE BAKING DISH

THIS OLD-FASHIONED DISH IS ALSO KNOWN AS A STRATA BECAUSE OF THE LAYERS.
IT MAKES A COMFORTING SUPPER. ONCE ASSEMBLED, THIS DISH CAN BE REFRIGERATED
UP TO 24 HOURS BEFORE BAKING.

**SERVES** 4
**PREP:** 10 minutes
**BAKE:** 40 to 45 minutes

**PER SERVING:** 470 cal,
24 g pro, 44 g car, 3 g fiber,
22 g fat (11 g sat fat), 260 mg
chol, 938 mg sod

10 slices white sandwich bread
4 tomatoes, cut in ½-in.-thick slices
1 cup (4 oz) shredded Cheddar cheese
½ cup sliced scallions
2 cups milk
4 large eggs
½ tsp salt

**1** Lightly grease an 8-in. square baking dish.

**2** Place 4 slices bread over bottom of dish. Top with half the tomato
slices, cheese and scallions. Cover with 6 slices bread (overlapping),
remaining tomatoes, cheese and scallions. Put milk, eggs and salt in
a bowl. Whisk until blended; pour over bread. Cover and refrigerate
up to 24 hours.

**3** Heat oven to 350°F. Uncover and bake 40 to 45 minutes until
puffed and golden, and knife inserted near the center comes out clean
(see *Clean Knife Test*, page 183).

# Apple Bread Pudding

## EGGS OR EGG SUBSTITUTE · OVEN · 9-IN. SQUARE BAKING DISH

SERVE THIS DISH WARM WITH A DRIZZLE OF APRICOT PRESERVES FOR BREAKFAST
OR AS A DESSERT WITH A SMALL SCOOP OF FROZEN VANILLA YOGURT.

8 slices stone-ground 100% whole-wheat bread

¼ cup sugar

1 tsp ground cinnamon

2 cups 1% lowfat milk

1 cup fat- and cholesterol-free egg substitute (or the
equivalent in eggs)

1 Tbsp packed brown sugar

1½ tsp vanilla extract

2 large apples, cored and diced (see Tip, right)

**SERVES** 8
**PREP:** 15 minutes
**BAKE:** 40 to 50 minutes

**PER SERVING:** 167 cal,
7 g pro, 31 g car, 2 g fiber,
2 g fat (1 g sat fat), 2 mg chol,
223 mg sod

TIP: Cortland, McIntosh or
Rome Beauty apples would
work well here.

**1** Heat oven to 375°F. Lightly grease a 9-in. square baking dish.

**2** Toast the bread and cut each slice in half diagonally. Mix sugar
and cinnamon in a small bowl. In a larger bowl, blender or food
processor, whisk or blend milk, egg substitute (or eggs), brown sugar
and vanilla extract.

**3** Arrange half the toast in baking dish; sprinkle with half the cinnamon-sugar and apples. Repeat layers. Pour milk mixture over top.

**4** Bake uncovered 40 to 50 minutes until a knife inserted in center
comes out clean.

**5** Cut in squares to serve.

Substitutes:
White bread
½ c sugar / 2 tsp cinnamon
raisins <u>or</u> apples - 2 c.

# Spanish Omelet with Cheese

**SERVES** 6
**PREP:** 5 minutes
**COOK:** About 18 minutes

**PER SERVING:** 229 cal,
15 g pro, 10 g car, 1 g fiber,
14 g fat (5 g sat fat), 304 mg
chol, 527 mg sod

Tɪᴘ: The omelet is finished
under the broiler. If your skillet has a plastic or wood
handle, double-wrap it with
foil to protect it.

1 Tbsp oil
3 cups frozen O'Brien potatoes
¼ tsp salt
¼ tsp freshly ground pepper
1 cup (4 oz) diced ham
8 large eggs
½ cup (2 oz) shredded Monterey Jack or Cheddar cheese

**1** Heat oil in a 10- to 11-in. nonstick skillet over medium heat (see Tip, left). Add frozen potatoes, salt and pepper. Cover and cook as pkg directs. Add ham and stir until hot. Reduce heat to medium-low.

**2** Heat broiler. Whisk eggs in a large bowl. Pour into skillet and stir to mix with potatoes and ham.

**3** Cover and cook 6 minutes or until eggs are set on bottom. Sprin-kle with cheese.

**4** Broil 4 to 5 in. from heat source 1 to 2 minutes until eggs set and cheese melts. Slide onto serving plate and cut into wedges.

# Enchilada Frittata

## EGGS, HAM · SKILLET

AN ITALIAN-STYLE OMELET WITH TEX-MEX FLAVOR AND THE CRUNCH OF CORN TORTILLA CHIPS.
SERVE WITH SOUR CREAM FOR A SATISFYING DINNER.

8 large eggs
8.75-oz can corn kernels, drained
4.5-oz can chopped green chiles, drained (see Tip, right)
1 Tbsp oil
1 cup (4 oz) diced ham
3 scallions, sliced, white and green parts kept separate
2 tsp minced garlic
10-oz can enchilada sauce
30 baked corn tortilla chips
1½ cups (6 oz) shredded Monterey Jack cheese

**SERVES** 4
**TOTAL TIME:** About 25 minutes

**PER SERVING:** 504 cal,
33 g pro, 27 g car, 2 g fiber,
30 g fat (12 g sat fat), 487 mg
chol, 1,728 mg sod

TIP: Instead of a 4.5-oz can
of chopped green chiles, you
can use a 4.25-oz jar of
diced green chiles.

**1** Put eggs, corn and chiles in a large bowl; whisk to blend.

**2** Heat oil in a 10- to 11-in. nonstick skillet over medium heat. Add ham, white part of scallions and garlic; cook, stirring, 3 to 4 minutes until scallions are soft.

**3** Add egg mixture; stir to mix. Reduce heat to medium-low, cover skillet and cook 10 minutes or until eggs set on top.

**4** Top with enchilada sauce, tortilla chips, cheese and green part of scallions.

**5** Cover and cook about 1 minute to melt cheese. Cut in wedges to serve.

## WHAT IS A FRITTATA?

A frittata is an Italian omelet and differs from the French version in that added ingredients are usually mixed and cooked with the beaten eggs rather than folded inside after the eggs are cooked.
A frittata is cooked much more slowly than an omelet and is served flat, whole or cut in wedges, not folded over. Italian families there and in the U.S. often serve egg dishes for dinner.
In Spain, an omelet is called a tortilla and made like a frittata. There, tortillas are a popular snack in every tapas bar.

# Chorizo Frittata

**SERVES 4**
**TOTAL TIME:** 15 minutes

**PER SERVING:** 420 cal,
26 g pro, 11 g car, 2 g fiber,
30 g fat (12 g sat fat), 474 mg
chol, 834 mg sod

## CHORIZO

Chorizo is a highly seasoned chile- and garlic-flavored sausage, commonly made of pork, but also of beef or goat. Originally from Spain, distinctive varieties have evolved in Mexico and the American Southwest. Although available fresh, it's the hard smoked version that is usually found in supermarkets. Smoked chorizo keeps for weeks in the refrigerator. Add a few slices to a paella, chili or refried beans. Or dice a small amount and fry quickly in a skillet before adding beaten eggs and scrambling them.

1 Tbsp olive oil

3 oz chorizo sausage diced (see *Chorizo*, left)

2 cups chopped onions

¼ cup thinly sliced jalapeño pepper (see *Handling Hot Peppers*, page 52)

8 large eggs

1 cup (4 oz) shredded Monterey Jack cheese

2 Tbsp chopped fresh cilantro

½ tsp ground cumin

½ tsp salt

Toppings: **salsa, sour cream and chopped cilantro**

**1** Heat oil in a large nonstick skillet over medium-high heat (see Tip, facing page). Add sausage, onions and jalapeño and cook 4 to 6 minutes, stirring several times, until onion is almost tender.

**2** Whisk eggs, cheese, cilantro, cumin and salt in a medium bowl. Pour into skillet, shaking pan gently to distribute evenly.

**3** Reduce heat to medium and cook, without stirring, 3 to 5 minutes until set on bottom and sides (eggs will be runny in the center).

**4** Broil 4 to 6 in. from heat source 2 minutes or until frittata is firm in the center.

**5** Loosen edges with a rubber spatula; invert onto a serving platter. Cut in wedges and serve with Toppings.

Ham & Egg Hash Brown Pie *(page 171)*

Tomato & Cheese Casserole *(page 172)*

Enchilada Frittata *(page 175)*

Roast Vegetable Rancheros
*(page 181)*

# Mixed Vegetable Frittata

EGGS · SKILLET · BROILER

1 Tbsp olive oil
2 cups sliced zucchini
½ cup sliced red onion
½ cup sliced mushrooms
½ cup sliced red or green pepper
1 Tbsp minced garlic
8 large eggs
1 cup (4 oz) shredded mozzarella cheese
2 Tbsp chopped parsley
½ tsp salt
¼ tsp freshly ground pepper
TOPPINGS: heated marinara sauce and chopped fresh basil or
     parsley

**1**  Heat broiler. Heat oil in a large nonstick skillet (see Tip, right).

**2**  Add zucchini, onion, mushrooms, red pepper and garlic; sauté 4 to 6 minutes over medium-high heat until almost tender.

**3**  Whisk eggs, cheese, parsley, salt and pepper in a medium bowl. Pour into skillet, shaking pan gently to distribute evenly.

**4**  Reduce heat to medium and cook, without stirring, 3 to 5 minutes until set on bottom and sides (eggs will be runny in center).

**5**  Broil 4 to 6 in. from heat source 2 minutes or until frittata is firm in the center.

**6**  Loosen edges with a rubber spatula; invert onto a serving platter. Cut in wedges and serve with Toppings.

SERVES 4
TOTAL TIME: About 30 minutes

PER SERVING: 286 cal, 20 g pro, 8 g car, 1 g fiber, 20 g fat (7 g sat fat), 447 mg chol, 527 mg sod

TIP: The omelet is finished under the broiler. If your skillet has a plastic or wood handle, double-wrap it with foil to protect it.

**STUCK IN THE CARTON?**
If eggs are stuck to the carton, fill the indentations with a little cool water and let stand for about 5 minutes. You should be able to lift out the eggs easily. Make sure to cook stuck eggs completely.

# Ham, Potato and Swiss Frittata

**SERVES** 4
**TOTAL TIME:** 25 minutes

**PER SERVING:** 391 cal, 31 g pro, 10 g car, 1 g fiber, 24 g fat (10 g sat fat), 476 mg chol, 1,362 mg sod

1 Tbsp olive oil
1 cup diced potato
1 cup diced Virginia ham (see *Specialty Hams*, page 135)
½ cup sliced scallions
8 large eggs
1 cup (4 oz) shredded Swiss cheese
2 tsp Dijon mustard
¼ tsp salt
¼ tsp freshly ground pepper
TOPPINGS: **dollops of whipped chive cream cheese**

**1** Heat broiler. Heat oil in a large nonstick skillet (see Tip, left).

**2** Add potato, ham and scallions; sauté 6 to 8 minutes over medium-high heat until potato is almost tender.

**3** Whisk eggs, cheese, mustard, salt and pepper in a medium bowl. Pour into skillet, shaking pan gently to distribute evenly.

**4** Reduce heat to medium and cook, without stirring, 3 to 5 minutes until set on bottom and sides (eggs will be runny in center).

**5** Broil 4 to 6 in. from heat source 2 minutes or until frittata is firm in the center.

**6** Loosen edges with a rubber spatula; invert onto a serving platter. Cut in wedges. Top with whipped chive cream cheese.

TIP: The omelet is finished under the broiler. If your skillet has a plastic or wood handle, double-wrap it with foil to protect it.

# Florentine Eggs Diavolo

**HARD-COOKED EGGS · OVEN · SHALLOW 2-QT BAKING DISH**

FLORENTINE IN A RECIPE TITLE USUALLY INDICATES SPINACH, WHILE DIAVOLO MEANS DEVIL.
IN THIS BRUNCH OR SUPPER DISH DEVILED EGGS ARE PAIRED WITH SPINACH IN A CREAMY SAUCE.

10-oz box frozen chopped spinach, thawed and squeezed dry

9 eggs, hard cooked and peeled (see Tip, right)

3 Tbsp light mayonnaise

1 Tbsp cider vinegar

2 tsp instant minced onion

½ tsp mustard powder or prepared mustard

½ tsp salt

¼ tsp ground red pepper (cayenne)

16-oz jar Alfredo sauce

2 Tbsp stick butter

1 cup fresh bread crumbs (see *Fresh Bread Crumbs,* page 66)

**SERVES** 6
**PREP:** 30 minutes
**BAKE:** 25 to 30 minutes

**PER SERVING:** 348 cal, 14 g pro, 11 g car, 1 g fiber, 27 g fat (12 g sat fat), 394 mg chol, 1,053 mg sod

**1**  Heat oven to 350°F. Lightly coat a shallow 2-qt baking dish with cooking spray. Scatter spinach evenly in baking dish.

**2**  Cut eggs in half and scoop yolks into a bowl. Add mayonnaise, vinegar, onion, mustard, salt and red pepper and mash smooth with a fork. Spoon into hollow of each white.

**3**  Arrange yolk side down on spinach. Pour Alfredo sauce over eggs to cover.

**4**  Melt butter; stir in crumbs. Sprinkle over sauce.

**5**  Bake uncovered 25 to 30 minutes until sauce is bubbly.

TIP: Hard cook the eggs one or two days ahead and crackle the shells (see *How to Hard Cook Eggs Perfectly,* page 18) but don't peel them until just before.

TIP: Except for sprinkling on the buttered crumbs you can prepare this dish the day before, cover and refrigerate. Add 15 to 20 minutes to the baking time; insert a knife in the middle of the casserole and if it comes out very hot the casserole is ready.

# Egg & Pepper Enchiladas

## HARD-COOKED EGGS · OVEN · SHALLOW 3-QT BAKING DISH

**SERVES 8**
**PREP:** About 30 minutes
**BAKE:** 30 minutes

**PER SERVING:** 386 cal,
19 g pro, 39 g car, 2 g fiber,
17 g fat (7 g sat fat), 235 mg
chol, 1,122 mg sod

2 tsp oil

16-oz bag frozen mixed pepper strips

Eight 7- to 8-in. flour tortillas

16-oz can refried beans with green chiles

8 hard-cooked eggs, sliced

1½ cups (6 oz) shredded Cheddar or pepperjack cheese
   (or mix of both)

15-oz can mild green enchilada sauce

Toppings: green salsa, sour cream and minced red onion

**1** Heat oven to 350°F. Lightly coat a shallow 3-qt baking dish with cooking spray.

**2** Heat oil in a large nonstick skillet over medium-high heat. Add peppers and cook 7 to 8 minutes, stirring occasionally, until liquid that comes out of peppers evaporates.

**3** Spread each tortilla with a scant ¼ cup refried beans. Arrange 1 sliced egg on half of each tortilla, top egg with a scant ¼ cup peppers and sprinkle with 1½ Tbsp cheese.

**4** Spread ⅓ cup enchilada sauce in baking dish. Roll up tortillas starting from egg and pepper edge. Place seam side down in dish. Spoon on remaining sauce; cover tightly with foil.

**5** Bake 25 minutes. Uncover; sprinkle with remaining cheese. Bake 5 minutes to melt cheese. Serve with Toppings.

# Roast Vegetable Rancheros

8 small (9 oz) red-skinned potatoes, quartered

2 small (4 oz each) red onions, cut in 8 wedges

1 red pepper, cut in 8 wedges

1 orange pepper, cut in 8 wedges

6 oz zucchini, cut in 1½-in. chunks

6-oz summer squash, cut in 1½-in. chunks

Cooking spray

1 tsp chili powder

1 tsp salt

1 cup salsa

Four 7- to 8-in. flour tortillas

8 slices (about 5 oz) Canadian bacon (see *Canadian Bacon*, page 188)

4 large eggs

Garnish: sour cream and chopped fresh cilantro

**SERVES** 4
**PREP:** 25 minutes
**COOK & BAKE:** About 48 minutes

**PER SERVING:** 382 cal, 20 g pro, 47 g car, 5 g fiber, 13 g fat (3 g sat fat), 230 mg chol, 1,752 mg sod

**1** Heat oven to 400°F. Have ready a large rimmed baking sheet and a baking sheet large enough to hold 4 tortillas without overlapping.

**2** Put vegetables in a large bowl and lightly coat with cooking spray. Add chili powder and salt; toss to mix and coat. Spread in a single layer on rimmed baking sheet.

**3** Bake vegetables 20 minutes, stir and turn vegetables, then bake 20 minutes more or until tender and very lightly browned. Return to bowl, add salsa and toss gently to coat. Cover to keep warm.

**4** Coat both sides of tortillas with cooking spray. Place on another baking sheet and bake 5 minutes; turn over and bake 3 minutes longer or until brown and crisp. Top each with 2 overlapping slices bacon, return to oven, turn oven off and remove tortillas after 2 minutes.

**5** Meanwhile coat a large nonstick skillet with cooking spray. Place over medium heat and gently break eggs into skillet (see Tip, right). Cover and cook 3 to 4 minutes, just until yolks are set.

**6** Place each tortilla on a plate. Top with an egg, then vegetables. Garnish with cilantro and sour cream.

Tip: To avoid getting pieces of shell in with the egg, crack each egg into a cup and gently slide it into the skillet.

# Apple Dutch Baby

EGGS · OVEN · 9-IN. PIE PLATE OR PAN · BLENDER OR FOOD PROCESSOR · SKILLET

Prepare the apples while the Dutch Baby bakes.
Serve it promptly to catch the full effect of the crisp, puffed brown sides.

**SERVES 6**
**TOTAL TIME:** About 50 minutes

**PER SERVING:** 305 cal,
7 g pro, 43 g car, 3 g fiber,
12 g fat (5 g sat fat), 158 mg
chol, 118 mg sod

1 Tbsp oil
4 large eggs
⅔ cup flour
⅔ cup 1% lowfat milk
2 Tbsp cold stick butter, cut in small pieces
1 tsp vanilla extract

SAUTÉED APPLES
   4 medium (1½ lb) Golden Delicious, Cameo or
      Pink Lady apples
   1 Tbsp stick butter
   ½ cup sweetened dried cranberries
   ¼ cup packed light-brown sugar
   ½ tsp ground cinnamon

GARNISH: **confectioners' sugar**

**1** Heat oven to 450°F. Have ready a 9-in. pie plate.

**2** Pour oil into pie plate. Heat in oven 5 minutes.

**3** Meanwhile, put eggs, flour, milk, butter and vanilla in a blender or food processor and process, scraping down sides occasionally, until well blended. Pour into hot pie plate.

**4** Bake 20 minutes without opening the oven door until sides are puffed and high. Reduce oven temperature to 350°F; bake 20 minutes longer or until sides are browned and crisp.

**5** SAUTÉED APPLES: While Dutch Baby bakes, peel, halve and core the apples and cut in thin wedges (about 7 cups). Melt butter in a large nonstick skillet. Add apples, cranberries, sugar and cinnamon. Stir over medium-high heat 8 to 10 minutes until apples are glazed and tender. (Add up to ¼ cup water 1 Tbsp at a time if pan becomes dry.)

**6** Spoon apples into Dutch Baby. Dust with confectioners' sugar tapped through a strainer. Using 2 forks, tear in wedges and serve directly from the pan.

# Spring Vegetable Quiche

PIE CRUST · EGGS · OVEN · 9-IN. PIE PLATE

1 refrigerated ready-to-bake pie crust (from a 15-oz box of 2)

2 cups whole milk

0.9-oz box spring vegetable soup, dip and recipe mix

4 large eggs

1 cup (4 oz) shredded Swiss cheese

**1** Following directions on box, line a 9-in. pie plate with pie crust and prebake if desired (see Tip, right).

**2** Pour milk into a 4-cup measure, add soup mix and let soak at least 10 minutes.

**3** Heat oven to 350°F.

**4** Beat eggs in a medium bowl with a fork until blended. Stir in milk mixture.

**5** Sprinkle ¾ cup cheese over crust. Add egg mixture; sprinkle rest of cheese on top.

**6** Bake 45 minutes or until tip of a knife inserted in center comes out clean (see *Clean Knife Test*, right). Let stand 10 minutes before cutting in wedges.

SERVES 6
**PREP:** 15 to 20 minutes
**BAKE:** About 45 minutes
**STAND:** 10 minutes

**PER SERVING:** 336 cal, 13 g pro, 24 g car, 0 g fiber, 20 g fat (10 g sat fat), 177 mg chol, 547 mg sod

TIP: For a crisper crust, pre-bake the pie shell as directed on box.

**CLEAN KNIFE TEST**
To see if a liquid egg mixture has baked long enough, insert a knife in the center. If the egg mixture has set, the knife will come out clean, that is, without uncooked egg mixture clinging to it. If the knife comes out with liquid egg mixture clinging to it, further cooking is in order.

# Grains & Beans

Long a primary staple and source of protein for many countries, grains and beans have finally moved into a position of importance in the American diet—and it is easy to see why. Both are low in fat, high in fiber and complex carbohydrates and rich in vitamins and minerals. They offer a healthy alternative to meat dishes or a way to reduce the amount of meat in a meal. At one time dried beans might have been seen as a food that required thinking ahead (to soak the beans) and long cooking. But the availability of a wide range of canned beans has moved them into the quick-food category. Although even plain rice doesn't take very long to cook, that time has been reduced by converted and instant rice and packaged mixes where the seasonings are already mixed in. And our interest in grains has grown to include barley, bulgur and couscous. Grains and beans offer a wide variety of tastes and textures to meal planning. Use them often, as side and main dishes.

# Down-Home Beans & Greens

### HAM HOCK, DRIED BEANS · MAIN DISH

SERVE OVER RICE WITH HOT SAUCE ON THE SIDE.

**SERVES** 4
**BEANS** (short soak): 1 hour;
(long soak): 12 to 24 hours
**PREP:** 15 minutes
**COOK:** About 3¼ hours

**PER SERVING:** 320 cal,
23 g pro, 54 g car, 32 g fiber,
2 g fat (1 g sat fat), 12 mg chol,
547 mg sod

**TIP:** To quickly remove tough stems from collard, kale or turnip greens, hold stem in one hand. With other hand quickly fold leaf over at bottom and pull it off the stem. Wash leaves well in warm water before cutting and cooking.

1 lb small dried white beans, such as Great Northern, cannellini or navy beans, picked over, rinsed and drained (see *Searching for Stones*, page 162)

1 smoked ham hock (about 1 lb), split

1 cup sliced onions

2 medium cloves garlic

4 chicken bouillon cubes

2 bay leaves, each about 2 in. long

½ tsp dried thyme

1 lb collard, kale or turnip greens

**1** SHORT SOAK: Put beans in a large pot with cold water to cover by 2 in. Bring to a boil, remove from heat and let stand 1 hour. Drain and rinse. LONG SOAK: Put beans in a large pot with cold water to cover by 2 in. Let stand at room temperature at least 12 hours. Beans can soak up to 24 hours, but for that long put them in the refrigerator. Drain and rinse.

**2** TO COOK: Put ham hock and 8 cups water in a heavy 5-qt pot. Bring to a boil; skim off and discard foam from top. Reduce heat and add onions, garlic, bouillon cubes, bay leaves and thyme. Bring to a simmer and cook, uncovered, 1½ hours or until ham hock is tender.

**3** Stir in soaked beans, return to a simmer and cook, uncovered, 45 minutes.

**4** Meanwhile, stack the greens and cut crosswise in 1-in.-wide ribbons. Stir in greens, adding more water if mixture seems dry. Cook 45 minutes or until meat falls off the bones and beans are tender. Before serving, remove bones and cut or shred meat into small pieces.

## HOW MANY DRIED BEANS TO COOK
Yield from dry beans depends a little on the type and size of bean but as a general guide
   1 cup dried beans = 3 cups cooked beans
   1 lb dried beans (about 2½ cups beans) = 5½ to 6 cups cooked beans
   One 15-oz can of red or white kidney beans = about 1½ cups drained

# Ham & Broccoli Grits

## HAM, QUICK-COOKING GRITS · MAIN DISH · SHALLOW 2-QT BAKING DISH

4 cups (1 qt) 1% lowfat milk

½ tsp salt

1 cup quick-cooking grits

16 oz frozen broccoli cuts, thawed

6 oz ham, cut in ½-in. pieces (1⅔ cups)

1 small onion, shredded (see Tip, right)

1 large egg

1 cup (4 oz) shredded Cheddar cheese

**1** Heat oven to 350°F. Lightly grease a shallow 2-qt baking dish.

**2** Bring milk and salt to a gentle boil in a 3-qt saucepan, then slowly whisk in grits. Reduce heat and simmer, stirring often, 7 to 8 minutes until thickened.

**3** Meanwhile, press thawed broccoli between paper towels to dry.

**4** Add ham, broccoli, onion, egg and all but 2 Tbsp cheese to grits. Stir until well blended. Pour into prepared dish.

**5** Bake uncovered 15 minutes. Sprinkle with reserved cheese and bake 10 to 15 minutes until bubbly.

SERVES 6
PREP: 20 minutes
COOK: 8 minutes
BAKE: 30 minutes

PER SERVING: 328 cal, 20 g pro, 34 g car, 3 g fiber, 13 g fat (6 g sat fat), 78 mg chol, 794 mg sod

TIP: Shred the onion on the large holes of a four-sided grater. You'll get mushy juice, but that's what you want.

TIP: Have hot-pepper sauce on the table to sprinkle on the grits.

# Apple Rice & "Ham"

LEAN CANADIAN BACON IS ALREADY COOKED AND JUST NEEDS TO WARM THROUGH.

**SERVES** 4
**TOTAL TIME:** 45 minutes to
1 hour

**PER SERVING:** 367 cal,
13 g pro, 66 g car, 3 g fiber,
6 g fat (2 g sat fat), 26 mg chol,
771 mg sod

2¼ cups apple juice
1 Golden Delicious apple, peeled and diced
¼ cup raisins
1 Tbsp stick butter
¼ tsp salt
¼ tsp freshly ground pepper
1 cup brown rice
4 scallions, sliced, white and green parts kept separate
6 oz Canadian bacon, chopped (see *Canadian Bacon*, below)

**1** Put apple juice, apple, raisins, butter, salt and pepper in a medium saucepan. Bring to a boil, then stir in rice and the white part of the scallions. Return to a boil; reduce heat, cover and simmer 30 to 45 minutes until rice is tender and liquid is absorbed.

**2** Remove from heat; add Canadian bacon and green part of scallions. Toss to mix, cover and let stand 5 minutes.

**CANADIAN BACON**
Although it is called bacon, Canadian bacon is closer to ham. The cut comes from the lean, tender eye of the loin. It may seem expensive, but it is already cooked so there's virtually no shrinkage and it can be used straight from the package, sliced for sandwiches or salad, or heated gently.

# Lentils with Spinach & Walnuts

VEGETARIAN · SKILLET · MAIN DISH OR SIDE DISH

SERVE WITH WARM WHOLE-WHEAT PITA AND A SALAD.

1 cup brown lentils, picked over, rinsed and drained (see *Searching for Stones*, page 162)

Salt

2 tsp oil

1 cup diced onion

½ cup diced carrot

5 oz baby spinach

¼ cup fresh lemon juice

2 Tbsp finely chopped fresh dill

¼ cup crumbled feta cheese

½ cup chopped walnuts, toasted (see *Toasting Nuts*, right)

**SERVES** 2 as a main dish
**TOTAL TIME:** 45 minutes

PER SERVING: 685 cal, 37 g pro, 82 g car, 19 g fiber, 28 g fat (5 g sat fat), 15 mg chol, 926 mg sod

## TOASTING NUTS

Heat the oven to 350°F. Spread nuts on a rimmed baking sheet (or any other baking pan with a rim so the nuts don't roll off). Bake nuts 10 to 12 minutes, shaking pan gently once or twice, until nuts smell toasted and have taken on some color.

**1** Bring lentils, 2½ cups water and ½ tsp salt to a boil in a medium saucepan. Cover and simmer 20 to 30 minutes or until lentils are tender. Drain.

**2** Meanwhile heat oil in a large nonstick skillet over medium heat. Add onion and carrot and cook about 8 minutes, stirring often, until onions are lightly browned. Add spinach; stir until wilted.

**3** Add lentils, lemon juice, chopped dill and ¼ tsp salt. Stir gently to mix.

**4** Sprinkle servings with the cheese and nuts.

## COOKING BEANS AND LENTILS

Many dried beans require soaking before cooking. But not all. Dried split peas cook in about 30 minutes without a presoak, even if the package says to soak them. (Let them go a little longer if you want them mushy for soup.) Black beans can be cooked without soaking and may retain their shape and color better. Always keep plenty of lentils on hand. Even the largest ones cook in about 30 minutes. Add vegetables as the lentils cook and perhaps leftover ham just before serving. Lentils also make a quick and delicious salad. (The exception here is red lentils, which fall into a purée almost before they are cooked.) Don't be tempted to try and to cook dried beans or lentils in tomato or other high-acid medium because they will not soften. It's even best to add salt toward the end of cooking time.

# Tofu, Potatoes & Asparagus in Curry Sauce

## FIRM TOFU · COCONUT MILK · SKILLET · MAIN DISH

**SERVES 5**
**TOTAL TIME:** 45 minutes

**PER SERVING:** 173 cal,
14 g pro, 22 g car, 6 g fiber,
5 g fat (2 g sat fat), 0 mg chol,
755 mg sod

TIP: Look for coconut milk
(not cream of coconut or
coconut water) and the yellow curry base in the Thai
foods section of your market.

1 lb asparagus, woody ends broken off, spears cut in thirds
1½ cups thinly sliced onions
14.5-oz can diced tomatoes with basil, garlic and oregano
1 lb red-skinned potatoes, sliced ¼ in. thick
1 cup lite coconut milk (not cream of coconut, see Tip, left)
2 tsp yellow curry base (from 3.5-oz pkg)
½ tsp salt
14-oz pkg firm tofu
⅓ cup fresh basil strips

**1** Bring 1 in. lightly salted water to a boil in a large nonstick skillet. Add asparagus and boil 2 to 3 minutes until crisp-tender. Drain, rinse with cold water and set aside.

**2** Coat skillet with cooking spray. Add onion and cook over medium heat about 6 minutes, stirring often, until golden brown. Stir in tomatoes, potatoes, coconut milk, curry base and salt. Bring to a boil, reduce heat, cover and simmer 10 minutes or until potatoes are tender. Meanwhile pat tofu dry with paper towels and cut in 1-in. cubes.

**3** Stir tofu and asparagus into the skillet; cover and simmer until hot. Sprinkle with basil.

## SOY POWER

Not so long ago soy sounded strange to American ears, but fueled by health claims, soy is going mainstream, as a food and as a snack. Here's a brief guide to some of the soybean products available:

Edamame. Green soybeans sold cooked and still in the shell for snacking. Edamame are also available, shelled, near green beans and green peas in the frozen food section.

Miso. A salty, earth-tasting paste made from boiled soybeans that are crushed and fermented. There are several varieties of miso, made by adding another grain to the soybeans. Yellow miso is made from soybeans and rice and is slightly sweet. Barley goes with the soybeans to make red miso; its hearty flavor is often found in soups. There is also a very dark, thick miso made almost entirely from soybeans. Miso is sold packed in tubs, jars, plastic bags, even in tubes, and is usually found in the refrigerated section of the market. Miso keeps for many months. Use it sparingly at first.

Soy milk. A creamy, dairy-free beverage that tastes fairly close to whole milk with half the fat. Enjoyed by people who want to increase their soy intake and also by those who have trouble digesting milk. Try soy milk in cooking and baking, and pour it over cereal. Look for calcium-fortified soy milk.

Soybean oil. Often the main oil in bottles labeled "vegetable oil" because it heats to a high temperature for frying before it burns and has a bland taste.

Soy "meat" products. In addition to milk in the dairy case many excellent meat-like soy products are now available. Some resemble cooked ground beef, others are formed into sausages or burgers.

Soy sauce. Next time you open a little plastic pouch of soy sauce to enjoy with Chinese or Japanese food, remember that soy sauce goes back about 2,000 years in China. The good stuff is made from soybeans mixed with a roasted grain and fermented for several months (make sure the label says "brewed").

Tempeh. A firm but tender soybean cake, made by fermenting soybeans, with a nutty, slightly smoky flavor. It is high in protein, low in fat and, like all pure-soy products, contains no cholesterol. It holds its shape well and makes a good vegetarian stand-in for meat. Sold in the refrigerator case or frozen food section.

Tofu. A soft, cheese-like product made by curdling soy milk and draining off the whey, tofu may also be called "bean curd." Firm tofu can be cut into chunks and used instead of meat in many recipes; soft tofu can be blended into many creamy dishes. Tofu has little flavor on its own but takes well to spices. Look for tofu in the produce section, either as a thick rectangular cake in a tub of water or sealed in plastic packages. Flavor tends to vary from manufacturer to manufacturer, so try different brands and compare.

# Middle Eastern Chickpeas with Couscous

## VEGETARIAN · SKILLET · MAIN DISH OR SIDE DISH

**SERVES** 4 as a main dish
**TOTAL TIME:** About 35 minutes

**PER SERVING:** 431 cal,
13 g pro, 66 g car, 8 g fiber,
14 g fat (2 g sat fat), 0 mg chol,
1,809 mg sod

**FYI:** Pitted marinated Greek kalamata olives are available in jars.

1 medium yellow squash (about 6 oz)
1 medium zucchini (about 6 oz)
1 Tbsp olive oil
Two 14.5-oz cans diced tomatoes with onion and garlic
19-oz can chickpeas, drained and rinsed
20 pitted kalamata olives (see FYI, left)
⅓ cup raisins
1 tsp ground cumin
1 tsp ground coriander (optional)
½ tsp freshly ground pepper
5.6-oz box couscous with toasted pine nuts (see *Couscous*, below)

**1** Cut yellow squash and zucchini in half lengthwise, then into ½-in.-thick slices. Heat oil in a large nonstick skillet over medium heat. Add all the squash and cook about 5 minutes, stirring occasionally, until lightly browned.

**2** Add tomatoes, chickpeas, olives, raisins, cumin, coriander and pepper; stir to mix. Bring to a boil, reduce heat, cover skillet and simmer 5 minutes to blend flavors.

**3** Uncover and simmer 8 to 10 minutes longer until a little of the liquid has evaporated.

**4** Meanwhile, prepare couscous as box directs.

**5** Serve chickpea stew over couscous.

### COUSCOUS

Couscous is neither a grain nor a pasta. It's a granular product made out of semolina (ground durum wheat) like pasta, but couscous is partially cooked during the manufacturing process, whether labeled "instant" or not. If you try boiling couscous as you do pasta, you will end up with a porridgy mess. Couscous, the staple grain dish of North Africa, takes little time to prepare. Properly steamed, it is light and delicious to eat, a perfect foil for flavorful sauces and stews.

Down-Home Beans & Greens *(page 186)*

OPPOSITE: Italian Lentil Stew *(page 193)*
ABOVE: Mozzarella & Black Bean Salad *(page 193)*

Mushroom Risotto with Spinach *(page 198)*

# Italian Lentil Stew

VEGETARIAN · SLOW COOKER · MAIN DISH

SERVE WITH GRATED PARMESAN CHEESE. THE OLIVE OIL IS STIRRED IN AT THE END FOR FLAVOR.

1½ cups brown lentils, picked over, rinsed and drained
   (see *Searching for Stones*, page 162)
1¼-lb butternut squash, peeled and cut in 1-in. chunks
   (about 3 cups)
2 cups marinara sauce
8 oz green beans, ends trimmed, beans cut in half (2 cups)
1 medium red pepper, cut in 1-in. pieces
1 large all-purpose potato, cut in 1-in. chunks
¾ cup chopped onion
1 tsp minced garlic
1 Tbsp olive oil, preferably extra-virgin

> **SERVES** 5
> **PREP:** 10 minutes
> **COOK:** 8 to 10 hours on low
>
> **PER SERVING:** 383 cal,
> 21 g pro, 66 g car, 12 g fiber,
> 7 g fat (1 g sat fat), 0 mg chol,
> 644 mg sod

**1** Mix lentils and 3 cups water in a 3-qt or larger slow cooker. Put remaining ingredients except olive oil in a large bowl; mix well then spoon over lentils.

**2** Cover and cook on low 8 to 10 hours until the vegetables and lentils are tender. Stir in the oil. Serve in soup plates or bowls.

# Mozzarella & Black Bean Salad

VEGETARIAN · MAIN DISH · NO COOK

19-oz can black beans, drained and rinsed
1 pt grape, cherry or pear tomatoes, halved
9-oz tub cherry-size balls fresh mozzarella cheese
1½ cups diced Kirby cucumber (1 large)
8.75-oz can vacuum-packed kernel corn
6-oz jar marinated artichoke hearts, drained
½ cup Italian dressing
½ cup chopped cilantro
4 lettuce leaves

> **SERVES** 4
> **TOTAL TIME:** 15 minutes
>
> **PER SERVING:** 521 cal,
> 22 g pro, 29 g car, 7 g fiber,
> 34 g fat (13 g sat fat), 56 mg
> chol, 1,102 mg sod

Put all ingredients except lettuce into a large bowl. Toss to mix and coat. Serve on lettuce-lined plates.

# Bean & Bacon Salad

MAKE AHEAD · COMPANY DISH

GREAT FOR A COOKOUT BECAUSE IT CAN BE MADE AHEAD AND WON'T WILT.

**SERVES** 12
**TOTAL TIME:** 20 minutes

**PER SERVING:** 238 cal,
13 g pro, 25 g car, 7 g fiber,
10 g fat (3 g sat fat), 10 mg
chol, 980 mg sod

**TIP:** Use one kind of bean or
a can each of light- and dark-
red kidney beans, small white
beans and black beans, plus
the black-eyed peas.

**FYI:** You can serve this right
away, or refrigerate it for up
to 6 hours. If you do, cook
the bacon ahead so it's not
a last-minute task, or buy
already-cooked bacon.

DRESSING
  ¼ cup olive oil
  ¼ cup red-wine vinegar
  1 Tbsp Dijon mustard
  2 tsp salt
  2 tsp hot pepper sauce

4 tomatoes, cut in chunks
¾ cup thinly sliced red onion
Five 15- to 16-oz cans beans or black-eyed peas, drained and
  rinsed (see Tip, left)
10 oz spinach, tough stems removed, leaves chopped
6 slices bacon, cooked crisp, crumbled
4 oz blue, feta or soft goat cheese, crumbled

**1** Whisk Dressing ingredients in a large serving bowl. Stir in tomatoes, onion, and the 5 cans of peas and beans. Serve, or cover and
refrigerate up to 6 hours.

**2** Shortly before serving, add spinach; toss to mix. Sprinkle with
bacon and cheese.

# Chili-Orange Bean Salad

VEGETARIAN · NO COOK

**SERVES** 4
**TOTAL TIME:** 25 minutes

**PER SERVING:** 354 cal,
10 g pro, 33 g car, 8 g fiber,
22 g fat (2 g sat fat), 0 mg chol,
512 mg sod

15- to 16-oz can black beans, drained and rinsed
15- to 16-oz can chickpeas, drained and rinsed
1 navel orange, peel and white pith removed, quartered lengthwise,
  sliced
1 small yellow pepper, diced
⅓ cup finely chopped fresh cilantro
½ cup vinaigrette dressing
¾ tsp chili powder
6 red radishes, sliced thin
1 ripe avocado, cut in small chunks

**1** Put beans, chickpeas, orange, yellow pepper, cilantro, dressing and chili powder into a large bowl; toss to mix and coat. If desired, cover and refrigerate up to 3 hours.

**2** Shortly before serving, add radishes and avocado. Toss to mix and coat.

**TIP:** Good with tortilla chips and pepperjack cheese.

# Tuna, Barley & Black Bean Salad

### VEGETARIAN · MAIN DISH

THE SALAD CAN BE MADE UP TO 2 DAYS AHEAD, BUT ADD THE LETTUCE AND TUNA JUST BEFORE SERVING. SERVE SLIGHTLY CHILLED OR AT ROOM TEMPERATURE.

**1 cup quick-cooking barley**

DRESSING
 3 Tbsp oil
 2 Tbsp distilled white vinegar
 2 tsp grated fresh ginger (see *Fresh Ginger*, page 61)
 2 tsp soy sauce (see *Soy Power*, page 191)
 ½ tsp sugar
 ¼ tsp minced garlic

**15- to 16-oz can black beans, drained and rinsed**

**1 small red pepper, finely chopped**

**2 cups thinly sliced romaine lettuce**

**6.5-oz can water-packed chunk light tuna**

**SERVES** 4
**TOTAL TIME:** About 30 minutes

**PER SERVING:** 349 cal, 21 g pro, 8 g fiber, 41 g car, 12 g fat (1 g sat fat), 17 mg chol, 504 mg sod

**1** Cook barley as directed on box. Cool, stirring occasionally.

**2** Whisk Dressing ingredients in a large bowl until blended. Add black beans, red pepper and cooled barley. Toss gently to mix and coat. Add romaine and tuna just before serving.

# Bulgur & Roasted Vegetable Salad

## VEGETARIAN · MAIN DISH OR SIDE DISH

**SERVES** 4 as a main dish
**TOTAL TIME:** About 45 minutes

**PER SERVING:** 286 cal,
11 g pro, 51 g car, 13 g fiber,
6 g fat (1 g sat fat), 0 mg chol,
748 mg sod

### BULGUR

Bulgur, also known as burghul, is one of the oldest forms of convenience food, widely eaten in West Asia and North Africa. Wheat grains are steamed, dried and then cracked into coarse, medium or fine grind (medium is the most useful). Because it is already partly cooked, bulgur is very easy to prepare; it needs only hydrating. It can be mixed with ground meat, shaped into meatballs and either grilled or simmered in a sauce. It also makes excellent salads. Use 1 cup of bulgur and 2 cups of liquid for 3 cups of prepared bulgur. For a side dish, add it to boiling liquid or chicken broth. Cover and let stand (off heat) for 20 to 25 minutes. For salad, soak the bulgur in water in the refrigerator overnight.

1 cup uncooked bulgur wheat (see *Bulgur*, left)
Salt
1 large onion
1 red pepper
1 yellow pepper
1 zucchini (about 8 oz)
Cooking spray
Freshly ground pepper
16-oz can chickpeas, drained and rinsed
1½ cups chopped fresh flat-leaf (Italian) parsley
3 Tbsp red-wine vinaigrette dressing
1 tsp minced garlic

**1** Heat oven to 450°F. Have ready a medium roasting pan. Bring 2 cups water to a boil.

**2** Mix bulgur and ½ tsp salt in a large bowl. Add boiling water, cover tightly and let stand 20 minutes until bulgur is tender.

**3** Meanwhile, cut onion in rings, peppers in strips and zucchini in ¼- in.-thick rounds. Scatter in roasting pan, coat with cooking spray and sprinkle with ¼ tsp pepper and ¼ tsp salt.

**4** Roast, stirring once, about 20 minutes until vegetables are lightly browned and tender.

**5** Drain bulgur in a strainer, then dry between layers of paper towels. Return to bowl; add vegetables, chickpeas, parsley, dressing, garlic and ¼ tsp pepper. Toss gently.

# Spicy Rice Dish

### VEGETARIAN · MAIN DISH OR SIDE DISH · OVEN · 8-IN. SQUARE BAKING DISH

Two 1-lb eggplants, cut in ½-in.-thick rounds

Olive oil cooking spray

¼ tsp salt

¼ tsp freshly ground pepper

1 cup diced onion

2½ cups diced plum tomatoes

16-oz jar tomato salsa

¾ cup currants or raisins

1½ tsp ground cinnamon

1½ tsp ground cumin

2½ cups cooked brown rice

MINT SAUCE

    1 cup plain lowfat yogurt

    2 Tbsp chopped fresh mint

    1½ tsp freshly grated lemon peel

    1 tsp minced garlic

    ⅛ tsp salt

    ⅛ tsp freshly ground pepper

**SERVES** 6 as a side dish
**TOTAL TIME:** 50 minutes

**PER SERVING:** 348 cal, 10 g pro, 70 g car, 8 g fiber, 4 g fat (1 g sat fat), 3 mg chol, 1,050 mg sod

**1** Heat broiler. Have a shallow 8-in. square baking dish ready.

**2** Place eggplant in a large bowl; coat all sides with cooking spray. Sprinkle with salt and pepper. Arrange half on broiler rack. Broil 4 in. from heat 6 to 8 minutes each side until lightly browned and tender. Repeat with remaining eggplant.

**3** Meanwhile coat a large nonstick skillet with cooking spray. Heat over medium heat. Add onion; cook about 5 minutes until golden. Stir in tomatoes, salsa, raisins, cinnamon, cumin and rice.

**4** Turn oven to 375°F. Line baking dish with half the eggplant. Top with rice mixture; cover with remaining eggplant. Cover dish and bake 30 minutes until hot.

**5** MINT SAUCE: Mix ingredients in a bowl; serve at the table.

### WASH RICE?

Most of the rice sold today is clean and free of chaff, the outside husk, making washing unnecessary. However, in many cultures, washing rice in several changes of water before cooking it—even soaking it for hours—is a traditional part of preparing it even if there is no real culinary reason. Much of the rice sold here is enriched with iron and B vitamins (thiamine and folic acid). Wash the rice and you wash them away. Check the package for the word "enriched."

# Mushroom Risotto with Spinach

## VEGETARIAN · SKILLET · MAIN DISH OR SIDE DISH

A GOOD WAY TO SERVE THIS WOULD BE AS A COURSE ON ITS OWN,
FOLLOWED BY GRILLED FISH OR ROAST MEAT AND A SALAD OF MIXED GREENS.

**SERVES** 4 as a main dish
**TOTAL TIME:** About 55 minutes
(and worth it)

**PER SERVING:** 436 cal,
14 g pro, 65 g car, 9 g fiber,
14 g fat (5 g sat fat), 16 mg
chol, 1,279 mg sod

TIP: A good assortment
would include white, shiitake
and crimini mushrooms. If
using shiitake discard the
tough stems. High-starch
Arborio rice gives this classic Italian dish its lush,
creamy texture.

2 Tbsp olive oil
12 oz assorted mushrooms (see Tip, left), sliced (about 4½ cups)
6 oz baby spinach
1½ cups thinly sliced onions
4 cups chicken broth
3 cloves garlic, sliced
1½ cups Arborio rice (see *Rice 101*, facing page)
½ cup grated Parmesan cheese
1 Tbsp stick butter

**1** Heat 1 Tbsp oil in a deep 11- or 12-in. nonstick skillet over medium high heat. Add mushrooms and cook, stirring often, until lightly browned. Add spinach a few handfuls at a time, adding more as it cooks down, until all the spinach is wilted. Remove to a bowl.

**2** Heat remaining 1 Tbsp oil in same skillet. Add onion and cook over medium heat about 15 minutes, stirring occasionally, or until very well browned.

**3** Meanwhile bring broth and 1¾ cups water to a simmer (not a boil) in a 2-qt saucepan.

**4** Remove and reserve ⅓ cup onion. Stir garlic into onion remaining in skillet; stir a few seconds until aromatic. Add rice; stir until grains are completely coated with oil.

**5** Add 1 cup of the simmering broth and gently boil, stirring often to keep rice from sticking, 4 minutes or until liquid is almost completely absorbed.

**6** Repeat Step 5 four times. Rice should be tender but still have a little "bite."

**7** Remove skillet from heat; stir in the mushrooms and spinach, then the cheese, butter and remaining ¾ cup simmering broth. Let stand briefly for rice to absorb the broth before serving. Top with reserved browned onion.

## RICE 101

Rice is a treasured staple for at least one-third of the earth's population. A common greeting in China is, "Have you had your rice today?"

Rice comes in different shapes, sizes and even colors, and varies in its cooking characteristics and sometimes subtle flavor. Many formerly uncommon rices are now sold in, and many grown in, the U. S. as a check of the supermarket rice section shows.

**Long grain.** Kernels are 4 to 5 times longer than they are wide, and cooked grains are separate and light. Often used in recipes requiring a distinct shape and texture.

**Medium grain.** A shorter, wider kernel that long grain. Cooked grains are moist and tender and have a greater tendency to cling together. Often used in place of short grain in sushi since it's more readily available.

**Short grain.** Plump, almost round grains that are soft and cling together when cooked. Often used for sushi.

**Sweet.** Also called sticky rice or mochi, these short, plump opaque kernels lose their shape to some extent when cooked and become extremely sticky and glutinous. Although not sweet, it's so named because it's used almost exclusively in Asian desserts. Japanese cooks pound it to a paste, add color and flavor and form the paste into beautiful shapes.

**Brown rice.** Kernels with the outer hull removed, but not the coating of brans that gives it a tan color, chewy texture and nut-like flavor. It's slightly more nutritious than white rice and has more fiber. Great in stuffings, hearty salads and vegetarian entrées.

**Wild.** This isn't a member of the rice family, but a tall marsh grass native to the Midwest. Long, almost black grains expand to 3 to 4 times their size when cooked. Wild rice is cultivated in Minnesota and California.

**Parboiled.** Also called "converted," the rice has undergone a special steam-pressure process that forces more of the whole-grain nutrients into the grain than regular white rice. It produces extra-separate grains when cooked. Available in both white and brown forms.

**Precooked.** Rice that has been cooked and dehydrated so that boiling water can penetrate the grains more readily, completing the cooking in a short time. Available in white, brown, wild rice and blends. Also known as "instant" rice. There is also totally precooked rice, packed in plastic pouches, that requires no refrigeration, but only a brief heating in the microwave.

**Arborio.** Large, bold rice that originated in Italy. Grains are translucent and plump with a characteristic white dot in the center. Most often used in risotto, it develops a creamy texture around a slightly chewy center.

**Basmati.** Aromatic long-grain rice native to India. When cooked, grains swell only lengthwise, resulting in long, slender grains that are dry and separate. Often used in pilafs. Served with sauced and grilled meats and vegetables.

**Jasmine.** Long-grain, fragrant rice native to Thailand. Similar to basmati in flavor and aroma. When cooked, it's soft, moist and somewhat sticky. Ideal for rice desserts.

**Texmati.** A cross between American long-grain and basmati rice. Aroma is similar to basmati; however, cooked grains swell in both length and width.

# Thai Rice

VEGETARIAN · SKILLET · SIDE DISH

**SERVES** 6
**TOTAL TIME:** About 35 minutes

**PER SERVING:** 36 cal, 8 g pro, 70 g car, 2 g fiber, 7 g fat (3 g sat fat), 0 mg chol, 627 mg sod

TIP: Make sure the label on the can says coconut milk, not cream of coconut or coconut water.

2 tsp oil

1 cup diced red pepper

2 scallions, sliced, white and green parts kept separate

1 Tbsp chopped garlic

14-oz can lite coconut milk (see Tip, left)

1½ cups jasmine rice (see *Rice 101*, page 199)

1 tsp salt

8 oz fresh snow peas, halved crosswise (see *Sugar Snaps and Snow Peas*, page 263)

2 tsp freshly grated lime peel

GARNISH: lime wedges and cilantro

**1** Heat oil in a large nonstick skillet over medium heat. Add diced pepper, white part of scallions and garlic. Cook 1 to 2 minutes, stirring often, until aromatic.

**2** Add coconut milk and 1⅔ cups water; bring to a boil. Add rice and salt, reduce heat to a gentle simmer, cover and cook 12 minutes or until rice is nearly tender.

**3** Stir in snow peas, lime peel and, if rice looks dry, another ¼ cup water. Bring to a simmer, cover and cook 3 to 4 minutes until snow peas are crisp-tender. Remove from heat; stir in green part of scallion. Garnish with lime wedges and cilantro.

# Spicy Black Beans

VEGETARIAN · MAIN DISH · SKILLET

**SERVES** 4
**TOTAL TIME:** 25 minutes

**PER SERVING:** 517 cal, 19 g pro, 88 g car, 15 g fiber, 9 g fat (1 g sat fat), 0 mg chol, 596 mg sod

2 Tbsp olive oil

1 cup chopped onion

2 small jalapeño peppers, finely chopped (see *Handling Hot Peppers*, page 52)

1 Tbsp minced garlic

Two 15-oz cans black beans in seasoned sauce (see Tip, facing page)

1⅓ cups chopped tomato (1 large)

¼ cup picante sauce

4 cups hot cooked rice (see Tip, facing page)

**1** Heat oil in a large nonstick skillet. Add onion, peppers and garlic and cook about 5 minutes, stirring occasionally, until onion is tender. Stir in black beans in seasoned sauce, the tomato and the picante sauce. Bring to a simmer, cover and cook 8 minutes to develop flavors.

**2** Serve over rice or toss with the rice.

> TIP: Look for black beans in seasoned sauce in the Hispanic foods section of your market.

> TIP: The black beans take only a short while to prepare so start cooking the rice before the beans.

# Cowboy Beans & Sausage

## SMOKED SAUSAGE · MAIN DISH OR SIDE DISH · SKILLET

TASTES LIKE BEANS THAT BAKED FOR HOURS, BUT NEVER SEES THE INSIDE OF AN OVEN.
THIS EASY DISH IS ALWAYS A SUCCESS AT COVERED DISH (OR POTLUCK) SUPPERS.

8 oz smoked sausage links or frankfurters, sliced ½ in. thick
1½ cups coarsely chopped onions
¾ cup barbecue sauce
2 Tbsp pancake syrup or sugar
2 Tbsp water
1 Tbsp cider vinegar
15- to 16-oz can red kidney beans, drained and rinsed
15- to 16-oz can pinto beans, drained and rinsed
15- to 16-oz can black beans, drained and rinsed
GARNISH: **sliced scallions**

> **SERVES** 4 as a main dish
> **TOTAL TIME:** 35 minutes
>
> **PER SERVING:** 461 cal, 23 g pro, 52 g car, 11 g fiber, 18 g fat (6 g sat fat), 38 mg chol, 1,496 mg sod

**1** Heat a large skillet over medium-high heat. Add sausage; cook, turning slices once, 3 minutes or until browned. Remove to a bowl.

**2** Add onions to drippings in skillet. Reduce heat, cover and cook about 8 minutes, stirring occasionally, until tender and golden.

**3** Add barbecue sauce, syrup, water and vinegar; bring to a boil. Stir in beans and sausage. Heat covered, over medium heat, 15 minutes, stirring often, for flavors to blend. Sprinkle with scallions if desired.

# Pizzas & Breads

latbreads are one of the world's oldest prepared foods; wherever there has been a plentiful supply of grain (corn, barley, millet, wheat) humans, probably fed up with eating husky grain out of hand, have pounded grain into flour, mixed the flour with water, smoothed out the resulting dough and baked it on heated stone or clay (as in a tandoor oven). Today, more and more flatbreads are finding a place at our tables, the three most popular perhaps being pizza, pita and tortillas. Homemade pizza is always a favorite and making it at home allows you to create just the kind you or your family likes best. And with refrigerated or prebaked crusts easily available, you don't even have to make bread dough (let alone pound wheat into flour). In addition to delicious ways with pizza, pita and tortillas you will also find recipes that call for, among others, Italian bread and hard rolls. And there are two surprise recipes: one for cornmeal spoon bread, the second for bread stuffing made in a slow cooker.

# Grilled Chicken Pizza

## BONELESS BREAST HALVES · GRILL · BAKING SHEET

**SERVES** 4
**PREP:** 10 minutes
**GRILL:** About 12 minutes

**PER SERVING:** 411 cal,
35 g pro, 36 g car, 2 g fiber,
14 g fat (5 g sat fat), 70 mg
chol, 1,151 mg sod

3 boneless, skinless chicken-breast halves (about 12 oz)
¼ cup balsamic vinaigrette dressing
Garlic-flavor cooking spray
10-oz can refrigerated pizza crust
1 cup (4 oz) shredded part-skim mozzarella cheese
¼ cup (1 oz) grated Parmesan cheese
1 cup diced plum tomatoes
1 cup lightly packed torn arugula or basil leaves

**1** Heat outdoor grill. While grill heats, place chicken and dressing in a large ziptop bag and turn to coat.

**2** Line a baking sheet with foil; coat foil with cooking spray. Unroll pizza dough on foil; press into a 12 x 9-in. rectangle. Coat dough with cooking spray.

**3** Remove chicken from bag and grill 7 to 8 minutes, turning once, until lightly charred and cooked through. Put on a cutting board.

**4** Invert pizza dough onto grill; peel off foil. Grill 1 minute or until the underside is lightly browned. Turn crust over and grill 30 seconds or until underside stiffens. Meanwhile, cut chicken crosswise in ½-in.-thick slices.

**5** Scatter ¾ cup mozzarella cheese over crust, then the chicken, remaining mozzarella cheese and the Parmesan cheese.

**6** Cover and grill 1 to 2 minutes until cheese melts, making sure underside of pizza doesn't burn.

**7** Transfer to a cutting board; top with tomato and arugula, then cut in 4 pieces.

# Muffaletta Stromboli

SOPPRESSATA, VIRGINIA HAM · OVEN · BAKING SHEET

10-oz can refrigerated pizza crust

4 oz thinly sliced soppressata (an Italian salami)

1 cup (4 oz) shredded part-skim mozzarella cheese

4 oz thinly sliced Virginia ham (see *Specialty Hams*, page 135)

⅓ cup sliced pimiento-stuffed olives

**SERVES** 4
**TOTAL TIME:** 25 to 30 minutes

**PER SERVING:** 505 cal,
23 g pro, 42 g car, 4 g fiber,
25 g fat (9 g sat fat), 36 mg
chol, 1,977 mg sod

**1** Heat oven to 400°F. Coat a baking sheet with cooking spray. Unroll crust on sheet; pat into a 14 x 9-in. rectangle.

**2** Arrange overlapping slices soppressata lengthwise 1 in. from edge of 1 long side and either end of dough. Top with ½ cup cheese, the slices of ham folded in half, rest of cheese, then olives. Pull dough over filling; press edges to seal. Cut four 2-in. slits in top.

**3** Bake 15 minutes or until golden. Remove to cutting board; cut in 4 pieces.

# Olive Pizza

VEGETARIAN · OVEN · BAKING SHEET · FOOD PROCESSOR

A QUICK AND DELICIOUS SUPPER.

**SERVES 4**
**TOTAL TIME:** 20 minutes

PER SERVING: 556 cal,
8 g pro, 50 g car, 7 g fiber,
35 g fat (7 g sat fat), 12 mg
chol, 1,015 mg sod

10-oz pkg baked thin pizza crust
Two 6-oz cans pitted black (ripe) olives, drained
¼ cup olive oil
1 large clove garlic
½ tsp dried oregano
½ tsp crushed red pepper
¾ cup (3 oz) shredded part-skim mozzarella cheese

FRESH TOMATO TOPPING
    1 cup diced tomatoes
    2 Tbsp chopped onion
    2 Tbsp fresh basil
    2 tsp olive oil
    ½ tsp minced garlic

**1** Heat oven to 450°F. Put pizza crust on a baking sheet (see FYI, facing page).

**2** Put olives, olive oil, garlic, oregano and crushed red pepper in food processor; pulse until olives are finely chopped. Spread on crust; top with cheese.

**3** Bake 10 minutes until crust is crisp.

**4** Meanwhile mix Fresh Tomato Topping ingredients in a bowl. Cut pizza in wedges; serve with topping.

# Pepperoni & Spinach Pizza

PEPPERONI · OVEN · BAKING SHEET

SERVE WITH A TOSSED SALAD.

10-oz pkg baked thin pizza crust

8 oz sliced mushrooms

10- to 12-oz pkg fresh spinach, coarsely chopped

⅛ tsp salt

⅛ tsp freshly ground pepper

¾ cup pizza sauce

42 slices 70%-less-fat turkey pepperoni (from a 6-oz pkg)

½ cup shredded part-skim mozzarella cheese

**SERVES** 6
**TOTAL TIME:** About 25 minutes

**PER SERVING:** 262 cal,
10 g pro, 33 g car, 5 g fiber,
9 g fat (3 g sat fat), 22 mg chol,
602 mg sod

**FYI:** For crisper crust this pizza can be baked directly on the oven rack.

**1** Heat oven to 475°F. Put pizza crust on a baking sheet (see FYI, right).

**2** Coat a large nonstick skillet with cooking spray. Heat over medium heat. Add mushrooms and cook about 8 minutes, stirring often, until very lightly browned and tender. Stir in spinach, salt and pepper. Cook, stirring occasionally, until spinach wilts.

**3** Top crust with pizza sauce, mushroom-spinach mixture, pepperoni and cheese.

**4** Bake 8 to 10 minutes until hot.

# Turkey Enchiladas Suizas

COOKED TURKEY BREAST · OVEN · SHALLOW 2- TO 2½-QT BAKING DISH

IN THIS CLASSIC RECIPE FOR ENCHILADAS SUIZAS (SWISS-STYLE ENCHILADAS) TORTILLAS ARE FILLED, ROLLED AND BAKED. FOR AN EASY STOVETOP VERSION WITH SHRIMP, SEE SKILLET ENCHILADAS SUIZAS (PAGE 104). THE PRELIMINARY WARMING OF THE TORTILLAS SOFTENS THEM AND MAKES THEM EASIER TO ROLL UP.

**SERVES** 4
**TOTAL TIME:** 40 minutes

**PER SERVING:** 399 cal, 33 g pro, 34 g car, 3 g fiber, 15 g fat (9 g sat fat), 89 mg chol, 479 mg sod

**TIP:** You can also use leftover cooked turkey or chicken.

**FYI:** Suiza is Spanish for Swiss. When you see it describing enchiladas expect a filling that's rich and creamy with soft cheese or sour cream, as here.

8 corn tortillas, stacked and wrapped in foil
1¼ cups green salsa (salsa verde)
½ cup reduced-fat sour cream
¼ cup chopped fresh cilantro
1½ cups (8 oz) diced cooked turkey breast (see Tip, left)
1½ cups (6 oz) shredded reduced-fat Swiss cheese
7-oz jar roasted red peppers, drained and sliced
GARNISH: **diced tomato and sliced scallion**

**1** Place tortillas in oven. Heat to 425°F. Have a shallow 2- to 2½-qt baking dish ready.

**2** Mix salsa, sour cream and cilantro in a medium bowl. Spread ½ cup over bottom of baking dish. In another bowl, mix turkey, 1 cup cheese and the roasted peppers. Remove tortillas from oven.

**3** Spoon scant ½ cup turkey mixture down center of each tortilla. Roll up; place seam side down in baking dish. Pour remaining salsa mixture over top.

**4** Cover with foil and bake 15 minutes until bubbly. Uncover; sprinkle with remaining cheese and bake 10 minutes, or until cheese has melted.

Muffaletta Stromboli *(page 205)*

LEFT: Olive Pizza *(page 206)*
RIGHT: Grilled Eggplant Parmesan Pizzas *(page 215)*

Burritos with Rice & Beans *(page 210)*

Eggplant, Pepper & Basil Sandwiches *(page 214)*

# Soft & Crunchy Tacos

**GROUND BEEF · OVEN · 2 BAKING SHEETS · SKILLET**

8 taco shells

8 soft taco- or fajita-size flour tortillas

1 cup (4 oz) shredded Cheddar cheese

1 lb lean ground beef

1.25-oz pkt taco seasoning mix

1 cup shredded romaine lettuce

1 cup taco sauce

¼ cup chopped red onion

**SERVES** 4
**TOTAL TIME:** 15 minutes

**PER SERVING:** 808 cal,
35 g pro, 73 g car, 4 g fiber,
42 g fat (16 g sat fat), 115 mg
chol, 1,876 mg sod

**1**  Turn oven to 375°F. Put taco shells on 1 baking sheet. Spread flour tortillas on another and sprinkle each tortilla with 1 Tbsp cheese.

**2**  Brown ground beef in a large nonstick skillet, breaking up chunks with a spoon. Stir in taco seasoning mix and ¾ cup water. Simmer uncovered, stirring occasionally, 3 minutes until slightly thickened.

**3**  Meanwhile put baking sheets in oven (if it's not yet at 375°F, that's OK). Bake 3 minutes until cheese melts.

**4**  Center a taco shell in each flour tortilla; bring up sides of tortillas. Fill tacos with beef mixture, then shredded lettuce, rest of cheese, taco sauce and onion.

Tip: Wrapping the soft flour tortilla around the crisp taco shell makes for neat eating—no scattered, shattered taco shells. And they taste great together.

## TACOS AND BURRITOS

Tacos are crisp U-shaped shells of deep-fried corn tortillas that have a filling spooned into them. Toppings are then sprinkled or spooned on. Ready-to-heat taco shells can be bought in the Mexican food section of the supermarket, as can taco "kits," which contain shells, seasoning (for the meat) and sauce.

Burritos are soft flour tortillas rolled up around a filling. Most supermarkets carry a wide selection in a range of sizes and even flavors. For burritos look for those labeled "burrito-size," about 8 or 9 in. in diameter.

Heat tacos shells and burritos before serving. Heating brings out the flavor and crispness of taco shells; it makes tortillas soft and easy to fold. To heat taco shells in the oven: Heat the oven to 200°F. Separate the shells and arrange them on a paper-towel-lined baking sheet. Heat them for 15 minutes. To heat in a micro-wave oven: Separate the shells and fan 10 or 12 at a time on a large round plate lined with paper towels. Microwave on high for 1 minute. Rotate dish one-quarter turn and microwave on high for 1 minute more. To warm flour tortillas in the oven: Heat oven to 325°F. Wrap a stack of flour tortillas in foil and heat for 10 to 15 minutes. To warm in a microwave: Poke several holes in the plastic wrapper of purchased tortillas and microwave on high for 1 to 1½ minutes. Or stack 4 to 6 and wrap in moist paper towels, then microwave on high for 10 to 20 seconds. Keep the shells or tortillas warm covered with a napkin in a napkin-lined basket or on a napkin-lined platter.

# Buffalo Chicken Wraps

**SERVES** 4
**PREP:** 10 minutes
**BAKE:** About 11 minutes

**PER SERVING:** 392 cal, 21 g pro, 43 g car, 5 g fiber, 14 g fat (6 g sat fat), 200 mg chol, 1,909 mg sod

Two 9-oz pkg fully cooked breaded chicken tenders
2 Tbsp stick butter
3 Tbsp hot pepper sauce
Four 8- to 9-in. spinach and basil–flavored wraps or plain burrito-size flour tortillas
¼ cup lowfat blue cheese dressing, plus extra for dipping
2 cups baby spinach leaves
2 ribs celery, cut in narrow 3-in.-long strips
2 carrots, cut in narrow 3-in.-long strips
1 medium zucchini (about 6 oz), cut in narrow 3-in.-long strips

**1** Heat oven to 400°F. Arrange chicken on a rimmed baking sheet.

**2** Melt butter in a small bowl or pan; stir in hot pepper sauce and brush on both sides of chicken. Bake as pkg directs.

**3** Spread each tortilla with 1 Tbsp blue cheese dressing, then arrange ½ cup spinach leaves and some celery, carrot and zucchini sticks down center. Top each with 3 tenders placed end to end. Scatter remaining vegetables on top and around chicken. Roll up tightly; cut diagonally in half. Serve with extra dressing for dipping.

# Burritos with Rice & Beans

VEGETARIAN

**SERVES** 4
**TOTAL TIME:** About 35 minutes

**PER SERVING:** 392 cal, 11 g pro, 77 g car, 6 g fiber, 4 g fat (1 g sat fat), 0 mg chol, 1,005 mg sod

8-oz pkg seasoned rice & red bean mix
1 medium red pepper, cut in thin strips
4.5-oz can chopped green chiles
½ cup chopped fresh cilantro
4 burrito-size flour tortillas (see FYI, top of facing page)

**1** Cook rice in a saucepan following pkg directions but omitting any oil or butter. Add red pepper 3 minutes before rice is done. Remove from heat, let stand 10 minutes, then stir in chiles and cilantro.

**2** FOR EACH BURRITO: Place a tortilla on work surface. Spoon one-quarter of the rice mixture (about 1 cup) on bottom third. Roll bottom over filling, fold sides over filling then continue rolling up. Place seam side down on plate.

**FYI:** Burrito-size flour tortillas come in a variety of flavors. Spinach with garlic and pesto is a good choice. Of course, you can also use plain.

# Moo Shu Pork

PORK TENDERLOIN · SKILLET

2 large eggs

2 Tbsp oil

12-oz pork tenderloin, cut diagonally in thin slices (see Tip and FYI, right)

½ cup stir-fry sauce

6 oz shiitake or white mushrooms, sliced (see Tip, right)

12-oz bag broccoli slaw

4 scallions, trimmed, cut in thirds, then in long thin strips

15-oz can whole baby corn on the cob, drained (see Tip, right)

12 taco- or fajita-size flour tortillas, warmed (see *Tacos and Burritos*, page 209)

**SERVES** 6
**TOTAL TIME:** About 20 minutes

PER SERVING: 436 cal, 23 g pro, 55 g car, 6 g fiber, 15 g fat (3 g sat fat), 108 mg chol, 908 mg sod

TIP: Use plain tenderloin, or buy teriyaki-marinated.

TIP: If using shiitake mushrooms, twist off and discard the tough stems.

TIP: If some of the ears of baby corn seem on the large side, cut them in half.

**1** Beat eggs in a bowl. Heat 1 tsp oil in a large nonstick skillet over medium-high heat. Pour in eggs, swirling pan to form a thin layer on the bottom. Cover, reduce heat to low and cook 1 to 2 minutes until eggs are set. Invert onto a cutting board. Cut in half, then into ½-in.-wide strips.

**2** Heat 2 tsp oil in same skillet over medium-high heat. Add pork and stir-fry 1 minute or until no longer pink. Remove to a bowl; toss with 1 Tbsp stir-fry sauce.

**3** Heat remaining 1 Tbsp oil in skillet. Add mushrooms and stir-fry 2 minutes or until just starting to brown. Add broccoli slaw and scallions. Stir-fry 3 to 4 minutes until crisp-tender. Stir in corn, egg strips, pork and remaining stir-fry sauce. Toss to mix and coat. Pour into a serving bowl.

**4** Let diners fill and roll their own warmed tortillas.

**FYI:** To slice the meat diagonally, instead of cutting parallel to the face of the tenderloin turn the tip of the knife about 45° to the left (if you're right-handed). After a few "starter" slices, the slices will come out wider, more oval.

# Hot Reuben Heros

CORNED BEEF FROM THE DELI · OVEN · BAKING SHEET

**SERVES** 4
**TOTAL TIME:** About 10 minutes

**PER SERVING:** 629 cal, 30 g pro, 61 g car, 4 g fiber, 29 g fat (12 g sat fat), 93 mg chol, 1,396 mg sod

One 12- to 14-in.-long loaf Italian bread (about 14 oz), split horizontally
2 Tbsp Russian dressing
8 oz thinly sliced corned beef
4 slices (5 oz) Swiss cheese
About 2½ cups (8 oz) deli coleslaw
½ cup thinly sliced red onion

**1** Turn oven to 500°F. Have a baking sheet ready.

**2** Place bread, cut sides up, on baking sheet. Spread Russian dressing on bottom half. Top with corned beef and Swiss cheese.

**3** Place in oven (if it hasn't reached 500°F yet, that's OK). Bake 3 to 4 minutes until cheese melts.

**4** Cover cheese with coleslaw, onion and top of loaf. Press down gently; cut crosswise in 4 sections.

# Pork Sandwiches Italiano

PORK TENDERLOIN · SKILLET

**SERVES** 4
**TOTAL TIME:** 35 minutes

**PER SERVING:** 401 cal, 31 g pro, 40 g car, 4 g fiber, 13 g fat (3 g saturated fat), 74 mg chol, 850 mg sod

SEASONING
  ¾ tsp dried oregano, crumbled
  ¾ tsp dried rosemary, crumbled
  ¾ tsp salt
  ¼ tsp freshly ground black pepper
  ¼ tsp crushed red pepper

1-lb pork tenderloin
2 Tbsp olive oil
1½ cups halved and thinly sliced onion
1 each green and yellow pepper or 3 Italian frying peppers, cut in thin strips
4 medium plum tomatoes, cut in chunks
8 slices crusty Italian bread
1 clove garlic, cut in half

**1** Mix Seasoning ingredients in a cup.

**2** Cut tenderloin on an angle (see *Cutting at an Angle*, page 92) into twelve ½-in.-thick slices. Sprinkle slices with 2 tsp Seasoning, pressing it on the meat.

**3** Heat oil in a large nonstick skillet over medium-high heat. Add pork and cook 2 to 3 minutes per side until lightly browned and just barely pink in the center. Transfer to a plate.

**4** Add onion, peppers and remaining Seasoning to skillet. Cook 10 minutes, stirring often, or until vegetables are tender and lightly browned. Add tomatoes and, stirring often, cook 3 minutes or until soft.

**5** Return pork and juices to skillet; heat through. Remove from heat.

**6** Rub bread slices with cut sides of garlic; arrange bread on plates (see Tip, right). Spoon pork mixture over bread or alongside.

TIP: This can be eaten as a knife-and-fork sandwich, or the pork and vegetables can be spooned alongside the bread and the bread can be used to sop up the juices.

# Bella Burgers

### VEGETARIAN · GRILL OR STOVETOP GRILL PAN

IF YOU WISH YOU CAN TOAST THE BUNS AND TOP THE BURGERS WITH CHEESE.

4 large portobello mushroom caps (about 3 oz each)
1 large red pepper, quartered and cored
1½ cups ½-in.-thick slices red onion
Garlic-flavored cooking spray
3 Tbsp reduced-fat Italian dressing
3 Tbsp light mayonnaise
4 hamburger buns, split
4 lettuce leaves
4 slices tomato

**SERVES** 4
**TOTAL TIME:** About 20 minutes

**PER SERVING:** 234 cal, 7 g pro, 34 g car, 3 g fiber, 9 g fat (1 g sat fat), 4 mg chol, 459 mg sod

**1** Heat outdoor grill or a large stovetop grill pan.

**2** Coat mushrooms, red pepper and onion with cooking spray. Grill onion slices 4 minutes on each side and mushrooms and peppers 5 to 6 minutes on each side, turning everything over once, until lightly charred and tender.

**3** Meanwhile, whisk dressing and mayonnaise in a small bowl until blended and smooth. Spread buns with dressing mixture.

**4** To assemble, top bottoms of each roll with: lettuce, tomato, a mushroom cap, a piece of red pepper and onion. Cover with bun tops.

# Pesto Chicken Sandwiches with Tomato-Feta Salad

CHICKEN-BREAST CUTLETS · STOVETOP GRILL PAN OR BROILER

**SERVES** 4
**TOTAL TIME:** 15 minutes

**PER SERVING:** 521 cal,
31 g pro, 37 g car, 2 g fiber,
28 g fat (6 g sat fat), 67 mg
chol, 978 mg sod

3 plum tomatoes, sliced (about 2 cups)
½ cup (2 oz) crumbled feta cheese
⅓ cup balsamic vinaigrette dressing
⅓ cup sliced scallions
Four 3-oz chicken-breast cutlets
½ cup purchased refrigerated basil pesto
4 kaiser or other hard rolls, split

1  Heat broiler or stovetop grill pan. Coat broiler-pan rack with cooking spray.

2  Put tomatoes, cheese, dressing and scallions in a bowl and toss to mix.

3  Brush cutlets lightly with 1 Tbsp of the pesto; place on broiler-pan rack or grill pan. Broil or grill 3 to 4 minutes, turning once, until cooked through.

4  Spread rolls with remaining 7 Tbsp pesto. Place a cutlet on bottom of each. Top with tomato-feta salad, including any dressing remaining in bowl. Cover with roll tops.

# Eggplant, Pepper & Basil Sandwiches

VEGETARIAN · BROILER

THIS IS ESPECIALLY GOOD MADE WITH LOCAL VEGETABLES AT THEIR BEST.

**SERVES** 4
**TOTAL TIME:** 40 minutes

**PER SERVING:** 320 cal,
8 g pro, 46 g car, 5 g fiber,
12 g fat (2 g sat fat), 7 mg chol,
799 mg sod

1¼-lb eggplant, cut lengthwise in ½-in.-thick slices
1 Tbsp olive oil
½ tsp salt
¼ tsp freshly ground pepper
2 red peppers, cut in half
2 yellow peppers, cut in half
⅓ cup light mayonnaise
2 tsp minced garlic
Eight ½-in.-thick slices round Italian bread
16 medium to large fresh basil leaves

**1** Heat broiler.

**2** Lightly brush eggplant slices with oil; sprinkle with salt and pepper. Place in a single layer on broiler-pan rack. Add peppers, skin sides up.

**3** Broil about 4 in. from heat source, eggplant 12 to 14 minutes, turning over once, until charred and soft, and peppers, without turning, 15 to 20 minutes until skins blister and blacken. Remove eggplant to a plate. Place peppers in a bowl and cover. When cool enough to handle, pull off skin.

**4** Mix mayonnaise and garlic in a small bowl. Toast 1 side of bread in broiler pan under broiler. Spread other side with garlic mayonnaise and broil just until toasted.

**5** Layer vegetables and basil between bread slices; cut sandwiches in half.

# Grilled Eggplant Parmesan Pizzas

VEGETARIAN · GRILL

4 baby eggplants (about 5 oz each), cut in ½-in.-thick rounds
4 pocketless pitas
Olive-oil cooking spray
1 cup marinara sauce
1 cup (9 oz) part-skim ricotta cheese
1 cup (4 oz) shredded part-skim mozzarella cheese
2 Tbsp grated Parmesan cheese
GARNISH: chopped fresh basil leaves

> **SERVES** 4
> **TOTAL TIME:** 25 minutes
>
> **PER SERVING:** 427 cal, 23 g pro, 53 g car, 4 g fiber, 15 g fat (7 g sat fat), 37 mg chol, 976 mg sod

**1** Heat outdoor grill. Coat eggplant and pitas with cooking spray.

**2** Grill eggplant 10 minutes, turning as needed until tender, then remove from grill. Grill pitas 1 minute until bottoms are lightly charred. Transfer to a platter; spread grilled sides with the sauce. Top with grilled eggplant and spoonfuls of ricotta; sprinkle with mozzarella and Parmesan cheeses.

**3** Return to grill. Cover and grill 1 to 2 minutes until cheeses melt. Serve whole or cut each in 4 wedges for easier eating. Garnish with basil.

# Nana's Spoon Bread

VEGETARIAN · OVEN · SHALLOW 1½- TO 2-QT BAKING DISH

SPOON BREAD IS A SOUTHERN CORNMEAL SPECIALTY THAT IS SOFT AND PUDDING-LIKE.
IT IS SERVED WITH A SPOON AND EATEN WITH A FORK AND MAKES A GOOD SIDE DISH FOR
HAM, TURKEY OR CHICKEN.

**SERVES** 4
**PREP:** 10 minutes
**BAKE:** 25 minutes

**PER SERVING:** 341 cal,
14 g pro, 37 g car, 2 g fiber,
15 g fat (8 g sat fat), 190 mg
chol, 883 mg sod

3 cups milk
3 Tbsp stick butter
3 large eggs
½ tsp salt
1 cup cornmeal (preferably stone-ground)
1 Tbsp baking powder

**1**  Heat oven to 450°F. Grease (or coat with cooking spray) a shallow
1½- to 2-qt baking dish

**2**  Heat 2 cups milk and the butter in a saucepan over medium heat
until boiling.

**3**  Meanwhile whisk eggs, remaining 1 cup milk and the salt in a
bowl until thoroughly blended.

**4**  Gradually whisk cornmeal into boiling milk. Then stir with whisk
until mixture returns to a boil and thickens slightly.

**5**  Whisk cornmeal mixture into egg mixture until blended; stir in
baking powder. Pour into prepared dish.

**6**  Bake 25 minutes or until slightly puffed, a light crust forms on top
and the inside has a custard-like consistency.

# Slow-Cooker Mushroom-Herb Bread Stuffing

VEGETARIAN · SLOW COOKER

1 stick (½ cup) butter
2 cups chopped onion
2 cups chopped celery
12 oz mushrooms, sliced
⅔ cup chopped fresh parsley
2 tsp dried sage, crumbled
1 tsp poultry seasoning
1 tsp dried thyme
½ tsp dried marjoram
1½ tsp salt
½ tsp freshly ground pepper
1¼ cups chicken broth
2 large eggs
1 loaf (1 lb) whole-wheat bread, torn in pieces,
   left out overnight to dry (see FYI, right)

**SERVES** 8 with leftovers
**TOTAL TIME:** 5½ to 6½ hours
(plus one day for bread to dry)

**PER CUP:** 200 cal, 6 g pro, 23 g car, 4 g fiber, 10 g fat (5 g sat fat), 56 mg chol, 699 mg sod

**FYI:** The bread needs to dry for a day before you make the stuffing. Tear it in pieces onto a baking sheet, cover loosely (so it can dry out) and leave at room temperature.

**1** Have ready a 5-qt or larger slow cooker.

**2** Melt butter in a large skillet over medium heat. Add onions and celery; cook 8 to 10 minutes, stirring several times, until translucent. Add mushrooms; cook 5 minutes. Stir in parsley, sage, poultry seasoning, thyme, marjoram, salt and pepper. Transfer to cooker (or refrigerate overnight).

**3** Whisk broth and eggs in a bowl to blend. Pour into cooker, add bread and stir until eggs, bread and mushroom mixture are blended. Cook on high 45 minutes then reduce heat to low and cook 4 to 6 hours.

**TIP:** If you are making this for Thanksgiving or another big-production occasion, you probably want to get as much as possible done ahead. Up to two days ahead you can chop the onion and celery (store them together) and the parsley. One day ahead you can cook the onions, celery and mushrooms; stir in the parsley and seasonings; and refrigerate overnight.

# Soups

There is nothing more satisfying than a bowl of homemade soup. But don't think homemade soup means endless preparation and simmering. The recipes in this chapter use a wide range of fresh and prepared ingredients, canned broth and some shortcut methods to create a selection of easy-to-prepare flavorful soups, both hot and cold. For a main dish, try Creamy Vegetable Chowder. If you have leftover chicken, Mexican Tortilla Soup or Hearty Chicken Noodle Soup will turn those leftovers into another filling meal. There are chilled soups, too. For ease and speed (sandwich recipe included) check out Chilled Pea Soup & Smokey Joe Clubs; the soup takes less than 5 minutes to make, including partly thawing the green peas. When the weather is steamy try the Gazpacho with Avocado Shrimp Salad or start a meal with Chilled Moroccan Vegetable Soup. For centuries cooks have looked to soups for warm, filling meals, with little in the way of preparation. Our collection provides plenty of those recipes. Check under the recipe title for those marked Main Dish.

# Creamy Vegetable Chowder

### VEGETARIAN · MAIN DISH · 4-QT POT

A GREAT WAY TO ENJOY THE VEGETABLES OF SUMMER,
THIS SOUP IS GOOD SERVED WITH WARM BISCUITS.

**SERVES** 4 (makes 9 cups)
**TOTAL TIME:** About 55 minutes

**PER SERVING:** 345 cal,
12 g pro, 54 g car, 9 g fiber,
11 g fat (6 g sat fat), 33 mg
chol, 605 mg sod

2 Tbsp stick butter

1 bunch scallions, sliced, white and green parts kept separate

4 medium carrots, cut in ½-in. chunks

12 oz red-skinned potatoes, cut in ½-in. chunks (about 2¼ cups)

¾ tsp salt

½ tsp freshly ground pepper

2 Tbsp flour

2 cups whole milk

8 oz green beans, ends trimmed, cut in quarters (about 2 cups)

3 ears corn, kernels cut off cobs (1½ cups, see *Cutting Off the Kernels*, page 264), or one 15-oz can corn, drained

1 cup fresh or frozen green peas

2 Tbsp coarsely chopped fresh thyme

**1** Melt butter in a 4-qt or larger pot over medium heat. Add white part of scallions, the carrots, potatoes, salt and pepper. Cover and cook 6 minutes, stirring occasionally, until vegetables are slightly soft but not browned.

**2** Add flour; stir to mix with vegetables. Add 3 cups water; stir to scrape up flour on bottom of pot. Bring to a boil, reduce heat, cover and simmer 10 minutes or until vegetables are almost tender.

**3** Stir in green part of scallions, the milk, green beans, corn, green peas and thyme. Bring to a boil, reduce heat and simmer uncovered 5 minutes until vegetables are tender.

# Florentine Chicken & Rice Soup

## CHICKEN THIGHS · MAIN DISH · 4- TO 5-QT POT

SERVE THIS MAIN DISH SOUP WITH CRUNCHY GARLIC BREAD AND GRATED PARMESAN CHEESE.

6 chicken bouillon cubes (for 6 cups broth, see FYI, right)

3 chicken thighs (about 1 lb)

1½ tsp Italian seasoning

1 Tbsp chopped garlic

1½-lb butternut squash, peeled and cut in ¾-in. cubes (about 4 cups, see Tip, right)

10-oz box frozen chopped spinach

15-oz can chickpeas, drained and rinsed

1 cup converted white rice

**1** Bring 8 cups water and the broth cubes to boil in a 4- to 5-qt pot, stirring to dissolve cubes. Add chicken thighs, seasoning and garlic. Reduce heat, cover and simmer 20 minutes or until chicken is cooked through.

**2** Remove chicken to a cutting board; let stand until cool enough to handle. Skim fat off broth.

**3** Stir squash and frozen spinach into broth. Increase heat to medium and cook 8 minutes or until spinach thaws.

**4** Add chickpeas and rice; cook 15 minutes or until squash and rice are tender.

**5** Meanwhile remove skin, bones and fat from chicken. Cut chicken in bite-size pieces; add to pot. Ladle soup into bowls.

---

**SERVES 5**
**TOTAL TIME:** About 50 minutes

---

**PER SERVING:** 333 cal, 19 g pro, 56 g car, 6 g fiber, 4 g fat (1 g sat fat), 43 mg chol, 1,344 mg sod

---

**FYI:** Bouillon "cubes" also come in tablet and granular form. Use the amount for 6 cups of broth. Or use 8 cups canned chicken broth and add salt to taste.

---

**TIP:** (See *Peeling Butternut Squash,* page 21). Butternut squash can also be purchased peeled and cut up, at certain times of the year.

# Mexican Tortilla Soup

**SERVES** 6
**TOTAL TIME:** About 35 minutes

**PER SERVING:** 234 cal,
18 g pro, 22 g car, 4 g fiber,
9 g fat (2 g sat fat), 42 mg chol,
1,158 mg sod

**TIP:** (See *Peeling Butternut Squash,* page 21). Butternut squash can also be purchased peeled and cut up, at certain times of the year.

4 corn tortillas
2 Tbsp oil
6 cups chicken broth
1½-lb butternut squash, peeled and cut in ½-in. cubes
    (about 4 cups, see Tip, left)
1 Tbsp minced garlic
14.5-oz can diced tomatoes with green chiles
2 cups (8 oz) shredded cooked chicken
GARNISH: diced avocado, lime wedges and chopped fresh cilantro

**1** Stack tortillas and cut in half, then in very narrow strips. Heat 1 Tbsp oil in a large nonstick skillet over medium-high heat. Fry half the tortilla strips, turning often, 5 minutes or until lightly browned and crisp. Remove to paper towels to drain. Repeat with remaining oil and strips.

**2** Bring broth, squash and garlic to a boil in a 3-qt pot. Cover, reduce heat and simmer 5 minutes or until squash is almost tender. Add tomatoes and chicken; simmer, uncovered, 5 minutes or until squash is tender.

**3** Place half the tortilla strips in soup bowls. Ladle in soup; top with remaining tortilla strips. Serve with small bowls of avocado, lime and cilantro.

# Hearty Chicken Noodle Soup

**SERVES** 4
**TOTAL TIME:** About 25 minutes

**PER SERVING:** 351 cal,
34 g pro, 28 g car, 3 g fiber,
11 g fat (3 g sat fat), 105 mg
chol, 1,639 mg sod

6 cups chicken broth
1 cup sliced carrots
1 cup sliced celery
4 oz (1½ cups) extra-wide egg noodles
½ cup frozen green peas
2½ cups (10 oz) large shreds cooked chicken
¼ cup chopped fresh parsley

**1**  Put broth, carrots, celery and 1 cup water in a 3- to 4-qt pot. Bring to a boil, add noodles and boil 6 minutes or until noodles are almost tender.

**2**  Add peas; boil 1 minute until noodles and vegetables are tender. Stir in chicken and parsley; heat through.

> TIP: No cooked chicken in the house? If you have about 12 oz raw chicken breast or tenders, cut it into small pieces and add with the noodles. There's more than enough time for small pieces of chicken to cook.

# Mom's Meatball and Escarole Soup

### TURKEY MEATBALLS · MAIN DISH · 4- TO 5-QT POT

THE MOM HERE IS THE MOTHER OF ONE OF OUR FOOD EDITORS.
SERVE THIS SOUP WITH CRUSTY BREAD FOLLOWED BY CHEESE AND FRUIT FOR DESSERT.

4 cups chicken broth
12 oz escarole, cut into 1-in.-wide strips (6 cups)
1½ cups sliced carrots
¾ cup chopped onion
2 tsp minced garlic
¼ tsp salt
¼ tsp freshly ground pepper
19-oz can cannellini beans, drained and rinsed
12-oz pkg fully cooked turkey meatballs, cut in quarters
3 Tbsp grated Parmesan cheese

> **SERVES** 4
> **TOTAL TIME:** 20 to 25 minutes
>
> **PER SERVING:** 319 cal, 26 g pro, 34 g car, 11 g fiber, 9 g fat (3 g sat fat), 49 mg chol, 1,250 mg sod

**1**  Bring broth, escarole, carrots, onion, garlic, salt and pepper to a boil in a 4- to 5-qt pot. Reduce heat, cover and simmer 7 minutes until vegetables are almost tender.

**2**  Add beans and meatballs and simmer 3 minutes until vegetables are tender. Remove from heat; stir in cheese.

# Gazpacho with Avocado Shrimp Salad

COOKED SHRIMP · NO COOK · BLENDER · MAIN DISH

SERVE WITH TORTILLA CHIPS FOR A SPECIAL LUNCH OR LIGHT SUPPER.

**SERVES** 4
**PREP:** 20 minutes
**CHILL:** At least 1 hour

**PER SERVING:** 280 cal,
23 g pro, 23 g car, 3 g fiber,
13 g fat (3 g sat fat), 176 mg
chol, 1,059 mg sod

**FYI:** A blender makes a finer
purée than a food processor.

**FYI:** Soups and other liquid
foods chill more quickly in a
stainless-steel bowl than in
plastic, glass or pottery.

**FYI:** The acid in the lime
juice will keep the cut-up
avocado from darkening.

SOUP
- 12-oz jar roasted red peppers, drained
- 1 cucumber, peeled, halved lengthwise; seeds scraped out
- 2 cups tomato juice

2 Tbsp fresh lime juice
½ tsp salt
¼ tsp freshly ground pepper
2 plum tomatoes, cut in small chunks (about 1 cup)
1 Hass avocado, cut in ½-in. pieces
1 small green pepper, finely diced
¼ cup finely chopped red onion
3 Tbsp minced fresh chives or parsley
12 oz cooked peeled and cleaned medium shrimp,
    cut in ½-in. pieces
8 Tbsp reduced-fat sour cream

**1** SOUP: Put roasted peppers, cucumber and tomato juice in a blender (see FYI, left). Blend at medium speed 1 minute or until smooth. Pour into a large bowl (see FYI, left) and chill, stirring occasionally, about 1 hour. (Longer is fine.)

**2** Meanwhile, mix lime juice, salt and pepper in a large bowl. Add tomatoes, avocado, green pepper, red onion and chives. Stir gently to mix. Gently stir in shrimp.

**3** TO SERVE: Mound ½ cup shrimp mixture in center of each of 4 soup plates. Pour 1 cup soup around each mound. Pat mounds down slightly, top each with 2 Tbsp sour cream, then remaining shrimp mixture.

Mexican Tortilla Soup *(page 222)*

Hearty Chicken Noodle Soup *(page 222)*

Split Pea Soup *(page 228)*

Caribbean Pumpkin Soup *(page 235)*

# Russian Borscht

2 tsp oil
2 Tbsp flour
1 lb beef chuck for stew, cut in ¾-in. pieces
2 cups chopped red onions
6 cups beef broth
1 small bay leaf
5 cups (about 1 lb) coarsely shredded green cabbage
1¼ lb small red-skinned potatoes, cut in ¾-in. cubes (3⅓ cups)
1½ cups (8 oz) thinly sliced carrots
1 lb beets, cut in ½-in. pieces (about 2 cups, see Tip, right)
½ cup red-wine vinegar
GARNISH: sour cream, chopped fresh dill

SERVES 6 (makes 14 cups)
TOTAL TIME: 2 hours 45 minutes

PER SERVING: 387 cal, 21 g pro, 37 g car, 5 g fiber, 17 g fat (6 g sat fat), 54 mg chol, 1,152 mg sod

TIP: Peel beets before cutting them up. If the beets you buy come with stems and leaves, you may use them instead of the cabbage, or save them to serve as a side dish up to 4 days later. Cook as you would spinach.

**1** Heat oil in a heavy 5- to 6-qt pot over medium-high heat. Put flour and beef in a plastic bag; shake to coat beef. Add to pot and cook, stirring often, 4 minutes or until browned.

**2** Stir in onions and cook 2 to 3 minutes, until they start to soften. Add beef broth and 2 cups water. Bring to a boil, scraping up any brown bits on bottom of pot. Add bay leaf. Reduce heat, cover and simmer 2 hours or until the beef is tender.

**3** Stir in cabbage, potatoes, carrots and beets. Cover and simmer 30 minutes or until vegetables are tender. Remove bay leaf. Stir in vinegar.

**4** Ladle into soup bowls. Top with a spoonful of sour cream and sprinkle with the fresh dill.

# Beef, Barley & Mushroom Soup

BEEF CHUCK FOR STEW · MAIN DISH · SLOW COOKER

SERVE WITH SOUR CREAM.

**SERVES 6**
PREP: 20 minutes
COOK: 7 to 9 hours on low

**PER SERVING:** 264 cal,
19 g pro, 36 g car, 8 g fiber,
5 g fat (2 g sat fat), 37 mg chol,
682 mg sod

**FYI:** Shallots are mild members of the onion family.

12 oz beef chuck for stew
4 cups chicken broth
14.5-oz can diced tomatoes with roasted garlic and onion
12 oz shiitake mushrooms, stems discarded; caps sliced
1½ cups diced and peeled white turnip (1 large)
1½ cups diced carrot
1 cup barley (not quick cooking)
½ cup chopped shallots or onion (see FYI, left)
½ tsp freshly ground pepper
½ tsp dried thyme
½ cup chopped fresh dill

**1** Put all ingredients except dill in a 4-qt or larger slow cooker. Add 2 cups water and stir to mix. Cover and cook on low 7 to 9 hours or until beef and vegetables are tender.

**2** Stir in dill before serving.

# Pizza in a Bowl

PEPPERONI · MAIN DISH · SLOW COOKER

**SERVES 4**
PREP: 10 minutes
COOK: 6 to 8 hours on low

**PER SERVING:** 462 cal,
23 g pro, 25 g car, 3 g fiber,
30 g fat (12 g sat fat), 61 mg
chol, 2,493 mg sod

28-oz can diced tomatoes with roasted garlic
2 cups beef broth
8 oz stick pepperoni sausage, diced
1½ cups sliced fresh mushrooms
1 large green pepper, diced
1½ cups chopped red onion
1 Tbsp Italian seasoning
1 cup shredded part-skim mozzarella cheese

**1** Put all ingredients except cheese in a 3-qt or larger slow cooker. Add 1 cup water and stir to mix. Cover and cook on low 6 to 8 hours or until vegetables are tender.

**2** Ladle into soup bowls and sprinkle with cheese.

# Tlalpeño Soup

## CHICKEN THIGHS · MAIN DISH · SLOW COOKER

THIS CALDO TLALPEÑO (SOUP FROM TLALPEÑO) HAS A LIGHT BUT INTENSE FLAVOR.

4 chicken thighs (1¼ lb), skin removed
   (see *Off with the Skin*, page 65)
3½ cups chicken broth
2 cups chopped plum tomatoes (about 1 lb)
1 cup chopped green pepper
1 cup chopped onion
½ cup converted rice
½ cup canned chickpeas, drained and rinsed
1 Tbsp chopped garlic
2 canned chipotle chiles in adobo sauce, diced (see FYI, right)
½ tsp salt
½ tsp freshly ground pepper
1 bay leaf
GARNISH: shredded Monterey Jack cheese, diced avocado,
   chopped chipotle chiles in adobo sauce

**SERVES 4**
PREP: 15 minutes
COOK: 7 to 9 hours on low

PER SERVING: 280 cal,
22 g pro, 34 g car, 4 g fiber,
6 g fat (1 g sat fat), 67 mg chol,
1,286 mg sod

**FYI:** Chipotles are jalapeño peppers that were allowed to ripen, then were dried and smoked. Canned chipotles in an adobo—mild, red chile—sauce are popular in Mexico as a condiment. The heat level of chipotles is high so use a light hand to begin with.

**1**  Mix all ingredients in a 3-qt or larger slow cooker. Cover and cook on low 7 to 9 hours until chicken and rice are tender.

**2**  TO SERVE: Place a chicken thigh in each of 4 soup bowls. Add soup and, if desired, top with cheese, avocado and chiles.

# Split Pea Soup

SERVE WITH CORNBREAD, OR CUT CORNBREAD IN CUBES, TOAST IN OVEN AND SERVE AS CROUTONS.

**SERVES 4**
**PREP:** 15 minutes
**COOK:** About 6 hours on high,
12 hours on low

**PER SERVING:** 551 cal,
40 g pro, 84 g car, 10 g fiber,
8 g fat (2 g sat fat), 32 mg chol,
1,528 mg sod

1 lb dried green split peas
2 cups chopped onions
1½ cups diced carrots
1 cup diced celery
2 tsp minced garlic
½ tsp freshly ground pepper
3 cups chicken broth
1¼ lb ham hock(s)

**1** Put all ingredients and 7 cups water in a 5½-qt or larger slow cooker.

**2** Cover and cook on high 6 hours or low 12 hours until peas are very soft and fall apart.

**3** Remove ham hock. When cool enough to handle, cut meat off the bone, dice and return to soup.

## ACCOMPANIMENTS
The next time you serve soup, try one of these instead of serving crackers.

### CRISPY CROUTONS
3 slices day-old white bread
2 Tbsp olive oil

**1** Heat oven to 350°F. Have a rimmed baking sheet ready.
**2** Stack bread and cut into ½-in. squares. Put in a bowl, add olive oil and toss thoroughly to coat.
**3** Spread out on ungreased baking sheet. Bake 5 to 7 minutes, stirring twice, until golden brown and crisp.

## CHILI PITAS
2 Tbsp olive oil
¾ tsp chili powder
¾ tsp ground cumin
⅛ tsp salt
4 drops hot pepper sauce
Six 3- to 4-in. pita breads

**1** Heat broiler. Have a baking sheet ready.
**2** Mix oil, chili powder, cumin, salt and hot pepper sauce in a small cup. Brush over both sides of each pita.
**3** Broil on baking sheet (or broiler pan rack) 1 to 2 minutes on each side, until lightly browned and puffed.

## CHEESE TOASTS
12-inch long baguette
   (French bread)
1 cup (4 oz) grated Parmesan
   cheese
½ cup mayonnaise

**1** Heat broiler. Have a baking sheet ready.
**2** Cut bread in ¼-inch thick slices. Mix Parmesan and mayonnaise in a small bowl. Spread over one side of each slice of bread. Put spread side up on baking sheet.
**3** Broil 1 to 2 minutes or until the topping bubbles and edges are toasted.

# Pasta & Chickpea Soup

## MAIN DISH · 4- TO 5-QT POT

SERVE WITH GRATED PARMESAN CHEESE. FOLLOW WITH CHEESE, FRUIT AND BREAD OR CRACKERS.

1 Tbsp olive oil

2 slices bacon, diced

1 cup diced carrots

1 cup diced celery

1 cup chopped onion

1 Tbsp minced garlic

6 cups chicken broth

¼ tsp Italian seasoning

¼ tsp freshly ground pepper

1 cup elbow macaroni

19-oz can chickpeas, drained and rinsed

4 cups packed fresh spinach leaves, coarsely torn, or 10-oz pkg frozen leaf spinach, thawed

**SERVES 6**
**TOTAL TIME:** About 50 minutes

**PER SERVING:** 259 cal, 11 g pro, 32 g car, 6 g fiber, 10 g fat (3 g sat fat), 5 mg chol, 1,178 mg sod

**1** Heat oil in a large pot over medium-high heat. Add bacon; cook 5 minutes, stirring often until browned. Remove with a slotted spoon.

**2** Add carrots, celery, onion and garlic to fat in pot. Cook, stirring often, 7 to 8 minutes until vegetables are tender.

**3** Add bacon, chicken broth, 2 cups water, the Italian seasoning and pepper. Bring to a boil, reduce heat, cover and simmer 10 minutes.

**4** Add pasta; cook 8 minutes or until pasta is slightly underdone. Stir in chickpeas and spinach, return to a simmer and cook 2 minutes or until hot. Serve with Parmesan cheese.

**BUMPING UP SOUP**
To turn a hot vegetable soup into a main dish serve it with a poached egg (or two) in each bowl.

# North African Lamb & Couscous Soup

LAMB NECK · MAIN DISH · 4- TO 5-QT POT

SERVES 6
PREP: 15 to 20 minutes
COOK: About 2 hours 40 minutes

PER SERVING: 721 cal, 57 g pro, 69 g car, 14 g fiber, 24 g fat (7 g sat fat), 126 mg chol, 2,156 mg sod

TIP: Look for Israeli couscous in the grains section of your market. Israeli couscous is rounder and larger—almost the size of small pearls—than regular couscous. Although it's toasted during the manufacturing process, package directions suggest toasting it again, as in this recipe, before cooking it.

TIP: You can cook the lamb in the broth 2 or 3 days before you want to serve the soup. The fat will rise to the top and harden when chilled and be easy to lift off.

9 cups chicken broth
3 lb lamb neck for stew
2 cloves garlic, halved
½ lemon, cut in thin slices
2½ cups (8 oz) sliced carrots
1 medium onion, cut in thin wedges
2 tsp ground cumin
½ tsp salt
½ tsp caraway seeds
½ tsp turmeric
¼ tsp ground cinnamon
¼ tsp ground red pepper (cayenne)
1 Tbsp olive oil
¾ cup large toasted Israeli couscous (see Tip, left)
29-oz can chickpeas, drained and rinsed
10 oz fresh baby spinach

**1** Put broth, 1 cup water, lamb, garlic and lemon in 4- to 5-qt pot. Bring to a boil, reduce heat and simmer, uncovered, 2 hours or until lamb is tender. Strain broth, return to pot and skim off fat (see Tip, left).

**2** Bring broth to a gentle boil. Add carrots, onion, cumin, salt, caraway seeds, turmeric, cinnamon and red pepper. Reduce heat and simmer 20 minutes or until vegetables are tender.

**3** When lamb is cool enough to handle, remove meat from bones and shred.

**4** Heat oil in a nonstick skillet over medium-high heat. Add couscous and cook about 4 minutes, stirring often, until golden brown. Remove from heat.

**5** Stir chickpeas, couscous and lamb into soup. Gently boil 10 minutes or until couscous is firm-tender. Stir in spinach a handful at a time, stirring down each batch as it wilts. Ladle soup into bowls.

# Chilled Pea Soup & Smokey Joe Clubs

SMOKED SALMON, WHITEFISH SALAD · SOUP AND SANDWICH · NO COOK · BLENDER

THINK OF THIS AS SOFT-SERVE SOUP: DELIVERED FRESHLY MADE AND CHILLED,
ALL AT THE SAME TIME.

**SOUP**
- 16-oz bag frozen green peas, slightly thawed
- 1 cup chicken broth
- 1 cup fat-free half & half
- ½ tsp salt

**SANDWICH**
- 8 slices pumpernickel bread
- 4 slices rye bread
- ½ cup chive-and-onion cream cheese
- 4-oz pkg thinly sliced lox or smoked salmon
- 28 very thin slices seedless cucumber
- 8-oz tub smoked whitefish salad

GARNISH: freshly ground pepper and chives

SERVES 4
TOTAL TIME: 25 minutes

PER SERVING: 688 cal,
28 g pro, 71 g car, 10 g fiber,
29 g fat (16 g sat fat), 66 mg
chol, 2,102 mg sod

**1** SOUP: Purée ingredients in a blender.

**2** SANDWICHES: Lay 4 slices pumpernickel on a cutting board. Spread each with 1 Tbsp cream cheese; top with lox and cucumber. Spread 4 slices rye bread with rest of cream cheese. Place spread side down on cucumber; spread top slice with whitefish salad. Cover with remaining pumpernickel. Cut corner to corner.

**3** TO SERVE: Sprinkle soup with pepper; garnish with chives.

# Cucumber Soup with Turkey Sandwiches

## SMOKED TURKEY BREAST · SOUP AND SANDWICH · NO COOK

**SERVES 4**
**TOTAL TIME:** 30 minutes

**PER SERVING:** 488 cal, 35 g pro, 54 g car, 5 g fiber, 15 g fat (5 g sat fat), 55 mg chol, 1,827 mg sod

**TIP:** Scrape out the cucumber seeds with a teaspoon. A melon baller works well, too.

**CUCUMBER SOUP**

2 medium cucumbers, peeled
3 cups plain lowfat yogurt
1 cup 1% lowfat milk
¼ cup finely chopped fresh dill
2 Tbsp fresh lemon juice
2 tsp minced garlic
½ tsp salt
¼ tsp freshly ground black pepper
½ cup finely diced yellow pepper
½ cup finely diced red pepper

⅓ cup light mayonnaise
8 slices pumpernickel bread
12 oz thinly sliced smoked turkey breast
4 red- or green-leaf lettuce leaves

**1** CUCUMBER SOUP: Line a rimmed baking sheet with a double layer of paper towels and place box grater on top. Cut cucumbers in half lengthwise and scrape out seeds (see Tip, left). Shred cucumbers using large holes of box grater. Cover with more paper towels and press down to absorb moisture. Put yogurt, milk, dill, lemon juice, garlic, salt and pepper into a large bowl; whisk until blended. Add cucumber and peppers. Refrigerate while making sandwiches.

**2** Spread mayonnaise on 4 slices bread. Top with turkey and lettuce and remaining bread. Cut each sandwich in half and serve with bowls of the chilled soup.

# Fresh Tomato Soup

TOMATOES · VEGETARIAN · 3- TO 4-QT POT · FOOD PROCESSOR OR BLENDER

GOOD HOT, CHILLED OR AT ROOM TEMPERATURE, AND PERFECT WITH
THE EGGPLANT, PEPPER & BASIL SANDWICHES (PAGE 214).
MAKE PLENTY WHEN YOUR GARDEN IS OVERFLOWING WITH TOMATOES.

1 Tbsp olive oil
1 cup coarsely chopped onion
1 Tbsp minced garlic
3 lb ripe tomatoes, cored and coarsely chopped (7 cups)
1¼ tsp salt
½ tsp freshly ground pepper
GARNISH: fresh basil leaves

**SERVES** 4 (makes 6 cups)
**TOTAL TIME:** About 35 minutes

**PER SERVING:** 114 cal,
3 g pro, 19 g car, 5 g fiber,
4 g fat (1 g sat fat), 0 mg chol,
755 mg sod

**1** Heat oil in 3- to 4-qt pot over medium heat. Add onion and garlic; sauté 3 to 4 minutes just until onion starts to brown slightly.

**2** Stir in tomatoes, salt and pepper. Bring to a boil; reduce heat, cover and simmer 15 minutes, stirring occasionally, until tomatoes are very soft.

**3** Remove from heat and let cool slightly. Pulse 2 or 3 cups at a time in a food processor or blender until still slightly chunky. Serve hot or chilled.

# Chilled Moroccan Vegetable Soup

CARROTS · VEGETARIAN · 3- TO 4-QT POT · FOOD PROCESSOR OR BLENDER

**MAKES** 6 cups
**PREP TIME:** 35 to 40 minutes
**CHILL:** 1 hour, up to 4 days

**PER CUP:** 111 cal, 2 g pro, 16 g car, 4 g fiber, 5 g fat (1 g sat fat), 0 mg chol, 616 mg sod

**TIP:** Remove lemon peel for garnish with a vegetable peeler before you cut the lemon for squeezing. Cut the peel in thin strips; wrap tightly in plastic and refrigerate.

2 Tbsp olive oil
1 lb carrots, coarsely chopped (2½ cups)
2 yellow peppers, coarsely chopped
2 cups chopped sweet onions
4 cloves garlic, sliced
2 tsp ground cumin
2 tsp sweet paprika
About 1½ tsp salt
About ¼ cup fresh lemon juice (see Tip, left)
GARNISH: thin strips lemon peel and fresh chives

**1** Heat oil in a 3- to 4-qt pot over medium heat. Add carrots, yellow peppers, onion, garlic, cumin and paprika. Cover and cook about 15 minutes, stirring occasionally, until vegetables are very soft but not brown. Add 4 cups water and 1½ tsp salt. Simmer covered 10 minutes to blend flavors.

**2** Purée 2 or 3 cups at a time in food processor or blender until as coarse or fine as preferred. Pour into a container. Stir in lemon juice; taste soup, add more salt or lemon juice if you wish. Cover and refrigerate until cold, or up to 4 days.

**3** Garnish servings with lemon peel and chives.

# Caribbean Pumpkin Soup

### CANNED PUMPKIN · 3- TO 4-QT POT

⅔ cup chopped onion
⅔ cup chopped red pepper
2 tsp minced garlic
1 tsp ground cumin
2½ cups chicken broth
15-oz can 100%-pure pumpkin
15-oz can black beans, drained and rinsed
14.5-oz can diced tomatoes, drained
¼ tsp salt
¼ tsp freshly ground pepper
GARNISH: sour cream and chopped cilantro

> SERVES 4 (makes 5 cups)
> TOTAL TIME: 20 to 25 minutes
>
> **PER SERVING:** 146 cal,
> 9 g pro, 28 g car, 6 g fiber,
> 1 g fat (0 g sat fat), 0 mg chol,
> 878 mg sod

**1** Coat a 3- to 4-qt pot with cooking spray; heat over medium heat.

**2** Add onion and pepper and cook about 5 minutes, stirring occasionally, until vegetables are tender. Stir in garlic and cumin and cook 1 minute. Stir in broth, pumpkin, beans, tomatoes, salt and pepper. Bring to a boil; reduce heat, cover and simmer 5 minutes to blend flavors.

# Salads

Long ago, or maybe not so long ago, a salad meal was thought of as an inescapably "light" meal, and as such bound to be inherently unsatisfying. Certainly it was something men didn't choose on their own. But, perhaps because of the advent of "salad" bars in supermarkets and takeout shops, a salad meal has gone male and mainstream. In this chapter you'll find only one side-dish salad (check the line directly under the recipe title), and two more that can go either way. The others are definitely main dishes starring pork, steak, ground beef, eggs, pasta and brown rice, among other ingredients. Even chicken salad is no big deal these days with so many cooked chicken items ready to fill your shopping cart. What makes a great main-dish salad are filling ingredients (beans, rice, meat) and a mix of textures: crisp (lettuce, shredded carrots), crunchy (nuts, taco chips) and creamy (avocado, cheese). To bring it all together you need a good piquant dressing, homemade or one of the incredible variety available on store shelves.

# Thai Steak Salad Platter

## SIRLOIN STEAK · MAIN DISH · GRILL OR STOVETOP GRILL PAN

IF THIS THAI WAY OF EATING IS NEW TO YOU HERE IS HOW IT GOES: EACH PERSON HOLDS A LETTUCE LEAF IN ONE HAND, TOPS IT WITH SLICED STEAK, CUCUMBER, MINT, CARROTS, PEANUTS AND PEANUT DRESSING, ROLLS UP THE LEAF AND EATS IT OUT OF HAND. THE PITA IS EATEN SEPARATELY; YOU COULD SERVE WITH RICE INSTEAD, OR GRILL CHUNKS OF FOCACCIA BREAD.

**SERVES 4**
PREP: 20 minutes
GRILL: About 15 minutes

**PER SERVING:** 510 cal, 31 g pro, 44 g car, 4 g fiber, 23 g fat (6 g sat fat), 68 mg chol, 981 mg sod

**PEANUT DRESSING**
⅓ cup Oriental salad dressing
1 Tbsp creamy peanut butter

About 12 large, green-leaf lettuce leaves
1 cup thinly sliced seedless cucumber
½ cup fresh mint leaves
½ cup shredded carrots
¼ cup unsalted dry-roasted peanuts, coarsely chopped
One 1-lb boneless sirloin steak (about 1 in. thick)
Cooking spray
½ tsp salt
½ tsp freshly ground pepper
4 pocketless or regular pitas

**1** Heat outdoor grill or stovetop grill pan.

**2** PEANUT DRESSING: Whisk salad dressing and peanut butter in a small bowl to blend; scrape into a serving dish.

**3** On a large serving platter arrange lettuce leaves in a pile and mounds of cucumber, mint, carrots and peanuts. Refrigerate.

**4** Coat both sides of steak with cooking spray; season with salt and pepper. Grill, turning once, 8 to 10 minutes for medium-rare (140°F on a meat thermometer inserted in middle). Remove to a cutting board; let rest 5 minutes (meat will continue to cook).

**5** Meanwhile grill pitas 1 to 2 minutes, turning once, until lightly toasted.

**6** TO SERVE: Thinly slice steak across the grain (see *Across the Grain*, page 89); add to serving platter. Serve with pitas separately.

# Beef Taco Salad

## GROUND BEEF · MAIN DISH · SKILLET

VEGETABLE OR TORTILLA CHIPS ADD A NICE CRUNCH TO THE SALAD.

12 oz lean ground beef

1 Tbsp minced garlic

DRESSING

    ½ cup Italian dressing

    2 Tbsp lime juice

    1 tsp ground cumin

10-oz bag leafy romaine lettuce

16-oz can kidney beans, drained and rinsed

8-oz can whole-kernel corn, drained

1 pt grape, cherry or pear tomatoes

1 cup (4 oz) shredded Cheddar cheese

1 cup fresh cilantro

1 avocado (preferably Hass), cut in chunks

2 cups mixed vegetable chips or baked tortilla chips

**SERVES** 4
**TOTAL TIME:** 20 minutes

**PER SERVING:** 722 cal,
35 g pro, 52 g car, 9 g fiber,
43 g fat (12 g sat fat), 79 mg
chol, 953 mg sod

**1** Brown ground beef and garlic in a nonstick skillet. Drain off any fat.

**2** Put Dressing ingredients in a large bowl. Whisk to blend. Add beef mixture and remaining ingredients; toss to mix and coat.

---

### WASHING GREENS

Many wonderful greens are sold triple-washed and ready to eat.
But it's still nice to buy fresh lettuce and getting it clean is not a big chore. Drying the washed greens is easy with a salad spinner.
(The ones that have a handle on the top work well.)
Fill a big bowl with cold water. Separate the lettuce leaves,
discarding any very damaged ones or any with soft brown spots.
Put the leaves into the bowl of water and leave for 10 to 20 minutes.
Pour off the water and fill bowl with fresh water to rinse the leaves again. Drain the leaves then dry them well in a salad spinner.
If space permits, refrigerate leaves in the salad spinner. Or put them in a bowl (cover with plastic wrap) or ziptop bag with a few pieces of paper towel to absorb any remaining moisture and refrigerate.

# Layered Salad

### HARD-COOKED EGGS, COOKED CHICKEN · MAIN DISH

THIS MAKES A SPECIAL SUMMER LUNCH OR DINNER ESPECIALLY IF YOU WILL BE COMING HOME HUNGRY WITH NO DESIRE TO COOK. THE SALAD CAN BE PUT TOGETHER 24 HOURS AHEAD.

**SERVES** 6
**PREP:** 20 minutes
**CHILLING:** 2 to 24 hours

**PER SERVING:** 394 cal, 27 g pro, 14 g car, 3 g fiber, 27 g fat (8 g sat fat), 241 mg chol, 952 mg sod

TIP: A 2-lb rotisserie chicken will give you about 3½ cups chicken. Take off the skin then tear the meat into bite-size pieces.

TIP: Get the cheese, nuts and bacon ready while you are putting the salad together. Wrap airtight and refrigerate next to the salad.

TIP: To make preparation even simpler, buy already-cooked bacon.

DRESSING
½ cup light mayonnaise
½ cup reduced-fat sour cream
1 Tbsp plus 1 tsp fresh lemon juice
1 tsp minced garlic
¼ tsp mustard powder (see FYI, page 42)
¼ tsp salt
¼ tsp freshly ground pepper
¼ tsp sugar

SALAD
2 cups baby spinach
About 3½ cups bite-size pieces roast chicken (see Tip, left)
1 red pepper, cut in 2 x 1-in. strips
4 hard-cooked eggs, quartered
1 small head iceberg lettuce, coarsely chopped
2 cups shredded carrots

½ cup (2 oz) shredded Cheddar cheese
¼ cup pecans, toasted and coarsely chopped (see *Toasting Nuts*, page 189)
3 slices bacon, fried crisp, drained on paper towels and coarsely crumbled (see Tip, left)

**1** Have ready a 4- to 5-qt serving bowl, preferably clear glass so layers are visible.

**2** Put Dressing ingredients in a small bowl and whisk until blended. Refrigerate until ready to use.

**3** Spread spinach over bottom of serving bowl. Top with the chicken. Place a row of red pepper strips around sides of bowl; scatter remaining strips in middle. Place egg wedges against side of bowl; put rest in middle. Top with layers of lettuce and carrots. Spread Dressing completely over carrots, right to the edges of the bowl to keep air out. Refrigerate at least 2 hours or cover airtight and refrigerate overnight.

**4** TO SERVE: Sprinkle cheese, pecans and bacon on top. Toss salad or spoon through the layers.

Spicy Island Roast Pork & Fruit Salad *(page 243)*

Mexican Tuna Salad *(page 246)*

Mediterranean Pasta Salad *(page 248)*

Asian Chicken Salad *(page 241)*

# Asian Chicken Salad

⅓ cup Asian sesame dressing and marinade
2 Tbsp fresh lime juice
2 cups (8 oz) shredded cooked chicken
4 cups (6 oz) coleslaw mix
1 small cucumber, halved lengthwise, seeds scraped out, thinly sliced
1 small red pepper, quartered and cut in narrow strips
¼ cup coarsely chopped fresh cilantro
¼ cup coarsely chopped fresh mint leaves
5 oz Asian or other salad blend
¼ cup cashews or peanuts, chopped

**SERVES** 4
**TOTAL TIME:** 15 minutes

**PER SERVING:** 248 cal, 19 g pro, 23 g car, 3 g fiber, 11 g fat (2 g sat fat), 63 mg chol, 832 mg sod

**1** Whisk dressing and lime juice in a large bowl. Add chicken, coleslaw, cucumber, pepper, cilantro and mint; toss to mix and coat.

**2** Serve on greens; sprinkle with nuts.

# Chicken Salad with Pears & Grapes

A SALAD WITH CHICKEN AND FRUIT OFTEN HAS A MAYONNAISE DRESSING.
A VINEGAR AND OLIVE OIL DRESSING MAKES THIS SALAD EXTRA REFRESHING.

2 cups (8 oz) shredded cooked chicken
⅓ cup finely diced red onion
1 cup red seedless grapes, cut in halves
2 ribs celery, sliced
2 ripe pears, cored and cut in thin wedges (see Tip, right)
½ cup red-wine vinegar and olive oil dressing
4 leaves romaine lettuce

**SERVES** 4
**TOTAL TIME:** 15 minutes

**PER SERVING:** 298 cal, 18 g pro, 30 g car, 4 g fiber, 13 g fat (3 g sat fat), 50 mg chol, 491 mg sod

**1** Put chicken, onion, grapes, celery and pears in a large bowl. Add dressing and toss to mix and coat.

**2** Serve on lettuce-lined plates.

TIP: Except for the pears (which would brown) you can prepare the ingredients into a bowl 2 or 3 hours ahead and refrigerate covered. Before serving cut them up and add to the bowl.

# Chicken with Cuban Mojo Sauce & Papaya Slaw

PURCHASED ROAST CHICKEN-BREAST HALVES · NO COOK

PAPAYA SEEDS ARE EDIBLE AND ADD A PEPPERY TOUCH.
BUY COOKED CHICKEN BREASTS, OR USE LEFTOVER ROAST CHICKEN.

**SERVES** 4
**TOTAL TIME:** 20 minutes

**PER SERVING:** 397 cal,
28 g pro, 25 g car, 2 g fiber,
22 g fat (5 g sat fat), 84 mg
chol, 1,070 mg sod

## SHREDDING GREEN CABBAGE

Choose firm heads of
green cabbage that feel
heavy for their size. Pull
off any wilted outer leaves
and trim the stem end.
With a large, sharp knife
cut the head lengthwise in
quarters and cut out the
hard white core. Then slice
each wedge as thin as
possible from top to
bottom (the easier way) or
across each wedge.

PAPAYA SLAW
- ¼ cup light mayonnaise
- ¼ cup orange juice
- 2 tsp distilled white vinegar
- ½ tsp salt
- ½ tsp freshly ground pepper
- 1 ripe papaya (about 1 lb), peeled and quartered lengthwise
- 4 cups (6 oz) coleslaw mix or shredded green cabbage (see *Shredding Green Cabbage*, left)
- 1 small red pepper, thinly sliced
- ½ cup coarsely chopped fresh cilantro

MOJO SAUCE
- 1 cup fresh cilantro
- ⅓ cup orange juice
- 2 Tbsp olive oil
- 1 clove garlic
- ¼ tsp salt
- ¼ tsp paprika
- ¼ tsp ground cumin

4 purchased roast chicken-breast halves (about 4½ oz each), boned and sliced

**1** PAPAYA SLAW: Put mayonnaise, orange juice, vinegar, salt and pepper in a large bowl. Whisk to mix. Scoop out and save papaya seeds. Slice papaya, and add to bowl with coleslaw mix, bell pepper and cilantro; toss to mix and coat.

**2** MOJO SAUCE: Blend ingredients in a blender or food processor until cilantro is very finely chopped.

**3** Spoon Mojo Sauce over chicken. Sprinkle slaw with the papaya seeds and serve with the chicken.

# Spicy Island Roast Pork & Fruit Salad

PORK TENDERLOIN · OVEN · MAIN DISH · ROASTING PAN

1-lb pork tenderloin
1 Tbsp Caribbean jerk seasoning (see *What's Jerk?*, right)
8-oz can pineapple chunks in juice

DRESSING
   1 tsp freshly grated lime peel
   ¼ cup fresh lime juice
   1 Tbsp honey
   1 tsp Caribbean jerk seasoning
½ cantaloupe, cut into 4 wedges
8 cups (9 oz) mixed salad greens (such as romaine, frisée, radicchio)

**1** Heat oven to 425°F. Place pork in a roasting pan; rub with 1 Tbsp jerk seasoning.

**2** Roast 30 minutes or until barely pink in middle and an instant-read meat thermometer inserted in center registers 155°F. Remove to cutting board, cover loosely with foil and let rest 8 to 10 minutes.

**3** DRESSING: Drain pineapple juice into a large bowl. Add lime peel and juice, honey and jerk seasoning. Whisk to blend.

**4** Cut each wedge of melon off the peel then slice thinly crosswise.

**5** Cut pork in ¼-in.-thick slices. Add to Dressing along with salad greens, cantaloupe and pineapple. Toss to mix.

---

**SERVES 4**
**TOTAL TIME:** 50 minutes

PER SERVING: 265 cal, 26 g pro, 27 g car, 2 g fiber, 6 g fat (2 g sat fat), 67 mg chol, 104 mg sod

---

## WHAT'S JERK?

Jerk refers to a seasoning blend, a method of cooking and to meat that has been cooked that way. No one is certain how it came by that name but the Caribbean, specifically Jamaica, is its place of origin. Jerk seasoning can be a powder, a dry paste or a more liquid marinade. Essential ingredients are allspice (which the Jamaicans call "pimiento" or pepper), fiery Scotch bonnet chiles, salt and thyme. Beyond that every competitive jerk cook has his own list, which may include garlic, cinnamon, nutmeg, ginger, brown sugar, tamarind and lime juice. Pit roasting is the preferred cooking method, low heat for hours over allspice branches, or it can be done over indirect heat on an outdoor grill.

---

## FARMER'S MARKET GREENS

Farmer's markets and green markets are good places to search out "new" salad greens. Farmers enjoy growing new-to-them greens as much as we enjoy tasting them. Look for uncommon lettuces; for greens popular in China and Japan such as mizuna and tatsoi; for young amaranth leaves and for pea shoots, the tips of green pea vines which are sweet and delicious in a salad. Straggly bunches of green or gold purslane often turn up in farmer's markets. The succulent leaves and stems are both edible and can be cooked or eaten raw. Wash purslane just before using it. If stored damp, purslane leaves quickly fall off the stems. To find farmer's markets near you: www.ams.usda.gov/farmersmarkets.

# Grilled Pork Waldorf Salad

BONELESS PORK CHOPS · MAIN DISH · GRILL OR STOVETOP GRILL PAN

**SERVES** 4
**TOTAL TIME:** 20 minutes

**PER SERVING:** 367 cal,
22 g pro, 25 g car, 4 g fiber,
20 g fat (4 g sat fat), 53 mg
chol, 249 mg sod

TIP: Choose a sweet apple
such as Mutsu, Cameo, Pink
Lady or Jonagold.

½ cup Dijon vinaigrette dressing
2 Tbsp light mayonnaise
12 oz boneless pork chops, ½ to ¾ in. thick
8 cups (9 oz) baby salad greens (mesclun)
2 apples, cored, cut in chunks (see Tip, left)
½ cup sliced celery
½ cup sliced scallions
½ cup chopped walnuts

**1** Heat outdoor grill or stovetop grill pan. Whisk dressing and mayonnaise in a cup; pour all but 1 Tbsp into a medium bowl. Brush the 1 Tbsp over the chops.

**2** Grill, turning once, 7 minutes or until barely pink in center and lightly charred. Remove from grill and let rest 3 or 4 minutes.

**3** While pork cooks, add greens, apples, celery, scallions and walnuts to dressing in bowl.

**4** Slice pork. Add to bowl and toss to mix.

## NON-GREEN SALADS
· Drain plain beets (from a can or jar). Toss with an herb vinaigrette and some sliced sweet onion. Beets are also delicious with sliced oranges.
· Toss sliced cucumbers (peeled or not) with plain yogurt seasoned with salt, pepper and lots of chopped fresh dill, cilantro or mint.
· Toss strips of roasted red peppers (from a jar) with marinated artichoke hearts and the marinade. No additional dressing is needed.
· Cook lots more carrots than you need one night. Toss the extra with a vinaigrette dressing and refrigerate for a delicious salad three or four nights later.
· Arrange sliced, peeled seedless oranges on plates with sliced sweet onion and sprinkle with a citrus vinaigrette. Add drained and rinsed canned black beans for a more filling salad.

# All-American Cowboy Salad

GOOD WITH BREAD SO CRUSTY YOU HAVE TO TEAR IT APART.

8-oz chunk fully cooked ham, cut in small pieces (1¾ cups)

3 medium tomatoes, cut in chunks (4 cups)

11-oz can corn kernels, drained

4-oz chunk Monterey Jack cheese, cut in long, thick strips

⅓ cup thinly sliced red onion

⅓ cup chopped fresh parsley

⅔ cup light ranch dressing

1 small head Boston lettuce, leaves separated

½ cup smoked almonds, coarsely chopped (see Tip, right)

**SERVES** 4
**TOTAL TIME:** 20 minutes

**PER SERVING:** 504 cal,
27 g pro, 27 g car, 5 g fiber,
35 g fat (9 g sat fat), 63 mg
chol, 1,658 mg sod

**1** Put ham, tomatoes, corn, cheese, onion and parsley in a large bowl. Add dressing and toss to mix and coat.

**2** Line a large serving platter with lettuce. Top with ham mixture, sprinkle with almonds and serve immediately.

TIP: Before chopping the almonds rub them between paper towels to get rid of some of the salt.

## IT'S EASY BEING GREEN

Who says it's not easy being green? Now with all the colorful salad leaves available, many washed and dried and ready to pop in the bowl, preparing a salad with a variety of colors, textures and flavors is easier than ever before. A salad of mixed greens complements just about any meal, as an appetizer or as an accompaniment to the main dish. Add fish, meat or eggs, and greens become the main dish.

Keep the following thoughts in mind when making a green salad:

Mild greens: romaine, green- and red-leaf lettuce, frisée, oak leaf lettuce, lolla rosa (a lettuce) and baby spinach. Use a large proportion of these in a mixed salad.

Peppery greens: For a pleasantly pungent taste add arugula (also known as rocket or roquette) or watercress. If you buy them by the bunch, cut off arugula roots, and wash and dry the leaves. Pluck sprigs of watercress off the thick stems. The thinner stems can be chopped and eaten.

For a pleasantly bitter flavor, add a small amount of escarole, or chicory (curly endive), Belgian endive, radicchio or dandelion.

Less common, but popular in Asia and becoming more available here, are tatsoi and mizuna. Mizuna has feathery leaves; it is eaten raw when young, cooked as a green when larger. The same is true of tatsoi.

# Mexican Tuna Salad

TUNA · MAIN DISH · NO COOK

**SERVES** 6
**PREP:** 20 minutes
**CHILL:** 30 minutes to 6 hours

**PER SERVING:** 144 cal,
20 g pro, 14 g car, 2 g fiber,
2 g fat (0 g sat fat), 29 mg chol,
73 mg sod

Two 7.06-oz pouches chunk white albacore tuna in water
3 cups (4 large) chopped tomatoes
½ cup finely diced red onion
1 cup chopped fresh cilantro
½ to ¾ cup fresh lime juice
2 jalapeño peppers, minced (optional)
1 tsp salt
1 head Boston lettuce
24 baked tortilla chips

**1** Place tuna in a medium bowl; break into large pieces with a fork. Add tomatoes, onion, cilantro, lime juice, jalapeños and salt. Stir to mix. Cover and refrigerate 30 minutes or up to 6 hours.

**2** Line plates with lettuce leaves and top with tuna salad; serve with the chips.

# Tuna Salad Provençal

TUNA · MAIN DISH

**SERVES** 6
**TOTAL TIME:** 25 minutes

**PER SERVING:** 233 cal,
11 g pro, 27 g car, 3 g fiber,
9 g fat (1 g sat fat), 5 mg chol,
679 mg sod

1½ lb small red-skinned potatoes, cut in ¾-in. pieces
8 oz fresh green beans, cut in thirds

DRESSING
   3 Tbsp olive oil
   2 Tbsp red-wine vinegar
   1 Tbsp Dijon mustard
   ½ tsp salt
   ½ tsp sugar
   ½ tsp freshly ground pepper
   ½ tsp minced garlic

12-oz jar roasted red peppers, drained
6-oz can light tuna in oil, drained
¾ cup chopped dill pickles
½ cup thinly sliced red onion

**1** Cook potatoes in water to cover 8 minutes. Stir in green beans and cook 5 to 7 minutes more until tender. Drain vegetables in a colander then put in a large bowl.

**2** Meanwhile, put Dressing ingredients in a small bowl. Whisk to blend. Pour half over potatoes and beans. Mix gently with a rubber spatula. Add red peppers, tuna, dill pickles and onion and remaining Dressing. Mix gently. Serve while vegetables are still warm or let cool to room temperature.

# Brown Rice & Pecan Salad

## VEGETARIAN · MAIN DISH OR SIDE DISH

1 cup brown rice
½ cup Italian dressing
2 tsp creamy Dijon mustard
1 cup sliced celery
1 cup shredded carrots
1 red pepper, quartered and thinly sliced
1 apple, any kind, diced
½ cup thinly sliced red onion
½ cup chopped fresh parsley
½ cup pecans, toasted and coarsely chopped (see *Toasting Nuts*, page 189)

**1** Cook rice as pkg directs omitting any butter called for.

**2** Spread cooked rice on a large plate to cool quickly.

**3** Whisk dressing and mustard in a large serving bowl. Add rice, celery, carrots, red pepper, apple, onion and parsley. Toss to mix and coat.

**4** Just before serving, stir in pecans.

> **SERVES** 6 (side dish)
> 4 (main dish)
> **PREP:** 20 minutes
> **COOK:** Depends on rice used
>
> **PER SERVING (AS SIDE DISH):** 284 cal, 6 g pro, 32 g car, 4 g fiber, 16 g fat (2 g sat fat), 0 mg chol, 224 mg sod

> TIP: Can be made through Step 3 up to three hours ahead. Refrigerate until about half an hour before serving.

# Mediterranean Pasta Salad

SERVE THE SALAD JUST THIS WAY AS A SIDE DISH FOR CHICKEN OR FISH.
ADD COOKED SHRIMP FOR A VERY SPECIAL MAIN DISH.

**SERVES** 8 (as a side dish)
**TOTAL TIME:** 25 minutes

**PER SERVING:** 365 cal,
10 g pro, 48 g car, 2 g fiber,
15 g fat (4 g sat fat), 14 mg
chol, 556 mg sod

**FYI:** Ricotta salata is ricotta that's been pressed and salted. It is firm, yet crumbles easily, just like feta.

1 lb gemelli (little twists) or fusilli (short-cut spirals) pasta
7-oz jar roasted red or yellow peppers, drained
6-oz jar marinated artichoke hearts, drained
¼ cup sundried tomatoes in oil
½ cup (2 oz) crumbled ricotta salata or feta cheese (see FYI, left)
¼ cup chopped fresh parsley
¼ cup olive oil
3 Tbsp quartered, pitted kalamata olives
1 Tbsp plus 1 tsp red-wine vinegar
1 tsp minced garlic
½ tsp freshly ground pepper

**1** Cook pasta as pkg directs.

**2** While water comes to a boil and pasta cooks, cut peppers and artichoke hearts bite size and put in a large bowl. Cut tomatoes in strips; add to bowl. Add cheese, parsley, oil, olives, vinegar, garlic and pepper. Stir gently to combine.

**3** Drain pasta. Rinse under running cold water; drain well. Add to bowl; toss to mix and coat. Serve salad at room temperature.

### MAKING SALAD A MEAL

Plain rice, pasta, bulgur and couscous all make great beginnings for a main-dish salad. Add chopped vegetables and a vinaigrette dressing. To make it even more substantial add leftover cooked meat or poultry, deviled eggs or canned tuna.

If you're grilling dinner, get started on another meal by cooking extra chicken, steak, shrimp or vegetables. They'll keep refrigerated for several days. To serve, toss with fresh greens and a vinaigrette dressing.

If you have stale bread on hand, don't throw it to the birds. Tear it in chunks, soak briefly in water then squeeze out the excess. Toss bread with chopped tomato, red onion, garlic and a vinaigrette dressing and you've produced what Italians call panzanella.

# That Illinois Salad

1 cup sliced almonds
¼ cup sugar
8 cups torn romaine lettuce
11-oz can mandarin orange segments, drained
2 Tbsp thinly sliced scallions

DRESSING
   ¼ cup oil
   2 Tbsp honey
   2 Tbsp cider vinegar
   1 Tbsp chopped fresh parsley

**1** Put a square of foil on work surface. Stir nuts and sugar (see Tips, right) in a small saucepan over medium heat for about 5 minutes, until most of the sugar has melted and turned golden. Pour onto the foil to cool and harden.

**2** Put lettuce in 4 salad bowls. Top with oranges and scallions.

**3** DRESSING: Put ingredients in a small jar and shake to blend; drizzle over salads.

**4** Break up the hardened sugar and almonds; scatter over salads.

**SERVES** 4
**TOTAL TIME:** 15 minutes

**PER SERVING:** 389 cal, 7 g pro, 37 g car, 4 g fiber, 26 g fat (2 g sat fat), 0 mg chol, 17 mg sod

TIP: Just keep the nuts and sugar on the move. Energetic stirring may cause the sugar to crystallize instead of just glazing the nuts.

TIP: Choose a saucepan made of stainless steel or other light-colored material so you can easily see when the melted sugar changes color.

TIP: The molten sugar is very hot. Be careful.

# Vegetables

The produce area is unquestionably the most astonishing department in any supermarket: fresh herbs, fresh ginger, lemongrass and "wild" mushrooms have become commonplace, peppers are present in every color, tomatoes in every size and shape, and potatoes. Green vegetables no longer mean just broccoli and cabbage, but also chard, dandelion, broccolini and two or three kinds of kale. Even cauliflower turns up in different colors and in a pyramid shape. For food editors who are constantly being told that people aren't cooking any more, the produce departments (along with the meat) reassure us otherwise. Because vegetables are low in fat and high in fiber, vitamins and minerals, they have taken on new importance in our lives. They add satisfying flavor and texture to meals and are easy to prepare, as a side dish or main dish (check the line right under the recipe title to see which a recipe is). Another excellent source of fresh fruits and vegetables are farmer's markets.

# Eggplant Parmigiana

**SERVES** 6
**TOTAL TIME:** 1 hour 50 minutes

**PER SERVING:** 346 cal,
16 g pro, 26 g car, 5 g fiber,
22 g fat (7 g sat fat),
27 mg chol, 1,451 mg sod

**TIP:** To keep cheese from sticking to the foil, use non-stick foil or coat foil with cooking spray.

2 eggplants (2½ lb), cut in ½-in.-thick rounds
¼ cup olive oil
¾ tsp salt
½ tsp freshly ground pepper
26-oz jar marinara sauce
1½ cups (6 oz) shredded part-skim mozzarella cheese
1 cup (4 oz) grated Parmesan cheese
GARNISH: chopped fresh parsley

**1**  Heat broiler. Have a shallow 9-in. square baking dish ready.

**2**  Spread half the eggplant slices on the broiler rack. Brush with 2 Tbsp oil; sprinkle with half the salt and pepper. Broil 4 in. from heat, 6 to 8 minutes on each side, until lightly browned and tender. Remove from pan and broil the remaining eggplant the same way

**3**  Heat oven to 350°F. Spread ½ cup marinara sauce in baking dish. Cover with first batch of eggplant. Spoon on 1¼ cups sauce; top with 1 cup mozzarella, ½ cup Parmesan, second batch of eggplant, remaining sauce and mozzarella. Sprinkle with remaining Parmesan; cover with foil.

**4**  Bake 45 minutes or until bubbly. Let rest 15 minutes. Sprinkle with parsley and serve.

---

### STORING EGGPLANT
Store whole eggplant unwrapped, or in a paper bag, in the refrigerator and use within 2 days. Or put it in a basket on the kitchen counter and enjoy its beauty. Use within 2 days. If not properly stored, eggplant will quickly develop a spongy flesh and rough skin.

# Chickpea & Sweet Potato Stew

VEGETARIAN · MAIN DISH · SKILLET

SERVE OVER COUSCOUS (SEE COUSCOUS, PAGE 192).

2 tsp olive oil
1½ cups chopped onion
1 yellow pepper, diced
1 Tbsp minced garlic
1½ tsp ground cumin
28-oz can whole tomatoes, chopped
1¼ lb sweet potatoes, cut in ¾-in. chunks (4 cups)
19-oz can chickpeas, drained and rinsed
¾ tsp salt
¼ tsp freshly ground pepper
½ cup chopped fresh cilantro

**SERVES** 6
**TOTAL TIME:** 40 minutes

**PER SERVING:** 195 cal, 6 g pro, 36 g car, 7 g fiber, 4 g fat (0 g sat fat), 0 mg chol, 618 mg sod

1   Heat oil in large nonstick skillet over medium heat. Add onions, yellow pepper and garlic; cover and cook about 6 minutes, stirring occasionally, until vegetables are tender.

2   Stir in cumin; cook 1 to 2 minutes until fragrant. Stir in tomatoes, sweet potatoes, chickpeas, salt and pepper. Bring to a boil, reduce heat, cover and simmer 10 to 15 minutes, stirring once or twice until sweet potatoes are tender. Stir in cilantro.

**BUYING SWEET POTATOES**
Shop for firm, unblemished sweet potatoes that are heavy in the hand. Keep them in a well-ventilated cool place (but not in the refrigerator) for up to 2 weeks.

## YAMS AND SWEET POTATOES: THE SAME?

The names are often used interchangeably but these tropical-vine tubers have no familial link. The yam is a member of the yam family (Dioscorea) while the sweet potato is an outcrop of the morning glory family (Convolvulaceae). Sweet potatoes come from Asia, yams from Africa where they are the most popular food in many countries, especially in Ghana and Nigeria. Usually what are called yams in the U.S. are actually sweet potatoes, with relatively moist texture and orange flesh. When true yams are sold in the U.S., often in Hispanic, African and Caribbean markets, they were probably grown in the Caribbean. To add to the confusion the USDA requires that canned yams also be labeled "sweet potatoes."

The sweet potato by itself is highly nutritious and low in calories. It's the addition of sweet stuff that loads on the calories. The more orange the flesh the more vitamins A and C it carries. There are over 150 species of yam grown and the flesh may be various shades of white, yellow, purple or pink. Yams can also grow to more than 6 feet long and weigh more than 100 pounds.

# Cheese & Corn-Stuffed Poblanos

**SERVES** 6
**TOTAL TIME:** 1 hour

PER SERVING: 185 cal,
10 g pro, 16 g car, 3 g fiber,
9 g fat (4 g sat fat), 23 mg chol,
392 mg sod

TIP: When poblano chiles are plentiful grill more than you need. Remove the skin, core and seeds and freeze the chiles slivered or chopped. Use them to quickly spice up dishes such scrambled eggs, chili or tomato soup.

FYI: Mostly-mild poblanos can also be grilled stovetop if you have gas (just put them on the flame and turn with tongs) or on a stovetop grill pan. A barbecue grill works great too.

6 poblano chiles
2 tsp stick butter
2 tsp oil
½ cup sliced scallions
2 tsp minced garlic
3 ears fresh corn, kernels cut from cobs (about 1½ cups, see *Cutting Off the Kernels*, page 264)
⅓ cup chopped fresh cilantro
¾ cup (6 oz) crumbled farmer cheese
½ tsp salt
½ cup (2 oz) shredded Cheddar cheese

**1** Heat broiler. Lightly coat a large rimmed baking sheet and a 2-qt shallow baking dish with cooking spray.

**2** Put the poblanos on the baking sheet. Broil about 5 in. from heat source 15 to 20 minutes, turning chiles often to char evenly. Transfer to a bowl, cover and let cool about 10 minutes.

**3** Meanwhile, heat butter and oil in a large nonstick skillet over medium-high heat. Add scallions and garlic; cook 1 to 2 minutes, stirring often, to wilt scallions. Add corn; cook 2 to 3 minutes then add cilantro. Remove from heat and stir in farmer cheese and salt.

**4** Heat oven to 350°F. Carefully remove the now-loose skin from the poblanos. Cut poblanos in half lengthwise; remove core and seeds. Arrange poblano halves in baking dish in 1 layer. Fill each with about ½ cup corn mixture.

**5** Bake 10 minutes, top with Cheddar cheese and bake 5 minutes to melt cheese.

# Noodlecakes

VEGETARIAN · SIDE DISH OR MAIN DISH · SKILLET OR GRIDDLE

GOOD WITH ROAST CHICKEN OR PORK AT DINNER OR SOLO FOR A LIGHT MEAL.

3-oz pkg any flavor ramen noodle soup mix

2 large eggs

1 cup (6 oz) shredded zucchini

2 scallions, cut in long, narrow strips

¾ cup shredded carrot

2 Tbsp flour

2 Tbsp oil

2 Tbsp lite soy sauce

2 Tbsp fresh lemon juice

**SERVES** 4 (2 pancakes each)
**TOTAL TIME:** 25 minutes

**PER SERVING:** 231 cal, 7 g pro, 21 g car, 1 g fiber, 13 g fat (4 g sat fat), 106 mg chol, 540 mg sod

**1** Break pkg of noodles in 4 sections (reserve seasoning packet). Cook as pkg directs, then drain.

**2** Beat eggs in a medium bowl. Stir in zucchini, scallions, carrot, flour, ½ tsp seasoning from packet and the noodles.

**3** Heat 1 Tbsp oil in a large nonstick skillet (see Tip, right) over medium-high heat. Make 4 pancakes, using about one-eighth mixture for each and frying 2 to 3 minutes on each side. Then make 4 more using remaining oil.

**4** Mix soy sauce and lemon juice. Serve with pancakes.

TIP: If you have a big pancake griddle you can make all 8 pancakes at one time.

## RAMEN NOODLES

Here's how to make ramen noodles more nutritionally valuable.

· Stir in leftover vegetables such as broccoli, carrots, peas or spinach.

· Add cut or shredded cooked chicken, pork or beef, or small meatballs.

· Toss the prepared noodles with shredded red cabbage, fresh spinach and an Asian-flavored salad dressing.

· Stir in a beaten egg for fresh egg-drop soup.

# Black Bean Chili

**SERVES** 4
**TOTAL TIME:** 20 minutes

**PER SERVING:** 339 cal, 12 g pro, 72 g car, 10 g fiber, 3 g fat (0 g sat fat), 0 mg chol, 1,028 mg sod

2 cups 10-minute brown rice
Two 10-oz cans diced tomatoes and green chiles
19-oz can black beans, drained and rinsed
10-oz box frozen corn and roasted red peppers (Southwestern style)
¼ cup tomato paste
3 Tbsp fresh lime juice
TOPPINGS: **sour cream and chopped fresh cilantro**

**1** Cook rice as pkg directs.

**2** While rice cooks, put remaining ingredients in a saucepan. Cover and heat over medium heat, stirring occasionally, about 8 minutes or until slightly thickened.

**3** Serve chili with rice and Toppings.

# Rosemary Roasted Potatoes

SIDE DISH · OVEN · RIMMED BAKING SHEET

GOOD WITH ROAST CHICKEN OR PORK.

**SERVES** 4
**PREP:** 8 minutes
**ROAST:** About 40 minutes

**PER SERVING:** 244 cal, 4 g pro, 41 g car, 4 g fiber, 7 g fat (1 g sat fat), 0 mg chol, 600 mg sod

2 lb (12 to 16) small red-skinned potatoes, quartered
2 Tbsp olive oil
1 to 1½ tsp dried rosemary, crumbled
1 tsp salt

**1** Heat oven to 425°F.

**2** Place potatoes on a rimmed baking sheet. Sprinkle with oil, rosemary and salt. Stir until evenly coated.

**3** Roast, stirring potatoes once, 40 minutes, or until nicely browned and soft when pierced.

Eggplant Parmigiana *(page 252)*

Grilled Vegetables on
Garlic Toast *(page 267)*

Onions Stuffed with Butternut Squash & Sage *(page 266)*

Garlic, Olive & Parmesan
Mashed Potatoes *(page 257)*

# Garlic, Olive & Parmesan Mashed Potatoes

GOOD WITH CHICKEN, LAMB, JUST ABOUT ANYTHING.

4 baking potatoes (about 8 oz each), peeled and quartered

3 medium cloves garlic, peeled

2 Tbsp olive oil, preferably extra-virgin

⅓ cup grated Parmesan cheese

¼ cup kalamata olives, pitted and chopped

½ tsp salt

½ tsp freshly ground pepper

GARNISH: olive oil and chopped fresh parsley

**SERVES** 5
**PREP:** 10 minutes
**COOK:** 25 to 30 minutes

PER SERVING: 203 cal,
5 g pro, 26 g car, 2 g fiber,
9 g fat (2 g sat fat), 4 mg chol,
460 mg sod

**1** Cook potatoes and garlic in gently boiling water to cover 20 to 25 minutes until tender. Scoop out ⅔ cup cooking water before draining potatoes.

**2** Put hot potatoes and garlic back in pot and mash with potato masher (or beat with handheld mixer on medium-high speed), adding olive oil and the ⅔ cup cooking water. Stir in cheese, olives, salt and pepper.

**3** Spoon into serving bowl. Drizzle with a little olive oil and sprinkle with parsley.

## BUYING POTATOES

Look for firm potatoes with few or no gashes or slashes. Don't buy potatoes with wrinkled skins or dark spots. Potatoes are more fragile than they appear so handle them carefully to prevent bruising. Keep them in a cool, dark, well-ventilated place for up to 2 weeks. Freshly dug new potatoes can be refrigerated to help maintain their sweetness, but do not refrigerate mature potatoes. Don't buy potatoes that have turned green on the outside; it's not mold but a result of too much exposure to light. If there's just a small patch of green, cut it off before cooking the potato.

# Mashed Potato Pancakes with Sautéed Onion

SIDE DISH · SKILLET

NEXT TIME YOU MAKE MASHED POTATOES, MAKE EXTRA FOR THESE.

**SERVES** 6
**TOTAL TIME:** 35 minutes

PER SERVING: 201 cal,
5 g pro, 22 g car, 2 g fiber,
11 g fat (4 g sat fat), 49 mg
chol, 529 mg sod

TIP: Shred onion on large
holes of a box grater. You'll
get mushy juice, but that's
what you want.

5 slices bacon

SAUTÉED ONION
   1 tsp stick butter
   1 cup thinly sliced onion
   ¼ tsp salt

3 cups cold mashed potatoes
1 large egg
2 Tbsp shredded onion (see Tip, left)
2 Tbsp flour
1 Tbsp stick butter
SERVE WITH: **sour cream**

**1** Fry bacon until crisp, and while it's cooking take ½ tsp of the fat and put it into a large nonstick skillet. Drain bacon on paper towels.

**2** SAUTÉED ONION: Add the 1 tsp butter to the ½ tsp bacon fat. Heat over medium heat until butter stops foaming. Stir in onion and salt. Cook 10 to 12 minutes, stirring often, until onion is browned. Remove to a small bowl; cover to keep warm. Don't clean skillet.

**3** While onion cooks, put potatoes, egg and shredded onion in a bowl. Crumble in 3 slices of the bacon and stir until blended. Sprinkle flour on wax paper. Form potatoes into 6 patties. Turn in flour to coat lightly.

**4** Add 1 Tbsp butter to the skillet and heat over medium heat. When butter stops foaming, add patties and fry 4 minutes on each side or until golden. Put on a platter. Top with onions. Crumble remaining 2 strips bacon over the onions. Serve with sour cream.

# Potato-Rosemary Galette

### SIDE DISH · SKILLET · FOOD PROCESSOR

FOR BEST FLAVOR AND TEXTURE SERVE THE GALETTE AS SOON AS IT IS COOKED.

2 lb (about 4 medium) baking potatoes, peeled (see Tip, right)
1 tsp dried rosemary, crumbled
1 tsp salt
1 tsp freshly ground pepper
3 Tbsp stick butter

**SERVES** 6
**TOTAL TIME:** About 30 minutes

**PER SERVING:** 142 cal,
2 g pro, 21 g car, 2 g fiber,
6 g fat (4 g sat fat), 16 mg chol,
454 mg sod

**1** Dry potatoes with paper towels then quickly shred using a food processor or the large holes of a 4-sided grater (see Tip, right). Put shredded potatoes in a dry bowl. Add rosemary, salt and pepper; toss to mix.

**2** Melt 2 Tbsp butter in a large nonstick skillet over medium-high heat until butter stops foaming. Add potatoes, pressing them with a spatula into an even layer.

TIP: Submerge the peeled potatoes in a bowl of cold water to prevent browning.

**3** Cook 2 to 3 minutes, pressing down occasionally with the spatula, until lightly browned on bottom. Cut remaining 1 Tbsp butter in small pieces and scatter over the top. Cover skillet, reduce heat to medium and cook 6 to 8 minutes until potatoes are tender.

**4** Uncover and invert a baking sheet over skillet. Holding both together with oven mitts or potholders, carefully invert galette onto the baking sheet. Slide galette back into skillet, increase heat to medium-high and cook 5 minutes or until browned on bottom. Slide onto serving plate, cut in wedges and serve promptly.

TIP: A food processor fitted with a shredding disk shreds the potatoes in seconds.

# Sweet Potato Puddin'

SIDE DISH · OVEN · 1½-QT SOUFFLÉ DISH OR DEEP CASSEROLE

**SERVES** 6
**PREP:** 25 minutes
**BAKE:** About 35 minutes

**PER SERVING:** 221 cal,
3 g pro, 34 g car, 2 g fiber,
8 g fat (4 g sat fat), 86 mg chol,
174 mg sod

1½ lb sweet potatoes, peeled and cut in 1½-in. chunks
3 Tbsp granulated sugar
3 Tbsp packed brown sugar
3 Tbsp stick butter
2 large eggs, yolks separated from whites, whites put into a
   medium bowl
1 tsp baking powder
1 tsp ground cinnamon
1 tsp vanilla extract

**1** Boil sweet potatoes in water to cover 15 minutes or until tender. Just before draining, scoop out ¼ cup of the cooking water.

**2** While sweet potatoes cook, heat oven to 350°F. Grease a 1½-qt soufflé dish or deep casserole and coat with 2 Tbsp granulated sugar.

**3** Mash the drained sweet potatoes until smooth, adding the ¼ cup cooking water, the brown sugar, butter, egg yolks, baking powder, cinnamon and vanilla.

**4** Beat egg whites until soft peaks form when beaters are lifted. Beat in remaining 1 Tbsp granulated sugar until whites are stiff and glossy. Fold into sweet potato mixture; transfer to prepared baking dish.

**5** Bake 35 minutes or until puffed and top is lightly browned. Serve immediately.

# Lemony Baked Sweet Potatoes

4 medium (8 oz each) sweet potatoes, scrubbed
1 Tbsp freshly grated lemon peel
1 Tbsp fresh lemon juice
2 Tbsp stick butter, melted

**SERVES** 4
**PREP:** 5 minutes
**BAKE:** About 45 minutes

**PER SERVING:** 224 cal,
3 g pro, 40 g car, 5 g fiber,
6 g fat (4 g saturated fat),
16 mg chol, 80 mg sod

**1** Heat oven to 350°F. Pierce sweet potatoes in several places with a knife. Bake directly on oven rack 45 minutes or until tender when pierced.

**2** Meanwhile, stir lemon peel and juice into melted butter.

**3** Cut a slit in top of each sweet potato; push ends toward center to open. Fluff with a fork. Add lemon butter, salt and pepper to taste.

# Mashed Butternut Squash & Apples

One 3-lb butternut squash, halved lengthwise, seeds and
    strings removed
3 large Golden Delicious apples (1½ lb), halved and cored
2 Tbsp sweetened dried cranberries
½ stick (¼ cup) butter, cut in small pieces
2 tsp freshly grated lemon peel
1 tsp salt
½ tsp freshly ground pepper

**SERVES** 6
**PREP:** 20 minutes
**BAKE:** About 40 minutes

**PER SERVING:** 175 cal,
2 g pro, 27 g car, 2 g fiber,
8 g fat (5 g sat fat), 21 mg chol,
468 mg sod

**1** Heat oven to 400°F. Coat a baking sheet with cooking spray and put squash and apples on it, cut sides down. Bake 40 minutes or until squash is fork-tender and apples are very soft. Let stand until cool enough to handle.

**2** Meanwhile, put cranberries in a small bowl, add 1 cup boiling water and let soak while squash and apples bake.

**3** Scoop squash and apple pulp into a bowl. Add butter, lemon peel, salt and pepper and mash with a potato masher or beat with a mixer. Drain cranberries and fold in.

**4** Spoon into a serving dish and, if needed, reheat in microwave.

**TIP:** Can be made up to 2 days ahead. Cover and refrigerate in a baking dish. Reheat, covered, in a 350°F oven 20 to 30 minutes, or in microwave.

# Tuscan Kale

**SERVES** 4
**TOTAL TIME:** About 20 minutes

**PER SERVING:** 133 cal,
4 g pro, 16 g car, 2 g fiber,
7 g fat (1 g sat fat), 0 mg chol,
321 mg sod

**TIP:** Keep a lookout in your market for Tuscan kale, which has flatter, darker leaves and a rich flavor.

**FYI:** Toasted almonds give this a delightful crunch, but if you can try it the Tuscan way: with toasted pignoli (pine nuts) instead.

2 tsp olive oil, preferably extra-virgin
¼ cup slivered almonds
1 large clove garlic, thinly sliced
1 lb fresh kale, leaves very coarsely chopped (see *Prepping Greens*, below)
¼ cup raisins
½ tsp salt

**1** Heat 1 tsp oil in a large nonstick skillet over medium heat. Stir in almonds and cook 2 minutes, shaking pan often, until lightly toasted. Put into a small bowl.

**2** Heat remaining 1 tsp oil in same skillet. Add garlic and cook 1 to 2 minutes, stirring often, until just starting to color. Add ⅓ cup water, the kale, raisins and salt.

**3** Cover and cook, stirring once, 5 to 6 minutes until greens are tender and water is nearly evaporated. Stir in almonds; serve immediately.

## PREPPING GREENS

Most of the dark-green leafy vegetable family has tough stems, but this problem is quickly resolved.

**For kale, collards and turnip greens:** Hold the stem in one hand. With the other fold the leaf over and pull it off, all in one quick motion. Discard the stems.

**Swiss chard and beet greens** have tender stems but stems are best removed as above, cut into 1-in. lengths and cooked for a minute or two before the leaves are added.

Wash all leaves in two or three changes of warm water. Then stack several leaves roughly together on a cutting board and cut them into approximately 1-in. widths.

**Broccoli rabe** also has tender stems and is easiest to cut before washing. Cut off and discard the bottom 2 in. or so (usually below the tie or string that holds the bunch). Remove the tie. Keeping the bunch together, cut into roughly 2-in. lengths. Then wash thoroughly.

# Snap Beans Gremolata

12 oz green beans, stem ends trimmed

12 oz yellow wax beans, stem ends trimmed

½ cup finely chopped fresh flat-leaf (Italian) parsley

1 Tbsp freshly grated lemon peel

1 Tbsp fresh lemon juice

1 Tbsp olive oil

2 tsp minced garlic

½ tsp salt

½ tsp freshly ground pepper

**SERVES** 6
**TOTAL TIME:** About 30 minutes

PER SERVING: 56 cal, 2 g pro, 8 g car, 2 g fiber, 2 g fat (0 g sat fat), 0 mg chol, 201 mg sod

**FYI:** See *Gremolata*, FYI, page 152.

1 Bring a large pot of water to a rapid boil, add beans and cook 7 to 8 minutes until just tender. Drain well.

2 Meanwhile put remaining ingredients in a serving bowl and stir until well blended.

3 Add hot beans; toss to mix and coat.

## SUGAR SNAPS AND SNOW PEAS

One wonderful attribute of sugar snap peas and snow peas is that there is no shelling. They are eaten crisp sweet pods and all. Flat-podded snow peas are often seen in Chinese dishes. Either pea is great added to carrots, green peas or broccoli rabe for the last minute of cooking time. Sugar snaps (also known as snap peas) and snow peas make a great snack for kids, good dippers or a crunchy addition to a salad. For crisper texture and brighter color blanch them first: Put them in a strainer and lower the strainer into a pan of boiling water. Count to 10, lift out the strainer and immediately rinse the peas under cold water to prevent further cooking.

Trim snow peas by nipping off the tip and the stem end. Sugar snaps—which are a cross between snow peas and shelling peas—may already have strings removed. Bend the tip of a sugar snap and pull it toward you; if there is a string, it will pull off with the tip. Bad news for family members usually assigned to shell green peas: If snap peas are too mature to eat raw, they may be shelled and cooked like regular green peas.

# Corn & Tiny Tomatoes

## SIDE DISH · SKILLET

GREAT WITH STEAK OR BURGERS. MAKE A LOT AND IT'S A CONVENIENT WAY TO
SERVE FRESH CORN TO A CROWD.

**SERVES** 4
**TOTAL TIME:** About 10 minutes

**PER SERVING:** 100 cal,
2 g pro, 14 g car, 3 g fiber,
5 g fat (2 g sat fat), 5 mg chol,
323 mg sod

TIP: Depending on what's in the market, you might want to mix small yellow tomatoes with the red ones.

TIP: The corn can be cut off the cobs (see *Cutting Off the Kernels*, right) a few hours ahead, covered and refrigerated.

2 tsp olive oil

2 tsp stick butter

3 ears fresh corn, kernels cut from cobs (about 1½ cups, see *Cutting Off the Kernels*, below)

1 pt mixed little tomatoes (such as grape, cherry and pear)

⅓ cup chopped chives

½ tsp salt

½ tsp freshly ground pepper

**1** Heat oil and butter in a large nonstick skillet over medium-high heat. Stir in corn and tomatoes and cook 2 to 3 minutes, stirring often, until tomatoes just begin to split.

**2** Remove from heat; stir in chives, salt and pepper.

### CUTTING OFF THE KERNELS

Pull husks off corn. Kernels tend to fly so work on a large plate or put a large piece of parchment or wax paper on a cutting board. Hold husk, stem end up, in one hand. Using a good sharp knife, cut kernels off cob from middle to tip, turning the ear of corn around as you cut. Then flip cob so tip is up and cut off remaining kernels the same way.

When corn is very fresh it is worth scraping the husk to remove any soft part still inside where the kernels came out. This is especially good to add to the kernels when making a corn chowder or other creamy corn dish.

# Swiss Chard with Walnuts

## SIDE DISH · SKILLET

¼ cup walnut pieces

1 Tbsp olive oil

1½ cups chopped onions

3 cloves garlic, thinly sliced

1½ lb Swiss chard, stems cut in 1-in. pieces, leaves coarsely
chopped, stems and leaves kept separate
(see *Prepping Greens*, page 262)

¼ tsp salt

¼ tsp freshly ground pepper

2 tsp fresh lemon juice, or more to taste

**SERVES** 4
**TOTAL TIME:** About 20 minutes

**PER SERVING:** 137 cal,
5 g pro, 14 g car, 4 g fiber,
8 g fat (1 g sat fat), 0 mg chol,
509 mg sod

**1** Stir walnuts in a large nonstick skillet over medium heat until toasted. Remove to a plate.

**2** Heat oil in skillet over medium heat. Add onions and garlic; cook about 4 minutes, stirring often, until onions are soft.

**3** Stir in chard stems and 3 Tbsp water. Cover and cook 4 minutes until stems are crisp-tender (add more water if onions are browning too much).

**4** Add chard leaves a handful at a time, adding more as they cook down. When all the leaves have cooked down, cook 2 to 3 minutes until tender. Season with salt, pepper and lemon juice. Serve sprinkled with walnuts.

# Onions Stuffed with Butternut Squash & Sage

VEGETARIAN · SIDE DISH OR MAIN DISH · OVEN · 13 X 9-IN. BAKING DISH

A FESTIVE SIDE DISH FOR THE HOLIDAYS.

**SERVES** 8 (side dish) or 4 (main dish)
**PREP:** 40 minutes
**BAKE:** 25 minutes

**PER SERVING** (as side dish): 275 cal, 12 g pro, 35 g car, 5 g fiber, 12 g fat (7 g sat fat), 35 mg chol, 365 mg sod

TIP: The onions can be stuffed up to 8 hours ahead, covered and refrigerated.

TIP: Only half the raw onion scraped out of each onion is cooked for the stuffing. If you can't use the rest right away, refrigerate or freeze it. You'll be glad you did another day when you are in a rush and need chopped onion.

6 cups ¾-in. chunks peeled butternut squash (from a 2¼-lb squash)

8 large, sweet onions (about 12 oz each)

3 Tbsp stick butter

Salt

3 Tbsp finely chopped fresh sage leaves (about 12 large), or 2 tsp dried

1½ cups (6 oz) shredded Gruyère cheese

GARNISH: **fresh sage leaves**

**1** Have ready a 13 x 9-in. baking dish.

**2** Put squash chunks in a medium saucepan; add water to cover. Bring to a boil, reduce heat, cover and simmer 15 to 20 minutes until tender. Drain well, then mash.

**3** While squash cooks, peel onions and cut a ½-in.-thick slice off the tops. Cut a smaller slice from root ends so onions can stand upright. With a melon baller or serrated teaspoon, scoop flesh from centers, leaving a ½-in.-thick shell. Reserve scooped flesh.

**4** Wrap 4 onions in dampened paper towels and put on a dish. Microwave on high 10 minutes or until just tender. Unwrap; place in the baking dish. Cook remaining 4 onions the same way.

**5** Chop half the scooped-out flesh. (The rest can be used for something else.)

**6** Heat oven to 375°F. While onion shells cook, melt butter in a large nonstick skillet over medium heat. Add chopped onion and ½ tsp salt. Cook 9 to 10 minutes, stirring often, until browned and tender. Stir in sage.

**7** Stir onion mixture and 1¼ cups cheese into the mashed squash. Sprinkle onion shells with ¼ tsp salt. Spoon squash mixture into onions, mounding slightly.

**8** Bake, uncovered, 20 minutes. Top with remaining ¼ cup cheese and bake 5 minutes or until cheese melts. Garnish with sage leaves.

# Grilled Vegetables on Garlic Toast

2 red or green peppers, quartered

1 yellow squash (about 8 oz), cut in half lengthwise

1 zucchini (about 8 oz), cut in half lengthwise

1 medium red onion, cut in 8 wedges (see Tip, right)

6 oz portobello mushroom caps

1 lb asparagus, woody ends snapped off

Cooking spray, preferably olive oil

½ tsp salt

½ tsp freshly ground pepper

4 slices frozen garlic Texas Toast (from an 11.25 oz box, see Tip, right)

½ cup Caesar dressing

4 oz arugula, large leaves torn in half

**SERVES** 4
**PREP:** 20 minutes
**GRILL:** About 25 minutes

**PER SERVING:** 375 cal, 9 g pro, 34 g car, 4 g fiber, 24 g fat (4 g sat fat), 3 mg chol, 917 mg sod

1  Heat outdoor grill or large stovetop grill pan.

2  Lightly coat vegetables with cooking spray; sprinkle with salt and pepper.

3  Grill vegetables, turning as needed: peppers and squash about 12 minutes, onions and mushroom caps 10 minutes and asparagus 5 minutes, until tender and lightly charred. Transfer to a cutting board; cut in bite-size pieces.

4  Grill garlic bread as pkg directs. Put a slice on each plate.

5  Put vegetables in a large bowl. Add dressing and arugula; toss to mix and coat. Spoon on bread.

TIP: To keep the onion wedges from falling apart, thread them on skewers (water-soaked if wood) before grilling.

TIP: Buy the garlic bread you prefer, from bakery section or freezer.

# Roasted Fall Vegetables

WHEN VEGETABLES ROAST AT A HIGH TEMPERATURE MOISTURE EVAPORATES AND SOME OF THEIR NATURAL SUGARS CARAMELIZE, LENDING THE VEGETABLES MARVELOUS FLAVOR.

**SERVES** 6
**PREP:** 20 minutes
**BAKE:** 45 minutes

**PER SERVING:** 166 cal, 4 g pro, 29 g car, 8 g fiber, 5 g fat (1 g sat fat), 0 mg chol, 555 mg sod

**TIP:** Young bunched carrots don't need peeling. Just scrape them with a small, sharp knife.

1-lb bunch or bag carrots (see Tip, left)
1 lb parsnips
2 medium beets (¾ lb, see *Beets*, below)
1 medium sweet onion
9-oz tub Brussels sprouts, trimmed
2 Tbsp olive oil
1¼ tsp salt
¼ to ½ tsp freshly ground pepper

**1** Position racks to divide oven in thirds. Heat to 450°F. Line 2 rimmed baking sheets with foil.

**2** Cut carrots and parsnips in 2½ x ½-in. sticks, beets and onion in ½-in.-thick wedges. Put in a large bowl with Brussels sprouts, oil, salt and pepper; toss to mix and coat. Spread half on each baking sheet.

**3** Bake, stirring once, 45 minutes or until vegetables are lightly charred and tender.

**BEETS**
If you are grilling or roasting beets as here, peel them first with a swivel-head vegetable peeler. If you are boiling them, do not peel them first as they will lose a great deal of their color. Just scrub the beets, then boil in water to cover. Medium size ones will be tender after about 30 minutes.
Drain the beets, fill the pan with cold water and let cool a few minutes. The skin will then slip off easily in your hands.

# Tomato Tart

10-oz can refrigerated pizza crust

8-oz brick ⅓-less-fat cream cheese (Neufchâtel), softened

½ cup finely chopped fresh basil leaves

1 tsp minced garlic

½ tsp dried thyme

6 ripe plum tomatoes, sliced ¼ in. thick

2 tsp olive oil

¼ tsp salt

GARNISH: freshly ground pepper and fresh basil leaves

**SERVES** 12
**TOTAL TIME:** 25 minutes

**PER SERVING:** 116 cal,
4 g pro, 12 g car, 1 g fiber,
6 g fat (3 g sat fat), 13 mg chol,
360 mg sod

**1** Heat oven to 425°F. Unroll crust on a lightly greased baking sheet; press into a 13 x 10-in. rectangle. Bake 12 to 14 minutes or until lightly browned. Reduce oven to 350°F.

**2** Mix cream cheese, basil, garlic and thyme in a small bowl until well blended. Spread evenly on crust. Top with tomatoes, drizzle with oil and sprinkle with salt.

**3** Bake 8 minutes to warm tomatoes and develop flavors.

**4** Cut tart in 24 pieces. Sprinkle with pepper and garnish with basil leaves. Serve warm or at room temperature.

# Cakes & Cookies

There is something inherently satisfying about pouring a batter into a pan or putting raw cookie dough onto a baking sheet and not so much later, as wonderful smells of baking flour, sugar and spice fill the air, taking a baked cake or cookies out of the oven. No matter how often you do this, the feeling of satisfaction is there. The only tough part: waiting for the cake or cookies to cool before sampling. In this chapter you will find a wide variety of cake and cookie flavors to choose from, including plenty of chocolate, of course. You will also find several cakes made from mixes, since we find that many readers like to let someone else hunt down the baking powder and cinnamon and do the measuring. Speaking of measuring, careful attention to it is important when baking. Check page 272 for details on how to measure flour, baking powder, spices and liquids. Measure all the ingredients before you start mixing them. Enjoy the baking. But most of all, enjoy the tasting.

## MEASURING

With a stew or a pasta dish, a little more or a little less meat, onion or broth isn't going to make or break the results. But when it comes to baking, accurate measuring of ingredients is essential to success.

For dry ingredients, including flour, sugar, baking powder and spices (also for small amounts of liquids such as vanilla and lemon juice), use nested measures that come in sets and are sized to the rim: ¼, ⅓, ½ and 1 cup; ⅛, ¼, ½, 1 teaspoon (tsp) and 1 tablespoon (Tbsp).

Buy good quality metal or plastic nested cups with sturdy handles that are clearly marked with the amount they hold. Have at least two sets of measuring cups and spoons (for ease). When you bake, especially if you are on the learning track, there are lots of distractions in your home or you are trying a recipe for the first time, measure all the ingredients before you begin and set them out, still in the measuring cups or spoons, on a tray or baking sheet. Do a final check against the recipe before you start mixing. That way, if you do get distracted, you can quickly tell whether or not you have added the baking powder to a cake batter.

FLOUR: If the recipe calls for ¾ cup flour, take a ½-cup measure and a ¼ cup. Put a strip of wax paper on the counter. Stir the flour in the bag or canister. Working over the wax paper (or the bag or canister), spoon flour lightly into the ½-cup measure until it is overflowing. Do not tap the cup on the counter, or press down the flour. Then take a metal spatula (or any straight edge) and sweep off the excess. Measure the ¼ cup in the same way. Use the wax paper to pour the spilled flour back into the bag.

Use this method also for measuring cocoa, confectioners' sugar and cornstarch.

SUGAR: Scoop up the sugar in the appropriate cup measure(s) and level off the surface. Use this method for other compact ingredients such as cornmeal and rice.

BROWN SUGAR: Since brown sugar does not find its own level if scooped or spooned, pack it firmly into a cup measure until level with the rim.

SPICES, BAKING POWDER, BAKING SODA: Use nested teaspoon/tablespoons to measure. Slip measuring spoon into container of baking powder or baking soda, then level off excess with a small metal spatula or other straight edge. If the neck of a spice jar is too narrow for a measuring spoon to pass through, pour the spice into the spoon over a small piece of wax paper until spoon is overflowing. Then sweep off the excess. Use the piece of wax paper to pour the excess spice back into the jar.

MILK, WATER AND OTHER LIQUIDS: Use a stainless steel or clear polycarbonate angled measuring cup that allows you to check the liquid level from the top. Or use clear glass or plastic measures and check the liquid level by looking through the side of the measure.

SOUR CREAM, YOGURT AND OTHER SEMISOLIDS: Use the nested cups. It's hard to get a level surface of sour cream in a glass or plastic measure.

BUTTER: To measure butter, use the marks on the paper each stick is wrapped in. If the wrapper is off center and you need to measure accurately for a cake or cookies, unfold it and reposition the butter before cutting.

## SOFTENING BUTTER AND CREAM CHEESE

The best way to soften butter or cream cheese so they can be beaten easily is to cut them up and leave them at room temperature for 15 or 20 minutes, depending on how warm or cold the room is. Butter is soft enough when it yields to gentle pressure from your fingertips. Do not leave it in a hot kitchen for hours; it will get too soft, too close to being melted butter and will not beat properly.

Butter can also be softened in the microwave, but be extremely careful. If you melt the butter instead of just softening it, it will not regain volume when beaten with sugar. Start again with fresh butter and save the melted butter for other cooking.

## STORING COOKIES

Storing cookies may never be a problem: The cookies may be eaten before baking day is out. However, should you be baking ahead for a party or the holidays, here are some general guidelines to follow, unless a recipe specifies otherwise:

- Store cookies airtight in tightly closed plastic bags, foil packets, tins, cookie jars with tight-fitting lids or rigid plastic storage containers. If cookies are moist or sticky, separate layers with wax paper or parchment paper.
- Don't store crisp and soft cookies in the same container.
- Unless a recipe states otherwise, all of the cookies in this book can be stored airtight at room temperature up to 2 weeks, or frozen in freezer bags or containers up to 3 months.
- Unwrap frosted or decorated frozen cookies before thawing or icing may stick to wrapping.

## SEPARATING EGGS

Recipes often call for separating the yolks of eggs from the whites so that the whites may be beaten separately and folded into the batter to help lighten it. When the cake bakes, the air beaten into the egg whites expands, helping to lighten the cake.

It is easiest to separate the yolks from the whites when the eggs are very cold. But the whites beat to a greater volume when they are at room temperature. Solution: When a recipe calls for separating yolks from whites do that first. Put the whites into the bowl in which they will be beaten, then let them come to room temperature while you organize the rest of the ingredients. Put the yolks in a small custard cup and cover to prevent a skin forming on the top.

An egg separator does the separating quickly. Look for one that is made of stainless steel, not plastic or (breakable) ceramic. Put the separator over a small bowl (a custard cup works fine) and carefully break an egg into it. The white will fall through to the cup and the yolk will stay on the top.

To separate eggs by hand, have two small cups, plus the bowl the egg whites will be beaten in. Crack open one egg by tapping it firmly but gently on the table. Pull shell apart while holding egg over a small cup and let the white fall in. Move the yolk back and forth two or three times from half shell to half shell so as to get out as much white as possible. Put the yolk into the other small cup. If there is a lot of white left in the shell, scoop it out with a finger.

With luck the yolk will be intact with no specks of yolk or bits of shell in with the white. Tip the white into the large bowl it will be beaten in and discard the shell. If there are specks of yolk or shell in with the white, scoop them out with a teaspoon.

## BAKING

Before turning on the oven check that the shelf or shelves are in the right position. Cakes and cookies should bake on a shelf in the middle of the oven. Allow time for the oven to heat.

If you are baking three cake layers at once, stagger them on the shelves. That is, put one layer in the middle of the top shelf; two other layers on a lower shelf, but toward the edge of the oven and not directly opposite each other. About halfway through baking, turn and change the pans around so the cakes bake evenly.

For even baking, bake only one sheet of cookies at a time. (Unless using a convection oven—the hot air continuously circulates making it possible to bake two or three sheets of cookies at a time.)

Always put unbaked cookies on a cold baking sheet. If you bake a lot of cookies, it's worth having two or three baking sheets for speed. Or while the first batch is baking shape the second batch and put the cookies on a sheet of foil. This way you can slide off the first batch and as soon as the sheet is cool slide on the next.

## BAKING PANS

When buying baking pans keep in mind that pans with a darker finish bake darker. For most cakes a light finish is best.

Nonstick pans are helpful for more complicated shapes, such a bundt or turk's head, but you still have to grease them.

If you are a beginning baker consider using disposable foil pans for your first attempts. When ready to graduate to cake pans proper, buy good quality, heavy aluminum ones that will last forever. Take a tape measure to the store; layer cake pans are not always the diameter they claim. Buy layer cake pans with straight sides that are 2 in. high, as many cakes need them.

## SPRINGFORM PAN

A springform pan consists of a bottom with removable wrap-around sides. It is invaluable for making cheesecakes and streusel-topped cakes where turning the cake upside down to get it out of the pan (as for most cakes) is not possible. A small catch fastens and releases the sides, and the cake can be served on the pan bottom or carefully eased onto a plate with a spatula.

## PASTRY BLENDER

A pastry blender is used for cutting butter up in a bowl of flour. The tool consists of six steel wires suspended from a handle. While slowly turning the bowl with one hand quickly draw the pastry blender through the flour over and over again, gradually chopping the butter into tiny, flour-coated pieces. When it's ready, the mixture should look like coarse cornmeal.

A food processor can also cut butter into flour very well. Put the flour and any salt called for into the work bowl. Pulse a few times to mix salt and flour. Cut the cold butter into small pieces and scatter it over the flour. A very few presses of the "pulse" button and the job is done.

# Oatmeal Superchip Cookies

## MIXER · BAKING SHEETS

How long will they keep? Room temperature, 1 week; freezer, 2 months.

2 sticks (1 cup) butter, softened
¾ cup packed light-brown sugar
½ cup granulated sugar
1 tsp ground cinnamon
2 large eggs
2 tsp vanilla extract
1 tsp baking soda
½ tsp salt
1½ cups all-purpose flour
3 cups old-fashioned or quick oats
11.5- or 12-oz bag semisweet chocolate chunks, chopped
1 cup pecans, chopped

**MAKES** 45
**PREP:** 10 minutes
**BAKE:** About 25 minutes

**PER COOKIE:** 151 cal,
2 g pro, 18 g car, 1 g fiber,
9 g fat (4 g sat fat), 20 mg chol,
101 mg sod

**1** Heat oven to 350°F. Have baking sheet(s) ready.

**2** Put butter, both sugars, cinnamon, eggs, vanilla, baking soda and salt in a large bowl. Beat with mixer, starting on low speed and increasing to high, until well blended. Reduce speed to low; beat in flour just until blended. Stir in oats, chocolate and pecans.

**3** Drop rounded tablespoons about 1 in. apart on ungreased baking sheet(s). Bake one sheet at a time, 10 to 12 minutes or until cookies are golden brown. Cool 1 minute on baking sheet, then remove to a wire rack to cool.

# Wickedly Good Whoopie Pies

HOW LONG WILL THEY KEEP? REFRIGERATOR, 1 WEEK; FREEZER, 1 MONTH.

**MAKES 30**
PREP: 1 hour 5 minutes
BAKE: About 35 minutes

**PER COOKIE:** 142 cal,
2 g pro, 21 g car, 1 g fiber,
6 g fat (4 g sat fat), 22 mg chol,
172 mg sod

**TIP:** Lightly grease the measuring cup and spoon before spooning marshmallow cream into them and it will come out very easily and cleanly. A quick wipe with a paper towel moistened with oil, butter or solid vegetable shortening, or use cooking spray.

**MAKING WHOOPIE PIES**

Whoopie Pies are a Pennsylvania Dutch treat. The name? One thought is that when Pennsylvania Dutch women were baking cakes they might pour spoonfuls of the batter onto a baking sheet and bake them for after-school treats. When excited kids saw the treats they called out "whoopee."

BATTER
  1 stick (½ cup) butter, softened
  1 cup granulated sugar
  1½ tsp baking soda
  ½ tsp baking powder
  ½ tsp salt
  1 large egg
  1 tsp vanilla extract
  ½ cup unsweetened cocoa powder
  1 cup 1% lowfat milk
  2 cups all-purpose flour

FILLING
  ¾ stick (6 Tbsp) butter, melted
  1 cup plus 2 Tbsp confectioners' sugar
  1 cup plus 2 Tbsp marshmallow cream (see Tip, left)
  1½ tsp vanilla extract

**1** Heat oven to 375°F. Coat baking sheet(s) with cooking spray.

**2** BATTER: Put butter, sugar, baking soda, baking powder and salt in a large bowl and beat with mixer on medium speed until fluffy. Beat in egg and vanilla, then cocoa until blended. With mixer on low speed, slowly beat in milk until blended. Stir in flour.

**3** Drop level tablespoons batter 2 in. apart on prepared baking sheet(s). Bake, one sheet at a time, 8 minutes or until tops spring back when lightly pressed. Cool on baking sheet 1 minute before removing to a wire rack to cool completely. Repeat with remaining batter.

**4** FILLING: Put all ingredients in a bowl and stir vigorously until blended and smooth.

**5** Spread 2 tsp filling onto flat side of half the cookies; sandwich with another cookie, pressing to adhere. Store with wax paper between layers.

# Cornmeal Lemon Drop Cookies

## MIXER · BAKING SHEET(S)

How long will they keep? Room temperature, 1 week.

2 sticks (1 cup) butter, softened
½ cup granulated sugar
½ cup packed light-brown sugar
½ tsp baking soda
¼ tsp salt
2 large eggs
2 tsp freshly grated lemon peel
1 Tbsp fresh lemon juice
1¾ cups all-purpose flour
¾ cup yellow cornmeal

ICING
1½ cups confectioners' sugar
2 Tbsp milk

40 lemon drop candies, finely crushed (see Tip, right)

**MAKES 48**
**TOTAL TIME:** 50 minutes

**PER COOKIE:** 98 cal, 1 g pro, 14 g car, 0 g fiber, 4 g fat (2 g sat fat), 19 mg chol, 68 mg sod

**1** Heat oven to 350°F. Have baking sheet(s) ready.

**2** Put butter, sugars, baking soda and salt in a large bowl. Beat with mixer on medium speed until pale and fluffy. Beat in eggs, lemon peel and juice until well blended.

**3** On low speed, gradually beat in flour and cornmeal until blended.

**4** Drop rounded measuring teaspoons dough 2 in. apart on (ungreased) baking sheet(s). Bake 6 to 8 minutes or until golden brown around edges. Cool on sheet 1 minute before removing to wire rack to cool completely.

**5** ICING: Whisk confectioners' sugar and milk in a small bowl until smooth. Scrape Icing into a ziptop bag. Snip tiny tip off 1 corner and pipe a spiral on each cookie. Before icing dries, spoon crushed candies into a wire strainer and dust tops. Let dry completely. Store with wax paper between layers.

**TIP:** To crush the hard lemon candies, put one large ziptop bag inside another. Fill inner bag with candies. Close bags and crush candies to powder with the flat side of a hammer.

**FYI:** You will need a wire strainer to sift the crushed candies over the cookies.

# Cinnamon Crisps

## MIXER · BAKING SHEET(S)

How long will they keep? Room temperature, 2 weeks; freezer, 3 months.

**MAKES 48**
**TOTAL TIME:** About 1 hour

**PER COOKIE:** 85 cal, 1 g pro, 14 g car, 0 g fiber, 3 g fat (2 g sat fat), 12 mg chol, 51 mg sod

**UNSALTED BUTTER**
Unsalted butter can be used in place of lightly salted butter in any recipe and without adding additional salt.

**Tip:** Pearl sugar can be found in stores selling baking supplies (especially Scandinavian ones). Or go to an online search engine and enter "pearl sugar."

1½ sticks (¾ cup) unsalted butter, softened
1 cup sugar
1 tsp baking powder
1 tsp baking soda
2½ tsp ground cinnamon
¼ tsp salt
1 large egg
¼ cup light (unsulphured) molasses
2⅔ cups all-purpose flour
Decoration: ¾ cup pearl sugar (see Tip, left) or coarse white (crystal) sugar

**1** Heat oven to 375°F. Line baking sheet(s) with foil.

**2** Put butter and sugar in a medium bowl and beat with mixer on high speed until pale and fluffy. Reduce speed; add baking powder, baking soda, cinnamon and salt; beat until well combined. Add egg; beat at medium speed until blended, then beat in molasses. On low speed, beat in flour until just blended.

**3** Shape dough in 1-in. balls; roll in pearl sugar. Place 2 in. apart on foil-lined baking sheet(s).

**4** Bake 8 to 10 minutes until cookies are light brown around edges and tops crackle. Transfer to a wire rack to cool.

# Hazelnut Snowballs

HOW LONG WILL THEY KEEP? REFRIGERATOR, 1 WEEK.

1 cup hazelnuts, toasted (see *Toasting Hazelnuts*, right)
2 sticks (1 cup) cold unsalted butter, cut in small pieces
1¾ cups confectioners' sugar
2 tsp vanilla extract
2 cups all-purpose flour

**MAKES 64**
**TOTAL TIME:** 1 hour

**PER COOKIE:** 64 cal, 1 g pro, 7 g car, 0 g fiber, 4 g fat (2 g sat fat), 8 mg chol, 1 mg sod

**1** Heat oven to 325°F. Have baking sheet(s) ready.

**2** Finely grind nuts in food processor (but watch, don't grind them into hazelnut butter). Add butter, ¼ cup confectioners' sugar and the vanilla. Process, scraping bowl often, just long enough to blend. Add flour; pulse for a few seconds, then process until combined.

**3** With lightly floured hands, roll dough into 1-in. balls. Place 1 in. apart on (ungreased) baking sheet(s).

**4** Bake about 15 minutes until bottoms are light brown. Cool on sheets on a wire rack 15 minutes. Gently (cookies are fragile) roll warm cookies in remaining confectioners' sugar. Cool, then roll in sugar again. Store with wax paper between layers.

**TOASTING HAZELNUTS**
Spread nuts on a rimmed baking sheet. Bake at 350°F 10 to 12 minutes until fragrant and the papery skins begin to flake. Cool slightly, wrap in a kitchen towel and rub off loosened skins. Cool, then pick out nuts.
Hazelnuts can occasionally be purchased already skinned and toasted.

# Almond-Cranberry Rugelach

## FOOD PROCESSOR · BAKING SHEET(S)

HOW LONG WILL THEY KEEP? ROOM TEMPERATURE, UP TO 4 DAYS.

MAKES 36
TOTAL TIME: 2 hours (includes
1 hour chilling dough)

PER RUGELACH: 105 cal,
2 g pro, 12 g car, 1 g fiber,
5 g fat (2 g sat fat), 14 mg chol,
28 mg sod

TIP: You can use the food processor to chop the almonds and the cranberries separately.

### DOUGH
½ of a 7-oz pkg almond paste (not marzipan)
1½ cups all-purpose flour
2 Tbsp packed light-brown sugar
¼ tsp salt
¾ stick (6 Tbsp) unsalted butter, cut in pieces
3-oz package cream cheese

### FILLING
1 cup almonds, toasted and very finely chopped
   (see *Toasting Nuts*, page 189, see Tip, left)
1 cup frozen or fresh cranberries, very finely chopped
   (see Tip, left)
⅔ cup packed light-brown sugar
½ tsp ground cinnamon

### TOPPING
1 large egg, lightly beaten
2 Tbsp granulated sugar
¼ tsp ground cinnamon

**1** DOUGH: Crumble almond paste into food processor. Pulse until fine crumbs. Add flour, sugar and salt; process until almond paste is incorporated into flour. Add butter and cream cheese; pulse until mixture starts to clump together to form a dough. Transfer mixture to work surface; press together and knead until a dough forms. Divide dough in thirds. On a lightly floured surface, shape each portion into a ½-in.-thick disk. Wrap individually in plastic wrap; refrigerate 1 hour.

**2** Heat oven to 350°F. Line baking sheet with parchment paper or nonstick foil. Mix Filling ingredients in a medium bowl.

**3** Take one disk dough from refrigerator. On floured surface, roll it into a 9-in. circle then trim to an even 8½-in. circle (see Tip, left). Spread a scant ½ cup filling over the dough, pressing lightly so it adheres. With pizza wheel or knife, cut circle in 12 wedges. Slide a

TIP: To trim dough to an even 8½-in. circle put a plate, bowl or other light object 8½ in. in diameter on top of dough and cut around it with a small knife.

spatula under one wedge and pull it out from the circle. Roll up from wide edge to point and place point-side down on prepared baking sheet. Repeat with remaining wedges, placing them 2 in. apart. (If there's room on the baking sheet, roll out another disk of dough now; if not, continue while first batch bakes.)

**4** TOPPING: Before baking, brush rugelach with some of the egg. Mix sugar and cinnamon in a cup; sprinkle over cookies.

**5** Bake 21 to 23 minutes, until lightly browned. Cool on rack on baking sheet.

# Pine Nut Macaroons

### FOOD PROCESSOR · BAKING SHEET(S)

How long will they keep? Best eaten within 2 weeks, or freeze up to 3 months.

8-oz can or 7-oz pkg almond paste (not marzipan),
    cut in small pieces
⅔ cup sugar
**Whites from 2 large eggs**
**1 tsp freshly grated lemon peel**
¾ cup pine nuts (see *Pine Nuts or Pignoli*, below)

**MAKES** 24
**TOTAL TIME:** About 1 hour

**PER COOKIE:** 87 cal, 2 g pro, 10 g car, 0 g fiber, 5 g fat (1 g sat fat), 0 mg chol, 6 mg sod

**1** Heat oven to 325°F. Line baking sheet(s) with foil.

**2** Crumble almond paste into food processor. Pulse until fine crumbs. Add sugar, egg whites and lemon peel. Process until smooth.

**3** Drop heaping teaspoons 1 in. apart on foil-lined baking sheet(s). Sprinkle with pine nuts to cover; press nuts gently to adhere.

**4** Bake 22 to 25 minutes until tops feel firm and dry when lightly pressed. Cool completely on baking sheet on a wire rack. Peel off foil.

**FYI:** Pine nuts packed in bags are less expensive than those in small jars. Look for them in health food and warehouse stores and in the bulk-food section of your supermarket.

### PINE NUTS OR PIGNOLI

Pine nuts ("pignoli" in Italian, "pinon" in Spanish) do indeed come from inside a pine cone, which is generally heated to release them. Several varieties of pine tree produce pine nuts, which are grown extensively in North Africa, Italy, Mexico and Southwestern United States. China is also a big producer of these nuts, generally shorter and fatter with a squat triangular shape and a more pungent flavor. Store pine nuts in the refrigerator and use them within a few months; because of their high fat content they turn rancid quickly. Italian cooks use them in pesto, and in macaroons such as these. They also are often served with kale (see Tuscan Kale, page 262)

# Pecan-Date Bars

## FOOD PROCESSOR · 13 x 9-IN. BAKING PAN

HOW LONG WILL THEY KEEP? REFRIGERATOR, 2 WEEKS; FREEZER. 1 MONTH.

**MAKES** 48
**TOTAL TIME:** 1 hour 5 minutes

**PER BAR:** 156 cal, 2 g pro, 19 g car, 1 g fiber, 9 g fat (4 g sat fat), 16 mg chol, 61 mg sod

TIP: The date filling can be prepared the day before. You can chop the pecans in the food processor before making the crust.

FILLING
    1 lb pitted dates, chopped (2½ cups)
    1½ cups orange juice

CRUST & TOPPING
    1½ cups all-purpose flour
    1½ cups old-fashioned oats
    ⅔ cup packed light-brown sugar
    1½ cups (6 oz) pecans, chopped (see Tip, left)
    2½ sticks (1¼ cups) cold butter, cut up

**1** FILLING: Bring dates and orange juice to a boil in a 3-qt saucepan. Reduce heat to low and simmer 15 minutes, stirring often, until dates are tender, orange juice is absorbed and mixture thickens. Let cool.

**2** Heat oven to 350°F. Line a 13 x 9-in. baking pan with foil, letting foil extend above pan at both ends. Lightly coat with cooking spray.

**3** CRUST AND TOPPING: Put flour, oats, brown sugar and ½ cup chopped pecans in food processor; pulse to blend. Add butter; pulse until mixture is crumbly. Transfer 2½ cups crumb mixture to a medium bowl. Press remaining crumbs over bottom of lined pan. Spoon Filling over crust and carefully spread in an even layer to within ¼ in. of pan sides. Stir the 1 cup pecans into the 2½ cups crumb mixture; sprinkle over filling and press down lightly with fingertips.

**4** Bake 35 minutes or until edges are brown. Place pan on a wire rack until completely cool.

**5** Lift by ends of foil to cutting board. Cut lengthwise in 6 strips, then cut each strip in 8. If putting in a container, put wax paper between layers.

# Chocolate-Banana Snackin' Bars

## MIXER · 15½ x 10½ x ⅝-IN. RIMMED BAKING SHEET

A BIG HIT IN SCHOOL LUNCH BOXES AND FOR AFTER-SCHOOL SNACKS.
HOW LONG WILL THEY KEEP? REFRIGERATOR, 1 WEEK; FREEZER, 3 MONTHS.

1 cup mashed ripe bananas (3 medium)
¾ cup packed light-brown sugar
⅓ cup oil
¼ cup milk
2 large eggs
1 tsp baking powder
1 tsp cinnamon
1 tsp vanilla extract
½ tsp baking soda
¼ tsp salt
1¾ cups all-purpose flour
½ cup chocolate mini chips

**MAKES** 40
**TOTAL TIME:** 30 to 35 minutes

**PER BAR:** 72 cal, 1 g pro, 11 g car, 0 g fiber, 3 g fat (1 g sat fat), 11 mg chol, 48 mg sod

**1** Heat oven to 350°F. Line a 15½ x 10½ x ⅝-in. rimmed baking sheet with foil, letting foil extend above pan at ends. Lightly coat with cooking spray.

**2** Put mashed bananas, sugar, oil, milk, eggs, baking powder, cinnamon, vanilla, baking soda and salt in a large bowl. Beat with mixer on medium speed until blended. On low speed beat in flour just until blended. Stir in chips.

**3** Spread batter in prepared pan. Bake 15 to 20 minutes until a wooden pick inserted near center comes out clean. Let cool in pan on a wire rack.

**4** Lift by ends of foil onto a cutting board. Cut lengthwise in 4 strips, then cut each strip in 10; remove from foil.

# Chocolate-Orange-Swirl Cheesecake Bars

## FOOD PROCESSOR · 9-IN. SQUARE BAKING PAN

How long will they keep? Refrigerator, 3 days; freezer, 1 month.

**MAKES** 24
**PREP:** 25 to 30 minutes
**BAKE:** 40 minutes
**CHILL:** 3 hours or longer

**PER BAR:** 94 cal, 3 g pro, 12 g car, 0 g fiber, 4 g fat (2 g sat fat), 27 mg chol, 97 m sod

CRUST
9 whole (2 squares each) chocolate graham crackers
1 Tbsp stick butter, cut up
White of 1 large egg

FILLING
8-oz brick ⅓-less-fat cream cheese (Neufchâtel), softened
1 cup nonfat sour cream
½ cup plus 2 Tbsp sugar
2 large eggs
2 tsp finely grated orange peel
¼ cup orange juice

3 Tbsp unsweetened cocoa powder

**1** Heat oven to 350°F. Line a 9-in. square baking pan with foil, letting foil extend above pan on opposite sides; coat with cooking spray.

**2** CRUST: Process crackers in food processor until fine crumbs form. Add butter and egg white; pulse until crumbs are moistened. Spread crumbs in prepared pan then press evenly in place using the bottom of a small measuring cup. Bake 10 minutes or until firm and set. Cool until Filling is ready.

**3** FILLING: Put cream cheese, sour cream, ½ cup sugar, the eggs, orange peel and juice in a large bowl. Whisk until smooth. Remove ¼ cup. Pour remaining Filling over crust.

**4** Stir cocoa, 1 Tbsp water and the 2 Tbsp sugar in a cup to mix. Stir into reserved ¼ cup Filling until blended. Spoon over Filling in crust, then drag a toothpick or skewer through filling in a spiral motion to create marbled effect.

**5** Bake 30 minutes or until firm around edges but slightly jiggly in center. Cool uncovered in pan on rack in refrigerator at least 3 hours until firm.

**6** TO SERVE: Lift by ends of foil onto cutting board. Cut lengthwise in 4 strips, then cut each strip in 6.

# Perfect Double-Chocolate Brownies

MIXER · 13 x 9-IN. BAKING PAN

HOW LONG WILL THEY KEEP? REFRIGERATOR, 2 WEEKS; FREEZER, 6 WEEKS.

8 oz unsweetened baking chocolate, chopped

1½ sticks (¾ cup) butter, cut up

2 cups sugar

4 large eggs

2 tsp vanilla extract

1½ cups all-purpose flour

1 tsp baking powder

1¼ cups chopped walnuts

1¼ cups white chocolate chips

**MAKES** 24
**PREP:** 10 minutes
**BAKE:** About 30 minutes

**PER BROWNIE:** 314 cal, 4 g pro, 34 g car, 2 g fiber, 19 g fat (10 g sat fat), 51 mg chol, 108 mg sod

**1** Heat oven to 350°F. Line a 13 x 9-in. baking pan with foil, letting foil extend about 2 in. at ends; coat foil with cooking spray.

**2** Microwave chocolate and butter in a medium bowl on high 1 minute, then stir. Repeat at 30-second intervals until melted and smooth. (Or melt chocolate and butter in a small saucepan over low heat, stirring until smooth.) Let cool until warm.

**3** Put sugar, eggs and vanilla in a large bowl and beat with mixer on medium-high speed 3 minutes until pale. Beat in chocolate mixture. Stir in flour, baking powder and 1 cup each nuts and chips. Spread in prepared pan; sprinkle with rest of nuts and chips.

**4** Bake 30 minutes or until a wooden pick inserted in center comes out with moist crumbs attached. Put pan on a wire rack until completely cool. Lift foil by ends onto cutting board. Cut lengthwise in 4 strips, then cut each strip in 6. Store with wax paper between layers.

**BAKING WITH MARGARINE**

If you wish, stick margarine (not spread) or soft baking butter with canola oil may be used instead of butter. Spreads are not suitable for baking because they contain a high proportion of liquid. Check the nutrition label: If 1 Tbsp of a product has 100 calories from fat, it can be used instead of butter for baking.

# Brownies

How long will they keep? Refrigerator, 2 weeks; freezer, 6 weeks.

**MAKES** 16
**PREP:** 10 minutes
**BAKE:** About 30 minutes

**PER BROWNIE:** 189 cal,
3 g pro, 23 g car, 1 g fiber,
11 g fat (6 g sat fat), 55 mg
chol, 72 mg sod

1 stick (½ cup) butter
4 oz unsweetened baking chocolate, chopped
1⅓ cups sugar
3 large eggs
1½ tsp vanilla extract
¾ cup all-purpose flour

**1** Heat oven to 350°F. Line an 8-in. square baking pan with foil, letting ends extend above pan on opposite sides. Coat foil with cooking spray.

**2** Melt butter and chocolate in a medium saucepan over low heat; stir until blended. Off heat, whisk in sugar, then eggs, one at a time. Stir in vanilla and flour.

**3** Spread in prepared pan. Bake 25 to 30 minutes until a wooden pick inserted in the center comes out with moist crumbs attached.

**4** Cool in pan on a wire rack. Lift foil by ends to cutting board. Cut in 4 each way.

**FYI:** These brownies are more fudge-y than cake-y.

# Baby Lemon-Rosemary Poundcakes

## MIXER · THREE 5¾ x 3¼ x 2-IN. FOIL LOAF PANS

HOW LONG WILL THEY KEEP? ROOM TEMPERATURE, I DAY; REFRIGERATOR, 4 DAYS; FREEZER, I MONTH.

2 sticks (1 cup) butter, softened

2½ tsp freshly grated lemon peel

2 tsp finely chopped fresh rosemary

1 tsp baking powder

¼ tsp salt

¾ cup sugar

4 large eggs, at room temperature

1 tsp vanilla extract

2 cups all-purpose flour

LEMON-SUGAR TOPPING

  ½ cup sugar

  ¼ cup fresh lemon juice

DECORATION: fresh rosemary sprigs and long strips lemon peel

MAKES 3 loaves, 8 slices each
PREP: About 25 minutes
BAKE: About 40 minutes, plus cooling

PER SLICE: 161 cal, 2 g pro, 19 g car, 0 g fiber, 9 g fat (5 g sat fat), 56 mg chol, 133 mg sod

**1** Heat oven to 325°F. Coat three 5¾ x 3¼ x 2-in. foil baby-loaf pans with cooking spray.

**2** Put butter, lemon peel, rosemary, baking powder and salt in a large bowl and beat with mixer on medium-high speed until creamy. Gradually beat in sugar; beat 2 minutes or until pale and fluffy. Beat in eggs, one at a time, then vanilla. On low speed, beat in flour until just blended. Half fill each prepared pan. Smooth tops and place pans on baking sheet.

**3** Bake 35 to 40 minutes until a wooden pick inserted in centers comes out clean. While cakes bake, mix sugar and lemon juice in a cup.

**4** Cool cakes in pans on a wire rack 5 minutes before inverting on rack. Turn cakes right side up. While still warm, pierce tops all over with a wooden pick. Gently brush or spoon on Topping, letting it soak in before adding more. Let cakes cool completely. Wrap tightly in plastic wrap to store.

**5** At serving, garnish cakes with rosemary and lemon peel.

TIP: Put the batter-filled pans on a rimmed baking sheet so they can be lifted in and out of the oven more easily.

# Apple Streusel Loaf Cake

HOW LONG WILL IT KEEP? ROOM TEMPERATURE, 1 DAY;
REFRIGERATOR, 4 DAYS; FREEZER, 1 MONTH.

**SERVES** 8
**PREP:** 20 minutes
**BAKE:** 1 hour 20 minutes

**PER SERVING:** 545 cal,
7 g pro, 74 g car, 2 g fiber,
25 g fat (15 g sat fat),
116 mg chol, 531 mg sod

STREUSEL
  1 cup all-purpose flour
  ½ cup packed light-brown sugar
  1 stick (½ cup) butter, melted
  2 tsp cinnamon

CAKE
  2 cups all-purpose flour
  ¾ cup sugar
  2 tsp baking powder
  ½ tsp salt
  2 large eggs
  1 stick (½ cup) butter, melted
  ½ cup 1% lowfat milk

  2 medium Granny Smith apples, peeled, halved, cored and
  cut in ½-in. dice

**1**  Heat oven to 350°F. Coat a 9 x 5 x 3-in. loaf pan with cooking
spray.

**2**  STREUSEL: Put all ingredients in a medium bowl and stir with a
fork until crumbly.

**3**  CAKE: Put flour, sugar, baking powder and salt in a large bowl and
stir until blended.

**4**  Beat eggs in a medium bowl with a fork just to blend. Stir in butter and milk. Add to flour mixture and fold with a spatula just until
dry ingredients are moistened. Spoon half the batter into prepared
pan; spread to cover bottom. Sprinkle with half the apples and half
the Streusel. Spoon on remaining batter, spreading to cover. Sprinkle
with half the remaining Streusel, the remaining apples and then the
last of the remaining Streusel.

**5**  Bake 1 hour 10 minutes to 1 hour 20 minutes or until a wooden
pick inserted in center comes out clean. Cool in pan on a wire rack
10 minutes. Run a thin knife around sides; invert cake onto rack.
Turn streusel side up and let cool completely. Store tightly covered.

FYI: Melting the butter for
the Streusel makes a
crunchier topping.

LEFT: Oatmeal Superchip Cookies *(page 275)*
RIGHT: Wickedly Good Whoopie Pies *(page 276)*

Chocolate-Orange-Swirl
Cheesecake Bars *(page 284)*

Baby Lemon-Rosemary Poundcakes *(page 287)*

Raspberry-Almond Streusel Coffee Cake *(page 290)*

# Orange Chiffon Cake

## MIXER · 10-CUP BUNDT PAN

OLIVE OIL ADDS FABULOUS FLAVOR TO A CHIFFON CAKE. HOW LONG WILL IT KEEP?
ROOM TEMPERATURE, 1 DAY; REFRIGERATOR, 4 DAYS; FREEZER, 1 MONTH.

2¼ cups cake flour (not self-rising)
1⅓ cups plus 2 Tbsp sugar
1 Tbsp baking powder
½ tsp salt
1 Tbsp freshly grated orange peel
½ cup fresh orange juice (see Tip, right)
Yolks of 3 large eggs
½ cup extra-virgin olive oil
Whites of 4 large eggs
4 cups fresh fruit salad
DECORATION: confectioners' sugar

**SERVES 14**
**PREP:** 25 minutes
**BAKE:** 40 minutes

**PER SERVING:** 276 cal,
4 g pro, 45 g car, 1 g fiber,
10 g fat (2 g sat fat), 46 mg
chol, 207 mg sod

**TIP:** You will need 2 to 3
oranges to get ½ cup juice.

**TIP:** Sift confectioners' sugar
over cake just before serving.

**NO DREDGER?**
If you want to sprinkle
cocoa or confectioners'
sugar over a cake but don't
have a sugar dredger or
shaker, a wire strainer
makes a good stand-in. Put
the confectioners' sugar (or
cocoa) in a plastic or metal
strainer, hold it in one hand
over the cake or pie to be
adorned, and gently tap the
rim of the strainer with the
other hand.

**1** Heat oven to 325°F. Coat a 10-cup (8¾-in.) nonstick bundt pan
with olive oil or cooking spray.

**2** Put flour, the 1⅓ cups sugar, the baking powder and the salt in a
large bowl; stir to mix well. Make a hollow in the center and in it put
the orange peel and juice, the 3 yolks and the oil.

**3** In a large bowl beat egg whites with mixer on high speed until
foamy. Gradually beat in the 2 Tbsp sugar, beating until stiff peaks
form when beaters are lifted.

**4** Using same beaters, beat flour mixture on low speed 1 minute,
incorporating the juice, yolks and oil. Gently fold into beaten whites.
Scrape into prepared pan.

**5** Bake 40 minutes or until a wooden pick inserted in center of cake
comes out clean (cake will rise to top of pan). Place pan on a wire
rack to cool 5 minutes.

**6** Loosen cake around edge with a thin knife. Unmold onto rack; let
cool completely. Sprinkle cake with confectioners' sugar shortly
before serving. Serve with fruit salad.

# Raspberry-Almond Streusel Coffee Cake

## MIXER · 9-IN. SPRINGFORM PAN · STARTS WITH A MIX

How long will it keep? Refrigerator, 2 days.

**SERVES** 12
**PREP:** 20 minutes
**BAKE:** 1 hour 10 minutes

**PER SERVING:** 389 cal,
6 g pro, 45 g car, 2 g fiber,
23 g fat (9 g sat fat), 71 mg
chol, 422 mg sod

CRUNCH TOPPING
½ cup (from an 18.25-oz box) classic white cake mix
⅓ cup packed light-brown sugar
3 Tbsp cold stick butter, cut in small pieces
¾ cup whole almonds (with skins), coarsely chopped

CAKE
Remaining classic white cake mix
1 cup reduced-fat sour cream
1 stick (½ cup) butter, softened
2 large eggs
1½ tsp almond extract

½ pt (6 oz) fresh raspberries
DECORATION: **confectioners' sugar**

1  Heat oven to 325°F. Lightly coat a 9-in. springform pan with cooking spray.

2  TOPPING: Put the ½ cup cake mix, the brown sugar and the butter in a small bowl. Cut with pastry blender (see *Pastry Blender,* page 274) until mixture resembles small peas. Stir in almonds.

3  CAKE: Put remaining cake mix, the sour cream, butter, eggs and almond extract into a large bowl. Beat with a mixer on low speed 1 minute to blend. Increase speed to medium and beat 2 minutes longer (mixture is very thick). Fold in berries; spread in prepared pan. Press Topping into a ball between hands. Break off small clumps; sprinkle evenly over cake and press lightly.

4  Bake 1 hour 10 minutes or until a wooden pick inserted in center comes out clean (cake settles in center; that's OK).

5  Put pan on wire rack; let cake cool completely. Run a thin knife around edge of pan; remove pan sides. Loosen cake from pan bottom with a wide spatula; slide cake onto serving plate. Sprinkle with confectioners' sugar. To store, leave in pan and wrap tightly.

# Tiramisù Cake

## MIXER · 13 x 9-IN. BAKING PAN · STARTS WITH A MIX

HOW LONG WILL IT KEEP? REFRIGERATOR, 3 DAYS.

**18.25-oz box devil's food cake mix**
**Strong coffee**

SOAK
 ¼ cup freshly made espresso or strong coffee
 2 Tbsp coffee-flavored liqueur (such as Kahlua, optional)

TOPPING
 Two 8-oz tubs mascarpone cheese
 ¼ cup plus 2 Tbsp espresso or strong coffee
 1 cup heavy (whipping) cream
 ⅓ cup sugar
 DECORATION: **unsweetened cocoa powder and coffee beans**

**SERVES** 16
**TOTAL TIME:** 1½ hours

**PER SERVING:** 400 cal,
5 g pro, 32 g car, 1 g fiber,
28 g fat (14 g sat fat), 84 mg
chol, 310 mg sod

TIP: To decorate the cake
use coffee beans or choco-
late-coated espresso beans

**1** Heat oven to 350°F. Line a 13 x 9-in. baking pan with foil, letting foil extend about 2 in. above pan at both ends. Coat foil with cooking spray.

**2** Prepare cake mix as pkg directs, using coffee instead of water. Spread batter in prepared pan. Bake as box directs. Cool completely in pan on a wire rack. Hold foil ends and lift cake from pan. Using a long serrated knife cut rounded top off cake. Lift cake back into pan.

**3** SOAK: Mix ¼ cup espresso and the liqueur in a small bowl; brush over top of cake.

**4** TOPPING: Stir mascarpone and espresso in a large bowl until blended. Beat cream and sugar in a medium bowl with an electric mixer on high speed until soft peaks form when beaters are lifted. Fold into cheese mixture until smooth. Spread over cake, making swirls with back of a spoon. Cover and refrigerate up to 3 days.

**5** TO DECORATE: Put a little cocoa powder in a strainer and tap sides so it falls on top of the cake. Lift cake out of pan and onto a cutting board. Cut lengthwise in 4 strips. Cut each strip in 4 then each piece into 2 triangles. Decorate with coffee beans.

**TIRAMISÙ**
The name of this cross
between a cake and a
dessert translates from the
Italian as "carry me up" or
"pick me up." When you
taste the espresso-soaked
cake with its rich creamy
topping you might imagine
that "to heaven" is left
unspoken.

# Margarita Cheesecake Bars

MIXER · 13 x 9-IN. BAKING PAN · STARTS WITH A MIX

How long will it keep? Refrigerator, 3 days.

**MAKES 42**
**PREP:** 1 hour
**CHILL:** 3 hours

**PER BAR:** 139 cal, 2 g pro, 13 g car, 0 g fiber, 9 g fat (4 g sat fat), 33 mg chol, 133 mg sod

18.25-oz box lemon cake mix, batter prepared as box directs
⅓ cup fresh lime juice (grate peel before cutting lime)
2½ tsp (1 pkt) unflavored gelatin
Three 8-oz bricks cream cheese, softened
½ cup sugar
1 Tbsp freshly grated lime peel
Decoration: lime

**1** Heat oven to 350°F. Line a 13 x 9-in. baking pan with foil, letting foil extend about 2 in. above pan at both ends. Coat foil with cooking spray.

**2** Spread cake batter in prepared pan. Bake as box directs. Cool completely in pan on a wire rack. Hold foil and lift cake from pan. With a long serrated knife cut rounded top off cake. Lift cake back into pan.

**3** Pour lime juice into a small saucepan; sprinkle with gelatin. Let stand 1 minute, then stir over low heat 3 minutes until liquid is almost boiling and gelatin is completely dissolved. Remove from heat.

**4** Beat cream cheese, sugar and lime peel in a large bowl with mixer on medium speed 2 minutes until fluffy. Slowly beat in gelatin mixture. Beat 1 minute to blend. Scrape onto cake, then spread evenly to edges. Refrigerate 1 hour to set, then cover loosely and refrigerate 2 hours or overnight.

**Tip:** Dipping a knife in very hot water and wiping it before cutting each square helps make neat, easy cuts through the topping.

**5** TO SERVE: Lift from pan. Cut lengthwise in 6, then cut each strip in 7 bars (dip knife in hot water; wipe clean between cuts).

**6** TO DECORATE: Remove lime peel with a vegetable peeler. Cut in thin shreds. Wrap in plastic wrap and sprinkle on cake shortly before serving.

# Rum Raisin Cake

## MIXER · 12-CUP BUNDT PAN · STARTS WITH A MIX

HOW LONG WILL IT KEEP? ROOM TEMPERATURE, 5 DAYS. UNGLAZED CAKE, FREEZER, 3 MONTHS.

1 cup golden raisins
¾ cup dark rum or fresh orange juice
18.25-oz box yellow cake mix
⅓ cup yellow cornmeal
1 cup reduced-fat sour cream
4 large eggs
¼ cup oil
2 Tbsp freshly grated orange peel

**ORANGE GLAZE**
  1½ cups confectioners' sugar
  2 Tbsp fresh orange juice
  1 tsp freshly grated orange peel
  ⅛ tsp vanilla extract

DECORATION: **golden raisins and orange peel slivers**

SERVES 12
**SOAK RAISINS:** At least 30 minutes
**PREP:** 20 minutes
**BAKE:** About 45 minutes

**PER SERVING:** 391 cal, 6 g pro, 66 g car, 1 g fiber, 13 g fat (4 g sat fat), 76 mg chol, 304 mg sod

**1** At least 30 minutes or up to 24 hours before baking cake, mix raisins and rum in a small bowl. Cover and leave at room temperature.

**2** Heat oven to 350°F. Lightly coat a 12-cup bundt pan with cooking spray.

**3** Mix cake mix and cornmeal in a large bowl. Drain liquid from raisins into bowl. Add sour cream, eggs and oil. Beat with mixer on low speed 1 minute to combine. Increase speed to medium and beat 2 minutes until thickened. Stir in the 2 Tbsp orange peel and the raisins. Pour into prepared pan.

**4** Bake 40 to 45 minutes until a wooden pick inserted in center of cake comes out clean. Remove to a wire rack. Cool cake in pan on rack 10 minutes. Invert on rack, remove pan and cool completely.

**5** ORANGE GLAZE: Stir ingredients in a small bowl until blended and smooth.

**6** Put cake on a serving plate; drizzle with glaze and decorate with raisins and peel.

# Banana Cream Cake

## MIXER · THREE 9-IN. ROUND CAKE PANS · STARTS WITH A MIX

How long will it keep? Cake layers: refrigerator, 2 days; freezer, 3 months.
Fill and glaze shortly before serving.

**SERVES** 12
**PREP:** 15 minutes
**BAKE:** 20 to 30 minutes
**ASSEMBLE:** 10 minutes

**PER SERVING:** 555 cal,
8 g pro, 75 g car, 2 g fiber,
28 g fat (9 g sat fat), 77 mg
chol, 380 mg sod

1⅓ cups mashed ripe bananas (3 large)

1 cup reduced-fat sour cream

½ cup packed light-brown sugar

18.25-oz box yellow cake mix

3 large eggs

⅓ cup oil

1 cup pecans, toasted and finely chopped (see *Toasting Nuts*, page 189)

GLAZE

⅓ cup heavy (whipping) cream

3.5-oz bar bittersweet chocolate, broken in small pieces

FILLING

2 large ripe bananas

22-oz tub refrigerated vanilla pudding

**1** Position racks to divide oven in thirds. Heat to 350°F. Coat three 9-in. round cake pans with cooking spray. Line bottoms of pans with wax paper.

**2** Put mashed bananas, sour cream and brown sugar in a large bowl and beat with mixer on low speed until sugar dissolves. Add cake mix, eggs and oil; beat 2 minutes on medium speed. Stir in pecans. Spread in prepared pans.

**3** Stagger pans on oven racks and bake 20 minutes (28 minutes in disposable pans) or until a wooden pick inserted in centers comes out clean. Cool in pans on a wire rack 10 minutes. Invert cakes on rack, remove paper and let cool completely.

**4** GLAZE: Heat ⅓ cup cream in a small saucepan (or bowl in microwave) just until steaming hot. Remove from heat and add chocolate; let stand 4 minutes. Stir until chocolate melts and blends with cream.

**5** FILLING: Thinly slice bananas. Put 1 cake layer on serving plate. Top with a sliced banana. Gently spread with half the pudding (about 1 cup). Top with another cake layer, cover with remaining banana and pudding. Put third cake layer in place.

TIP: Three 8½-in. foil pans can be used instead of the cake pans.

**6** Pour Glaze in the middle of the top layer; spread carefully to edges.

# Coffee Spice Cake

How long will it keep? Cake layers: room temperature, 5 days; finished cake: refrigerator, 3 days.

1 Tbsp instant coffee granules
18.25-oz box spice cake mix
⅓ cup oil
3 large eggs
1 tsp vanilla extract
2 oz semisweet baking chocolate, grated (see Tip, right)
1 pt heavy (whipping) cream
¼ cup coffee liqueur (such as Kahlúa, see Tip, right)

SERVES 12
PREP: 12 minutes
BAKE: About 36 minutes
ASSEMBLE: About 10 minutes

PER SERVING: 419 cal, 5 g pro, 42 g car, 0 g fiber, 27 g fat (13 g sat fat), 107 mg chol, 302 mg sod

**1** Heat oven to 350°F. Lightly coat two 8-in. round cake pans with cooking spray. Line bottoms with wax paper; lightly spray paper.

**2** Put 1⅓ cups water and coffee granules in a large bowl. Beat with mixer on low speed until dissolved. Add cake mix, oil, eggs and vanilla. Beat on low speed 1 minute to combine. Increase speed to medium and beat 2 minutes until thickened and smooth. Stir in grated chocolate. Spread in prepared pans.

**3** Bake 33 to 36 minutes until a wooden pick inserted near center of layers comes out clean. Cool in pans on a wire rack 10 minutes. Invert on rack; remove pans and paper. Cool completely.

**4** Put cream and liqueur in a medium bowl. Beat with mixer on high speed until soft peaks form when beaters are lifted and mixture is firm enough to spread.

**5** TO ASSEMBLE: Invert 1 cake layer on a serving plate. Spread top with 1 cup cream mixture. Top with remaining cake. Frost sides and top with remaining cream.

TIP: Grate the chocolate using the largest holes of a four-sided grater. A rotary grater works well too.

TIP: If not using liqueur, add 1 Tbsp sugar, 2 tsp instant coffee granules and 1 tsp vanilla extract to cream and stir until coffee and sugar dissolve.

# Desserts

In popular parlance, "save room for dessert" has changed! Now we joke "eat dessert first." Perhaps it means "think of dessert first." When we have company we may grill a steak and vegetables, make a salad and garlic bread… all of which we know how to do by heart. But when it comes to dessert (essential for company) we need a recipe. We want to make something new, different, special. A dessert that guests will rave about. The recipes in this chapter are designed to bring raves. Yet none of them is difficult, nor do they require special skills. Almost all of them can be made ahead, for peace of mind. There are recipes for rich desserts and not-so-rich. We know cheesecakes are a favorite; we offer recipes for three different kinds. There are pies: Chocolate Truffle Pie, Key Lime Pie and individual apple pies. There are old-fashioned fruit desserts, including a crisp and a cobbler, and "new" fruit desserts like Frozen Raspberry-Mango Terrine and Mojito Fruit Cocktail. Do you need any more reasons to get cooking and eat dessert, whether it be first or last?

# Chocolate Truffle Pie

How long will it keep? Refrigerator, 2 days.

SERVES 10
PREP: 25 minutes
CHILL: 4 hours

PER SERVING: 419 cal,
4 g pro, 41 g car, 2 g fiber,
28 g fat (14 g sat fat), 45 mg
chol, 166 mg sod

FYI: Instead of using a microwave you can melt the caramels with the evaporated milk in a small heavy saucepan over low heat, stirring often until smooth. The chocolate chips can be melted the same way.

½ cup pecan pieces, toasted and coarsely chopped (see *Toasting Nuts*, page 189)
One 6-oz ready-to-fill chocolate-flavored crumb crust

CARAMEL LAYER
17 individually wrapped square caramels (5 oz, ¾ cup), unwrapped
¼ cup canned evaporated milk (not sweetened condensed)

TRUFFLE LAYER
1½ cups (9 oz) semisweet chocolate chips
1 cup heavy (whipping) cream
3 Tbsp stick butter

Decoration: slightly-sweetened whipped cream (see *Whipping Cream*, below)

1 Sprinkle pecans on crust.

2 CARAMEL LAYER: Put caramels in a bowl with the evaporated milk. Microwave, stirring every 10 seconds until caramels are melted and mixture is smooth (see FYI, left). Pour over pecans.

3 TRUFFLE LAYER: Heat chocolate chips, cream and butter in a bowl in microwave, stirring every 10 seconds until chocolate is melted and mixture is smooth. Pour over Caramel Layer. Refrigerate about 4 hours until set.

4 TO SERVE: Pipe or spoon whipped cream around edge of pie.

## WHIPPING CREAM

To get the greatest volume out of cream start with very cold, heavy (whipping) cream. If you can, chill the bowl (metal is best) and beaters, too (5 or 10 minutes in the freezer or refrigerator will do it). As when beating egg whites, choose a bowl that is deep and narrow to ensure that the beaters have more contact with the cream. Pour the cream into the bowl. Add any sugar or flavoring (such as vanilla). Start beating at medium speed, then increase to high. If using a hand-held beater, keep moving the beater around the bowl to ensure evenly whipped cream. Once or twice scrape down the sides of the bowl. As the cream thickens and the beaters leave trails, keep a close watch. Stop the beater and lift it out of the bowl to check on how thick the cream is. Or lift some of the cream with a spatula. Stop as soon as the cream is as thick as you need it. Cover and refrigerate until ready to use.

# Pumped-Up Pecan Pie

STORE-BOUGHT PIE CRUST · 9-IN. PIE PLATE · OVEN

How long will it keep? Refrigerator, 4 days.

1 refrigerated ready-to-bake pie crust (from a 15-oz box of 2)

2 cups roasted and salted mixed nuts

1 cup sweetened dried cranberries

4 large eggs

½ cup packed light-brown sugar

½ cup light corn syrup

½ cup pure maple syrup

¼ cup all-purpose flour

2 Tbsp stick butter, melted

SERVES 14
PREP: 20 minutes
BAKE: 1 hour

PER SERVING: 352 cal,
5 g pro, 44 g car, 2 g fiber,
18 g fat (5 g sat fat), 68 mg
chol, 109 mg sod

**1** Heat oven to 350°F. Fit crust into a 9-in. pie plate. Flute edges.

**2** Set aside ½ cup mixed nuts and ¼ cup dried cranberries for decoration. Coarsely chop remaining nuts and cranberries. Sprinkle evenly in crust.

**3** Put eggs, brown sugar, corn syrup, maple syrup, flour and melted butter in a medium bowl. Whisk until blended. Pour over nut mixture. Arrange reserved nuts and cranberries on top.

**4** Bake 50 to 60 minutes until set. (If crust browns too quickly, cover loosely with foil.) Place on a wire rack to cool. If you're going to refrigerate the pie, let it cool, then cover it.

# Pineapple-Coconut Cream Pie

MIXER · FOOD PROCESSOR · 9-IN. PIE PLATE · OVEN

How long will it keep? Refrigerator, 2 days.

**SERVES 8**
**PREP:** 30 minutes
**CHILL:** At least 3 hours

**PER SERVING:** 656 cal,
5 g pro, 67 g car, 2 g fiber,
42 g fat (25 g sat fat), 197 mg
chol, 260 mg sod

TIP: If you don't have a food processor, put the cookies in a sturdy plastic food bag and crush them finely with a rolling pin. Add the butter; knead to mix.

## STORING AND USING EGG WHITES

Egg whites can be put into a clean, grease-free glass or plastic container and frozen. Try to label them first with the number of whites and the date. Use them for meringue, or for Pine Nut Macaroons (page 281). Let them thaw in the refrigerator. If you don't know how many whites are in a container measure them after they thaw: 1 cup is about 7 to 8 whites. To freeze egg yolks, see Tip, page 349.

CRUST
> 20 crisp oatmeal cookies, broken up
> ½ stick (4 Tbsp) butter, melted

FILLING
> Yolks from 5 large eggs
> ¾ cup sugar
> ⅓ cup cornstarch
> 14-oz can coconut milk (not cream of coconut)
> 20-oz can crushed pineapple, in its own juice, well drained, reserve juice
> 2 Tbsp stick butter, cut in small pieces
> 1 cup sweetened flaked coconut, chopped

1 cup heavy (whipping) cream
2 Tbsp sugar

DECORATION: sweetened flaked coconut, small pineapple chunks, mint sprigs

**1** Heat oven to 350°F. Coat a 9-in. pie plate with cooking spray.

**2** CRUST: Process cookies in food processor until fine crumbs form. Add butter; pulse until crumbs are moistened. Press over bottom and up sides of pie plate. Bake 12 minutes until toasted around edge. Cool on a wire rack.

**3** MEANWHILE MAKE FILLING: Have the egg yolks in a medium bowl. Mix ¾ cup sugar and the cornstarch in a 2-qt saucepan. Pour coconut milk into a 4-cup measure; add enough pineapple juice to equal 2½ cups. Stir with a whisk into sugar mixture, then bring to a boil over medium heat, stirring occasionally (don't stir too briskly or Filling will be thin), scraping bottom and corners of pan to prevent scorching. Boil 1 minute; remove from heat. Whisk yolks to mix. Gradually whisk in about half the hot mixture; pour back into the saucepan. Stir over low heat 2 minutes to cook yolks. Remove from heat; stir in butter until melted. Stir in crushed pineapple and coconut. Pour into crust. Cover surface with plastic wrap and refrigerate at least 3 hours.

**4** UP TO 2 HOURS BEFORE SERVING: Beat cream and sugar with mixer on high speed until stiff peaks form when beaters are lifted (see *Whipping Cream*, page 298). Spread over pie. Garnish with coconut, pineapple and mint.

# Key Lime Pie

MIXER · FOOD PROCESSOR · 9-IN. PIE PLATE · OVEN

How long will it keep? Refrigerator, 2 days.

CRUST
  12 whole graham crackers, broken up (see Tip, right)
  6 Tbsp stick butter, melted

FILLING
  Yolks from 4 large eggs
  14-oz can sweetened condensed milk (not evaporated milk)
  1½ tsp freshly grated lime peel
  ½ cup Key lime juice (see FYI, right)
  1 cup heavy (whipping) cream
  2 Tbsp sugar

DECORATION: strips of lime peel

**1** Heat oven to 350°F. Have a 9-in. pie plate ready.

**2** CRUST: Put crackers and butter in food processor. Process until fine moist crumbs. Press evenly over bottom and up sides of pie plate. Bake 8 minutes or until set. Cool completely on a wire rack.

**3** FILLING: Beat egg yolks in a medium bowl with mixer on medium speed until pale. Beat in sweetened condensed milk, lime peel and juice. Pour into crust. Bake 20 to 30 minutes until filling sets. Cool on wire rack, then refrigerate at least 4 hours. Cover when cold.

**4** UP TO 2 HOURS BEFORE SERVING: Beat cream and sugar in a medium bowl with mixer on high speed until peaks form when beaters are lifted. Spread cream over pie. Sprinkle with lime peel strips; refrigerate until serving.

SERVES 8
PREP: About 20 minutes
BAKE 20 to 30 minutes
COOL AND CHILL: At least 4 hours

PER SERVING: 451 cal, 7 g pro, 45 g car, 0 g fiber, 28 g fat (16 g sat fat), 187 mg chol, 261 mg sod

TIP: You can use 1½ cups store-bought graham cracker crumbs. Add melted butter. Stir to mix.

FYI: Key limes, from Florida, are smaller, rounder, yellower and more tart than regular limes, but you can use regular limes.

# Rustic Little Apple Pies

FOOD PROCESSOR · BAKING SHEET · OVEN

HOW LONG WILL THEY KEEP? ROOM TEMPERATURE, 1 DAY.

**MAKES** 6
**TOTAL TIME:** 1 hour 20 minutes

PER PIE: 341 cal, 4 g pro,
36 g car, 2 g fiber, 21 g fat
(12 g sat fat), 52 mg chol,
196 mg sod

PASTRY
  1¼ cups all-purpose flour
  1 stick (½ cup) cold butter, cut in small pieces
  1 Tbsp freshly grated orange peel
  ¼ cup ice water

3 small Golden Delicious apples
3 Tbsp granulated sugar
½ tsp ground nutmeg
3 Tbsp sliced skin-on almonds (see Tip, facing page)
6 tsp fresh orange juice
2 Tbsp stick butter, cut small
DECORATION: **confectioners' sugar**

## A DUSTING OF SUGAR

A dusting of confectioners' sugar over a pie, cake or cookies is a quick way to give a plain cake or pie a classy, finished look. Keep a filled sugar shaker ready to grab in your cupboard at all times. More formally known as a dredger, a sugar shaker is about the size of a soup can and may or may not have a handle. The top can be perforated, or it may be of wire mesh. A mesh top is best for sprinkling cakes with confectioners' sugar or cocoa. A perforated top can also be used for confectioners' sugar (although it doesn't yield as fine a dusting).

**1** TO MAKE PASTRY IN FOOD PROCESSOR: Put flour, butter and orange peel in processor; pulse until coarse crumbs form. Add water all at once; pulse just until dough begins to leave sides of bowl. BY HAND: Put flour in a bowl and cut in butter with a pastry blender (see *Pastry Blender*, page 274) until coarse crumbs form. Add peel and water; stir with a fork until mixture clumps together and a dough forms.

**2** Gather dough into a ball, flatten and cut in 6 equal pieces. Form each piece into a ball, flatten, then place between sheets of plastic wrap and roll with a rolling pin to a 6-in.-diameter circle (circles don't have to be perfect). Refrigerate while preparing remaining ingredients.

**3** Peel apples. Cut in half, cut small wedges to remove stem and bud ends; scoop out core. Turn halves cut side down and slice thin.

**4** Heat oven to 425°F. Have a large baking sheet ready. Mix sugar and nutmeg in a small bowl.

**5** Take out one circle of dough, peel off the plastic and place circle on baking sheet. Leaving a 1- to 1½-in. border, fan apple slices overlapping on dough. Sprinkle with ½ Tbsp each almonds and sugar mixture and 1 tsp orange juice. Fold edges of pastry over apples. Make 5 more pies the same way. Dot apples with butter.

**6** Bake 10 minutes, reduce oven temperature to 375°F and bake 25 to 30 minutes more until pastry is lightly browned and apples are tender. Remove pies to wire rack to cool until just warm. Just before serving, dust with confectioners' sugar (see *A Dusting of Sugar*, facing page).

> **TIP:** If you make the pies a day ahead, leave the almonds off. Cover loosely when cool. Before serving, sprinkle the pies with the almonds and bake them for 5 to 10 minutes at 375°F to recrisp them.

# Lemon Sour Cream Tarts

## STORE-BOUGHT MINI GRAHAM CRACKER CRUSTS · NO BAKE

*HOW LONG WILL THEY KEEP? REFRIGERATOR, 2 DAYS.*

½ cup sugar

2 Tbsp cornstarch

⅔ cup whole milk

Yolks from 2 large eggs

3 Tbsp fresh lemon juice

2 tsp freshly grated lemon peel (see Tip, right)

2 Tbsp stick butter

⅔ cup reduced-fat sour cream

6 ready-to-fill mini graham cracker crusts

DECORATION: whipped cream and lemon slices

> **SERVES 6**
> **PREP:** 35 minutes
> **CHILL:** 4 hours
>
> **PER TART:** 311 cal, 5 g pro, 38 g car, 1 g fiber, 15 g fat (6 g sat fat), 94 mg chol, 216 mg sod

> **TIP:** Grate peel before cutting lemon for juice (see *Grating Lemon Peel*, page 21)

**1** Whisk sugar and cornstarch in a 1-qt saucepan to mix. Whisk in milk, egg yolks and lemon juice until smooth.

**2** Bring to a boil over medium heat, stirring gently with a silicone spatula. Boil 30 seconds, stirring constantly, or until translucent and thick. Remove from heat. Add lemon peel and butter; stir until butter melts. Cover surface directly with wax paper to prevent a skin from forming. Cool to room temperature.

**3** Fold in sour cream until well blended. Spoon about ⅓ cup into each crust. Cover loosely and refrigerate at least 4 hours until set.

**4** TO SERVE: Garnish with whipped cream and lemon slices.

> **KEEPING BOWLS STEADY**
> To steady a bowl while whipping cream or eggs or making cake batter, put a damp kitchen towel between bowl and counter.

# Crunchy Crumb Apple Pie

BAKING SHEET · 9-IN. PIE PLATE · FOOD PROCESSOR · OVEN

THERE ARE LOTS OF APPLES IN THIS PIE, BUT THEY COOK DOWN DURING BAKING.
THIS PIE IS BEST THE DAY IT'S BAKED.

**SERVES 8**
**PREP:** 30 minutes
**BAKE:** 1 hour

**PER SERVING:** 489 cal,
3 g pro, 79 g car, 3 g fiber,
19 g fat (10 g sat fat), 38 mg
chol, 257 mg sod

1 refrigerated ready-to-bake pie crust (from a 15-oz box of 2)

CRUNCHY CRUMB TOPPING
  ½ cup plus 2 Tbsp all-purpose flour
  ½ cup packed light-brown sugar
  ⅓ cup granulated sugar
  1 tsp ground cinnamon
  1 stick (½ cup) cold butter, cut in small pieces

FILLING
  7 medium to large tart apples (about 3¼ lb), such as
    Granny Smith, Pippins or Greenings
  1 Tbsp fresh lemon juice
  ½ cup granulated sugar
  3 Tbsp all-purpose flour
  ½ tsp ground cinnamon
  ⅛ tsp ground nutmeg

**1** Have ready a 9-in. pie plate and a baking sheet. Place oven rack in lowest position in oven. Heat oven to 450°F.

**2** Line pie plate with pie crust as pkg directs. Flute or crimp edge.

**3** CRUNCHY CRUMB TOPPING: Put flour, sugars and cinnamon in food processor work bowl (see Tip, left); pulse to mix. Add butter; pulse until mixture forms moist, coarse crumbs that clump together easily.

**4** FILLING: Peel, halve and core apples. Cut in ⅛-in.-thick slices by hand (or with the slicing disk of a food processor). Place in a large bowl, add lemon juice and toss to coat. Mix remaining ingredients in a small bowl, sprinkle over apple slices and toss to coat.

**5** Layer apple slices in pie shell, mounding them higher in center. Pat topping evenly over apples to form a top crust. Place pie on the baking sheet to catch any drips.

**6** Bake 15 minutes. Reduce oven temperature to 350°F and bake 45 minutes longer or until a skewer meets some resistance when center

**TIP:** To make the crumb topping by hand, mix flour, sugars and cinnamon in a medium bowl. Cut in butter with a pastry blender (or rub in with fingertips) until mixture forms moist, coarse crumbs that clump together easily.

Key Lime Pie *(page 301)*

Rustic Little Apple Pies *(page 302)*

Frozen Raspberry-Mango Terrine
*(page 316)*

of pie is pierced (apples will continue cooking after pie is removed from oven) and topping is golden brown. (If topping browns too quickly, drape a piece of foil loosely over the pie.) Cool completely on a wire rack before serving.

# New York–Style Cheesecake

MIXER · 8 x 3- OR 9 x 3-IN. SPRINGFORM PAN · FOOD PROCESSOR · OVEN

How long will it keep? Refrigerator, 3 days.

CRUST
  6 whole graham cracker (see Tip, right)
  3 Tbsp stick butter, cut up
  2 Tbsp sugar

FILLING
  1 cup sugar
  2 Tbsp cornstarch
  Five 8-oz bricks ⅓-less-fat cream cheese (Neufchâtel), softened
  2 large eggs
  2 tsp vanilla extract
  ½ cup heavy (whipping) cream

Decoration: fresh raspberries

**SERVES** 12
**PREP:** 25 minutes
**BAKE:** 55 minutes to 1 hour
**COOL:** 1½ hours
**CHILL:** At least 4 hours

**PER SERVING:** 356 cal, 12 g pro, 10 g car, 0 g fiber, 28 g fat (18 g sat fat), 123 mg chol, 486 mg sod

Tip: You can use ¾ cup store-bought graham cracker crumbs. Add sugar and melted butter. Stir to mix.

**1** Heat oven to 350°F. Coat bottom and sides of an 8 x 3- or 9 x 3-in. springform pan with cooking spray.

**2** CRUST: Break up crackers and put in food processor work bowl. Add butter and sugar. Process to fine crumbs. Press firmly over bottom of pan.

**3** FILLING: Mix sugar and cornstarch in a large bowl. Add cream cheese; beat with mixer on medium speed until smooth. Beat in eggs and vanilla, scraping down sides of bowl as needed. On low speed, add cream; beat just to blend. Pour over crust in pan.

**4** Bake 55 to 60 minutes until cake has risen, edges are very lightly browned and center still jiggles when pan is moved. Cool in pan on a wire rack about 1½ hours (cake will finish setting). Run knife around edge of pan. Cover pan loosely; refrigerate at least 4 hours.

**5** UP TO 1 HOUR BEFORE SERVING: Remove pan sides. Garnish with raspberries.

# Cappuccino Cheesecake

MIXER · 8-IN. SPRINGFORM PAN · FOOD PROCESSOR · OVEN

How long will it keep? Refrigerator, 3 days.

**SERVES** 16
**PREP:** 20 minutes
**BAKE:** About 1 hour 10 minutes
**CHILL:** At least 6 hours

**PER SERVING:** 350 cal,
6 g pro, 27 g car, 0 g fiber,
25 g fat (15 g sat fat), 105 mg
chol, 233 mg sod

**Tip:** Use regular, not reduced-fat, cream cheese and sour cream.

CRUST
   9 whole cinnamon graham crackers (see FYI, page 308)
   3 Tbsp stick butter, cut in small pieces

FILLING
   3 Tbsp instant-coffee granules
   1 Tbsp vanilla extract
   Three 8-oz bricks cream cheese, softened (see Tip, left)
   ½ cup granulated sugar
   ½ cup packed light-brown sugar
   2 Tbsp cornstarch
   1 tsp ground cinnamon
   3 large eggs
   ¾ cup sour cream (see Tip, left)

TOPPING
   1¼ cups sour cream (see Tip, left)
   ¼ cup granulated sugar

DECORATION: **1 Tbsp confectioners' sugar mixed with ⅛ tsp ground cinnamon; chocolate-covered espresso beans**

**1** Heat oven to 350°F. Lightly coat an 8-in. springform pan with cooking spray.

**2** CRUST: Break up crackers and put into food processor. Process until fine crumbs form. Add butter; pulse until blended. Press over bottom of prepared pan. Bake 8 minutes. Cool in pan on a wire rack.

**3** MEANWHILE MAKE FILLING: Stir coffee granules and vanilla in a large bowl until coffee dissolves. Add cream cheese and beat with mixer on high speed until smooth. Beat in sugars, cornstarch and cinnamon, scraping down sides of bowl often, until well blended. Reduce speed to low, add eggs and beat just until combined. Add sour cream; beat just until blended. Pour into crust; spread evenly.

**4** Bake 1 hour or until top is brown and puffed around edges but still jiggly in center. Remove from oven and let stand a few minutes until Filling sinks slightly.

**5** TOPPING: Stir sour cream and sugar in a small bowl until sugar dissolves. Carefully pour over filling, spreading evenly to edges. Bake 10 minutes or until sour cream sets. Cool completely in pan on a wire rack. Refrigerate at least 6 hours or up to 3 days.

**6** TO SERVE: Remove pan sides. Sift cinnamon-sugar over cake. Make a circle of espresso beans around the edge.

# Panna Cotta

### 6-CUP BUNDT PAN OR RING MOLD · NO BAKE

HOW LONG WILL IT KEEP? REFRIGERATOR IN MOLD, 3 DAYS.

1 qt whole milk
2 Tbsp (from 3 pkt) unflavored gelatin
1½ cups heavy (whipping) cream
¾ cup sugar
1 Tbsp vanilla extract
SERVE WITH: **fresh fruit such as grapes, berries, orange segments, cut-up melon**

**SERVES** 12
**PREP:** 20 minutes
**CHILL:** At least 8 hours

**PER SERVING:** 208 cal, 4 g pro, 17 g car, 0 g fiber, 14 g fat (9 g sat fat), 52 mg chol, 54 mg sod

**1** Have ready a 6-cup bundt pan or ring mold.

**2** Pour milk into a medium saucepan. Sprinkle with gelatin and let stand 5 minutes for gelatin to soften. Stir in cream and sugar. Place over medium-low heat and stir occasionally with a rubber spatula until mixture is hot but not boiling, has a thin layer of very fine foam on top and gelatin and sugar have dissolved (see Tip, right). Remove from heat and stir in vanilla.

**3** Set saucepan in a large bowl half-filled with ice and water. Stir with a rubber spatula until cold and thick enough so the spatula leaves a trace when the mixture is stirred. Pour into bundt pan or mold, cover loosely and refrigerate at least 8 hours, or until firm enough to unmold (mixture will wobble slightly when pan is moved). Cover the pan with plastic wrap once the gelatin has set.

**4** UP TO 2 HOURS BEFORE SERVING: Have platter beside you. Dip pan up to rim in warm (not hot) water about 5 seconds. Tip to check that custard is released. Put platter upside down over pan, turn pan and platter over and shake gently from side to side until custard drops onto platter and pan lifts off. (If custard doesn't drop, drape a hot damp kitchen towel over pan and shake again.) Refrigerate until serving. Serve with fruit.

**FYI:** This silky Italian dessert is soft and creamy. Think of it as a custard without eggs. Literally, "panna" means cream, "cotta" cooked.

**TIP:** To make sure gelatin has dissolved, rub some mixture between your thumb and fingertips. It should feel smooth and slightly slippery, without any swollen granules (of undissolved gelatin).

**TIP:** To serve the panna cotta, cut slices with a wet knife then lift onto serving plates with a pie or cake server.

# White-Chocolate Cheesecake

MIXER · 8-IN. SPRINGFORM PAN · FOOD PROCESSOR · OVEN

How long will it keep? Refrigerator, 3 days.

**SERVES** 16
**PREP:** 30 minutes
**BAKE:** About 1½ hours
**COOL:** About 1½ hours
**GLAZE:** 10 minutes
**CHILL:** At least 4 hours

**PER SERVING:** 326 cal,
7 g pro, 26 g car, 1 g fiber,
20 g fat (13 g sat fat), 85 mg
chol, 285 mg sod

**FYI:** A "whole" graham cracker means the two joined squares, just as they come out of the package.

**TIP:** No food processor? Break crackers into a large ziptop bag. Seal. Crush with a rolling pin. Melt and add butter. Knead to blend.

CRUST
    7 whole graham crackers (see FYI, left)
    2 Tbsp stick butter, cut up

FILLING
    Six 1-oz squares white baking chocolate
    Three 8-oz bricks ⅓-less-fat cream cheese (Neufchâtel), softened
    ⅔ cup sugar
    1 Tbsp cornstarch
    3 large eggs, at room temperature
    ¾ cup reduced-fat sour cream
    2 Tbsp fresh lemon juice
    2 tsp vanilla extract

CHOCOLATE GLAZE
    ¼ cup heavy cream
    ½ cup (3 oz) semisweet chocolate chips

**1** Heat oven to 350°F. Coat an 8-in. springform pan with cooking spray.

**2** CRUST: Break graham crackers into food processor (see Tip, left). Add butter and pulse until fine crumbs form. Pat firmly over bottom of springform pan.

**3** FILLING: Melt white chocolate as pkg directs and cool. Beat cream cheese, sugar and cornstarch in a large bowl with mixer on medium speed until smooth. Beat in eggs, one at a time, just until blended. Beat in sour cream, white chocolate, lemon juice and vanilla until well blended. Pour over Crust.

**4** Bake 15 minutes. Reduce oven temperature to 250°F and bake 1¼ hours longer or until center still jiggles slightly when shaken. Turn off oven (leave door closed); let cake cool 1 hour. Cool in pan on a wire rack. Carefully run a thin knife around edge of pan to release cake.

**5** CHOCOLATE GLAZE: Heat heavy cream in a small saucepan until steaming. Remove from heat; add chocolate chips and stir until melted and smooth. Let cool slightly.

**6** Remove pan sides; place cheesecake on serving plate. Spread glaze on top, cover and refrigerate at least 4 hours.

**7** Remove cheesecake from refrigerator about 1 hour before serving.

---

**KEEPING WRAP OFF A SURFACE**

For some foods it is important that plastic wrap touch the surface in order to prevent a skin from forming. Other times you want to cover the food but keep the wrap away from the surface. Stick wooden toothpicks in the pie or cake, about 5 around the edge and 3 toward the center. Lay the plastic wrap over the top and the toothpicks will suspend the wrap above the surface.

---

# Chocolate Soup

CEREAL BOWL · ICE CREAM SCOOP, SPOON

HOW LONG WILL IT KEEP? 30 SECONDS!

¼ cup plus 4 Tbsp chocolate-flavored syrup
2 cups milk (see Tip, right)
1 pt coffee ice cream

**1** Pour milk into a cup measure or bowl. Add the ¼ cup chocolate syrup; stir until blended. This can be done ahead.

**2** TO SERVE: Pour ½ cup chocolate milk into each soup plate or cereal bowl. Add a scoop of ice cream; drizzle with 1 Tbsp syrup.

**SERVES** 4
**TOTAL TIME:** 5 minutes

PER SERVING: 426 cal, 10 g pro, 51 g car, 0 g fiber, 21 g fat (12 g sat fat), 137 mg chol, 151 mg sod

TIP: You can buy chocolate milk instead of making it.

# Chocolate Cake with White Chocolate Frosting

MIXER · THREE 9-IN. OR 8 x 2-IN. ROUND CAKE PANS · OVEN

HOW LONG WILL IT KEEP? CAKE LAYERS, REFRIGERATOR, 3 DAYS; FREEZER 2 WEEKS.
FROSTING, REFRIGERATOR 3 DAYS. CHOCOLATE CURLS, COOL PLACE 1 WEEK.

**SERVES** 16
**PREP:** 45 minutes
**BAKE:** About 30 minutes

**PER SERVING:** 600 cal,
7 g pro, 88 g car, 2 g fiber,
26 g fat (16 g sat fat), 86 mg
chol, 461 mg sod

¾ cup unsweetened cocoa powder

1½ sticks (¾ cup) butter, softened

2⅓ cups sugar

3 large eggs

2 tsp vanilla extract

2½ cups all-purpose flour

2 tsp baking soda

¾ tsp salt

FROSTING

    8 oz white chocolate

    3¼ cups confectioners' sugar

    6 oz cream cheese, softened

    5 Tbsp stick butter, softened

    1½ Tbsp fresh lemon juice

DECORATION: **Chocolate Curls (directions follow)**

**FYI:** In 8-in. pans the cakes will rise higher than in 9-in. pans, therefore 2-in.-high sides are essential.

**1** Position racks to divide oven in thirds. Heat to 350°F. Coat three 9-in. or 8 x 2-in. round cake pans with cooking spray. Line bottoms with wax paper.

**2** Bring 2⅓ cups water to a boil. Stir in cocoa. When smooth, let cool.

**3** Put butter, sugar, eggs and vanilla in a large bowl and beat with mixer on high speed 5 minutes or until pale and fluffy. Meanwhile, mix flour, baking soda and salt in a bowl. Add cool cocoa to butter mixture; beat until blended. Scrape bowl. On low speed, beat in flour mixture just to blend, scraping bowl once or twice. Spoon into prepared pans; smooth surfaces. Stagger pans on oven racks.

**4** Bake 24 to 31 minutes (depending on pan size) until a wooden pick inserted in center of cakes comes out clean. Cool in pans on wire rack 10 minutes. Run knife around edges; invert on rack, remove paper and cool completely.

**5** FROSTING: Melt chocolate as pkg directs, put into a medium bowl and let cool. Add confectioners' sugar, cream cheese, butter and lemon juice. Beat on low speed to blend. Increase speed to high; beat 2 minutes until light and fluffy.

**6** TO ASSEMBLE: Place one cake layer on serving plate, bottom side up. Spread with one-third of the Frosting. Repeat with remaining layers, swirling frosting on top. Garnish with Chocolate Curls.

## CHOCOLATE CURLS

4 oz white chocolate
4 oz milk chocolate

Line 2 mini loaf pans with a double thickness foil or shape foil into 2 approximately 3½ x 2 x 1¼-in. pans. Melt white chocolate and pour into one pan; melt milk chocolate and pour into second pan. Chill until firm. Remove from pans and/or peel off foil. Let chocolate soften at room temperature 30 minutes. Starting with white chocolate, pull a swivel-blade vegetable peeler along side of bar to form curls (if curls break, soften chocolate more). Store white and milk chocolate curls in an airtight container.

# Mojito Fruit Cocktail

## MARTINI OR SIMILAR GLASSES

2 oranges, peeled, segments cut out and diced
1 cup diced peeled kiwi (2 kiwi)
¾ cup diced fresh pineapple
¾ cup diced fresh strawberries
2 Tbsp white rum (optional)
2 Tbsp chopped fresh mint
2 Tbsp sugar
½ tsp grated lime peel
DECORATION: **sugar, red liquid food color and lime slices**

**SERVES** 4
**TOTAL TIME:** 25 minutes

**PER SERVING:** 106 cal, 1 g pro, 26 g car, 4 g fiber, 1 g fat (0 g sat fat), 0 mg chol, 3 mg sod

**1** Mix all ingredients except garnish. Let stand, tossing occasionally, 10 minutes until juicy and sugar dissolves.

**2** TO SERVE: Put about 2 Tbsp sugar in a small plastic bag. Add 1 or 2 drops food coloring and knead bag with fingers until sugar is evenly pink. Dip rims of martini glasses in water, then the sugar. Spoon in fruit and juice. Garnish with a lime slice.

TIP: You can cut the oranges, kiwi, pineapple and lime slices up to 4 hours ahead (refrigerate each separately), and sugar the rims of the glasses. Dice the berries and chop the mint just before you use them.

# Nectarines in White Zinfandel

HOW LONG WILL IT KEEP? REFRIGERATOR, UP TO 1 DAY.

NOT ONLY DO NECTARINES HAVE A WONDERFUL FLAVOR, THEY DO NOT NEED TO BE PEELED.
A SMALL SCOOP OF VANILLA OR PISTACHIO ICE CREAM IS GOOD WITH THIS.

**SERVES** 4
**TOTAL TIME:** 30 minutes (plus 4 hours chilling)

**PER SERVING:** 173 cal, 1 g pro, 33 g car, 2 g fiber, 1 g fat (0 g sat fat), 0 mg chol, 6 mg sod

4 ripe nectarines, each cut in 12 wedges
⅓ cup sugar
2 cups white Zinfandel wine or nonalcoholic white Zinfandel

**1** Put nectarines and sugar in a large bowl. Stir gently. Let stand 30 minutes for sugar to dissolve. Add Zinfandel; cover and refrigerate at least 4 hours.

**2** Drain liquid from nectarines into a medium saucepan. Simmer over medium-high heat about 15 minutes until some of the liquid has evaporated and what's left has the consistency of maple syrup. Refrigerate until cold.

**3** TO SERVE: Spoon nectarines and syrup into individual serving dishes.

# Blueberry Cobbler

## SHALLOW, 2-QT BAKING DISH · OVEN

HOW LONG WILL IT KEEP? BEST EATEN FRESHLY MADE.

DROP BISCUITS ARE SO CALLED BECAUSE THE DOUGH IS SO SOFT IT CAN'T BE ROLLED OUT.
INSTEAD IT IS "DROPPED" IN SPOONFULS ON TOP OF THE FRUIT.

⅔ cup plus 2 tsp sugar

2 Tbsp cornstarch

¼ tsp plus ⅛ tsp freshly grated nutmeg

About 5¾ cups (2½ pt) fresh blueberries

2 tsp freshly grated lemon peel (see Tip, right)

2 Tbsp fresh lemon juice

CREAM DROP BISCUITS

    2 cups all-purpose flour

    3 Tbsp sugar

    2 tsp baking powder

    ½ tsp salt

    2 cups heavy (whipping) cream

    2 tsp freshly grated lemon peel (see Tip, right)

SERVES 8
PREP: 20 minutes
BAKE: 55 minutes

PER SERVING: 474 cal,
5 g pro, 65 g car, 3 g fiber,
23 g fat (14 g sat fat), 82 mg
chol, 297 mg sod

TIP: Grate the peel before
cutting the lemon to juice it
(see *Grating Lemon Peel*,
page 21).

**1** Heat oven to 400°F.

**2** Put ⅔ cup sugar, the cornstarch and ¼ tsp nutmeg in a shallow 2-qt baking dish. Stir with a whisk to blend. Add blueberries, lemon peel and juice. Stir gently with a spoon to coat. Cover tightly; bake 20 minutes.

**3** MEANWHILE PREPARE CREAM DROP BISCUITS: Put flour, sugar, baking powder and salt in a medium bowl and stir with a whisk until well blended. Just before blueberries are done, add cream and peel and stir just until a very soft dough forms.

**4** Remove dish from oven, uncover and stir berries. Drop 8 mounds of dough, not touching (they spread), on filling. Mix remaining 2 tsp sugar and ⅛ tsp nutmeg; sprinkle evenly on dough.

**5** Place baking dish in oven (on a piece of foil to catch any drips). Bake 35 minutes or until biscuits are golden and the filling bubbles. Cool on a wire rack. Serve warm or at room temperature.

# Apple-Cherry Crisp

FOOD PROCESSOR · SHALLOW 2-QT BAKING DISH · OVEN

HOW LONG WILL IT KEEP? BEST SERVED FRESHLY MADE.

SERVES 8
PREP: 15 minutes
BAKE: 50 to 55 minutes

PER SERVING: 318 cal, 2 g pro, 61 g car, 3 g fiber, 9 g fat (5 g sat fat), 23 mg chol, 97 mg sod

TIP: Try different combinations of apples. You need about 3 lb total.

TIP: The apple and streusel mixtures can be prepared 1 day ahead and refrigerated separately.

3 large Granny Smith apples (see Tip, left)
3 large Cortland or Mutsu/Crispin apples
¾ cup packed brown sugar
¾ cup all-purpose flour
¾ cup dried tart cherries
½ cup apple cider or juice
½ tsp ground cinnamon
¾ stick (6 Tbsp) butter, cut up

**1** Heat oven to 350°F. Have ready a shallow 2-qt baking dish.

**2** Peel, core and slice the apples and put them into a large bowl. Add 2 Tbsp of the brown sugar, 1 Tbsp of the flour and the cherries. Toss to mix, pour into baking dish and pour the cider over the top.

**3** Put the remaining brown sugar, the remaining flour and the cinnamon into a food processor. Pulse a few times until blended. Add butter and pulse until mixture is crumbly. Sprinkle evenly over the apples.

**4** Bake 50 to 55 minutes or until top is browned and apples are tender when pierced. Place baking dish on a wire rack to cool. Serve the Crisp warm or at room temperature.

**BEST APPLES FOR...**
Pies: These varieties won't fall apart or turn mushy. Try mixing two or three kinds. Cameo, Empire, Granny Smith, Gravenstein, Idared, Jonathan, Newtown Pippin, Northern Spy, Pink Lady, Rome Beauty, Winesap
Baking: These can bake without collapsing much. Idared, Cortland, Mutsu/Crispin, Rome Beauty, York Imperial
Snacking & Salads: Akane, Braeburn, Elstar, Empire, Fuji, Gala, Granny Smith, Jonagold, Macoun, McIntosh, Newtown Pippin, Red Delicious, Royal Gala

# Plum Plate Cake

FOOD PROCESSOR · 9-IN. ROUND CAKE PAN · OVEN

HOW LONG WILL IT KEEP? BEST EATEN WARM AND FRESH. THIS UPSIDE-DOWN COBBLER COMES BY ITS NAME BECAUSE IT'S TURNED OUT DIRECTLY ONTO A SERVING PLATE.

**TOPPING**
- ½ cup sugar
- ¼ tsp ground nutmeg
- 3 Tbsp stick butter, melted
- 1 lb plums (about 6), halved, pitted; each half cut in 4 wedges

**LEMON-CORNMEAL BISCUIT**
- 1 cup all-purpose flour
- ⅓ cup cornmeal
- 3 Tbsp sugar
- 1 Tbsp freshly grated lemon peel
- 1¼ tsp baking powder
- 5 Tbsp plus 2 tsp cold stick butter, cut in small pieces
- ½ cup milk
- 1 large egg

**SERVES 8**
**PREP:** 15 minutes
**BAKE:** 55 minutes

**PER SERVING:** 303 cal, 4 g pro, 42 g car, 2 g fiber, 14 g fat (8 g sat fat), 62 mg chol, 219 mg sod

**1** Heat oven to 400°F. Line bottom of a 9-in. round cake pan with wax paper.

**2** TOPPING: Mix sugar and nutmeg, then butter in a small bowl. Spread over paper in pan. Arrange plum wedges, on their sides, in circles, on the topping.

**3** LEMON-CORNMEAL BISCUIT: Put flour, cornmeal, sugar, lemon peel and baking powder in a food processor. Pulse briefly to mix. Add butter; pulse just until coarse crumbs form. Add milk and egg; pulse briefly until a soft dough forms. Spoon over plums, spreading to edges of pan to completely cover fruit.

**4** Bake 26 to 28 minutes until cake is lightly browned and fruit bubbles up around edge.

**5** Cool in pan on a wire rack 10 minutes. Turn serving plate upside down over pan. Hold plate and pan and turn them over together. Remove pan and wax paper. Serve cake warm, cut in wedges.

# Mocha-Hazelnut Granita

How long will it keep? At least 5 days. The icy crystals of the granita make a refreshing dessert.

**SERVES** 8
**PREP:** 10 minutes
**FREEZE:** 4 hours, stirring every 30 minutes

**PER SERVING:** 191 cal, 2 g pro, 32 g car, 0 g fiber, 7 g fat (1 g sat fat), 0 mg chol, 24 mg sod

Tip: Look for the hazelnut spread near peanut butter or preserves.

¾ cup chocolate-hazelnut spread (Nutella) (see Tip, left)
⅔ cup sugar
½ cup instant coffee granules

**1** Bring 3¼ cups water to boil in a medium saucepan.

**2** Add spread, sugar and coffee granules. Remove from heat and stir with a whisk until spread melts and sugar and coffee dissolve. Pour into an 8- or 9-in. square metal pan.

**3** Freeze at least 4 hours, stirring frozen edges into center of pan with a rubber spatula every 30 minutes until entire mixture is frozen hard.

**4** TO SERVE: Scrape surface with a large metal spoon. Mound in serving dishes.

# Frozen Raspberry-Mango Terrine

How long will it keep? Freezer, 3 weeks.

**SERVES** 16
**PREP:** 20 minutes
**FREEZE:** About 8 hours

**PER SERVING:** 152 cal, 2 g pro, 27 g car, 1 g fiber, 5 g fat (1 g sat fat), 7 mg chol, 18 mg sod

1 pt vanilla ice cream, slightly softened
1⅔ cups coarsely crushed Amaretti or other crisp almond cookies
½ cup plus 2 Tbsp toasted sliced almonds (see *Toasting Nuts*, page 189)
1 pt mango sorbet, very slightly softened
1 pt raspberry sorbet, very slightly softened
Decoration: mango slices, raspberries and mint sprigs

**1** Line a 9 x 5-in. loaf pan with plastic wrap, letting enough wrap extend above pan on all sides to cover top of pan when filled.

**2** Spoon half the ice cream into lined pan; press into a fairly even layer. Sprinkle with ⅓ cup cookie crumbs and 2 Tbsp almonds. Continue layers as follows: half the mango sorbet, crumbs, almonds; half the raspberry sorbet, crumbs, almonds. Then repeat the layers. There won't be any crumbs or almonds left for the last layer.

**3** Freeze 8 hours or until hard. Fold plastic wrap over top to cover. Freeze up to 3 weeks.

**4** TO SERVE: Unwrap top. Invert terrine onto serving plate. Peel off plastic wrap. Garnish with mango slices, raspberries and mint.

# Frozen Margarita Pie

MIXER · FOOD PROCESSOR · 9-IN. PIE PLATE · NO BAKE

How long will it keep? Freezer, 3 months.

CRUST
    4 oz (2½ cups) salted thin pretzel sticks
    ⅓ cup sugar
    1 stick (½ cup) butter, melted

14-oz can sweetened condensed milk (not evaporated milk)
1 Tbsp freshly grated lime peel
2 Tbsp fresh lime juice
1½ Tbsp tequila
1½ Tbsp Cointreau or other orange-flavor liqueur
4 drops green and 2 drops yellow liquid food color (optional)
1½ cups heavy (whipping) cream
DECORATION: thin pretzel sticks and lime slice

| |
|---|
| **SERVES** 12 |
| **PREP:** 15 minutes |
| **FREEZE:** 8 hours |
| |
| **PER SERVING:** 382 cal, 5 g pro, 39 g car, 0 g fiber, 23 g fat (14 g sat fat), 77 mg chol, 308 mg sod |

**1** Lightly coat a 9-in. pie plate with cooking spray.

**2** CRUST: Put pretzels and sugar in food processor and process until fine crumbs. Add butter; pulse to blend. Press on bottom and sides of pie plate. Place in freezer.

**3** Put condensed milk, lime peel and juice, tequila, Cointreau and food color into a small bowl. Stir to mix well. In a large bowl beat cream with mixer until soft peaks form when beaters are lifted. Gradually fold in lime mixture until blended. Pour into crust; freeze uncovered at least 6 hours. Wrap airtight; freeze at least 2 more hours.

**4** TO SERVE: Unwrap pie, garnish with pretzels and lime slice and refrigerate about 15 minutes for easier slicing.

# Entertaining

Entertaining revolves around the food. The drinks are rarely a surprise (although we offer some recipes that will change that), but what guests want to know is: What's to eat? Anyone can entertain, but it's no secret that when the host or hostess is relaxed and enjoying the party, everyone else usually has a great time, too. Even with today's relaxed approach to entertaining a little advance planning goes a long way to success. Make lists. Yes, lists. Lists are the only way to avoid last-minute trips to the store for such party basics as seltzer, paper napkins or plastic utensils. Make a list of the ingredients you need. Prepare the food as far ahead as your time and the recipe permit. We've selected easy-to-fix recipes for hearty food that everyone will enjoy. There are dips and spreads including a Smoked Salmon Mousse and a Double Egg Spread, a chili, a recipe for the ever-popular Jamaican Hot Wings and for Buffalo Shrimp. Serve the Sangria Surprise as a dessert or as a "drink" with a spoon. And enjoy your own parties.

# Antipasto Platter

THIS ITALIAN APPETIZER TRADITIONALLY CONSISTS OF MARINATED VEGETABLES,
MEATS AND CHEESES. ARRANGE THE FOODS ON A PLATTER OR WOODEN BOARD.
HERE'S ONE SELECTION YOU COULD ADD TO.

## MAKE A MEAL OF APPETIZERS

This is the kind of food everyone enjoys because they can eat as much or as little as they want and it's very informal. Plus it's usually served as an appetizer, leaving guests longing for more of it. The flavors are piquant and satisfying. Preparation requires little more than a trip to the store and setting all the foods out on platters or in bowls. Have baskets of bread or breadsticks, tiny plates of olive oil to dip the bread into and possibly sliced tomatoes or a bowl of salad greens.

Cherry-size fresh mozzarella balls sprinkled with chopped parsley and crushed red pepper

Two or three kinds of olives

Quartered marinated artichoke hearts

Roasted red pepper strips

Sliced prosciutto, salami, pepperoni

Sliced provolone cheese

Tuscan-style peperoncini

Italian bread, breadsticks

## GREEK PLATTER

Bowls of spreads/dips such as:
  Hummus (chickpea)
  Baba ghanoush (eggplant)
  Hot red pepper dip
  Taramasalata (salted cod roe dip)
Feta and other Greek-style cheeses
Greek olives
Cucumber salad
Flat breads, including pitas

## SOUTH OF FRANCE PLATTER

Country pâté or duck-liver pâté
Tuna packed in olive oil
Sardines packed in olive oil
Hard-cooked eggs
Marinated mushrooms
Salami
Two or three kinds of olives
French cheese
French bread

Antipasto Platter *(page 320)*
and White Sangria *(page 333)*

Baked Potato Skins *(page 323)*

Smoked Salmon Mousse *(page 329)*

Antipasto Tart *(page 325)*

# Buffalo Shrimp

SHRIMP · RIMMED BAKING SHEET · BROILER

2½ Tbsp stick butter

1 to 3 Tbsp hot-pepper sauce (see Tip, right)

1 tsp minced garlic

24 raw, peeled (tails left on) and deveined extra-large shrimp (about 1 lb; see *Deveining Shrimp*, page 103)

4 ribs celery, cut in sticks

GARNISH: lime wedges

**SERVES 8**
**TOTAL TIME:** 8 minutes

**PER SERVING:** 97 cal, 12 g pro, 1 g car, 0 g fiber, 5 g fat (2 g sat fat), 96 mg chol, 310 mg sod

**1** Line a rimmed baking sheet with foil; coat foil with cooking spray.

**2** Melt butter in small bowl in microwave or small saucepan. Remove from heat; stir in pepper sauce and garlic. Place shrimp on prepared baking sheet; drizzle and toss with 2 Tbsp of the butter mixture. Cook right away, or cover and refrigerate for up to 8 hours.

**3** Shortly before serving, heat broiler. Broil shrimp, turning once, about 2½ minutes or until just cooked through. Toss with remaining sauce. Arrange on platter; serve with celery. Garnish with lime wedges.

TIP: Hot-pepper sauces vary greatly in the "heat" they provide. Start with the minimum amount, taste and add more if a kick is desired.

# Jamaican Hot Wings

**SERVES** 12
**PREP:** 25 minutes
**MARINATE:** At least 4 hours
**BAKE:** 30 minutes

**PER SERVING:** 266 cal,
20 g pro, 15 g car, 0 g fiber,
14 g fat (4 g sat fat), 60 mg
chol, 111 mg sod

TIP: If wings still have tips, cut them off (freeze for broth later). If the two main parts are still joined, cut through joint with a cleaver or heavy knife.

TIP: Look for dry Caribbean jerk seasoning in the spice section of your market or paste jerk seasoning with barbecue and hot sauces.

TIP: To smash garlic, put the unpeeled cloves on a cutting board. Hold flat side of chopping knife on top of one or more cloves and "smash" down on the knife with the heel of the other hand. Garlic skins will pop open and can be removed easily; garlic cloves will be somewhat smashed, ready to add to the marinade.

MARINADE
 ⅔ cup fresh lime juice
 ⅔ cup honey
 ⅓ cup dry spice blend Caribbean jerk seasoning or paste jerk seasoning (see Tip, left, and *What's Jerk*, page 243)
 6 cloves garlic, smashed (see Tip, left)
 3 Tbsp minced fresh ginger (see *Fresh Ginger*, page 61)
 3 Tbsp Worcestershire sauce

5 lb chicken wings (25 to 28 wings), halved at center joint
GARNISH: lime wedges

**1** MARINADE: Put lime juice, honey, jerk seasoning, garlic, ginger and Worcestershire sauce in a large ziptop bag; seal and knead to mix ingredients. Add wings, seal and turn to coat. Refrigerate at least 4 hours or overnight, turning bag occasionally.

**2** Heat oven to 475°F. Line 2 rimmed baking sheets with foil (for easy cleanup). Set a large rectangular wire rack in each. Coat racks with cooking spray.

**3** Use tongs to transfer wings to prepared racks in a single layer. Pour Marinade into a medium saucepan.

**4** Bake wings 15 minutes. While wings bake, boil Marinade 6 to 8 minutes or until thick and syrupy.

**5** Brush syrupy Marinade on top of wings. (Discard any that's left.) Bake wings 15 minutes longer or until cooked through, crisp and brown.

**6** Spread out on one or two serving platters and garnish with lime wedges.

# Baked Potato Skins

How long will they keep? Refrigerator, up to 1 day prior to final baking.

10 medium baking potatoes, scrubbed
¼ cup olive oil
2 tsp garlic salt
1 tsp chili powder
5 slices bacon, cooked crisp and crumbled (see Tip, right)
⅓ cup thinly sliced scallions
⅔ cup shredded Cheddar cheese
For dipping: ranch dressing

**SERVES** 12
**BAKE:** 1 hour
**PREP:** 15 minutes
**BAKE:** 20 minutes just before serving

**PER SERVING:** 138 cal, 4 g pro, 13 g car, 1 g fiber, 8 g fat (2 g sat fat), 9 mg chol, 329 mg sod

**1** Heat oven to 350°F. Pierce potatoes in 2 or 3 places. Place directly on middle oven rack and bake 50 to 60 minutes until tender.

**2** When cool enough to handle, cut potatoes in quarters lengthwise. With a spoon, scoop pulp from skins, leaving ¼-in.-thick shells. Brush inside of shells with oil; sprinkle with garlic salt and chili powder. At this point, potatoes may be packed into rigid plastic containers (OK to stack them), covered and refrigerated up to 1 day.

**3** TO SERVE: Heat oven to 450°F. Spread potatoes skin side down on 2 rimmed baking sheets. Bake 15 to 20 minutes until hot and edges are crisp. Remove from oven; sprinkle with bacon, scallions and cheese. Bake 5 minutes or until cheese melts. Serve right away, with ranch dressing for dipping.

**TIP:** Buy cooked bacon instead of cooking it.

**TIP:** Use potato scooped from skins for Mashed Potato Pancakes with Sautéed Onion (page 258). Or make a quick soup: Simmer the potato in chicken broth for 10 to 15 minutes. Purée in food processor or blender then add a few Tbsp of cream or half-and-half. Leftover vegetables such as green peas or carrots can be added. Simmer them with the potato.

# Sausage & Pepper Sandwiches

RIMMED BAKING SHEET · ROASTING PAN · OVEN

How long will it keep? Refrigerator, 1 day.

**SERVES** 12
**PREP:** 20 minutes
**BAKE:** About 50 minutes

**PER SERVING:** 737 cal,
27 g pro, 83 g car, 6 g fiber,
32 g fat (10 g sat fat), 61 mg
chol, 1,720 mg sod

2½ lb sweet or hot Italian pork sausages
9 peppers, preferably 3 red, 3 yellow and 3 green, cut in ¾-in.-wide
    strips (about 12 cups total)
4 cups sliced onions
¼ cup olive oil
1 tsp dried oregano
1 tsp salt
1 tsp freshly ground pepper
3 long loaves French or Italian bread (about 1¼ lb each)
Garlic-flavor cooking spray
2 Tbsp red-wine vinegar

**1** Heat oven to 450°F. Line a rimmed baking sheet and a large roasting pan with foil (for easy cleanup).

**2** Place sausages on prepared baking sheet and prick each in two or three places with a fork. Roast 30 minutes, pouring off and discarding drippings after 15 minutes, until browned and cooked through. Remove sausages to a cutting board.

**3** While sausages cook, put peppers, onions, olive oil, oregano, salt and pepper in lined roasting pan; toss to mix and coat. Roast vegetables, tossing once, 40 minutes or until tender.

**4** With a serrated knife, cut breads lengthwise ¾ of the way through. Open each like a book; coat cut surfaces with cooking spray. Close loaves; wrap in foil

**5** Cut sausages in ½-in.-thick slices; add to pepper mixture along with the vinegar. Toss to mix and coat.

**6** Shortly before serving, bake wrapped breads (at 450°F) 8 minutes or until hot. Unwrap bread; cut each loaf in quarters. Serve with sausage and peppers, letting guests make their own sandwiches.

TIP: Get sausages cooking then slice the peppers and onions.

TIP: If made ahead, reheat sausages and peppers in microwave or in a large heavy skillet over low heat.

# Antipasto Tart

How long will it keep? Refrigerator, 2 days (before baking).

1 refrigerated ready-to-bake pie crust (from a 15-oz box of 2)
12-oz jar roasted yellow peppers, drained
6-oz jar marinated artichoke hearts, drained
½ cup (8 Tbsp) shredded mozzarella cheese
4 oz sliced 50%-less-fat salami or pepperoni
2 Tbsp store-bought refrigerated basil pesto
1 plum tomato, thinly sliced

**SERVES** 10
**PREP:** 20 minutes
**BAKE:** About 20 minutes

**PER SERVING:** 179 cal, 6 g pro, 14 g car, 1 g fiber, 12 g fat (4 g sat fat), 17 mg chol, 511 mg sod

**1** Unroll pie crust on a baking sheet or 12-in. pizza pan. Pat yellow peppers and artichoke hearts dry with paper towels.

**2** Leaving a 1-in. border around edge, sprinkle crust with 3 Tbsp mozzarella, top with salami, overlapping the slices, then spread salami evenly with pesto. Top with another 3 Tbsp mozzarella, the roasted peppers, tomato slices and artichokes. Sprinkle with remaining mozzarella.

**3** Brush edge of crust with water; fold over and flute, or crimp with a fork. Cover loosely with plastic wrap and refrigerate up to 2 days.

**4** TO SERVE: Heat oven to 425°F. Uncover tart and bake 20 minutes or until crust is golden brown and cheese has melted.

**5** Cool on baking sheet on a wire rack 5 minutes. Loosen edges of tart with a metal spatula, then carefully use spatula to slide tart onto a serving plate or cutting board. Cut in wedges (see Tip, right).

**TIP:** A pizza wheel makes a neat job of cutting this tart.

# Prosciutto Breadsticks

## NO-COOK

GREAT FOR A PARTY SINCE THEY CAN BE MADE AHEAD AND HANDED AROUND ON A PLATTER.
HOW LONG WILL THEY KEEP? REFRIGERATOR, I DAY.

**MAKES** 18
**TOTAL TIME:** About 10 to 15 minutes

**PER SERVING:** 45 cal, 2 g pro, 5 g car, 0 g fiber, 2 g fat (1 g sat fat), 7 mg chol, 152 mg sod

6 slices (about 3 oz) prosciutto (see *Specialty Hams*, page 135)
¼ cup chive-and-onion flavored cream cheese (from a tub), softened
18 long, thin breadsticks

**1** Lay 3 slices prosciutto on a large cutting board. Spread 2 tsp cream cheese on each slice. With a long, sharp knife, cut each slice prosciutto lengthwise in thirds. Wrap each strip around a breadstick, starting at top and wrapping toward the middle.

**2** Repeat with remaining prosciutto, cream cheese and breadsticks. To store, line up the wrapped breadsticks on a baking sheet lined with plastic wrap, putting wrap between the layers.

# Pepper Bruschetta

## NO-COOK · OVEN FOR TOASTING

AN EASY AND DELICIOUS APPETIZER. HOW LONG WILL IT KEEP? REFRIGERATOR, 2 DAYS.

**MAKES** About 15
**TOTAL TIME:** 10 minutes

**PER SERVING:** 60 cal, 1 g pro, 8 g car, 1 g fiber, 3 g fat (1 g sat fat), 0 mg chol, 120 mg sod

TIP: You can use 4 peppers of one color.

TIP: You can find the Italian toast in the cracker section of your supermarket.

2 bottled roasted red peppers (see Tip, right)
2 bottled roasted yellow peppers
2 Tbsp golden raisins
2 Tbsp toasted pine nuts (pignoli, see *Pine Nuts or Pignoli*, page 281; see *Toasting Nuts*, page 189)
2½ Tbsp olive oil, preferably extra-virgin
2 tsp balsamic vinegar
15 pieces (from a 4.25-oz bag) roasted-garlic oven-baked Italian toast (see Tip, left) or ½-in. thick slices French bread, toasted

**1** Dry peppers well on paper towels. Cut in narrow strips and put into a small bowl. Add raisins, pine nuts, olive oil and vinegar. Mix gently. Serve, or cover and refrigerate.

**2** Shortly before serving, spoon 1 Tbsp pepper mixture on each toast; drizzle with dressing left in bowl.

# Beef & Three-Bean Chili

## BEEF CHUCK FOR STEW

HOW LONG WILL IT KEEP? REFRIGERATOR, 4 DAYS; FREEZER, 2 WEEKS.

1 Tbsp olive oil

3 lb lean beef chuck, cut for stew (see *Cuts for Stew*, page 87)

2 cups chopped onions

Three 14-oz cans diced tomatoes with chiles

15-oz can tomato sauce

12 oz beer or water

⅓ cup chili powder

3 Tbsp minced garlic

1 Tbsp ground cumin

2 tsp salt

1 tsp dried oregano

½ tsp ground cinnamon

15- to 16-oz can black beans, drained and rinsed

15- to 16-oz can pinto beans, drained and rinsed

15- to 16-oz can kidney beans, drained and rinsed

½ cup chopped fresh cilantro

ACCOMPANIMENTS: **sour cream, chopped cilantro and red onion and shredded Monterey Jack or Cheddar cheese**

**SERVES 12** (makes 16 cups)
**TOTAL TIME:** About 2½ hours

**PER SERVING:** 310 cal, 29 g pro, 25 g car, 9 g fiber, 11 g fat (3 g sat fat), 74 mg chol, 1,340 mg sod

**1**  Heat 1½ tsp oil in a 5- to 6-qt pot over medium-high heat. Add half the beef; cook 5 to 6 minutes, stirring two or three times, until browned. Remove with a slotted spoon to a bowl. Add remaining 1½ tsp oil to pot and brown remaining beef; add to bowl.

**2**  Add onions to drippings in pot; cook about 5 minutes, stirring occasionally, until golden. Add tomatoes, 2 cups water, tomato sauce, beer, chili powder, garlic, cumin, salt, oregano and cinnamon. Stir, then bring to a boil. Add beef, partially cover the pot and simmer 2 hours, stirring every 20 to 30 minutes, until beef is very tender.

**3**  Stir in beans; heat through. Remove from heat. Just before serving, stir in cilantro. Serve with bowls of accompaniments.

TIP: If making the chili ahead, don't add the cilantro until just before serving.

# Southwestern Layered Dip

## 12-IN. OR LARGER ROUND OR SQUARE SERVING PLATTER · NO-COOK

How long will it keep? Refrigerator, 1 day.

SERVES 12
TOTAL TIME: 30 minutes

PER SERVING: 203 cal, 9 g pro, 18 g car, 4 g fiber, 12 g fat (4 g sat fat), 18 mg chol, 794 mg sod

**FYI:** Hass avocados are the dark, almost black when ripe, pebbly skinned variety.

BEAN LAYER

Two 16-oz cans lowfat refried black beans
¼ cup chopped fresh cilantro
½ tsp freshly grated lime peel
2 Tbsp fresh lime juice
1 Tbsp hot Mexican chili powder
1 tsp minced garlic

GUACAMOLE LAYER

2 ripe Hass avocados (see FYI, left)
2 Tbsp fresh lime juice
2 Tbsp minced red onion
1 tsp salt
1 tsp hot-pepper sauce

1 Tbsp chopped fresh cilantro
1 cup reduced-fat sour cream
1 cup (4 oz) shredded Monterey Jack cheese blend
2 cups store-bought refrigerated salsa
Garnish: cilantro sprigs
Serve with: a variety of tortilla chips

**1** BEAN LAYER: Put refried beans, cilantro, lime peel and juice, chili powder and garlic into a medium bowl. Stir to blend well. Scrape onto a 12-in. (larger is OK) square or round serving plate. Shape into a flat 9-in. square or round.

**2** GUACAMOLE LAYER: Halve avocados; scoop out seeds then scoop flesh into a medium bowl. Add lime juice, red onion, salt and hot sauce and mash until fairly smooth. Mound in center of bean layer; then spread level, leaving some of the bean layer showing around edge. Sprinkle guacamole with chopped cilantro.

**3** Spread sour cream almost to edge of guacamole. Sprinkle with cheese, almost to edge of sour cream. Serve, or cover and refrigerate.

**4** TO SERVE: Drain salsa in a strainer to get rid of excess juice. Spoon salsa over cheese and decorate with cilantro sprigs. Surround dip with chips.

# Smoked Salmon Mousse

## 8- OR 9-IN. ROUND CAKE PAN · FOOD PROCESSOR OR BLENDER

HOW LONG WILL IT KEEP? REFRIGERATOR, 3 DAYS.

8 oz thinly sliced smoked salmon

2 tsp unflavored gelatin (from 1 pkt)

15-oz can red salmon

½ cup reduced-fat sour cream

½ cup light mayonnaise

3 Tbsp fresh lemon juice

3 Tbsp finely chopped red onion

½ tsp or more hot-pepper sauce

GARNISH: cucumber and carrot strands (see Tip, right)

SERVE WITH: crostini (thin slices French bread toasted
  in oven) or crackers

> **SERVES** 12
> **PREP:** 25 minutes
> **CHILL:** At least 4 hours
>
> **PER SERVING:** 120 cal,
> 10 g pro, 2 g car, 0 g fiber,
> 8 g fat (2 g sat fat), 24 mg chol,
> 622 mg sod

**1** Lightly coat an 8- or 9-in. round cake pan with cooking spray. Line with plastic wrap, using enough wrap to extend 4 to 6 in. beyond sides of pan and keeping wrap smooth as possible.

**2** Line bottom of pan with half the smoked salmon, pressing slices thinner to cover bottom completely.

**3** Sprinkle gelatin over ½ cup cold water in a small saucepan. Let stand 1 minute. Stir over low heat 2 to 3 minutes until liquid is almost boiling and gelatin is completely dissolved. Remove from heat.

**4** Drain ¼ cup salmon liquid into a cup measure (discard the rest). Put salmon into a blender or food processor, removing any black skin as you do so. Add ¼ cup salmon liquid, remaining smoked salmon, the sour cream, mayonnaise, lemon juice, onion and hot pepper sauce. Process (or blend) until smooth.

**5** Add gelatin; process until blended. Pour over salmon in pan, fold plastic wrap over top to cover and refrigerate at least 4 hours.

**6** UP TO 10 HOURS BEFORE SERVING: Fold back wrap from top of mousse. Put serving plate upside down over pan. Hold tightly and turn pan and plate over together. Remove pan and plastic wrap. Smooth any rough edges with side of a knife. Garnish, cover loosely with plastic wrap and refrigerate. Serve with crostini and crackers.

> **TIP:** To make garnish, the day before the party, peel a cucumber in long strips with a vegetable peeler. Stack strips and cut into narrow strands. Slice a peeled carrot with the vegetable peeler. Cut as for cucumber strips. Wrap strips in paper towel and refrigerate in a plastic bag.

# Carrot Dip

How long will it keep? Refrigerator, 2 days.

**SERVES 8** (makes 2 cups)
**TOTAL TIME:** 30 minutes (plus at least 30 minutes chilling)
**CHILL:** 30 minutes

**PER ¼ CUP:** 90 cal, 1 g pro, 6 g car, 2 g fiber, 7 g fat (1 g sat fat), 0 mg chol, 143 mg sod

3 cups sliced carrots (1 lb)
1 cup chicken broth
⅓ cup cider vinegar
3 cloves garlic, thinly sliced
1 tsp ground cumin
¼ cup olive oil
Dippers: flavored or plain tortilla chips

**1** Put carrots, ¾ cup broth, the vinegar, garlic and cumin into a medium saucepan. Bring to a boil over medium-high heat. Cover pan, reduce heat to low and simmer 15 minutes until carrots are tender. Uncover pan, increase heat to medium-high and cook about 3 minutes longer until almost all the liquid has evaporated. Remove from heat; let cool a few minutes.

**2** Purée in food processor, scraping down sides of bowl a few times. With machine running, slowly add oil. Process, adding remaining ¼ cup chicken broth, until blended and fairly smooth. Taste dip, add a little more vinegar if you wish. Scrape into a bowl and refrigerate at least 30 minutes. Serve with chips.

# Hummus-Topped Cucumbers

How long will it keep? Room temperature, up to 3 hours.

**MAKES 32**
**TOTAL TIME:** 8 minutes

**PER 2-SLICE SERVING:** 22 cal, 1 g pro, 2 g car, 0 g fiber, 2 g fat (0 g sat fat), 0 mg chol, 70 mg sod

½ a long seedless cucumber, cut into 32 slices
⅔ cup store-bought refrigerated roasted red pepper hummus
¼ cup snipped chives

Top each cucumber slice with about 1 tsp hummus. Sprinkle with chives.

# Creamy Red Pepper Dip

## 3- TO 4-CUP SERVING BOWL · FOOD PROCESSOR

HOW LONG WILL IT KEEP? DIP, REFRIGERATOR, 3 DAYS; DIPPING VEGETABLES, 1 DAY.

4 medium red peppers (see Tip, right)
8-oz brick ⅓-less-fat cream cheese (Neufchâtel), softened
1 cup reduced-fat sour cream
1 tsp chopped garlic
½ tsp salt
DIPPERS: raw and blanched vegetables (see FYI, right)

**1** Roast red peppers directly over a gas burner or under a broiler, turning often until charred all over. Place in a bowl, cover and let steam 10 minutes to loosen skins. Pull off skins and remove stems and seeds.

**2** Put peppers in a food processor, add cream cheese, sour cream, garlic and salt and process until smooth. Scrape into a bowl; cover and refrigerate. Serve with dippers.

**SERVES** 12 (makes 3 cups)
**TOTAL TIME:** 30 minutes

**PER ¼ CUP:** 87 cal, 4 g pro, 3 g car, 0 g fiber, 7 g fat (4 g sat fat), 20 mg chol, 188 mg sod

TIP: You can use a 12-oz jar of roasted red peppers instead of fresh. Drain, blot dry with paper towels and put in food processor.

**FYI:** Blanching, that is giving vegetables such as green beans and broccoli a short dip in boiling water, brings out their flavor and brightens their color. Put them in a strainer and lower it into a pot of boiling water. When the water boils again, count to 10 then transfer the vegetables immediately to a bowl of cold water and ice to stop the cooking process.

# Double Egg Spread

## 4½- TO 5-CUP SERVING BOWL · FOOD PROCESSOR

How long will it keep? Refrigerator, 1 day.

Chicken-egg spread decorated with salmon eggs make this fun party fare.

**SERVES** 20 (makes 4½ cups)
**PREP:** 30 minutes
**CHILL:** At least 5 hours

**PER SERVING:** 114 cal,
7 g pro, 2 g car, 0 g fiber,
9 g fat (4 g sat fat), 179 mg
chol, 211 mg sod

12 large eggs, hard cooked and peeled

½ stick (¼ cup) butter, softened

1 tsp salt

½ cup thinly sliced scallions

1 cup (8 oz) reduced-fat sour cream

4 oz (half an 8-oz brick) ⅓-less-fat cream cheese (Neufchâtel),
softened

GARNISH: **5 oz salmon roe caviar and chives or flat-leaf Italian
parsley**

SERVE WITH: **crackers, crostini**

**1** Remove yolk from 1 hard-cooked egg. Press through a strainer into a small cup; cover and refrigerate to use for decoration. Put the egg white and the remaining eggs in a food processor and chop finely (or mash in a bowl). Add butter and salt and process (or mash) until well blended. Spoon into a 4½- to 5-cup serving dish and spread in an even layer. Cover and refrigerate at least 1 hour until firm.

**2** Sprinkle with scallions. Mix sour cream and cream cheese until well blended (it doesn't have to be completely smooth). Spoon over scallions, then spread evenly without disturbing scallions. Cover and chill at least 4 hours.

**3** UP TO 1 HOUR BEFORE SERVING: Spoon alternating lines of salmon roe and the sieved yolk on surface; arrange chives between. Refrigerate uncovered until ready to serve. Serve with crackers and one or two small spreaders.

# White Sangria

How long will it keep? Wine base, refrigerator, up to 1 day; fruit added, about 1 hour.

3 bottles (750 ml each) dry white wine

½ cup Triple Sec or other orange liqueur

1½ cups no-pulp orange juice

¼ cup fresh lemon juice

6 Tbsp sugar, or to taste

24 oz (2 pt) strawberries

4 ripe peaches

1 Golden Delicious apple

1 lemon

1 lime

1 orange

4 cups (2 trays) ice cubes

**MAKES** 22 cups
**PREP:** 5 minutes
**CHILL:** At least 1 hour
**PREP:** 15 minutes
**CHILL:** 1 hour

**PER CUP SANGRIA:** 125 cal, 1 g pro, 13 g car, 1 g fiber, 0 g fat (0 g sat fat), 0 mg chol, 6 mg sod

**1** Pour wine, Triple Sec, orange juice, lemon juice and sugar into a large bowl or stainless-steel pot. Stir until sugar dissolves. Refrigerate to chill, up to 1 day.

**2** ABOUT 1¼ HOURS BEFORE SERVING: Slice strawberries; cut peaches and apple in thin wedges. Cut lemon, lime and orange in half, then in thin slices.

**3** ONE HOUR BEFORE SERVING: Pour wine base into pitcher(s); add fruit. Refrigerate. Add ice just before serving.

**FYI:** For a nonalcoholic sangria, leave out the Triple Sec and sugar. Replace wine with 9 cups 100% white grape juice and add an extra ½ cup of orange juice.

# Raspberry Lemonade Tea

HOW LONG WILL IT KEEP? BEST FRESHLY MADE.

**MAKES** 4 cups
**TOTAL TIME:** 10 minutes

**PER SERVING:** 139 cal,
0 g pro, 36 g car, 0 g fiber,
0 g fat (0 g sat fat), 0 mg chol,
4 mg sod

3¼ cups boiling water
4 Raspberry Zinger tea bags
3 Tbsp sugar
6-oz can frozen lemonade concentrate
Ice cubes

Pour boiling water over tea bags. Steep 5 minutes. Remove tea bags. Stir in sugar until dissolved, then frozen lemonade concentrate. Serve over ice cubes.

# Tropical Smoothie

HOW LONG WILL IT KEEP? SERVE IMMEDIATELY.

**MAKES** 4 cups
**TOTAL TIME:** 10 minutes

**PER SERVING:** 142 cal,
2 g pro, 26 g car, 1 g fiber,
5 g fat (4 g sat fat), 0 mg chol,
14 mg sod

TIP: Look for cream of coconut (not coconut milk or coconut water) in the cocktail mix section of the market. Stir it in the can before pouring it into a cup measure.

1½ cups crushed ice
1⅓ cups chilled pineapple juice
2 ripe bananas
⅓ cup cream of coconut (see Tip, left)

Put all ingredients in a blender. Purée until blended and frothy.

# Watermelon Slush

BLENDER

How long will it keep? Serve immediately.

6 cups well-chilled 1-in. cubes watermelon
⅓ cup sugar
⅓ cup fresh lime juice
2 to 3 Tbsp coarsely chopped crystallized ginger

Purée watermelon, sugar, lime juice and crystallized ginger in a blender until smooth.

> SERVES 4
> TOTAL TIME: 15 minutes
>
> PER SERVING: 180 cal,
> 1 g pro, 44 g car, 1 g fiber,
> 0 g fat (0 g sat fat), 0 mg chol,
> 13 mg sod

# Summer Sunset

PITCHER FOR SERVING · TALL, CLEAR GLASSES

How long will it keep? Serve immediately.
Sip this while watching a real sunset.

2 cups chilled orange juice
1½ cups chilled peach nectar
½ cup fresh lime juice
Grenadine syrup (see Tip, right)

Mix orange juice, peach nectar and lime juice in a pitcher. Pour into glasses. Then pour a little grenadine into each glass; it will settle on the bottom.

> MAKES 4 cups
> TOTAL TIME: 10 minutes
>
> PER SERVING: 148 cal,
> 1 g pro, 37 g car, 0 g fiber,
> 0 g fat (0 g sat fat), 0 mg chol,
> 8 mg sod

> TIP: Look for grenadine syrup (it's red) in the cocktail-mix section.

# Minted Grapefruit Juice

PITCHER FOR SERVING

HOW LONG WILL IT KEEP? BEST WITHIN 1 HOUR.

**MAKES** 4 cups
**TOTAL TIME:** 10 minutes

**PER SERVING:** 251 cal,
6 g pro, 59 g car, 9 g fiber,
1 g fat (0 g sat fat), 0 mg chol,
44 mg sod

3 cups packed fresh mint leaves
4 cups grapefruit juice
½ cup sugar
Ice cubes

Boil mint leaves with 1 cup of the juice and the sugar in a small saucepan for 3 minutes, pushing mint down into juice if necessary. Meanwhile, pour remaining grapefruit juice into pitcher. Set a strainer over the pitcher; pour in mint mixture, pressing on leaves to extract juice. Discard mint leaves. Serve over ice cubes.

# Sangria Surprise

7-CUP PITCHER FOR SERVING

HOW LONG WILL IT KEEP? UP TO 2 DAYS.

**SERVES** 8
**PREP:** 25 minutes
**MACERATE:** About 4 hours
**CHILL:** At least 3 hours

**PER SERVING:** 223 cal,
2 g pro, 45 g car, 1 g fiber,
0 g fat (0 g sat fat), 0 mg chol,
62 mg sod

2 cups white wine or nonalcoholic wine
½ cup sugar
3 cups fruit (we used cut-up peaches, nectarines and plums, orange sections and grapes)
2 envelopes unflavored gelatin
2 cups cold white grape juice

**1** Put wine and sugar into a medium bowl; stir until sugar dissolves. Add fruit; stir to mix and coat. Cover surface of fruit with plastic wrap and macerate in refrigerator at least 4 hours or overnight.

**2** Sprinkle gelatin over ½ cup grape juice in a small saucepan. Let stand 1 to 2 minutes. Stir over medium-low heat until almost boiling and gelatin is completely dissolved.

**3** Drain liquid from fruit (about 2 cups) into a large bowl. Stir in remaining grape juice, then the gelatin until blended. Refrigerate until partially set (consistency of unbeaten raw egg whites).

**4** Fold fruit into gelatin; pour into a 7-cup capacity pitcher. Cover with plastic wrap and refrigerate at least 3 hours or up to 2 days. Spoon from pitcher into wine goblets.

TIP: "Macerate" is the term usually used when soaking fruits in a liquid to give them added flavor. "Marinate" refers to doing the same to meat, fish and vegetables.

# Fruit Smoothies

THESE WILL PLEASE CHILDREN AND ADULTS ALIKE. PUT INGREDIENTS IN BLENDER
IN ORDER LISTED. SERVE IN CHILLED GLASSES, WITH A STRAW.

## VANILLA BERRY

1 cup lowfat vanilla yogurt
1 small ripe banana, cut up
2 Tbsp honey
1 cup fresh or frozen strawberries
1 cup fresh or frozen raspberries
½ cup raspberry sherbet or sorbet

SERVES 2
TOTAL TIME: 10 minutes

PER SERVING: 322 cal,
8 g pro, 71 g car, 6 g fiber,
3 g fat (2 g sat fat), 8 mg chol,
99 mg sod

Purée all ingredients in a blender until thick and smooth.

## PIÑA LIMONADA

½ cup chilled lemonade
2 cups diced ripe fresh pineapple
1 small ripe banana, cut up
1 Tbsp honey
½ cup pineapple sorbet
½ cup coconut sorbet

SERVES 2
TOTAL TIME: 10 minutes

PER SERVING: 307 cal,
2 g pro, 74 g car, 3 g fiber,
3 g fat (1 g sat fat), 5 mg chol,
48 mg sod

Purée all ingredients in a blender until thick and smooth.

## MELLOW MELON

¼ cup chilled apple juice or white grape juice
2 cups diced ripe honeydew melon
1 small Granny Smith apple, peeled, cut up
1 small ripe banana, cut up
1 cup lime sherbet or sorbet

SERVES 2
TOTAL TIME: 10 minutes

PER SERVING: 279 cal,
2 g pro, 67 g car, 3 g fiber,
3 g fat (1 g sat fat), 5 mg chol,
63 mg sod

Purée all ingredients in a blender until thick and smooth.

# Celebrations

One of the best things about holidays such as Thanksgiving and the Fourth of July is that they make us take a break and spend time with family and friends. And where would those special celebrations be if it wasn't for the food? In fact, food often becomes the foundation of these occasions. In this chapter you will find delicious but easily manageable menus for Thanksgiving and July Fourth, as well as for Christmas and Easter. The Christmas menu offers a choice of main dishes: beef tenderloin or stuffed turkey breast. There are two cakes for Passover and a Brunch for 8 that would be perfect for Mother's Day, Father's Day or a simple family get-together for a graduation. Once again we suggest list-making and preparing food as far ahead as time and the recipe permit. If someone offers to make a dish and bring it, do not demur; send them the recipe immediately. You will have more time and the contributor will feel even more part of the occasion. Here's a toast from our family to yours: Enjoy time together.

## Thanksgiving for 12

## Christmas Menu for 8

## Easter Menu for 8

## Two Passover Cakes

## Fourth of July Picnic for 8

## Brunch for 8

# Thanksgiving *for* 12

APPLE & BLUE-CHEESE SALAD

ROAST TURKEY

SAUSAGE & CORNBREAD STUFFING

MAKE-AHEAD TURKEY GRAVY

ROSEMARY-GARLIC MASHED POTATOES

HONEY-GINGER SWEET POTATOES

CORN PUDDING

GREEN BEANS WITH FRENCH FRIED ONIONS

FRESH CRANBERRY-ORANGE-RASPBERRY RELISH

PUMPKIN-CHOCOLATE CHEESECAKE

PEAR-ALMOND TART WITH CRANBERRIES

## Thanksgiving Dinner Timetable

### THREE TO FOUR WEEKS AHEAD

- Check supply of chairs, dishes, glasses and utensils, and arrange to borrow or rent what you don't have.
- Prepare Make-Ahead Turkey Gravy. Freeze in airtight container.
- Bake Pumpkin-Chocolate Cheesecake. Cool, cover pan airtight and freeze.

### TWO WEEKS AHEAD

- Order turkey to be sure you get the size you want. Check that it will fit in your refrigerator and oven.
- Make shopping list. Shop for nonperishable food.
- Plan table settings and centerpiece.
- Bake crust for Pear-Almond Tart with Cranberries. Freeze airtight.

### ONE WEEK AHEAD

- Toast and chop walnuts for Apple & Blue Cheese Salad and pecans for Sausage & Cornbread Stuffing. Dice apricots for stuffing. Store separately at room temperature.
- Make Fresh Cranberry-Orange-Raspberry Relish. Refrigerate in covered serving bowl.

### SATURDAY BEFORE THANKSGIVING

- Pick up turkey if frozen.
- Get out china, glassware, serving dishes and serving utensils. Polish silver if necessary.
- Make Apple Vinaigrette for Apple & Blue Cheese Salad. Refrigerate.

## MONDAY BEFORE THANKSGIVING
- Shop for perishable food.
- Put frozen turkey in refrigerator to thaw.

## TUESDAY BEFORE THANKSGIVING
- Prepare onions, celery and parsley for Sausage & Cornbread Stuffing. Wrap separately and refrigerate.
- Transfer Make-Ahead Turkey Gravy from freezer to refrigerator to thaw.
- Prepare Honey-Ginger Sweet Potatoes. Cover and refrigerate in microwave safe serving dish or oven-to-table baking dish.
- Prepare and bake Pear-Almond Tart with Cranberries. Refrigerate tightly covered. Also cook and refrigerate cranberries for tart (Step 7).
- Transfer Pumpkin-Chocolate Cheesecake from freezer to refrigerator to thaw.
- Start making extra ice.

## DAY BEFORE THANKSGIVING
- Buy flowers.
- Pick up turkey if fresh. Refrigerate.
- Prepare Sausage & Cornbread Stuffing. Refrigerate airtight.
- Prepare Rosemary-Garlic Mashed Potatoes. Cover and refrigerate in microwave-safe serving dish or oven-to-table baking dish.
- Prepare Corn Pudding through Step 3. Refrigerate covered. Store buttered cracker crumbs airtight at room temperature.
- Prepare Green Beans with French Fried Onions through Step 2. Refrigerate covered.
- Set table.
- Chill beverages.

## THANKSGIVING MORNING
- Stuff turkey with Sausage & Cornbread Stuffing. Spoon extra stuffing into baking dish. Cover and refrigerate.
- Start roasting 12- to 14-lb turkey so it will be done 45 minutes before dinner. Check Turkey Roasting Chart (page 344), for roasting time.

## 1½ TO 2 HOURS BEFORE DINNER
- Remove Honey-Ginger Sweet Potatoes and Corn Pudding from refrigerator to come to room temperature.
- Cut apples for Apple & Blue Cheese Salad.

## 1 HOUR BEFORE DINNER
- Add cranberry garnish to Pear-Almond Tart with Cranberries. Remove tart from pan to serving plate. Leave at room temperature.
- Prepare garnishes for turkey platter.
- Start testing turkey for doneness.

## 45 MINUTES BEFORE DINNER
- Transfer turkey from oven to serving platter. Cover loosely with foil.
- Increase oven temperature to 350°F.
- Put covered baking dish of stuffing in oven.

## ABOUT 40 MINUTES BEFORE DINNER
- Sprinkle the Corn Pudding with the buttered cracker crumbs. Place in oven.

## 30 MINUTES BEFORE DINNER
- Place the covered Honey-Ginger Sweet Potatoes and Rosemary-Garlic Mashed Potatoes in oven (if not heating in microwave).

## 15 MINUTES BEFORE DINNER
- Uncover stuffing in baking dish; bake 15 minutes longer or until browned.
- Heat Make-Ahead Turkey Gravy. Add turkey drippings, if desired.
- Reheat Green Beans with French Fried Onions on stovetop (if not heating in microwave).
- Garnish turkey platter and serving dishes.

## JUST BEFORE SERVING DINNER

- Assemble Apple & Blue Cheese Salad. Divide among serving plates.
- Recrisp onions for Green Beans with French Fried Onions. Stir half into beans; sprinkle rest on top.
- Pour gravy into gravy boat.
- Set out Fresh Cranberry-Orange-Raspberry Relish.

## JUST BEFORE SERVING DESSERTS

- Place cheesecake on serving platter.

# Apple & Blue Cheese Salad

### BLENDER OR FOOD PROCESSOR

How long will it keep? Vinaigrette dressing, refrigerator, 5 days.
Toasted nuts, room temperature, 1 week.

**SERVES** 12
**TOTAL TIME:** 30 minutes

**PER SERVING:** 188 cal, 5 g pro, 11 g car, 2 g fiber, 14 g fat (4 g sat fat), 11 mg chol, 334 mg sod

**Tip:** Choose a good-quality blue cheese such as Gorgonzola or Roquefort.

**Tip:** The apples can be cut up to 2 hours ahead. Immerse the slices in a bowl of cold water and add 1 Tbsp lemon juice. Before adding to the salad, drain the slices and blot dry with paper towels.

APPLE VINAIGRETTE
- ½ cup unsweetened applesauce
- ⅓ cup olive oil
- ¼ cup cider vinegar
- 3 scallions, cut up
- 1 Tbsp Dijon mustard
- ½ tsp salt

3 Golden Delicious apples
21 to 24 oz romaine, curly endive and radicchio salad mix
1½ cups (6 oz) crumbled blue cheese (see Tip, left)
⅔ cup walnuts, pecans or hazelnuts, toasted and chopped
   (see *Toasting Nuts*, page 189 and *Toasting Hazelnuts*, page 279)

**1** VINAIGRETTE: Put all the ingredients in a blender or food processor; process until smooth. Pour into a jar, cover and refrigerate.

**2** TO SERVE: Halve and core the apples and cut in thin wedges (see Tip, left). Put in a large bowl with the salad greens, blue cheese and nuts. Shake dressing, pour over salad; toss and serve.

# Roast Turkey

One 12- to 14-lb turkey, thawed if frozen
Sausage & Cornbread Stuffing (see recipe, page 344)
1 Tbsp stick butter, melted
½ tsp salt
½ tsp freshly ground pepper
1 cup chicken broth
GARNISH: grapes and fresh herbs

**SERVES** 12
**PREP:** 30 minutes
**ROAST:** 3½ to 4 hours
(plus intermittent basting)
**REST:** 30 to 45 minutes

**PER 4-OZ SERVING** cooked lean meat: 191 cal, 33 g pro, 0 g car, 0 g fiber, 5 g fat (2 g sat fat), 87 mg chol, 84 mg sod

**1** Heat oven to 325°F. Have ready a shallow roasting pan with a rack. Take out giblets, neck and any fat from turkey body and neck cavities. Discard fat. Dry turkey inside and out with paper towels.

**2** Lightly spoon some stuffing into neck cavity. Fold skin flap under back; fasten with skewers or toothpicks. Loosely stuff body. Tie or clamp legs together. Twist wing tips under back. Brush skin with butter; sprinkle with salt and pepper.

**3** If using a standard meat thermometer (not an instant-read) insert it in center of a thigh next to body (not touching bone). Add broth to pan.

**4** Roast 3½ to 4 hours, basting every 30 minutes with pan juices, adding more broth or water if pan seems dry. If breast gets too brown, cover loosely with foil.

**5** About two-thirds through roasting time, untie drumsticks so heat can better penetrate body cavity.

**6** About 1 hour before turkey should be done, start checking for doneness. When thermometer reads 180°F in thigh and center of stuffing registers 165°F, remove turkey to a serving platter or carving board. Let rest about 45 minutes (at least 30) for juicier meat and easier carving. Garnish platter before serving.

PLANNING TIP: Plan to have turkey done about 45 minutes before rest of meal. Once cooked, a whole turkey will stay warm for at least 1 hour. See *Turkey Roasting Chart* (page 344) for roasting times.

## TURKEY ROASTING CHART

Because turkey body shapes differ, these cooking times are approximate. The times are based on open-pan roasting of a chilled turkey (with a starting internal temperature of 40°F) in a 325°F oven.

| WEIGHT (lb) | UNSTUFFED (hours) | STUFFED (hours) |
|---|---|---|
| 8 to 12 | 2¾ to 3 | 3 to 3½ |
| 12 to 14 | 3 to 3¾ | 3½ to 4 |
| 14 to 18 | 3¾ to 4¼ | 4 to 4¼ |
| 18 to 20 | 4¼ to 4½ | 4¼ to 5 |
| 20 to 24 | 4½ to 5 | 5 to 5¼ |

Roasting times based on recommendations from the Department of Agriculture.

# Sausage & Cornbread Stuffing

### SKILLET · BAKING DISH · OVEN

HOW LONG WILL IT KEEP? REFRIGERATOR, 1 DAY. STUFF BIRD JUST BEFORE ROASTING.

**SERVES** 12
**PREP:** 20 minutes
**BAKE:** 45 minutes

**PER SERVING:** 482 cal, 12 g pro, 63 g car, 4 g fiber, 20 g fat (5 g sat fat), 19 mg chol, 1,487 mg sod

TIP: Chop apricots and pecans up to 1 week ahead. Wrap; keep at room temperature. Prepare onion, celery and parsley up to 2 days ahead; wrap and refrigerate.

TIP: Sweetened dried cranberries can replace the dried cherries.

TIP: If you don't have a bowl large enough to mix the stuffing in, try a large pot instead.

Three 6-oz boxes stovetop cornbread stuffing mix
6-oz box stovetop savory herb stuffing mix
1 cup dried cherries, preferably tart (see Tip, left)
6 oz dried apricots, diced (2⅓ cups)
1 cup pecans, toasted, coarsely chopped (see *Toasting Nuts*, page 189)
1 cup chopped fresh parsley
12-oz roll pork sausage, thawed if frozen
2 cups chopped celery
1½ cups quartered and sliced red onion
4 cups chicken broth

**1** Put stuffing mixes, cherries, apricots, pecans and parsley in a large bowl or pot; toss to mix.

**2** Heat a large, deep nonstick skillet over medium-high heat. Add sausage, celery and onion and cook 5 to 7 minutes, stirring to break up sausage, until sausage is no longer pink and vegetables are crisp-tender. Add broth; bring to a boil.

**3** Pour over the stuffing mixture; toss to mix and moisten evenly. Stuff neck and body cavity of turkey.

**4** Spoon extra stuffing into a greased shallow baking dish. Cover with foil and refrigerate. Before serving, bake 30 minutes (at 350°F). Uncover and bake 15 minutes longer until lightly browned.

# Make-Ahead Turkey Gravy

ROASTING PAN · OVEN

How long does it keep? Refrigerator, 5 days; freezer, 1 month.

3 to 4 lb turkey wings
2 medium onions, quartered
8 cups chicken broth
¾ cup chopped carrots
½ tsp dried thyme
¾ cup flour
2 Tbsp stick butter
½ tsp freshly ground pepper
Turkey drippings

**MAKES** 8 cups
**PREP:** 10 minutes (plus 10 minutes before serving)
**ROAST AND SIMMER:** About 3 hours

**PER ¼ CUP:** 29 cal, 1 g pro, 3 g car, 0 g fiber, 1 g fat (1 g sat fat), 2 mg chol, 263 mg sod

**1** Heat oven to 400°F. Have ready a large roasting pan, 5- to 6-qt pot and 3-qt saucepan.

**2** Put wings in a single layer in roasting pan; scatter onions on top. Roast 1¼ hours or until wings are browned.

**3** Transfer wings and onions to pot. Add 1 cup water to roasting pan and stir to scrape up any brown bits on bottom. Add to pot. Add 6 cups broth (refrigerate remaining 2 cups), the carrots and thyme. Bring to a boil, reduce heat and simmer, uncovered, 1½ hours.

**4** Remove wings. (If you wish, when wings are cool, discard skin and bones and refrigerate meat to use later, see Tip, right.)

**5** Strain broth into saucepan, pressing vegetables to extract as much liquid as possible. Discard vegetables; skim fat off broth. (Or, if time permits, refrigerate overnight so fat solidifies and can be removed easily.)

**6** Add flour to remaining 2 cups broth; whisk until blended and smooth.

**7** Bring broth in saucepan to a gentle boil. Whisk in flour mixture and boil 4 to 5 minutes to thicken gravy and remove floury taste. Stir in butter and pepper.

**8** After the Thanksgiving turkey is out of the roasting pan, skim the fat off the pan drippings and add the drippings to the heated gravy.

TIP: For another meal, use meat from the cooked wings for a main-dish salad, or add it to a creamy sauce and serve with biscuits.

# Rosemary-Garlic Mashed Potatoes

MIXER · SHALLOW BAKING DISH

How long will they keep? Refrigerator, 1 day.

**SERVES** 12
**PREP:** 10 minutes
**COOK:** 25 to 30 minutes
**FINISH:** 5 minutes

**PER SERVING:** 182 cal,
4 g pro, 28 g car, 2 g fiber,
6 g fat (3 g sat fat), 16 mg chol,
173 mg sod

**FYI:** Mash potatoes with a potato masher or electric mixer. Do not use food processor to mash potatoes.

Tip: If making ahead, refrigerate in the dish they will be reheated and served in.

4½ lb Yukon Gold or all-purpose potatoes, peeled and quartered
6 large cloves garlic, peeled
2 sprigs fresh rosemary or ½ tsp dried
½ stick (4 Tbsp) butter
3 oz ⅓-less-fat cream cheese (Neufchâtel)
½ tsp salt
½ tsp freshly ground pepper
Garnish: **rosemary sprigs**

**1** Cook potatoes, garlic and rosemary in a large pot in liberally salted water to cover 25 to 30 minutes until potatoes are tender when pierced. Just before draining the potatoes in a colander, scoop out 1 cup of the cooking water. Discard the 2 rosemary sprigs, if using.

**2** Return potatoes and garlic to pot. Add butter, cream cheese, salt and pepper; mash potatoes until almost smooth. Gradually add the 1 cup cooking water and mash until smooth and fluffy. Spoon into serving dish, garnish and serve. Or refrigerate covered. Reheat in microwave, covered with lid or vented plastic wrap or in covered dish in 350°F oven 30 minutes.

# Honey-Ginger Sweet Potatoes

RIMMED BAKING SHEET · 2-QT BAKING DISH · OVEN

How long will they keep? Refrigerator, 2 days.

**SERVES** 12
**PREP:** 15 minutes
**BAKE:** 50 minutes to 1¼ hours
**FINISH:** 10 to 30 minutes

**PER SERVING:** 193 cal,
2 g pro, 38 g car, 4 g fiber,
4 g fat (2 g sat fat), 10 mg chol,
202 mg sod

5 lb sweet potatoes
½ stick (¼ cup) butter
3 Tbsp honey
1½ tsp grated fresh ginger (see *Fresh Ginger*, page 61)
¾ tsp salt
¾ tsp freshly ground pepper
Garnish: **chopped parsley**

**1** Heat oven to 400°F. Pierce each potato once with a fork; place on a rimmed baking sheet.

**2** Bake 50 minutes to 1¼ hours until very tender.

**3** Split open potatoes, and when cool enough to handle, scrape pulp into a large bowl. Add butter, honey, ginger, salt and pepper; mash until smooth. Spoon into serving bowl; sprinkle with parsley and serve. Or spoon into a 2-qt baking dish, cover and refrigerate. Reheat, covered, in a 350°F oven 25 to 30 minutes, or in microwave.

# Corn Pudding

FOOD PROCESSOR · 3-QT BAKING DISH · OVEN

How long will it keep? Pudding, unbaked, refrigerator, 1 day; crumbs, room temperature, 1 day.

12 saltine crackers, broken up
2 Tbsp stick butter, cut up
1.8-oz pkg leek soup and dip mix
2 tsp mustard powder (see FYI page 42)
½ tsp ground nutmeg
1 cup heavy (whipping) cream
2 large eggs
Yolks from 2 large eggs
Two 15.5-oz cans whole-kernel corn, drained
Two 14.75-oz cans cream-style corn
12-oz jar roasted red peppers, drained

SERVES 12
PREP: 15 minutes
BAKE: 35 to 40 minutes

PER SERVING: 235 cal, 5 g pro, 29 g car, 2 g fiber, 13 g fat (7 g sat fat), 104 mg chol, 637 mg sod

**1** Heat oven to 350°F. Lightly grease a shallow 3-qt baking dish.

**2** Put saltines and butter in food processor. Pulse until fine, evenly coated crumbs (see Tip, right).

**3** Put soup mix, mustard powder and nutmeg in a large bowl; whisk to blend. Whisk in cream, eggs and egg yolks until very well blended. Add all the corn. Blot peppers dry with paper towels; chop and add to bowl. Stir to mix well. Pour into prepared baking dish. (If desired, cover and refrigerate 1 day; let stand at room temperature 1 hour before baking.)

**4** Sprinkle cracker crumbs on pudding near edges of dish. Bake 35 to 40 minutes until a knife inserted near center comes out clean and temperature at center just registers 160°F on an instant-read thermometer. (Center will jiggle when dish is moved; that's OK.)

Tip: Instead of using a food processor, you can put the saltine crackers in a heavy ziptop bag and crush them with a rolling pin. Melt the butter and stir in the cracker crumbs.

# Green Beans with French Fried Onions

HOW LONG WILL IT KEEP? REFRIGERATOR, 1 DAY.

**SERVES** 12
**TOTAL TIME:** 20 minutes

**PER SERVING:** 101 cal,
2 g pro, 10 g car, 2 g fiber,
6 g fat (3 g sat fat), 8 mg chol,
199 mg sod

3 lb fresh green beans, stem ends trimmed
3 Tbsp stick butter
½ tsp salt
¼ tsp hot pepper sauce, or to taste
1½ cups French fried onions (from a 6-oz can)

**1** Cook green beans in lightly salted water to cover 7 to 9 minutes until crisp-tender. Drain well; transfer to a large bowl.

**2** Melt butter in a small saucepan over low heat. Cook about 6 minutes, swirling pan gently until butter browns. (Don't let butter burn or it will taste bitter.) Remove from heat; stir in salt and pepper sauce. Immediately pour over beans. Toss gently to mix and coat. (Cover and refrigerate if desired. Reheat in microwave or on stovetop in a large skillet.)

**3** JUST BEFORE SERVING: Recrisp onions as can directs. Gently stir half into beans; sprinkle rest on top.

# Fresh Cranberry-Orange-Raspberry Relish

FOOD PROCESSOR

HOW LONG WILL IT KEEP? REFRIGERATOR, 1 WEEK. RASPBERRY JAM GIVES A FLAVORFUL TWIST TO THE TRADITIONAL RECIPE, WHICH IS MADE WITH JUST CRANBERRIES, ORANGE AND SUGAR.

**SERVES** 12 (makes 3½ cups)
**PREP:** 5 minutes

**PER SERVING:** 69 cal, 0 g pro,
18 g car, 2 g fiber, 0 g fat (0 g
sat fat), 0 mg chol, 8 mg sod

**FYI:** The orange is not peeled (just scrubbed) and the relish is not cooked.

12 oz fresh or frozen cranberries
1 navel orange, unpeeled, cut in chunks
¾ cup seedless raspberry jam

**1** Put cranberries, orange and raspberry jam in a food processor and pulse until finely chopped.

**2** Cover and refrigerate.

# Pumpkin-Chocolate Cheesecake

FOOD PROCESSOR · 8-IN. SPRINGFORM PAN · OVEN · MIXER

How long will it keep? Frozen, 1 month (thaw 2 days in refrigerator).

CRUST

7 whole chocolate graham crackers, broken up
2 Tbsp sugar
2 Tbsp stick butter

FILLING

5 oz semisweet chocolate or ¾ cup semisweet chocolate chips
Three 8-oz bricks ⅓-less-fat cream cheese (Neufchâtel), softened
1 cup sugar
1 Tbsp cornstarch
¾ tsp ground cinnamon
½ tsp ground ginger
⅛ tsp ground cloves
⅛ tsp ground nutmeg
1 tsp vanilla extract
2 large eggs
Whites from 2 large eggs (see Tip, right)
15-oz can 100% pumpkin

**SERVES** 12
**PREP:** 20 minutes
**BAKE:** 1 hour 25 minutes
**CHILL:** At least 4 hours

**PER SERVING:** 360 cal, 9 g pro, 38 g car, 2 g fiber, 21 g fat (12 g sat fat), 84 mg chol, 321 mg sod

Tip: You can save the yolks for the Corn Pudding (see page 347). If using the yolks within 2 days, cover tightly and refrigerate. For longer storage: Stir 1¹⁄₁₆ tsp salt or ¾ tsp sugar or corn syrup into the yolks to prevent them from thickening or gelling. Label container with number of yolks and whether you added salt or sugar, and freeze. Thaw in refrigerator. See index for other recipes using egg yolks or whites.

**1** Heat oven to 350°F. Lightly coat an 8-in. springform pan with cooking spray.

**2** Put graham crackers, sugar and butter in food processor. Pulse until evenly coated crumbs. Press over bottom of pan. Bake 8 minutes. Cool in pan on a wire rack.

**3** Meanwhile, melt chocolate according to pkg directions. Keep warm.

**4** Beat cream cheese in a large bowl with mixer on high speed until smooth. Add sugar, cornstarch, cinnamon, ginger, cloves, nutmeg and vanilla. Reduce mixer speed to medium and beat mixture until very well blended. Scrape bowl and beaters, add eggs and egg whites, and beat just until mixed.

**5** Add pumpkin and beat on low speed until well blended. Stir 2 cups pumpkin mixture into chocolate. Take out another ½ cup before pouring rest into crust.

**6** Pour chocolate mixture onto pumpkin batter in a thick ring about ½ in. from sides of pan. Drop the ½ cup pumpkin batter in spoonfuls over the chocolate mixture. Run a knife through both batters for a marbled effect. (Don't overdo or effect will be muddied.)

**7** Bake 1 hour 15 minutes or until a wooden pick inserted near center comes out clean. Remove from oven and run a knife carefully between cake and pan.

**8** Cool cake in pan on a wire rack. Cover and refrigerate at least 4 hours before removing pan sides. Leave cheesecake on pan bottom, or carefully loosen bottom with a metal spatula and slide cake onto a serving plate.

# Pear-Almond Tart with Cranberries

FOOD PROCESSOR · 9-IN. FLUTED TART PAN WITH REMOVABLE BOTTOM · OVEN

How long will it keep? Crust, freezer, 2 weeks; tart, refrigerator, 2 days.

**SERVES** 10
**PREP:** About 30 minutes
**BAKE:** 16 minutes plus 45 to 50 minutes

**PER SERVING:** 451 cal, 7 g pro, 58 g car, 2 g fiber, 23 g fat (10 g sat fat), 104 mg chol, 170 mg sod

CRUST
 1¼ cups all-purpose flour
 1 stick (½ cup) cold butter, cut in small pieces
 3 Tbsp sugar
 Yolk of 1 large egg

FILLING
 8-oz can or 7-oz almond paste (not marzipan)
 ⅓ cup sugar
 ¼ cup all-purpose flour
 5 Tbsp stick butter, softened
 2 large eggs
 3 ripe, firm Bosc or Anjou pears
 3 Tbsp apple jelly, melted

1 cup fresh or frozen cranberries
½ cup sugar

**1** Have ready an ungreased 9-in. fluted tart pan with removable bottom.

**2** CRUST: Put flour, butter, sugar and egg yolk in food processor. Pulse until ingredients clump together. With lightly floured fingers, press dough evenly over bottom and up sides of tart pan to about ⅛ in. above top of rim. Prick bottom and sides with a fork. Chill in freezer at least 15 minutes.

**3** Heat oven to 400°F. Bake crust 16 minutes or until golden. (When cool, crust may be left in pan, wrapped airtight and frozen up to 2 weeks.)

**4** FILLING: Break up almond paste and put in food processor with the ⅓ cup sugar, the flour, butter and eggs. Process until completely smooth. Spread evenly in crust.

**5** Peel, halve and core the pears. Thinly slice each half but keep the slices together. Arrange halves on top of filling, fanning the slices slightly.

**6** Bake 45 to 50 minutes until pears are tender and filling is puffed and browned. Melt jelly and brush on the pears (but not the filling). Cool in pan on a wire rack.

**7** Meanwhile boil cranberries with remaining ½ cup sugar and 3 Tbsp water in a saucepan 5 minutes or until berries burst. Cover and set aside until tart cools, or refrigerate.

**8** Not more than one hour before serving spoon cranberries around edge of tart and in center. Put pan on a small, sturdy bowl; let sides fall down (see Tip, right). Gently slide tart onto serving plate (see Tip, right).

TIP: This tart is delicious even without the cranberries.

TIP: To remove the sides from this kind of pan, place the pan on a small bowl and the sides will fall off.

TIP: When choosing a plate to serve the tart on, select one that has at least 9 level inches inside the rim so the tart is on a flat surface. If you don't have one, a board could be a good alternative.

# Christmas Menu *for* 8

SALAD GREENS WITH FENNEL, TANGERINE & CANDIED WALNUTS

BEEF TENDERLOIN WITH MADEIRA SAUCE

OR

CRANBERRY-PISTACHIO-STUFFED TURKEY BREAST
WITH GRAVY

SCALLOPED POTATOES

BUTTERED SUGAR SNAPS & GREEN PEAS

HONEY-ROASTED CARROTS

PEAR-ALMOND TART WITH CRANBERRIES (PAGE 350)

## Salad Greens with Fennel, Tangerine & Candied Walnuts

HOW LONG WILL IT KEEP? CANDIED WALNUTS, ROOM TEMPERATURE, 4 DAYS; DRESSING, REFRIGERATOR, 8 HOURS; SALAD INGREDIENTS, REFRIGERATOR IN OWN BAGS OR CONTAINERS, 8 HOURS.

**SERVES 8**
**TOTAL TIME:** 50 minutes

**PER SERVING:** 245 cal, 3 g pro, 23 g car, 4 g fiber, 17 g fat (2 g sat fat), 0 mg chol, 397 mg sod

TIP: The caramelized sugar is very hot so have an oven mitt ready to lift the pan off the heat.

CANDIED WALNUTS
⅓ cup sugar
¾ cup walnut pieces

DRESSING
¼ tsp freshly grated tangerine or clementine peel
¼ cup fresh tangerine or clementine juice
¼ cup extra-virgin olive oil
2 tsp cider vinegar
¼ tsp salt
¼ tsp freshly ground pepper

1 medium bulb fennel (anise), stalks and leaves removed
½ cup halved and thinly sliced red onion
9 oz (8 cups) mixed baby salad greens
4 small tangerines or clementines, peeled and broken into segments
⅓ cup oil-cured black olives, pitted

**1** CANDIED WALNUTS: Line a baking sheet with nonstick foil (see Tip, right). Put sugar and 2 Tbsp water in small saucepan. Swirl pan slightly to moisten sugar evenly. Put over medium heat and cook until sugar melts and caramelizes to a rich amber-brown color (watch carefully that it does not blacken and burn). Immediately remove from heat, add walnuts and stir with a fork to coat nuts. Quickly lift nuts onto prepared baking sheet, separating the individual pieces with the fork. Let cool until caramel hardens. (When cold, nuts can be stored airtight at room temperature.)

**2** Put Dressing ingredients in a large bowl. Cut fennel in half lengthwise, across in thin slices. Whisk Dressing to blend, add fennel and red onion and let stand 15 minutes to soften slightly.

**3** TO SERVE: Add salad greens, tangerine segments, olives and walnuts; toss to mix. Transfer to a serving bowl or serving plates and serve at once.

> TIP: Nonstick foil is a good choice when you don't want food to stick to a pan (as here). It's also a good idea when you don't want foil to stick to food, as in a cheese-topped baked dish.

# Beef Tenderloin with Madeira Sauce

RIMMED BAKING SHEET · OVEN

HOW LONG WILL IT KEEP? HERB MIXTURE, ROOM TEMPERATURE, 10 HOURS.

One 3-lb center-cut beef tenderloin, trimmed
⅓ cup whole-grain mustard
1 Tbsp chopped fresh rosemary or 1 tsp dried
1 Tbsp chopped fresh thyme or 1 tsp dried
2 tsp minced garlic
2 tsp olive oil
1 tsp salt
1 tsp freshly ground pepper
GARNISH: **rosemary and thyme sprigs, small red tomatoes**
**Madeira Sauce (recipe follows)**

> SERVES 8
> PREP: 10 minutes
> ROAST: About 35 minutes
>
> PER BEEF SERVING: 233 cal, 26 g pro, 1 g car, 0 g fiber, 12 g fat (4 g sat fat), 78 mg chol, 468 mg sod

**1** Heat oven to 450°F. Liberally coat a large rimmed baking sheet with cooking spray.

**2** Spread beef with mustard. Mix rosemary, thyme, garlic, oil, salt and pepper in a cup; press on mustard. Place beef on prepared baking sheet.

**3** Roast 28 to 35 minutes or until a meat thermometer inserted in center of thickest part of tenderloin registers 145°F. Remove to

**PLANNING TIP:** Sauce can be made up to 1 day ahead. Refrigerate covered. Reheat over low heat just until hot, not boiling.

**MAKES** 2¼ cups
**TOTAL TIME:** 15 minutes

**PER ¼ CUP:** 70 cal, 1 g pro, 5 g car, 1 g fiber, 3 g fat (2 g sat fat), 7 mg chol, 323 mg sod

**FYI:** Madeira is a fortified wine like Sherry and Port, which means brandy or other spirit has been added as part of the maturing process. Madeira comes from the island of that name but some is also made in the U.S. As with Sherry and Port, Madeira comes in a range of flavors, from pale gold and dry (try it as an aperitif) to dark and sweet and excellent as an after-dinner drink.

cutting board, cover loosely with foil and let rest about 15 minutes (temperature will rise to 150°F for medium-rare).

**4** TO SERVE: Cut in ¼-in.-thick slices, arrange on a serving platter and garnish with herb sprigs and tomatoes. Serve with Madeira Sauce.

## MADEIRA SAUCE

    2 Tbsp stick butter
    8 oz sliced cremini or white buttom mushrooms
    ¾ cup dry Madeira wine
    1 tsp minced garlic
    2½ tsp cornstarch
    1½ cups beef broth
    2 Tbsp tomato paste
    1 tsp chopped fresh thyme or ¼ tsp dried
    ½ tsp salt
    ½ tsp freshly ground pepper

**1** Melt butter in large skillet over medium-high heat. Add mushrooms and cook about 4 minutes, stirring often, until golden. Stir in Madeira and garlic; boil 2 minutes or until most of the liquid evaporates.

**2** Stir cornstarch into broth until well blended. Add to skillet with tomato paste, thyme, salt and pepper. Stir until boiling, then reduce heat and boil 1 minute, until thickened and glossy. Pour into gravy boat and serve with the beef.

# Cranberry-Pistachio-Stuffed Turkey Breast with Gravy

LARGE ROASTING PAN · OVEN

HOW LONG WILL IT KEEP? STUFFED BUT NOT COOKED, REFRIGERATOR, 1 DAY.

TURKEY/STUFFING
    4 Tbsp stick butter
    4 cups chopped onions
    4 slices firm whole-wheat or white bread, cut in ¼-in. cubes
    ½ cup pistachio nuts, chopped
    ½ cup sweetened dried cranberries, chopped

½ cup dried apricots, chopped

2 Tbsp chopped fresh thyme or 2 tsp dried

½ cup chicken broth

2 skinless, boneless turkey-breast halves (about 2½ lb each, see Tip, right)

12 slices reduced-sodium bacon

GRAVY

3 cups chicken broth

⅔ cup dry white wine

2 Tbsp cornstarch

2 tsp chopped fresh thyme or ½ tsp dried

GARNISH: herb sprigs and dried cranberries

SERVES 12
PREP: 25 minutes
ROAST: 60 to 70 minutes

PER SERVING: 400 cal, 52 g pro, 19 g car, 3 g fiber, 11 g fat (4 g sat fat), 133 mg chol, 436 mg sod

**1** TURKEY/STUFFING: Heat oven to 375°F. Oil a large roasting pan.

**2** Melt butter in a large nonstick skillet over medium heat. Stir in onions; cover and cook 12 to 15 minutes, stirring occasionally, until golden. Off heat, stir in bread, pistachios, cranberries, apricots and thyme. Stir in broth; toss until moist.

**3** Place one turkey breast half on work surface between double layers of plastic wrap, with the skinned side down and one long side facing you. With meat pounder or rolling pin, pound thicker parts of meat until ½ in. thick. Remove wrap from top; mound half the stuffing crosswise down middle. Fold sides of turkey over stuffing into a tight roll. Skewer with toothpicks to help keep stuffing enclosed. Place pick side down in pan; wrap bacon around meat, tucking ends under. Repeat with the remaining breast half.

**4** Roast 60 to 70 minutes until thermometer inserted in center registers 160°F. Transfer to a cutting board; cover loosely with foil and let rest while preparing gravy (internal temperature will rise to 165°F).

**5** GRAVY: Discard fat from roasting pan. Place pan on stove over 2 burners. Add 2½ cups chicken broth and the wine. Cook over medium-high heat, scraping up browned bits on bottom of pan until boiling. Boil 2 minutes.

**6** Mix remaining broth and cornstarch in a small cup until smooth. Stir along with the thyme into pan. Stir until boiling; boil 1 minute until slightly thickened and clear.

**7** TO SERVE: Remove toothpicks from turkey. Cut in ½-in.-thick slices; place on serving platter or plates; garnish. Pour gravy into gravy boat and serve alongside.

TIP: Chances are you wouldn't be able to buy a boneless turkey breast half large enough to serve 8 comfortably, so we decided to err on the side of too much, rather than too little. It's easy enough to make more of the salad and vegetables, and the Scalloped Potatoes (see page 356) already serve 10. For dessert, you could make two tarts, or cut one into smaller slices and serve a fresh fruit and cheese course (perhaps one blue, one ripe and creamy and one firmer one) between the main course and dessert.

# Scalloped Potatoes

FOOD PROCESSOR · 13 x 9-IN. BAKING DISH OR OTHER · OVEN

How long will it keep? Baked, refrigerator, 1 day.

**SERVES** 10
**PREP:** 20 minutes
**BAKE:** 1 hour 35 minutes

**PER SERVING:** 231 cal, 10 g pro, 27 g car, 2 g fiber, 10 g fat (6 g sat fat), 36 mg chol, 649 mg sod

5 Tbsp flour

3 cups milk

2 cups (8 oz) shredded American and Cheddar Jack cheese blend

4 Tbsp grated Parmesan cheese

2 tsp Dijon mustard

1 tsp salt

¾ tsp paprika

3 lb (6 large) baking potatoes, peeled

¼ cup sliced scallions

**1** Heat oven to 375°F. Grease or coat a 13 x 9-in. or other shallow 3- to 4-qt baking dish with cooking spray.

**2** Put flour in a large saucepan. Whisk in milk until blended, making sure to get into corners of pan. Place over medium-high heat and stir until boiling. Reduce heat to low and simmer, stirring several times, 2 minutes or until thickened.

**3** Remove from heat; stir in 1½ cups cheese blend, 2 Tbsp Parmesan, the mustard, salt and ½ tsp paprika.

**4** Slice potatoes in food processor or in ⅛-in.-thick slices with a knife. Put potatoes in baking dish, add sauce and toss to coat. Spread evenly. Cover tightly with foil.

**5** Bake 1 hour. Uncover; bake 35 minutes or until potatoes are tender.

**6** Shortly before serving, sprinkle with remaining cheeses and ¼ tsp paprika; bake 15 minutes or until cheese melts. Sprinkle with sliced scallions.

Tip: If you have only one oven, you need a plot.
Turkey: Bake the Scalloped Potatoes along with the turkey. While turkey rests, increase heat to 450°F and roast the carrots.
Beef: Bake the Scalloped Potatoes first, then up the heat and roast the beef and carrots at the same time. The Scalloped Potatoes will keep warm just sitting on top of your stove.

**FYI:** To reheat this dish, put it, covered, in a 325°F oven for 30 minutes. Sprinkle with the remaining cheeses and the ¼ tsp paprika. Bake uncovered 15 minutes longer, until potatoes are hot and cheese has melted.

# Buttered Sugar Snaps & Green Peas

SKILLET

How long will it keep? Refrigerator, 1 day.

1 lb sugar snap peas, trimmed
10-oz box (2⅓ cups) frozen petite green peas
2 Tbsp stick butter
¼ tsp salt
⅛ tsp freshly ground pepper
2 Tbsp chopped fresh mint (optional)

SERVES 8
TOTAL TIME: 30 minutes

PER SERVING: 77 cal, 3 g pro, 9 g car, 3 g fiber, 3 g fat (2 g sat fat), 8 mg chol, 144 mg sod

**1** Half fill a large skillet with water, salt lightly and bring to a boil. Add snap peas and green peas. When boiling, boil 1 minute or until snap peas are crisp-tender. Drain; rinse with cold water and drain well. (Cover up the vegetables and refrigerate for 1 day, if desired.)

**2** Melt butter in skillet. Add vegetables, ¼ tsp salt and the pepper. Stir over medium-high heat until hot. Put into a serving bowl; sprinkle with mint.

# Honey-Roasted Carrots

TWO RIMMED BAKING SHEETS · OVEN

Very young carrots generally do not need peeling, just a good scrub. Trim tops so a tiny bit of the green remains. How long will they keep? Carrots, trimmed, refrigerator, 2 days.

2 lb very young carrots, trimmed; or 2 lb baby-cut carrots
¼ cup honey
2 Tbsp stick butter, melted
½ tsp salt
⅛ tsp ground red pepper (cayenne)

SERVES 8
PREP: 20 minutes
ROAST: 15 to 20 minutes

PER SERVING: 101 cal, 1 g pro, 18 g car, 2 g fiber, 3 g fat (2 g sat fat), 8 mg chol, 214 mg sod

**1** Heat oven to 450°F. Line 2 rimmed baking sheets with foil; coat with cooking spray. Divide carrots and rest of ingredients between pans. Toss to coat; spread into an even layer.

**2** Roast 15 to 20 minutes, tossing once or twice, until tender. Remove to a serving bowl or platter.

## Spiral-Cut Ham with Horseradish-Mustard Sauce

**TIP:** Save the bone to make split pea or bean soup.

Spiral-cut hams are a delicious and popular choice for Easter (or any other occasion) because they come already cooked and sliced and can be served cold, or heated accordingly to package directions. Some hams are already glazed; others come with a packet of glaze.

**HOW MUCH TO BUY:** Plan on 2 or 3 servings per lb of fully cooked bone-in ham (4 to 5 servings for boneless). Spiral-cut hams are bone-in; half hams (shank or butt) weigh 7 to 8 lb and will feed 8 with ample leftovers for other meals.

**MAKES** 1¼ cups
**TOTAL TIME:** 5 minutes

**PER SERVING:** 77 cal, 0 g pro, 2 g car, 0 g fiber, 7 g fat (2 g sat fat), 11 mg chol, 262 mg sod

**TIP:** Look for prepared horseradish in the refrigerated section of your market.

### HORSERADISH-MUSTARD SAUCE

½ cup light mayonnaise
½ cup reduced-fat sour cream
3 Tbsp Dijon mustard
2 Tbsp snipped chives or green part of scallions
1 Tbsp prepared white horseradish (from a jar)
¼ tsp freshly ground pepper

Put all ingredients in a bowl and whisk or stir to mix. Cover and refrigerate up to 2 days.

# Wild Rice & Orzo

How long will it keep? Refrigerator, 2 days.

1 cup wild rice
1 cup orzo (rice-shaped pasta)
3 Tbsp stick butter
2 cups chopped onions
1½ cups frozen green peas, thawed
½ tsp salt
½ tsp freshly ground pepper
⅓ cup thinly sliced scallions

**SERVES 8**
**TOTAL TIME:** About 1 hour

**PER SERVING:** 226 cal,
8 g pro, 38 g car, 4 g fiber,
5 g fat (3 g sat fat), 12 mg chol,
224 mg sod

**1** Cook wild rice and orzo separately as pkgs direct.

**2** Meanwhile melt 1 Tbsp butter in a large nonstick skillet. Add onions; cover and cook over medium heat, stirring occasionally, 15 minutes or until tender. Stir in remaining butter, the peas, salt and pepper; cook 1 minute.

**3** Drain rice and orzo; pour into serving dish. Stir in onion mixture and scallions.

**Tip:** If you make this ahead, refrigerate it, tightly covered, in a microwave-safe serving dish ready for reheating.

# Roasted Asparagus with Pine Nuts

ROASTING PAN · OVEN

How long will they keep? Toasted pine nuts, room temperature, 1 week; trimmed asparagus and shaved cheese, refrigerator, 2 days.

3 lb asparagus, woody ends snapped off
2 Tbsp olive oil
¾ tsp salt
¼ tsp freshly ground pepper
¼ cup (about 1½ oz) pine nuts (pignoli), toasted (see FYI, below and Tip, page 360)
2 oz Parmesan cheese, shaved from a chunk with a vegetable peeler

**SERVES 8**
**PREP:** 5 minutes
**ROAST:** 15 minutes

**PER SERVING:** 118 cal,
8 g pro, 6 g car, 2 g fiber,
8 g fat (2 g sat fat), 5 mg chol,
335 mg sod

**FYI:** To toast pine nuts, spread in a shallow pan. Bake in a 325°F oven 10 to 15 minutes, until light golden.

TIP: Buy extra pine nuts and make the Pine Nut Macaroons (page 281). Top each with an almond M&M before baking for festive Easter touch.

1  Heat oven to 425°F. Line a roasting pan with foil.

2  Place asparagus, oil, salt and pepper in pan; toss to mix and coat.

3  Bake 12 to 15 minutes, stirring once, until asparagus are crisp-tender. Arrange on platter; sprinkle with nuts and cheese.

# Corn & Cheddar Cornbread

## 9-IN. ROUND CAKE PAN · OVEN

HOW LONG WILL IT KEEP? CORNBREAD, ROOM TEMPERATURE, 1 DAY;
SCALLION BUTTER, REFRIGERATOR, 3 DAYS.

**SERVES** 8
**PREP:** 10 minutes
**BAKE:** 30 to 35 minutes

**PER SERVING:** 400 cal, 10 g pro, 53 g car, 2 g fiber, 17 g fat (7 g sat fat), 80 mg chol, 817 mg sod

Two 8.5-oz boxes corn muffin mix
11-oz can vacuum-packed Mexican-style corn
⅔ cup milk
2 large eggs
2 Tbsp stick butter, melted
1 cup (4 oz) shredded Cheddar cheese
SERVE WITH: **Scallion Butter (recipe follows)**

1  Heat oven to 375°F. Lightly coat a 9-in. round cake pan with cooking spray.

2  Put corn muffin mix, corn, milk, eggs and melted butter into a bowl. Stir to mix well. Fold in cheese. Scrape into prepared pan.

3  Bake 30 to 35 minutes until golden brown. Cool in pan on a wire rack. If making ahead, store airtight. Cut in wedges. Serve with the Scallion Butter.

## SCALLION BUTTER

**PER SERVING:** 102 cal, 0 g pro, 0 g car, 0 g fiber, 11 g fat (7 g sat fat), 31 mg chol, 121 mg sod

1 stick (½ cup) butter, softened
2 Tbsp minced scallions
¼ tsp hot pepper sauce

Mix ingredients in small bowl. Refrigerate tightly covered.

# Two Passover Cakes

## Chocolate Cake with Raspberry Sauce

10-IN. TUBE PAN WITH REMOVABLE TUBE INSERT · FOOD PROCESSOR · MIXER · OVEN

How long will it keep? Cake, covered, room temperature, 3 days, or frozen, wrapped airtight, 3 months; sauce, refrigerator, 3 days.

4 oz unsweetened baking chocolate

¾ cup pecans, toasted and cooled (see *Toasting Nuts*, page 189)

½ cup matzo cake meal (also just called cake meal)

¼ cup unsweetened cocoa powder

2 Tbsp potato starch (found among Passover foods)

½ tsp salt

10 large eggs, whites and yolks in separate large bowls, whites at room temperature

2 cups sugar

1 tsp vanilla

RASPBERRY SAUCE

    12-oz bag unsweetened frozen raspberries, thawed

    2 tsp sugar

    ½ tsp freshly grated orange peel

Decoration: **fresh raspberries and mint**

**SERVES** 12
**PREP:** 25 minutes
**BAKE:** 1 hour 10 minutes
**COOL:** 10 minutes

PER SERVING: 340 cal, 8 g pro, 50 g car, 3 g fiber, 15 g fat (5 g sat fat), 177 mg chol, 151 mg sod

**1** Heat oven to 325°F. Grease bottom, sides and tube of 10-in. tube pan with removable tube insert; line bottom with wax paper.

**2** Heat chocolate with ⅔ cup water in microwave on high 1 minute until chocolate has melted and mixture becomes smooth when stirred. If necessary, repeat at 30-second intervals. Or heat chocolate and ⅔ cup water over medium heat, stirring until chocolate melts and mixture is smooth. Let cool.

**3** Put pecans, cake meal, cocoa, potato starch and salt in food processor; pulse until nuts are finely ground.

**4** Beat egg whites with mixer on high speed until soft peaks form when beaters are lifted. Gradually (1 to 2 minutes) beat in sugar until stiff, shiny peaks form.

**5** Using same beaters (no need to wash), beat egg yolks and vanilla to blend. On low speed beat in chocolate mixture. Beat in nut mixture until combined (batter is very thick). Thoroughly beat in one-third the egg whites. With a silicone spatula, fold in remaining whites in 2 additions just until blended. Pour into prepared pan; smooth surface.

**6** Bake 1 hour 10 minutes or until a wooden pick inserted in middle of cake comes out with moist crumbs attached. Place pan on a wire rack. Gently run a long thin knife around edge of pan and inner tube. Let cool 10 minutes, invert cake on rack and remove wax paper; cool cake completely.

**7** SAUCE: Stir and press raspberries with back of a wooden spoon through a strainer set over a bowl. Discard seeds. Add sugar and peel; stir until sugar dissolves.

**8** TO SERVE: Place cake on serving plate. Decorate with raspberries and mint. Serve with the Sauce.

# Lemon-Almond Cake

10-IN. TUBE PAN WITH REMOVABLE TUBE INSERT · FOOD PROCESSOR · MIXER · OVEN

How long will it keep? Refrigerator airtight, up to 2 days.
Bring to room temperature to serve.

**SERVES** 12
**PREP:** 30 minutes
**BAKE:** 55 minutes

**PER SERVING:** 282 cal, 7 g pro, 32 g car, 1 g fiber, 15 g fat (2 g sat fat), 159 mg chol, 145 mg sod

1 cup (4 oz) blanched almonds, lightly toasted (see *Toasting Nuts*, page 189)

1½ cups sugar

½ cup matzo cake meal (also just called cake meal)

½ tsp salt

9 large eggs, yolks and whites in separate bowls, whites at room temperature

1½ tsp plus ¼ cup fresh lemon juice

⅓ cup oil (olive, canola or safflower)

1 Tbsp freshly grated lemon peel

DECORATION: Candied Lemon Slices (recipe follows), mint sprigs and raspberries

SERVE WITH: fresh fruit salad

**1** Heat oven to 350°F. Have ready a 10-in. tube pan with a removable tube insert.

**2** Process almonds and ¼ cup sugar in a food processor until nuts are finely ground. Add matzo meal and salt; pulse briefly to blend.

**3** Beat whites with mixer on high speed until foamy. Add 1½ tsp lemon juice; beat until soft peaks form when beater is lifted. Gradually (1 to 2 minutes) add ¼ cup sugar; beat just until stiff (tilt bowl sideways; if whites slide slightly, they're perfect).

**4** Using same beater, beat yolks, 1 cup sugar, ¼ cup lemon juice, the oil and peel just to blend. Fold in one fourth of the whites, then nut mixture. Fold in remaining whites. Pour into ungreased pan and smooth surface.

**5** Bake 55 minutes or until top is browned and dry and cake springs back when gently touched. Place upside down on neck of a bottle to cool.

**6** TO UNMOLD: Gently run a knife around edge and inner tube. Invert pan on serving plate; shake sharply to release cake.

**7** JUST BEFORE SERVING: Decorate with Candied Lemon slices, mint and raspberries. Serve with fresh fruit salad.

## CANDIED LEMON SLICES
  2 cups sugar
  2 thin-skinned lemons

Pour sugar and 2 cups water into a wide skillet. Bring to a boil. Scrub and thinly slice the lemons. Add slices to skillet, reduce heat to very low and simmer 25 minutes or until slices are translucent. Cool in syrup. To use, remove slices, let excess syrup drip off and arrange on cake.

# Fourth of July Picnic *for* 8

CRAB & AVOCADO DIP

REAL RIBS WITH HONEY-GINGER BBQ SAUCE

FINGER-LICKIN' CHICKEN WITH CHIPOTLE-ORANGE
BBQ SAUCE

RED, WHITE & BLUE POTATO SALAD

CELEBRATION LAYERED SALAD

SUMMER TOMATO PLATTER

WATERMELON & NECTARINES IN LIME SYRUP

OLD GLORY CUPCAKE FLAG

## Crab & Avocado Dip

How long will it keep? Dip, refrigerator, 4 hours.

**SERVES** 8
**TOTAL TIME:** About 20 minutes

**PER SERVING:** 216 cal,
6 g pro, 16 g car, 3 g fiber,
16 g fat (3 g sat fat), 14 mg
chol, 348 mg sod

Tip: Prepare all the other
ingredients while the water
for the corn comes to a boil
and the corn cooks.

4 ears of corn, husked

¼ cup finely chopped red onion

3 Tbsp fresh lime juice

1 tsp salt

4 ripe avocados, diced

1 cup diced plum tomato

1 large jalapeño pepper, halved, seeded and minced (see *Handling Hot Peppers*, page 52)

4 oz (1 cup) lump crab meat, picked over

Serve with: **tortilla chips**

**1** Bring a large pot of water to a boil, add corn and once it comes back to a boil cook 4 minutes. Quickly remove with tongs and put into a large bowl of cold or ice water to stop cooking. Cut kernels off cobs (see *Cutting Off the Kernels*, page 264) with a sharp knife (you'll have about 2 cups).

**2** Mix onion, lime juice and salt in a large bowl. Let stand about 10 minutes.

**3** Add avocado to bowl along with the corn, tomatoes and jalapeño pepper. Stir until blended, then stir in crab meat. Serve with chips.

TIP: The corn can be cooked and kernels cut off the cob a day ahead. Refrigerate airtight.

# Real Ribs with Honey-Ginger BBQ Sauce

## 2 RIMMED BAKING SHEETS · OVEN · GRILL

HOW LONG WILL IT KEEP? BAKED RIBS, REFRIGERATOR, 2 DAYS.

⅓ cup BBQ Rub (see recipe, page 367)
6 lb pork spareribs
Honey-Ginger BBQ Sauce (see recipe, page 366)

**1** Sprinkle ribs on both sides with BBQ Rub, then rub all over. Wrap ribs tightly in plastic wrap and place on a rimmed baking sheet. Refrigerate 4 hours or overnight.

**2** Position racks to divide oven in thirds. Heat to 300°F. Unwrap ribs and place on 2 rimmed baking sheets. Cover loosely with foil.

**3** Bake 1 hour. Brush with ½ cup Honey-Ginger BBQ Sauce and bake uncovered 2 hours longer or until ribs are very tender.

**4** Heat a covered charcoal or gas grill to medium. Brush ribs with some of the remaining sauce and grill, turning often, 10 to 15 minutes until glazed and brown. Cut into individual ribs.

**5** Heat remaining sauce; serve with the ribs.

SERVES 8
PREP: 5 minutes
CHILL: At least 4 hours
BAKE: About 3 hours
GRILL: About 15 minutes

PER SERVING: 834 cal, 43 g pro, 44 g car, 2 g fiber, 55 g fat (19 g sat fat), 194 mg chol, 2,154 mg sod

TIP: Look for St. Louis, baby-back or hors d'oeuvre-style pork spareribs, which are smaller than regular spareribs.

# Honey-Ginger & Chipotle-Orange BBQ Sauces

HOW LONG WILL THEY KEEP? REFRIGERATOR, 1 WEEK.

**MAKES** 2½ cups of each sauce
**TOTAL TIME:** 40 minutes

**PER ¼ CUP HONEY-GINGER BBQ SAUCE:** 168 cal, 2 g pro, 33 g car, 1 g fiber, 4 g fat (1 g sat fat), 0 mg chol, 1,272 mg sod

**PER ¼ CUP CHIPOTLE-ORANGE BBQ SAUCE:** 146 cal, 2 g pro, 27 g car, 1 g fiber, 4 g fat (1 g sat fat), 0 mg chol, 1,282 mg sod

STARTER SAUCE
  3 Tbsp olive oil
  1 Tbsp minced garlic
  2 cups tomato ketchup
  12-oz bottle chili sauce
  ¾ cup cider vinegar
  2 Tbsp packed brown sugar
  2 Tbsp hot-pepper sauce
  2 Tbsp Worcestershire sauce
  2 Tbsp Dijon mustard
  1 Tbsp BBQ Rub (see recipe, facing page)

HONEY-GINGER BBQ SAUCE
  2 Tbsp minced crystallized ginger
  2 Tbsp honey

CHIPOTLE-ORANGE BBQ SAUCE
  1 canned chipotle chile in adobo sauce, minced
  1½ tsp freshly grated orange peel

**1** STARTER SAUCE: Heat oil in 3-qt saucepan over medium heat. Add garlic and stir 1 minute or until fragrant. Add remaining ingredients and ¾ cup water. Bring to a boil, reduce heat and simmer 15 minutes, stirring often, to blend flavors. Pour half (about 2½ cups) into a cup measure.

**2** HONEY-GINGER BBQ SAUCE: To Starter Sauce remaining in saucepan, add crystallized ginger and honey. Simmer 5 minutes. Pour into a bowl or jar. Makes about 2½ cups.

**3** CHIPOTLE-ORANGE BBQ SAUCE: Put the other 2½ cups Starter Sauce back in the saucepan. Add chipotle chile and simmer 5 minutes. Stir in orange peel; pour into a bowl or jar. Makes about 2½ cups.

**4** Cover sauces; refrigerate until using.

# Finger-Lickin' Chicken with Chipotle-Orange BBQ Sauce

*Prepare through Step 1 at least 4 hours ahead or overnight.*

3 Tbsp BBQ Rub (see recipe, below)

4 lb cut-up chicken parts, skin removed
  (see *Off with the Skin*, page 65)

Chipotle-Orange BBQ Sauce (see recipe, facing page)

**1** Sprinkle chicken with BBQ Rub, then rub all over. Place in a large ziptop bag; refrigerate 4 hours or overnight.

**2** Heat a covered charcoal or gas grill to medium.

**3** Place chicken on grill bone-side down, close lid and grill 15 minutes. Turn chicken over, cover and grill 10 minutes longer. Brush with some of the Chipotle-Orange BBQ Sauce. Grill another 5 to 10 minutes per side until juices run clear when thigh is pierced.

**4** Heat remaining sauce; serve with the chicken.

> **SERVES 8**
> **PREP:** 35 minutes
> **CHILL:** At least 4 hours
> **GRILL:** About 35 minutes
>
> **PER SERVING:** 400 cal, 26 g pro, 46 g car, 3 g fiber, 13 g fat (3 g sat fat), 72 mg chol, 2,149 mg sod

## BBQ RUB

¼ cup paprika

2 Tbsp packed brown sugar

2 Tbsp chili powder

2 Tbsp ground cumin

1 Tbsp salt

1 Tbsp freshly ground black pepper

2 tsp ground red pepper (cayenne)

Put all ingredients in a jar or plastic container. Stir to blend well. Cover and store at room temperature up to 3 months.

> **MAKES** about ¾ cup
>
> **PER TBSP:** 25 cal, 1 g pro, 5 g car, 1 g fiber, 1 g fat (0 g sat fat), 0 mg chol, 598 mg sod

# Red, White & Blue Potato Salad

LARGE POT · SKILLET

How long will it keep? Refrigerator, 1 day.

**SERVES** 8
**TOTAL TIME:** 1 hour

**PER SERVING:** 271 cal,
6 g pro, 36 g car, 3 g fiber,
12 g fat (3 g sat fat), 9 mg chol,
711 mg sod

**TIP:** If blue potatoes are unavailable, use additional red-skinned.

1 lb medium red-skinned potatoes
1 lb medium blue potatoes (see Tip, left)
1 lb medium all-purpose potatoes
Salt
8 oz sliced bacon, cut into ¾-in.-wide pieces
1 cup chopped red onion
1 small red pepper, coarsely chopped
5 Tbsp cider vinegar
1 Tbsp maple or maple-flavored pancake syrup
3 Tbsp olive oil
1 Tbsp Dijon mustard
¾ tsp freshly ground pepper
2 Tbsp snipped chives

**1** Put potatoes and 1 tsp salt in a large pot; add cold water to cover. Bring to a boil, cover and simmer 20 to 25 minutes, until tender. Drain in a colander. Let stand until cool enough to handle but still warm.

**2** Meanwhile, cook bacon in a large skillet over medium heat until crisp. Remove with a slotted spoon to a paper-towel-lined plate. Pour off all but 2 Tbsp drippings.

**3** Add onion and red pepper to drippings. Cook over medium-high heat about 3 minutes, stirring two or three times, until soft and onion is golden. Add 2 Tbsp vinegar and the maple syrup; cook 1 minute, stirring to scrape up brown bits on bottom of pot. Remove from heat.

**4** Put 1¼ tsp salt, the oil, 3 Tbsp vinegar, the mustard and pepper in a large bowl. Whisk to blend.

**5** Peel only the blue and the all-purpose potatoes; cut all the potatoes in chunks, add to bowl and stir gently to coat.

**6** Add onion mixture; stir gently to mix. Cover loosely and leave at room temperature up to 3 hours or refrigerate overnight.

**7** TO SERVE: Bring salad to room temperature. Microwave bacon briefly to reheat. Stir into salad; sprinkle with chives.

# Celebration Layered Salad

## 4- TO 5-QT SERVING BOWL, PREFERABLY GLASS

How long will it keep? Refrigerator, 1 day. Make this salad the day before serving.

DRESSING
- ½ cup light mayonnaise
- ½ cup reduced-fat sour cream
- ¼ cup buttermilk
- 1 Tbsp fresh lemon juice
- ½ tsp minced garlic
- ¼ tsp salt
- ⅛ tsp freshly ground pepper

SALAD
- 6 cups bite-size pieces romaine lettuce
- 1 yellow pepper, diced
- 1 cup walnut pieces
- 1½ cups finely shredded red cabbage
- 10-oz box frozen tiny (petite) peas (2 cups)
- 1½ cups shredded carrots
- 1½ cups thinly sliced celery
- 1½ cups thinly sliced red radishes
- 4 oz (1 cup) crumbled blue cheese

GARNISH: 1 scallion, thinly sliced

**SERVES** 8
**PREP:** 25 minutes
**CHILL:** Overnight

**PER SERVING:** 287 cal, 10 g pro, 16 g car, 5 g fiber, 22 g fat (6 g sat fat), 23 mg chol, 521 mg sod

1 Have ready a 4- to 5-qt serving bowl, preferably glass (so the layers are visible).

2 Put Dressing ingredients in a small bowl and whisk until blended.

3 Layer Salad ingredients in bowl in order given. Spread dressing over the top to touch side of bowl. Cover with plastic wrap; refrigerate overnight.

4 TO SERVE: Sprinkle with scallions. Toss salad to mix or spoon through the layers.

# Summer Tomato Platter

How long will it keep? Dressing, room temperature, 2 hours.
Here's a wonderful, couldn't-be-simpler way to enjoy some of the heirloom
varieties of tomatoes found in farmer's markets and produce stores in summer.
Some are striped, some are very dark green when ripe.

**SERVES** 8
**TOTAL TIME:** 20 minutes

**PER SERVING:** 49 cal, 0 g pro,
1 g car, 0 g fiber, 5 g fat (1 g sat
fat), 0 mg chol, 146 mg sod

3 lb tomatoes, two or more varieties

DRESSING
    3 Tbsp olive oil, preferably extra-virgin
    3 Tbsp balsamic vinegar
    2 Tbsp chopped fresh basil
    ½ tsp salt
    ¼ tsp freshly ground pepper

1 cup yellow or red grape, cherry or pear tomatoes

**1** Finely dice enough tomato for ½ cup. Place in a jar; add Dressing ingredients, cover and shake to mix.

**2** Slice remaining large tomatoes and arrange on serving platter. Shake dressing and pour over. Scatter small tomatoes over the top.

# Watermelon & Nectarines in Lime Syrup

GLASS SERVING BOWL

How long will it keep? Watermelon and syrup, refrigerator, 4 hours.
Mix shortly before serving.

**SERVES** 8
**PREP:** 20 minutes
**CHILL:** At least 1 hour

**PER SERVING:** 96 cal, 1 g pro,
23 g car, 1 g fiber, 1 g fat (0 g
sat fat), 0 mg chol, 3 mg sod

⅓ cup sugar
2 Tbsp fresh lime juice (see Tip, facing page)
1 tsp freshly grated lime peel
6 cups seedless or seeded watermelon chunks
3 ripe nectarines

**1** Put sugar and 3 Tbsp water in a small saucepan. Bring to a boil; reduce heat and simmer 2 to 3 minutes, stirring until sugar dissolves. Remove from heat; stir in lime juice. Refrigerate until cold. Refrigerate watermelon in serving bowl.

**2** SHORTLY BEFORE SERVING: Cut nectarines in wedges; add to watermelon. Stir lime peel into syrup, drizzle over fruit and toss to mix and coat.

> TIP: Grate the lime peel before cutting the lime for juice. Put peel in a small cup or bowl, cover tightly and refrigerate until ready to use.

# Old Glory Cupcake Flag

MUFFIN PAN · OVEN · MIXER

HOW LONG WILL IT KEEP? FROSTED CUPCAKES, REFRIGERATOR, 3 DAYS; ASSEMBLED CAKE, 3 HOURS.

1½ sticks (¾ cup) butter
1 cup buttermilk
2 large eggs
2 tsp vanilla extract
2 cups all-purpose flour
1¼ cups sugar
1 tsp baking powder
½ tsp baking soda
½ tsp salt
White Chocolate Buttercream (recipe follows)
DECORATION: 3 cups fresh raspberries, 1 cup blueberries and 1½ cups sweetened flaked coconut

> **MAKES** 24 cupcakes
> **PREP:** 30 minutes
> **BAKE:** 30 to 36 minutes
>
> **PER SERVING:** 260 cal, 2 g pro, 32 g car, 1 g fiber, 14 g fat (9 g sat fat), 48 mg chol, 185 mg sod

**1** Heat oven to 350°F. Line 12 muffin cups with paper liners.

**2** Melt butter in a small saucepan over low heat or in a bowl in microwave. Pour into a large bowl and when cool add buttermilk, eggs and vanilla extract. Whisk until blended.

**3** Meanwhile, put flour, sugar, baking powder, baking soda and salt in a medium bowl; whisk until blended. Add to butter mixture; whisk until smooth. Spoon half the batter (about 2 cups) into the lined muffin cups, filling each half full.

**4** Bake 15 to 18 minutes or until tops spring back when pressed lightly. Cool in pan on a wire rack 10 minutes, then remove cupcakes from pan to rack.

**5** Repeat with remaining batter. Let cupcakes cool completely. Frost with White Chocolate Buttercream.

**6** TO SERVE: Arrange cupcakes on a large platter in 4 rows, 6 cupcakes in a row. Decorate top left quarter of cupcakes with blueberries. Decorate rest of cake with alternating rows of raspberries and coconut to resemble the stripes on the flag.

## WHITE CHOCOLATE BUTTERCREAM
   **4 oz white baking chocolate**
   **1½ cups confectioners' sugar**
   **10 Tbsp plus 2 tsp (⅔ cup) unsalted stick butter (not margarine), softened**
   **2 Tbsp buttermilk**

Melt chocolate as pkg directs. Stir smooth, scrape into a large bowl and let cool. Add confectioners' sugar, butter and buttermilk. Beat with mixer on low speed until blended. Increase speed to high; beat about 2 minutes until light and fluffy. Makes 2⅓ cups.

# BRUNCH *for* 8

PINK GRAPEFRUIT SPRITZERS

BACON & EGG BREAD PUDDING

MASHED HASH BROWNS

CHOPPED VEGETABLE SALAD

CRANBERRY BISCUITS WITH STRAWBERRY BUTTER

## Pink Grapefruit Spritzers

### GLASS PITCHER

HOW LONG WILL IT KEEP? SECTIONED CITRUS, REFRIGERATOR, 1 DAY.

1 pink grapefruit

1 navel orange

5 cups grapefruit-tangerine juice cocktail (such as Ruby Tangerine), well chilled

1 liter bottle club soda, well chilled (see Tip, right)

½ cup fresh raspberries

DECORATION: **mint sprigs**

**SERVES 8**
**TOTAL TIME:** 10 minutes

**PER SERVING:** 96 cal, 0 g pro, 25 g car, 1 g fiber, 0 g fat (0 g sat fat), 0 mg chol, 48 mg sod

**1** With a sharp knife cut a thin slice off top and bottom of grapefruit and orange. Place cut side down and cut off peel and white part (pith) from sides. Holding grapefruit and orange over a bowl, cut between membranes to release sections into bowl. Squeeze juices from membranes into bowl.

**2** TO SERVE: Drain juices from bowl into a large pitcher; add juice cocktail and club soda. Divide citrus sections and raspberries among glasses or goblets; add juice mixture and garnish with mint.

TIP: Instead of club soda, you can use sparkling wine or Champagne.

# Bacon & Egg Bread Pudding

SHALLOW 2½- TO 3-QT BAKING DISH · OVEN

How long will it keep? Before baking, refrigerator, 24 hours.

SERVES 8
PREP: 25 minutes
CHILL: At least 3 hours or overnight
BAKE: About 1 hour
STAND: 10 minutes

PER SERVING: 424 cal, 24 g pro, 32 g car, 1 g fiber, 22 g fat (12 g sat fat), 221 mg chol, 1,011 mg sod

TIP: Ask the deli clerk to slice the cheese thinly enough so that 4 oz Swiss cheese yields at least 5 slices and 4 oz American cheese yields 10.

3 Tbsp stick butter, softened

8 regular-size English muffins, split

4 oz thinly sliced Swiss cheese, slices cut in half crosswise (see Tip, left)

4 oz thinly sliced American cheese (see Tip, left)

6-oz pkg (10 slices) Canadian-style bacon (see *Canadian Bacon*, page 188)

6 large eggs

3 cups milk

¼ tsp salt

¼ tsp freshly ground pepper

**1**  Coat a shallow 2½- to 3-qt baking dish with 2 tsp butter. Toast the muffins and lightly spread remaining butter over split sides. Make sandwiches with 5 of the muffins, half the cheese and half the Canadian bacon. Cut each sandwich in half.

**2**  Arrange remaining 6 muffin halves split side up over bottom of prepared baking dish, cutting to fit if necessary. Coarsely chop remaining Canadian bacon; sprinkle over muffins. Top with alternating and overlapping slices of remaining cheese. Finish with the sandwiches overlapping the halves slightly to fit.

**3**  Put eggs, milk, salt and pepper in a large bowl; whisk until blended. Pour evenly over sandwiches. Press sandwiches down, so egg mixture is evenly distributed. Cover with plastic wrap and refrigerate 3 to 24 hours.

**4**  Heat oven to 350°F. Uncover pudding. Bake 55 to 60 minutes until puffed and browned; if browning too much during last 10 minutes, cover loosely with foil. Let stand 10 minutes before serving.

# Mashed Hash Browns

## 12-IN. NONSTICK SKILLET

HOW LONG WILL IT KEEP? REFRIGERATOR, COVERED, I DAY.
BRING TO ROOM TEMPERATURE BEFORE HEATING IN MICROWAVE OR OVEN.

2½ lb baking potatoes
1 large sweet potato (about 12 oz)
Salt
3 Tbsp stick butter
2 Tbsp olive oil
1½ cups chopped onion
2 medium red peppers, chopped (see Tip, right)
½ tsp freshly ground black pepper
⅛ to ¼ tsp ground red pepper (cayenne)
2 scallions, sliced

> **SERVES** 8
> **TOTAL TIME:** 1 hour 5 minutes
>
> **PER SERVING:** 202 cal,
> 3 g pro, 31 g car, 3 g fiber,
> 8 g fat (3 g sat fat), 12 mg chol,
> 639 mg sod

> **TIP:** Use 1 red pepper and
> 1 yellow pepper if you prefer.

**1** Peel baking and sweet potatoes, then cut in 1½-in. chunks. Place in a large heavy pot; add cold water to cover and 1 tsp salt. Bring to a boil, cover and simmer 12 minutes or just until tender. Drain in a colander and return to pot. With edge of a large spoon, break most into coarse chunks.

**2** Heat butter and oil in a 12-in., preferably deep, nonstick skillet over medium heat until hot. Add potatoes, 1½ tsp salt, onion, chopped red peppers and the ground black and red pepper; stir to mix.

> **TIP:** For best results, the skillet should be about 12 in. across the bottom.

**3** Cook, turning mixture often with a spatula, 23 minutes or until vegetables are tender and potatoes are browned in spots. Transfer to a serving dish; sprinkle with scallions.

# Chopped Vegetable Salad

HOW LONG WILL IT KEEP? DRESSING, REFRIGERATOR, 2 DAYS; ASPARAGUS AND CARROTS, BLANCHED, REFRIGERATOR, 1 DAY; CARROTS, CELERY, RADISHES AND CUCUMBER, CHOPPED, REFRIGERATOR, 1 DAY. CHOP TOMATO AND ONION A FEW HOURS AHEAD.

**SERVES** 8
**TOTAL TIME:** About 37 minutes

**PER SERVING:** 173 cal, 3 g pro, 11 g car, 3 g fiber, 14 g fat (2 g sat fat), 0 mg chol, 412 mg sod

DRESSING
- 2 Tbsp Dijon mustard
- 2 Tbsp cider or red-wine vinegar
- 1 tsp salt
- ½ tsp freshly ground pepper
- ⅓ cup olive oil

- 1 bunch (about 1 lb) asparagus, woody ends snapped off, spears cut into ½-in. pieces
- 1½ cups diced carrots
- 1⅓ cups diced celery
- 1 cup chopped radishes
- 1 medium cucumber, peeled, halved lengthwise, seeded and diced
- 1½ cups diced tomatoes
- ½ cup finely chopped red onion
- 1 firm-ripe Hass avocado, diced

**1** DRESSING: In a small bowl, whisk mustard, vinegar, salt and pepper until combined. Whisking constantly, slowly add oil until well blended.

**2** Bring a large saucepan of water to a boil. Set a colander in sink. Add asparagus to boiling water; cook 1½ minutes. Add carrots, immediately drain in colander and cool under running cold water. Drain well; turn out onto paper towels and pat dry. Transfer to a serving bowl.

**3** UP TO 1 HOUR BEFORE SERVING: Add remaining vegetables to bowl. Whisk (or shake) dressing, add to bowl and toss to mix vegetables and coat.

# Cranberry Biscuits with Strawberry Butter

How long will it keep? Biscuits, wrapped in foil, room temperature, 1 day; Strawberry Butter, refrigerator, 1 day.

BISCUITS

2 cups all-purpose flour

1 Tbsp sugar

1 Tbsp baking powder

½ tsp salt

1 stick (½ cup) cold butter, cut in small pieces

⅓ cup dried sweetened cranberries, chopped

¾ cup milk

STRAWBERRY BUTTER

½ stick (¼ cup) butter, softened

1 Tbsp strawberry spreadable fruit

1 Tbsp honey

**MAKES** about 12
**PREP:** 30 minutes
**BAKE:** About 11 minutes

PER BISCUIT: 210 cal, 3 g pro, 23 g car, 1 g fiber, 12 g fat (7 g sat fat), 33 mg chol, 343 mg sod

**1** Heat oven to 425°F. Have ready a 3-in. round or scalloped cookie cutter and a baking sheet.

**2** Put flour, sugar, baking powder and salt in a medium bowl and whisk until blended. Using a pastry blender (see *Pastry Blender*, page 274), cut butter into flour mixture until it resembles cornmeal with some tiny pieces of butter remaining. Stir in cranberries. Add milk and stir with a fork until dough clumps together. Gather into a ball.

**3** Place on a lightly floured work surface; knead lightly about 5 times. With a rolling pin, roll out to ½ in. thick. Using cutter, cut out biscuits; place on ungreased baking sheet. Gather scraps, reroll and cut more biscuits.

**4** Bake 9 to 11 minutes or until bottoms are lightly browned and tops are pale golden. Transfer to a wire rack to cool. To store, wrap in foil; to reheat, leave in foil and heat about 15 minutes in a 350°F oven.

**5** STRAWBERRY BUTTER: Mix ingredients until blended. Spoon into a serving dish. Serve at room temperature.

# Herbs & Spices

While herbs are usually the leaves from grassy plants (herba is the Latin for grass), spices can be from bark (cinnamon), buds (cloves), fruit (allspice, cardamom, vanilla), roots or rhizomes (galangal, ginger, turmeric) or seeds (anise, caraway, cumin, fennel, mustard, nutmeg). Many home cooks grow and cultivate their own herbs; few of us grow our own spices.

Herbs include familiar specimens such as basil, cilantro, parsley, rosemary, tarragon and thyme. Fresh herbs are increasingly accessible all year in large supermarkets, produce markets and specialty stores, and the variety goes way beyond big bunches of parsley and cilantro to include just several sprigs of rosemary, thyme, sage or other fresh herbs packed in rigid containers. Look for moist (but not wet), fresh-looking herbs without drooping leaves or black spots. If the herb has thick stems (rosemary, thyme and oregano are examples), discard the stems and use only the leaves. Fresh herbs are usually chopped to release the flavor before being added to a dish

Many herbs grow year round in flowerpots set on sunny kitchen windowsills. During warm months, they are easy to grow in containers on decks or planted in gardens. Nothing compares to the flavor and aroma of an herb snipped moments before use. But dried herbs add excellent flavors to dishes, too. In most instances, a teaspoon of dried herb can be used in place of a tablespoon of a chopped fresh herb—which translates to one-third the amount. It's a good idea to rub the dried herb between your fingertips before adding it to the dish to help release the herb's essential oils and flavors. Store dried herbs in their containers, in a cool, dark cupboard, away from the warmth of the stove.

Like dried herbs, spices should be stored in a cool, dark cupboard. Whole, unground spices (such as cloves, nutmeg, peppercorns, coriander and anise) will keep indefinitely. But write the date on jars of ground spices when you open them and be ruthless: Toss those that have been open for a year. (Or put them in a bowl and enjoy the last vestiges of aroma as a potpourri.) If you won't be using a spice often, buy it in small quantities. For example, depending on your cooking interests, you may prefer large containers of cinnamon and pepper but small ones of poppy seeds and cardamom.

## PRESERVING FRESH HERBS

Most fresh herbs can be dried or frozen and used later, with little loss of flavor or aroma. Cilantro is an exception.

## TO DRY HERBS

Tie the washed herbs in a bunch at the stem end and hang them, stem ends up, in a warm, dry, well-ventilated section of the kitchen or pantry. Or you can dry them by laying them on a screen and leaving them in a dry, well-ventilated place, indoors or out (protect them from morning dew and evening moisture). Depending on the size and type of herb, it will dry in one to two weeks. Make sure the herbs are completely dry before storing them in a glass or rigid plastic container. If not completely dry, mold may grow.

## TO FREEZE HERBS

Dill, parsley, chervil and fennel freeze well. Wash and dry them thoroughly. Discard large stems. Put the herbs in an airtight, rigid plastic container and freeze them. Date the container and use the herbs within a year, using them as you would fresh herbs (no need to defrost). Basil also freezes beautifully and many people like to make and freeze huge amounts of basil pesto when basil is at its best. At the least, purée the basil with olive oil and a little salt before freezing it

## HERBS

BASIL: Sweet and aromatic with a faint licorice flavor, basil is found most often in Italian and Mediterranean cooking but is also important in Thai cooking. Its marriage with tomatoes is legendary, and its presence in pesto imperative. Basil may have large or small leaves and may be green or purplish-red. All sizes and colors are equally aromatic. Fresh basil is easy to find all year long. Store-bought basil that has been washed and packaged is often a good bet. If you buy bunches of basil at a farmer's market, plan to use them promptly, especially if they are wet from rain. Pluck leaves from stems, then wash and drain them. Dry the leaves in a salad spinner, or wrap in kitchen towels or paper towels. Refrigerate until ready to use. Fresh basil is best for serving with sliced fresh tomatoes and mozzarella cheese, or to top a pizza. You can chop the leaves in the usual way like parsley, but to decrease bruising with the knife, stack several leaves and cut them across in thin strips. Dried basil is usually added to cooked preparations such as tomato sauces, soups and stews.

BAY LEAVES: Bay leaves are also called bay laurel and sweet bay. They are slightly spicy, very aromatic and one of the three herbs used (with parsley and thyme) in a classic *bouquet garni*. Bay leaves, which are fairly large, grayish-green specimens, are usually sold dried, and are added to stews and other savory dishes. They should be discarded before serving. Turkish leaves are greatly preferable to the Californian variety.

CHERVIL: Chervil is sold both dried and fresh and adds a light anise flavor to dishes such as cream soups, dressings and sauces. Chervil leaves are lacy and pale green.

CHIVES: Long, green and grassy-looking, chives are a member of the onion family and are available fresh all year long. Freeze-dried chives are not as flavorful as fresh. Chives' mild onion flavor is delicious in salads and sprinkled on top of chilled soups or mixed into creamy dips and spreads.

CILANTRO/FRESH CORIANDER: Fresh cilantro resembles flat-leaf parsley and is also called fresh coriander and even Chinese parsley. Cilantro finds its way into Mexican, Indian, Asian, North African and Caribbean cooking, where the roots, stems and leaves are often used. Some call cilantro the love-it-or-hate-it herb. Its distinctive, pungent flavor is easy to discern in salsa and other uncooked preparations. It is less powerful when cooked. Cilantro has little flavor when dried. Coriander seeds (page 381) come from the same plant but impart a very different flavor.

DILL WEED: Fragrant, fresh dill has a sharp lemony flavor; dried dill imparts a similar flavor. Dill weed is used in German, Scandinavian and Middle Eastern cooking often with fish or lamb. It's very good with potato soups and rice salad as well as with cream cheese for a spread. Greeks use it to flavor stuffed grape leaves. See also dill seed (page 382): same plant, very different flavor.

LEMONGRASS: Lemongrass is a pale green stalk with a bulbous base. Only this base is used to infuse dishes with a lovely lemon flavor. Lemongrass is becoming more available as Thai and Vietnamese restaurants become more common, creating a desire among adventurous home cooks to try recipes from those countries.

LEMON THYME: A member of the thyme family, this herb has tiny green leaves and a subtle but recognizable lemony scent and flavor. It is used with meat and fish, as well as salads. Lemon thyme is only available fresh.

MARJORAM: Sometimes called sweet marjoram, it is sold both fresh and dried. Its flavor somewhat resembles oregano and it may be used in place of it in many dishes. Fresh marjoram leaves are small and grayish-green.

MINT: Mint is one of the most common and recognizable herbs; it is also the easiest to grow and can often take over a garden. Mint's cool, fresh flavor adds to lemonade, iced tea, mint juleps, desserts, chocolate and lamb dishes. It is also used very often for garnish. Mint is easy to buy fresh, but spearmint is also sold dried.

OREGANO: Oregano is most readily associated with Italian, Greek and Mexican cooking and blends well with meat, vegetables and legumes. It has a pungent flavor and aroma and is available both fresh and dried. Fresh oregano has medium-sized dark green leaves.

PARSLEY: Whether curly- or flat-leafed, parsley is our most common herb, but is much more than just a finishing sprig. Parsley, with bay leaves and thyme, makes up traditional *bouquet garni,* herb flavoring for long-simmering pot roasts and rich stews. Parsley, with lemon juice and a little bulgur wheat, makes tabbouleh, the delicious Middle-Eastern salad. Mixed with garlic and butter it flavors baked snails; with garlic, clams and olive oil it is a great sauce for pasta. Parsley again teams with garlic in Argentinian chimichurri sauce, served with beef and chicken. Parsley is nearly always best used fresh, although it is sold dried.

ROSEMARY: Rosemary is characteristically found in Mediterranean cooking, where its spicy flavor and fragrant scent lend themselves to roast chicken and lamb. Rosemary and olives add delicious flavor to bread. But rosemary also has an unexpected sweet side: try the Baby Lemon-Rosemary Poundcakes, page 287. Rosemary is sold both fresh and dried. If purchased fresh, pull the leaves off the hard stems before chopping them.

SAGE: Sage's fuzzy gray-green leaves are easy to spot among the fresh herbs; its strong, slightly musty flavor is easy to recognize in pork sausage, sage and onion stuffing and other meat and poultry dishes. Dried sage comes in two forms: cut sage, when you want the leaf to show, and ground, which is closer to a powder. Ground sage loses its flavor much more quickly than do the leaves.

SAVORY: The small pointed green leaves of the savory plant add pleasantly sharp flavor to egg and fish dishes, lentils and beans and meats. Savory is also found in spice blends of the Mediterranean, including *herbes de Provence.* Savory is available fresh and dried and is often called summer savory.

TARRAGON: Pleasantly aromatic and tasting of licorice, tarragon's slender and somewhat spiky dark green leaves make it easily recognizable. Tarragon is used extensively in French cooking, in béarnaise sauce, with fish and with chicken (*poulet à l'estragon*) and is a common flavoring for vinegar. Tarragon is available both fresh and dried.

THYME: Thyme is one of the three herbs found in a classic *bouquet garni* (with bay leaves and parsley), a bundle of herbs used to flavor soups, stews and stocks. Its slightly strong pungent taste and spicy aroma are also frequently used to flavor chicken and other poultry dishes, including traditional bread stuffing. Thyme, readily available both fresh and dried, has tiny, dark green leaves.

# SPICES

ALLSPICE: Allspice is sold as whole berries or ground. It comes from the seed of a tree indigenous to the Western Hemisphere, which makes it unusual in the world of spices, most of which originate in Asia. It earned the name "allspice" because its flavor represents a combination of cinnamon, cloves and nutmeg. Allspice is used in fruit desserts, chutneys and pickles (it's a frequent ingredient in pickling spices). Allspice is essential in Jamaican jerk seasoning.

ANISE SEEDS: Anise tastes very similar to licorice, although the two are unrelated botanically. Anise is used to flavor cookies, cakes, fruit desserts, breads, stews and meat dishes. It is sold whole or ground.

ANNATTO SEEDS: Also called achiote, annatto are rusty red seeds with musky flavor. They are used mainly in Mexican and Southwestern cooking and impart a red-to-yellow color to foods. Annatto seeds are available whole or ground.

CARAWAY SEEDS: Caraway seeds taste sweet and nutty and are used to flavor breads, cheeses, coleslaw, sauerkraut, sausages and vegetable dishes. They are one of the oldest known spices and as such are integral to European and Asian cooking. Caraway seeds are available either whole or ground.

CARDAMOM: Cardamom is the dried, unripened fruit of a perennial. Enclosed in green, white or black pods are a dozen or so tiny, brownish-black aromatic seeds. Cardamom is available in the pod or ground, and is widely used in Scandinavian, Indian and Arab cuisines. In Scandinavia it is more popular than cinnamon for baked goods. Cardamom is an essential ingredient in dishes as diverse as Indian garam masala seasoning and Swedish meatballs and breads. The Arabs often flavor coffee with cardamom, a drink considered a symbol of hospitality. Cardamom is the third most costly spice—after saffron and vanilla.

CAYENNE: Cayenne, more properly called ground red pepper, is ground red chiles and adds noticeably spicy heat to dishes such as chilies and curries and in spice rubs for meats to be grilled. Use it sparingly at first. Cayenne is only available ground.

CELERY SEEDS: Celery seeds are tiny, light-brown seeds that provide celery flavor to soups, breads, sauces, stuffings, eggs and vegetables. However, they do not taste identical to celery; hints of nutmeg and parsley are detected in dishes seasoned with celery seeds. Celery seeds are usually sold whole, although they are available ground. Celery salt is a mixture of finely ground celery seeds and salt.

CHILI POWDER: Chili powder is deep red, ground seasoning mix that combines chiles, spices, herbs, garlic and salt. It may be mild, somewhat hot or fiery hot. Chili powder is used to flavor chilies and other Mexican and Southwestern dishes.

CINNAMON: Cinnamon, native to Sri Lanka, is a treasured spice used around the world to flavor desserts, baked goods and some meat dishes. Its warm, sweet flavor is recognizable to nearly everyone. Cinnamon is sold in rolled sticks in various lengths (part of the actual bark of a plant) or ground.

CLOVES: Cloves are the buds of furled flowers of an evergreen tree. The name comes from the French "clou," meaning nail, which whole cloves resemble. We think of them as something to stud ham with and as flavoring for cookies, but cloves are also an important flavor factor in tomato ketchup and Worcestershire sauce. Cloves are an important ingredient in the spice blends of Sri Lanka, North India (garam masala) and the Caribbean. Cloves are also use in Chinese and German cooking.

CORIANDER SEEDS: Coriander seeds are aromatic and sweet and are used extensively in North African, Mediterranean, Mexican, Indian and Southeast Asian cuisines. Whole coriander seeds are often found in pickling spice. Ground coriander is found in many spice blends including chili powder, garam masala, curry powder and Ethiopian berbere. It is often included in hot dogs and other sausages, as well as in pastries.

CUMIN: Cumin imparts a strong, aromatic, somewhat bitter flavor to foods. It is an essential ingredient in most chili powders and can also be found in curries, vegetable dishes, breads, soups and pickles. Cumin is available whole or ground.

CURRY POWDER: Curry powder is a blend of several spices and is used to flavor many dishes, particularly those referred to as curries inspired by Indian cooking. Not all curry powder blends are identical, but most commercially available in the United States include ginger, cumin, turmeric, black pepper, cayenne and coriander. Look in the Thai foods section of your market for red, yellow and green curry bases.

DILL SEED: Dill seed is used most often as a pickling spice, although it is also popular in breads and potato and vegetable dishes. Dill seeds are sold whole or ground.

FENNEL SEEDS: Fennel seeds taste of licorice and are used to flavor breads, fish dishes, soups and sweet pickles. They are available whole or ground. Fennel is the dominant flavor in Italian sausage.

GINGER: Ginger is sold fresh or ground. When fresh, it comes as gingerroot, a knobby, woody root (actually a rhizome) that is peeled and grated, sliced or chopped before being used. Ginger is used to flavor both savory and sweet dishes, including meat, poultry, fish, curries, winter squash, carrots and sweet potatoes. Ginger is essential to many Asian, Indian and African dishes. It is also used to flavor fruit, syrups and desserts. Crystallized ginger is candied ginger; it may be chopped and added to gingerbread or crème brulée, or enjoyed on its own.

JUNIPER BERRIES: Juniper berries are available both dried and fresh, although most recipes call for dried berries as the fresh berries are exceptionally pungent. Dried berries must be crushed before they are added to preparations. As the berries of an evergreen shrub, they taste somewhat of pine. Their strong flavor blends well with game and game birds, and they are used in the production of gin. Juniper berries are available whole.

MACE: Mace is the reddish-orange, lacy covering (called an aril) of a nutmeg seed and is usually ground into powder, although it is sometimes available whole. Mace imparts a nutmeg-cinnamon flavor to poultry and fish dishes, pickles, cakes, custard and puddings.

MUSTARD SEEDS: The seeds of the mustard plant are sold whole or ground into powder and are used to flavor coleslaw, curry, dressings and pickles, to say nothing of the yellow mustard that we slather on hot dogs. The most common mustard seeds are white, yellow or brown. Black mustard seeds, which are more pungent, are used in Indian cooking. White mustard seeds are used to make commercially prepared American mustards and some English mustards. Brown mustard seeds are used for Dijon mustards.

NUTMEG: Nutmeg is a favorite among spices and finds its way into any number of baked goods, sauces, fruit desserts and puddings. Eggnog is not official until it is topped with a sprinkling of nutmeg. Nutmeg is sold ground or whole, but for the best flavor it is advisable to buy the whole seed and grate it as needed. It grates very easily and can even be scraped with a small paring knife. Whole nutmegs keep their flavor almost indefinitely so grating it as you need it eliminates the pressure to toss opened ground spices after a year.

PAPRIKA: To those who know, paprika is not just a pretty red powder sprinkled on food as decoration. It is serious spice. Hungarians, for example, use lavish amount of paprika in many national favorites, including goulash soup and chicken paprikash. And paprika is used in seasoning blends for barbecue and chili. It is also essential to the cooking of India, Morocco and the Middle East. Paprika is made by grinding dried spicy red peppers to powder. Hungarian rose paprika ranges from mild and full-bodied to hot and spicy; Spanish paprika, ground from dried pimientos, is always mild.

PEPPER: Pepper is our most popular spice and accounts for 25% of the world's spice trade. The most common pepper is ground from black peppercorns, although white, red and dried green peppercorns are available and are often sold as a mixture. Some recipes specify white pepper because it does not add dark specks to the food. Although pepper is sold already ground, it tastes best when ground in a peppermill just before using. Pink peppercorns are dried berries of a rose plant and not true peppercorns.

POPPY SEEDS: Tiny slate-blue poppy seeds have a crunchy texture and provide a sweet, nutty topping to breads and bagels, and a crunchy addition to cookies and poundcakes. The seeds are also used in noodle dishes in Jewish, German and Slavic cooking. Ground, often after being toasted, and mixed with sugar and sometimes nuts, poppy seeds are used as a filling for strudel and Danish pastries. Poppy seeds are available whole, and also canned as a pastry filling.

SAFFRON: Saffron, the threadlike stigmas from a variety of Spanish crocus, is the world's most expensive spice. The stigmas must be plucked from the flowers by hand—and it takes 225,000 of them to make 1 pound of saffron. Saffron imparts a strong aroma and distinctive bitter honey-like taste to food as well as a deep yellow color. It is used for paella, for the rich French fish soup called bouillabaisse, and for chicken and fish dishes in Moroccan cooking. Saffron is also used in some sweet pastries. Saffron is sold whole and ground. Whole is the better way. A few stamens are usually soaked for a few minutes in warm water before being added to the dish.

SESAME SEEDS: Also known as benne seeds, sesame seeds were introduced to the Americas by African slaves. Sesame seeds are integral to African, Asian and Indian cooking and are used in the United States in baked goods. Favored for their nutty flavor, sesame seeds are also used to make the candy called halva. The white variety of sesame seed is the most common.

TURMERIC: A member of the ginger family, turmeric is ground into a bright yellow-orange powder and is used to flavor curries as well as vegetable, egg and fish dishes. Turmeric is a significant ingredient in curry powder and prepared mustard, and is also used in pickling. It gives food a pleasantly bitter, mild flavor.

VANILLA: Vanilla is a familiar and popular flavor, used in many desserts, confections, baked goods, beverages and some savory preparations. The long, thin pod is the fruit of an orchid that is the only one of more than 20,000 orchid varieties that bears anything edible. The long process of picking and curing the beans accounts for the high cost of vanilla beans and pure vanilla extract. Most of the vanilla beans grown today come from Mexico, Tahiti or, perhaps the best, from Madagascar, an island off the coast of Africa. Vanilla beans are richer tasting than vanilla extract, but extract can nearly always be used in recipes calling for the beans. Pure vanilla extract is far more flavorful than imitation vanilla extract. Vanilla is the second most expensive spice after saffron.

# Glossary of Cooking Terms

A LA CARTE: Term indicating that every item on a menu is priced separately.

AL DENTE: Term used to describe pasta, rice or vegetables that are cooked just to the point where they still offer resistance when bitten. In Italian, the term means "to the tooth."

AU GRATIN: French term referring to cooking food under a broiler or in a hot oven to form a lightly browned crust. The food can be left plain or topped with bread crumbs and/or grated cheese to make the crust.

BAIN-MARIE: The method of gently cooking food in a water bath. A bain-marie is made by placing a pan or dish of food (such as egg custard or crème brulée) in a larger, shallow pan and then adding enough water to the larger pan to come partway up the sides of the smaller dish. The food is then baked in the oven. A bain-marie can also be stovetop, when a saucepan or other metal container is placed inside a larger shallow pan over low heat.

BAKING POWDER: A raising agent or leavening used in baking. Double-acting baking powder has one ingredient that starts working when moisture is added and a second that works when the food is heated. Both agents create small air bubbles in the food that expand when heated. As the cake or pancakes "set" in the heat, the bubbles are trapped in the food, lightening the texture. Baking powder is not the same as baking soda.

BAKING SHEET: Also called cookie sheets, baking sheets have a raised rim on two sides to facilitate removing them from the oven. Choose heavy gauge (to prevent warping), light-colored baking sheets. A dark finish will produce dark rolls or cookies, which may not be what you want.

BAKING SODA: Bicarbonate of soda (baking soda) is used in baking as a leavening or raising agent when mixed with liquid and an acid (such as buttermilk) but it is frequently used with baking powder to neutralize acid ingredients such as brown sugar, honey or molasses. It cannot be used interchangeably with baking powder.

BAKING STONE: A heavy, thick round or rectangular stone designed to be used in a gas or electric oven to imitate a brick one. The stone absorbs and retains the oven's heat and promotes even baking. It is used most frequently for baking pizzas.

BASTE: To spoon or drizzle fat, a marinade or pan drippings over food while it cooks to add flavor and moisture.

BLANCH: To cook food (usually fruits and vegetables) in rapidly boiling water for a minute or less in order to set color, loosen skins (as when skinning tomatoes, peaches or almonds) or remove odors (blanching sliced scallions removes the onion-y odor, helpful if you want to slice them a day ahead). The blanched food is usually immediately rinsed with cold water to prevent further cooking.

BLIND BAKED: Term used to describe a prebaked, unfilled pie shell. The blind-baked pie shell may be baked further after filling or not, depending on the recipe.

BRAISE: To cook food slowly in a little liquid in a tightly covered pan on the rangetop or in the oven. This is a favored cooking method for tenderizing tougher cuts of meat.

BROCHETTE: The French term for a skewer; also refers to foods cooked on a skewer; *en brochette*.

BROIL: To cook food under a heat source.

BROWN: To cook food quickly over high heat—usually in a little fat—to give the food color and flavor. (Browning does not seal in juices.) Browning meat is often the first step in a stew or pot roast.

BUNDT PAN: A style of tube pan with fluted sides.

CARAMELIZE: To heat sugar until it liquifies, turns amber brown and acquires a caramel or "burnt" sugar flavor. Upon cooling, the caramelized sugar will harden. Sliced onions and other vegetables may be cooked slowly in a little fat until the natural sugars brown or caramelize, adding flavor and color to a finished dish. Natural sugars also cause grilled or roasted vegetables to brown.

CLARIFY: To separate and remove solids and sediment from a liquid to make it clear. Butter is clarified by heating it and pouring off the clear yellow fat, leaving behind the milk solids.

CHOP: To cut solid food into small pieces about the size of peas. Some recipes call for coarsely or finely chopped ingredients, which are pieces either larger or smaller than peas.

CORNED: Corned, as in corned beef, has nothing to do with corn, the vegetable. While today most corned beef is cured in a brine, in Anglo-Saxon times the meat was dry-cured by being rubbed with "corns" of salt. Corning, or brining beef, is a way of preserving less tender cuts of meat such as brisket, rump or round. Spices and herbs such as peppercorns, coriander seeds and bay leaf are often added to the brining mixture for extra flavor. The pink color of corned beef usually remains after cooking because nitrite used in the curing process fixes the pigment in the meat.

CREAM: To beat a fat such as butter or margarine either alone or with sugar until soft, smooth and fluffy. This method aerates the fat and will give baked goods a lighter texture. An electric mixture makes creaming ingredients easy.

CRIMP: To seal two pastry edges by pinching them together to form a decorative edge. The edges can also be pressed together with the tines of a fork.

CURDLE: To separate into lumpy curds and liquid. Egg custards tend to curdle when they are exposed to prolonged or too high heat, or in the case of milk, combined with acid. Cake batters can sometimes curdle if very cold eggs are added too quickly to beaten eggs and sugar. (Beating in a small amount of the flour will usually restore smoothness.)

CURE: To preserve meats and fish by smoking, salting, drying or a combination of two or three.

CUT IN: To incorporate cold, solid fat into a dry ingredient, such as flour, until the mixture resembles coarse crumbs. Most cooks use either a pastry blender (see page 274), or their fingertips to cut fat into flour. It can also be quickly done by pulsing the fat and flour in a food processor.

DEGLAZE: To scrape the browned bits of food from the bottom of the pan after adding liquid and heating it.

DICE: To cut solid food into small, uniformly sized cubes or squares.

DOUBLE BOILER: Two pots, one designed to fit partway inside the other, with a single lid. The bottom pan holds simmering water, which should not touch the base of the top pan. Used to cook custards and sauces where the mixture might curdle if cooked over direct heat.

**DREDGE:** To coat food with a powdery dry ingredient such as flour, sugar or cornmeal.

**DRIPPINGS:** The fat and juices left in a roasting pan or skillet after the meat has cooked.

**DUTCH OVEN:** The pot known as a Dutch oven has a heavy bottom and is made of materials that distribute heat evenly. Those made of enameled iron, known as French ovens, have thick walls as well. Two handles make it easy to lift the pot in and out of the oven, and a tight-fitting lid traps moisture inside. A wide bottom allows plenty of surface for browning food; it should be large enough to hold a whole chicken or a pot roast. If you are looking for a Dutch oven, check that it can be used stovetop as well as in the oven. These pots don't come cheap but are invaluable for cooking and should serve the cook well forever.

**FLUTE:** To make a decorative edge on a pie shell or other pastry, usually in a scalloped pattern.

**FOLD:** To incorporate a light, aerated mixture, such as beaten egg whites or whipped cream, into a heavier one while deflating the lighter mixture as little as possible. This is accomplished by gently but decisively cutting through both mixtures with a sharp-edged spoon or a silicone spatula from the top to the bottom of the bowl, lifting and folding the heavier mixture over the lighter one, rotating the bowl and repeating the process until both mixtures are incorporated. Sometimes a small amount of the lighter mixture is stirred into the heavier one to lighten it before the bulk of the lighter mixture is folded in.

**FRICASSÉ:** To cook meat (usually chicken) first in fat and then gently in liquid along with aromatic vegetables.

**FRITTER:** A small amount of thick batter, usually containing a food such as a sliced fruit (apple, banana, pineapple), that is deep fried.

**GANACHE:** A rich cake or chocolate filling made by melting chocolate in heavy cream. When the mixture is completely cold it can be whipped to lighten it.

**GARNISH:** To decorate a dish with a complementary attractive food, such as fresh herbs or lemon wedges.

**GLAZE:** To brush or spoon a sweet or savory liquid onto food that, after setting or cooking, will provide the food with a smooth, shiny surface. Glaze can also refer to the liquid itself.

**GRATE:** To turn solid food into particles by rubbing it against a serrated utensil, such as a common kitchen box grater or a Microplane. Foods may also be grated in rotating graters or mills. Hard foods such as Parmesan can be "grated" in a food processor, using the metal blade. (See also Shred.)

**JELLY ROLL PAN:** A rimmed baking sheet used most often to bake thin cakes. Once cooled, these cakes often are rolled around fillings or cut in strips and stacked. Most jelly roll pans are 15½ x 10½ x 1 in., although some are slightly smaller and others slightly larger. Jelly roll pans are also referred to as half sheet pans, although those are slightly larger, 16¾ x 11¾ in.

**JULIENNE:** Solid food (usually vegetables) cut into slender, uniformly sized strips, also called matchsticks.

**KNEAD:** To mix dough with the hands, a mixer fitted with a bread hook or in a bread machine so that the dough forms a cohesive mass and, at the same time, the gluten in the flour begins to develop (get more elastic).

**LUKEWARM:** A temperature divide between hot and cool, usually between body temperature (98°F) and 105°F.

**MACERATE:** To soak fruits in a liqueur, wine or syrup.

MARINATE: To soak foods, such as meat and fish, in a seasoned liquid. The liquid nearly always contains an acidic ingredient such as vinegar or lemon juice and flavors, but rarely tenderizes, the food. A dry mixture or paste of herbs, which is rubbed onto food before it is cooked, is also used as a marinade and is usually called a rub.

MINCE: To cut solid food into tiny pieces.

PANBROIL: To cook food (usually meat) in a hot skillet that may or may not contain fat.

PARBOIL: To partially cook food in boiling water, often for slightly longer than blanching (page 384). The cooking is usually completed by another method.

PARE: To remove the thin skin of fruit or a vegetable with a small knife or vegetable peeler.

PASTRY BLENDER: A tool fitted with rigid, curved wires that is used to cut fat into flour.

PASTRY SCRAPER: A tool fitted with a flat, rigid metal plate used to scrape dough from countertops and boards. Also made of more flexible plastic.

PINCH: A very small amount, usually less than ⅛ of a teaspoon.

PIPE: To squeeze a soft mixture (such as frosting) through a pastry bag or tube to make decorative shapes or borders.

POACH: To cook food in barely simmering liquid.

PROOF: In baking, this term refers to testing yeast to make sure it is alive and capable of leavening bread dough.

PURÉE: To blend in a blender or process in a food processor or food mill until food is smooth and lump-free. The term also refers to the food that has been puréed.

RAMEKIN: A small ovenproof dish used for individual portions of baked or chilled foods. Ramekins resemble soufflé dishes and are usually ceramic or porcelain.

REDUCE: To simmer slowly or boil a liquid in an uncovered pan so that water evaporates, volume decreases and flavors intensify.

RENDER: To cook food until it releases its fat in melted form.

RIMMED BAKING SHEET: Metal baking pan rimmed on all four sides. Used for roasting vegetables or baking chicken or cookies. A heavy one won't warp and a light-color metal will prevent foods from baking dark.

ROUX: A cooked mixture of flour and fat.

SAUTÉ: To cook gently in a little fat, stirring and shaking the ingredients for much of the cooking time. In French, the term translates "to jump."

SCALD: To heat liquid until it almost boils and just begins to form tiny bubbles around the rim of the pan.

SCALLOPED: A term that refers to baking food in (usually) a cream sauce (for example, scalloped potatoes).

SCALOPPINE: This refers to thin boneless slices of meat, usually veal. These cuts of meat can also be called scallops, for example veal scallops, or cutlets.

SCORE: To make elongated shallow cuts in meat or fish or on loaves of bread before baking.

SEAR: To brown food quickly over high heat.

SHEET CAKE PAN: Often the term used to describe a 13 x 9 x 2-in. baking pan.

SHRED: Reducing food (such as Cheddar cheese or carrots) to long thin pieces (as opposed to grating, in which food is turned into particles). Use the large V-shaped holes on a box grater or the shredding disk of a food processor.

SIFT: To remove lumps and aerate dry ingredients by passing them through a mesh sifter or strainer.

SIMMER: To boil very gently so that the liquid produces small, occasional bubbles around the edges of the pan and across the surface of the liquid.

SKIM: To use a spoon to remove the surface foam or fat from cooking liquid.

SPRINGFORM PAN: A round baking pan with a high straight side that can be released with a clamp.

STEAM: To cook a food with the steam produced by boiling liquid. The food is placed on a rack or in a basket so that it does not touch the liquid and the pot is covered to retain the steam.

STEEP: To soak an ingredient in very hot liquid so that its flavors are released into the liquid (as when making tea), or in order to soften it. Food can also be steeped in a cold liquid, such as raisins in rum.

STIR-FRY: To cook small, uniformly shaped pieces of food over high heat in only a small amount of fat, turning and stirring them continuously, until tender yet still with a "bite." The term also refers to the prepared dish.

STRAIN: To pour a mixture of liquid and solids into a strainer in order to remove the solids. Sometimes the solids are pushed through the strainer with the back of a spoon or spatula and the resulting purée is mixed with the strained liquid and becomes part of the dish.

TEMPER: To heat or warm food carefully and gently so that it may be incorporated into preparations requiring longer cooking. Eggs are often tempered by being mixed with a little hot liquid before they are stirred into a sauce or a soup.

TRUSS: To tie poultry or another meat with kitchen twine or to secure it with skewers so that it holds its shape during cooking.

WOK: A round-bottomed pan with curved sides used in Asian cooking for stir-frying, boiling and frying. Nowadays flat-bottom woks are easily available for use on an electric or gas range.

ZEST: The colored part of citrus peel that can be grated for flavor using a Microplane or a box grater. When grating citrus zest for a cake or other dishes take only the colored part. Referred to in this book as grated peel.

# Cheese Primer

## MAKING THE MOST OF CHEESE

**BREAKFAST:** Fill a hard roll with slices of a firm cheese such as Cheddar, Comte or Arina. Eat grape, cherry or pear tomatoes and fresh radishes with it. If you can't move out of the cereal bowl for breakfast, try the above mid-morning with coffee, instead of a pastry.

**LUNCH:** Fill olive and rosemary rolls with chêvre (soft goat cheese). Eat with a mound of fresh salad greens (with or without dressing) and fresh fruit.

Layer sliced pepperjack cheese with sliced fresh tomatoes and sweet onion on a plain roll.

Cut rosemary focaccia bread in half. Fill with thin-sliced roast beef, sliced (not crumbled) creamy blue cheese and lots of fresh arugula. No butter needed.

**CHEESE AS PART OF A SPECIAL DINNER:** More and more restaurants and home cooks are exploring cheese and fruit either as dessert (hand a box of chocolates at coffee time for a simple sweet finale) or as a course between the entrée and dessert. Either way, it's a simple but special course to put together.

First, the cheese: Have one or as many as you like, but three is a good number. Try a very rich triple-crème cheese, a blue, a soft goat cheese and then, if you like, something ripe and old. Arrange the cheeses on a board or platter, perhaps with an herb sprig or two for decoration, and have a separate spreader for each cheese. Take the cheeses out of the refrigerator about half an hour before serving so they can come to room temperature.

The fruit: Put apples, pears and grapes in a beautiful bowl and pass it around. In the winter, fresh tangerines or fuyu persimmons are a nice addition; in summer, fresh figs. (Dried fruit is good any season.) If you prefer to use cut-up fruit you might want to arrange it on each plate first, or on one large plate and pass it around.

The accompaniments: Supply plain water crackers, or a plain bread. Look for a simple bread that has no sugar or corn syrup added. Of course, sometimes a sweet bread is the perfect foil for a ripe cheese, but choose a bread that's sweet by nature, such as an Irish soda bread with raisins, bread with fennel seeds and raisin, or walnut and dried cranberry (or cherry) bread.

The tools: Give each person a knife to spread cheese on bread and maybe a fork, too, since some people enjoy eating cheese without bread and with a fork. The plate can be a dessert plate or larger, depending on what you have. Better to err on the size of largeness so there's room for cheese, bread, fruit and peels from the fruit.

The drink: Continue with wine served at dinner. Or if you prefer, serve a small glass of a sweet sherry or Marsala wine, or a sweet dessert wine.

**BIG BASH:** While a party is a great occasion to try something new, you don't want to intimidate the cheese-shy. So choose two or three crowd pleasers, then two or three unusual cheeses that are bound to get guests talking, even arguing.

Set the cheeses out with plenty of space around each one, or perhaps put them on separate boards and definitely with separate spreaders or cutters. While pre-cut cubes of cheese may seem like an easy idea for a party, the next time you have a piece of Cheddar on hand cut a cube and eat it. Then cut a thin slice and eat that. You will probably be surprised at how much richer and more flavorful the slice tastes.

If the guests are foodies you can have fun. Perhaps select just cheeses made from the milk of small animals, sheep and goats. There is a wide variety of textures and flavors available for each. Or ask the cheese manager to help you choose a selection of cheeses from mountainous regions. Or locate artisanal cheeses from local farms, whether made from cow, goat or sheep's milk; Wisconsin and California have outstanding small cheese-makers, as do Vermont and New York State, among others. So many wonderful cheeses, so little time to try them all.

## SOFT CHEESES

Rich and creamy with a wide range of flavors describes these spreadable cheeses. They can be broken down into two subcategories:

FRESH CHEESES: These are cheeses that have not been permitted to ripen (age). They have a mild flavor and a relatively short shelf life—check their freshness dates. These cheeses may be eaten plain (and are an exception to the rule that cheeses should be served at room temperature), mixed into dips or used in cooking.

| | |
|---|---|
| Boursin | Fromage blanc |
| Cottage cheese | Mascarpone |
| Cream cheese | Fresh mozzarella |
| Farmer cheese | Neufchâtel |
| Fresh goat cheese (chabis or tub) | Ricotta |

SOFT RIPENED CHEESES: These cheeses are ripened so that they develop fuller flavor than fresh cheeses. They do not keep for more than two weeks. These cheeses are generally eaten plain or simply with bread. They are rarely used in cooking.

| | |
|---|---|
| Boursault | Goat cheese |
| Brie | Bucherons |
| Brillat-Savarin | Limburger |
| Camembert | |

## SEMISOFT CHEESES

These cheeses are more ripened than soft cheeses. They are springy to the touch and, although soft textured, can be sliced. Semisoft cheeses will keep for up to three weeks in the refrigerator. They are often used in cooking, as many of these cheeses melt extremely well, with the exception of blue-veined cheeses (such as blue, gorgonzola and Stilton) and feta cheese.

| | |
|---|---|
| Blue | Mozzarella (packaged) |
| Feta | Muenster (American) |
| Fontina | Port Salut |
| Gorgonzola | Roquefort |
| Gouda | Stilton |
| Havarti | Taleggio |
| Monterey Jack | Tilsit |

## SEMIFIRM CHEESES

These cheeses are ripened to the extent that they develop a full, robust flavor. They have a firm but smooth texture and can be sliced. Ranging from mild to sharp, they are excellent eating cheeses and are often useful in cooking.

| | |
|---|---|
| Asiago | Edam |
| Beamont | Gruyere |
| Cheddar | Jarlsberg |
| Cheshire | Leyden |
| Colby | Provolone |
| Double Gloucester | Swiss |

## FIRM CHEESES

These cheeses are also called grating cheeses. They are aged until they are very dry and hard and will keep for months in the refrigerator. They range in flavor from mild to sharp and are almost always grated before being used in cooking or passed at the table for sprinkling over cooked dishes.

## ABOUT GOAT CHEESE

| | |
|---|---|
| Aged Asiago | Pecorino Romano |
| Locatelli | Sapsago |
| Parmesan | Sbrinz |

Making cheese from goats' milk is a time honored tradition in France and other parts of Europe, and it has become increasingly popular in the United States during the past decade. Although much of the goat cheese (chèvre) sold here is imported from France, a growing percentage is produced in this country.

When very fresh (generally less than a week old), goat cheese may be sold in a tub, sometimes mixed with herbs, or as a round, soft chabis. When it is aged a little longer, it is very often sold shaped into a log called a bucheron. This is the most popular shape for goat cheese. Cheese sold as bucheron is a little older than fresh cheese and has the distinctive yet mild sharp, salty flavor favored by goat cheese aficionados. Aged goat cheese is dry and very sharp-tasting and often is sold in a round, flattened disk called a crottin. Goat cheese is sometimes coated in ash or herbs and is sold in other shapes, too—the most common being a pyramid, which designates cheeses aged to about the same degree as bucheron.

## ABOUT BLUE-VEINED CHEESE

| | |
|---|---|
| Banon | Sainte-Maure |
| California chèvre | Arina (goat gouda) |
| Chabichou | Hoja Santa |
| Montrachet | Montasio |
| Saint-Christophe | Humboldt Fog |

We tend to classify all cheeses with blue streaks as "blue cheeses." In fact, they differ from one another in how and where they are made. The blue-green mold can occur naturally or from a strain of penicillin that is added during the curing process. The cheese is perforated with wire needles to allow the spread of mold veins. Roquefort, perhaps the most famous of the blue, is made from sheep's milk and is aged in cool, damp caves in a particular region of France. Stilton, England's revered cheese, requires long aging to acquire its strong, enticing flavor.

Blue-veined cheeses are excellent with bread and wine, crumbled over salads and accompanying fresh fruit. Bring the cheese to room temperature before serving. They should be well wrapped for storage as their potent aromas can mingle with other foods.

## LOWFAT CHEESES

| | |
|---|---|
| Bleu de Bresse | Oregon blue |
| Bleu de Castello | Pipo Crem' |
| Danish blue | Roquefort |
| Fourme d'Ambert | Saga blue |
| Gorgonzola | Stilton |
| Maytag blue | |

Cheese's big problem has always been its high fat content. But there are many truly delicious lowfat choices. Some, such as mozzarella and string cheese (especially part-skim), feta and some goat cheese are naturally lower in calories (about 75 calories per ounce) than Cheddar (at about 115 calories) or a triple crème (which tips the scale at 140 calories). Other lowfat selections include part-slim ricotta and reduced-fat cottage cheese.

## HOW TO STORE CHEESE

As a general rule, the harder the cheese, the longer it will remain fresh. Soft cheeses should be eaten within 1 to 2 weeks of purchase. Firmer, drier cheese such as Cheddar may be fine for a month or so, longer if sealed in its original wrapper. Hard grating cheeses may last indefinitely.

All cheese should be covered tightly in plastic wrap to prevent drying, then refrigerated. It is advisable to change the wrapping every few days to prolong the life of the cheese.

Strong-smelling ones such as Limburger should be wrapped and put into a tightly sealed container to prevent their odors from permeating other foods.

Even if cheeses are stored properly, they may develop surface molds. Make sure you slice off ¼ inch of the surface before serving.

If cheese has become dried out you may shred or grate it to use it in cooking.

# Coffee & Tea

## Coffee

### GOOD BREW CHECK

To make the best cup of coffee you can, keep in mind the following:

1.USE FRESH COFFEE: Coffee that's been sitting around in an open can for a month or more can't be expected to have full flavor. Try to buy no more than a week's supply of coffee at one time.

2.USE THE CORRECT GRIND FOR YOUR BREWING METHOD: The idea is to extract just the right amount of the oils from the ground coffee. If the coffee is ground too coarse, not enough of the oils will be extracted and you'll end up with a tasteless brew. Too fine and the flavor can lean toward bitter.

3. USE GOOD-TASTING COLD WATER: Brewed coffee is more than 98% water. If you don't drink the water from your faucet because of off-flavors, don't expect it to make good coffee. Use bottled or filtered water.

4. MEASURE THE COFFEE AND THE WATER: If you want your expectations to be met day after day, measure. Start with the amount of ground coffee the package suggests but in the end the amount of ground coffee you use per 6 fluid ounces of water is entirely up to you. Always make at least half the capacity of your coffee maker. If you make a pot of coffee and it turns out to be too strong for your taste, don't pour more water through the grounds; instead dilute what you've made with freshly heated water.

5. MAKE SURE YOUR COFFEE MAKER HEATS WATER TO PROPER BREWING TEMPERATURE (195°F to 205°F): Look for an electric drip coffee maker that's at least 1,200 watts. If you are boiling water (to pour into a manual drip coffee filter), bring it to a boil, then take the kettle or pan off the heat and let it stand briefly for the temperature to drop slightly.

6. BE PATIENT: Wait until the entire pot has brewed before pouring yourself a cup. Otherwise that first cup will be very strong, but the rest will be wishy-washy.

7. THEN BE IMPATIENT: Serve the coffee as soon as possible when its aroma and flavor are best. Freshly brewed means fresh taste; flavor starts to deteriorate after about 20 minutes. If you must keep it hot, use a vacuum carafe or flask.

8. KEEP YOUR COFFEE MAKER CLEAN: You know that stale coffee smell? If it's coming from old coffee oils on your brewing equipment, it can affect the flavor of the brew. Check the instructions that come with your coffee maker to learn how to properly clean it.

### BACK TO THE BEGINNING

While you inhale the aroma of brewing coffee and anticipate that first satisfying sip take a moment to reflect on some of the things that affect it:

The soil and climate where the coffee trees grew has a lot to do with how your java tastes. The same species grown in Africa will taste different from a coffee grown in Indonesia. Different, not better or worse, although generally coffee grown at an altitude of about 3,000 feet tastes best. Coffee beans don't grow in a pod; the fruit of the tree looks more like a paper-wrapped cherry. Inside each cherry nestle two beans. After the fruit is picked all the extraneous material is removed.

Coffees grown in Latin America (including Mexico, Peru, Brazil and Puerto Rico) have a bright, clean, straightforward flavor.

Those grown in African countries, including Yemen, Kenya, Ethiopia and Tanzania, have a distinctive, sharp, vibrant flavor, while those from Indonesia and New Guinea (including Sumatra, Sulawesi, Java and New Guinea) have a full, rich body.

Coffee is also grown in Hawaii and India.

These geographical differences help explain why most coffees are a blend of beans, rather than just a single flavor.

The color of coffee beans in their natural state ranges from gray-green to dark yellow but are called "green," meaning not roasted. Roasting causes sugars, fats and starches within the beans to caramelize and to release the oils that make some beans look shiny.

Although there are no hard and fast standards about roasting the following will give you some clues to look for:

CINNAMON ROAST: The beans are roasted to the color of cinnamon and smell more like toasted grain. Some tasters maintain that cinnamon-roasted beans often are sour and lack body.

AMERICAN ROAST: The roasted beans are light brown, with a flavor that's neither too heavy nor too light. This is the most popular roast in the eastern part of the U.S.

CITY OR MEDIUM ROAST: A darker roast popular in the western parts of the U.S.

FRENCH ROAST AND DARK FRENCH ROAST: Heavily roasted beans that are a deep chocolate brown and produce a rich coffee.

VIENNESE ROAST: One-third dark-roast beans blended with two-thirds American roast.

ITALIAN: Glossy, brown-black beans with strong flavor, used for espresso when very finely ground. Can be used for drip, too.

SPANISH: This is the darkest roast of all.

FLAVORED COFFEES: Vanilla, vanilla-almond, chocolate-hazelnut and chocolate-raspberry are some of the flavors that can be added to coffee beans.

If you think of coffee as bitter and astringent, try going for a darker roast. And keep in mind, it's not just the roast that determines the flavor. Coffee made with beans from Ethiopia will taste different than coffee brewed from beans grown in Mexico, even if both are French roast.

HISTORICAL NOTE: Around AD 600 to 900, the red cherry-like fruit of the coffee tree was fermented and made into wine. Another hundred or more years passed before the green beans (found inside the red berries) were boiled to make a beverage.

## NOT IN THE MOOD TO BREW?

Instant coffee is popular in many parts of the world, even in some coffee-producing countries. There are two kinds:

INSTANT COFFEE: Freshly brewed coffee is spray dried.

FREEZE-DRIED COFFEE: Freshly brewed coffee is frozen into a slush before the water is evaporated. Generally has a fresher flavor than instant because it is not exposed to high temperatures.

## DECAFFEINATED COFFEE

Caffeine is present in all coffee beans. The average cup of coffee has enough caffeine (about 115 milligrams in a 5-ounce cup) to stimulate the heartbeat, increase mental activity and cause sleeplessness in some coffee drinkers. Those who are sensitive to caffeine can chose to drink decaffeinated coffee. Not long ago, coffee lovers had little selection when it came to decaffeinated coffee, but today there is a wide variety of roasted decaffeinated beans and grinds so that no one who enjoys the flavor of coffee needs to feel deprived.

There are two methods of removing the caffeine from coffee beans. It can be removed by water or by solvents. Using water is more time consuming and therefore more costly than relying on solvents—even so, some coffee drinkers feel that water-decaffeinated beans are inferior. Regardless of the method, 97% of the caffeine is removed from the beans, rendering them essentially caffeine-free. The beans are then blended, roasted and ground. Surprisingly, a cup of inexpensive American coffee (the sort sold at diners and fast-food outlets) may have as much as 25% more caffeine than a cup brewed from specialty coffee beans. Espresso has slightly less caffeine than percolated coffee.

## CAFÉ COFFEES AND OTHER SPECIAL COFFEES

Coffee bars and restaurants serving specialty coffees are extremely popular. Following is a list of terms often used at these emporiums.

**CAFÉ AU LAIT:** This is the French term for coffee with milk and most often refers to equal portions of scalded milk and coffee.

**CAFÉ BRÛLOT:** Famous in New Orleans, this is spiced coffee flavored with citrus peel and brandy. The brandy is heated and ignited (flambéed) before being poured into the coffee.

**CAFFÈ LATTE:** Similar to cappuccino, this calls for a higher proportion of milk to coffee. In many coffee bars, you can request caffè latte with skim milk or soy milk.

**CAFÉ D'OLLA:** A Mexican coffee made in a special pot using a method similar to Turkish coffee.

**CAPPUCCINO:** Cappuccino is made by topping espresso with steamed milk, which is pressurized to create a thick, creamy foam. Some of the milk mixes with the coffee. Cappuccino can be topped with cinnamon or cocoa.

**ESPRESSO:** This dark, strong coffee is made from finely ground dark-roast coffee beans (often called Italian roast). During brewing, steam or hot water is forced through the grind, resulting in the characteristic thin layer of foam topping true espresso. In Southern Italy and the U.S., espresso is served in small cups with a piece of lemon peel, a custom that supposedly started during World War II when Italians used roast ground chicory instead of coffee and thought the touch of lemon made the chicory brew taste more like their beloved espresso.

**GREEK COFFEE:** Starts with a sweet blend of Brazilian coffee and roasted chicory root. Made the same way as Turkish coffee but of course no Greek would ever call it Turkish.

**IRISH COFFEE:** Usually served in restaurants and bars, this is a potent blend of strong coffee and Irish whisky, sweetened with sugar and topped with a generous spoonful of whipped cream.

**THAI COFFEE:** In Thailand, Vietnam and other countries where fresh dairy products are in short supply evaporated milk is used for coffee. When it comes to iced coffee, sweetened condensed milk is used for a hard-to-stop-sipping beverage.

**TURKISH COFFEE:** To make Turkish coffee, water and sugar are put into a special metal pot with a long handle called an "ibrik." Pulverized coffee is sprinkled on top and the whole is brought to a boil until the water foams up through the coffee layer. The boilings are repeated twice more, then the coffee is stirred before being immediately poured into tiny cups. Rich, thick Turkish coffee defies the common wisdom about never boiling coffee. In some parts of the Middle East, Turkish coffee is flavored with cardamom or cloves; in

North Africa coriander seed is preferred. In a restaurant coffee is ordered by the degree of sweetness desired.

Turkish coffee was invented during the 16th century and spread throughout the Middle East and into Europe and Russia. Today in the U.S. it can be found in Middle Eastern and Greek restaurants from New York to San Francisco. It is always sipped slowly. Turkish coffee can be made with any bean as long as it is pulverized (beyond finely ground).

In 15th-century Turkey it became legal for a woman to divorce her husband if he failed to provide her with her daily coffee quota.

# Tea

## HOW TO MAKE A PERFECT POT OF TEA

Tea may be brewed to be enjoyed either hot or cold. The preferred method for making a pot of tea is to use loose tea, although tea bags work nearly was well and are easier to use. Begin by filling a metal teakettle with cold tap water (see step 3, page 392). When the water gets close to the boiling point, pour some into a ceramic, porcelain or silver teapot to warm it. Just as the kettle boils, pour the hot water from the teapot and add the tea. Use one heaping teaspoon of loose tea or one tea bag for each cup. If you like tea very strong add an extra teaspoon or an extra tea bag "for the pot." Pour the boiling water over the tea. Those who like tea on the weak side pour their brew into a cup immediately. For a stronger brew, let it steep for 3 to 5 minutes, stirring once to distribute the flavor. While the length of steeping determines the strength of the tea, if you steep the tea for much longer than 5 minutes, black tea will be bitter. Pour the tea directly into the teacups or another warm pot for serving, straining it if necessary.

## HOW TO MAKE A PERFECT CUP OF TEA

Just as with a pot of tea, it's important to begin with good, cold tap water. Bring it to rapid boil and then pour it quickly over a tea bag, a tea ball filled with loose tea or over a heaping teaspoon of loose tea inside a warmed cup or mug.

Let the tea steep for 1 to 4 minutes.

White tea is the exception to the boiling water rule. White tea tastes best when the water is brought to a boil then removed from the heat and allowed to cool for a minute or two before being poured over the tea leaves or tea bag.

## TEA VARIETIES

Teas are made from the leaves of the tea plant, called *Camellia sinensis*, and are named according to their region of origin (Assam, Ceylon, Darjeeling), how the leaves are processed after picking or according to a special blending (Earl Grey, English Breakfast, Irish Breakfast). Tea is grown mainly in India, Sri Lanka (formerly Ceylon) and China.

The newly-picked leaves are spread out on racks and allowed to wither, making them soft and pliable. Next the leaves are rolled into twists and curls, something that is still done by hand for rare teas. The rolling breaks down the leaf cells. After rolling, the treatments vary according to the type of tea.

BLACK TEA means the leaves have been fermented before being heated and dried. Black tea produces a deep, reddish-brown brew. English Breakfast is a black tea as is the smoky Lapsang Souchong. (In China, black teas are called red teas.)

GREEN TEA is not fermented at all; instead it is steamed and dried. Gunpowder tea is a green tea, as are Lung Ching (China) and Bancha (Japan). It was green tea, 342 wooden chests of it, that got tossed overboard into Boston Harbor on December 16, 1773, as the colonists protested British oppression.

OOLONG tea leaves are partially fermented and the flavor, not surprisingly, is somewhere between black and green tea.

WHITE TEA is also not fermented. The difference here is that the leaves are picked before they are fully unfurled when the tips of the shoots are still covered with tiny white hairs, thus the name. White tea actually produces a slightly darker and more flavorful brew than green tea.

There are numerous teas, each with its distinct flavor, aroma and origin. Here are some of the best known:

ASSAM: This tea, from the Assam district of India, is a strong black tea.

CEYLON: Sri Lanka is known for its superlative teas, which often are referred to as Ceylon teas. Ceylon teas are black teas.

DARJEELING: Another black tea, Darjeeling is named after a region of India in the foothills of the Himalayas and is among the world's most prized teas.

EARL GREY: Named for Charles, the second Earl Grey of Britain, this tea is a favorite blending of black teas usually scented with bergamot.

ENGLISH BREAKFAST: This brisk tea is a blending of black teas from India and Sri Lanka.

FORMOSA OOLONG: An oolong tea from Taiwan, this is considered the best oolong by connoisseurs. Oolong teas are made from a partially fermented tea that is a cross between a green and black tea.

LAPSANG SOUCHONG: This black tea comes from China and has a distinctive smoky flavor.

ORANGE PEKOE: Although this term usually refers to a popular blending of Ceylon tea leaves, it is also a grade of tea leaf.

RED TEA, OR ROOIBOSS (ROY-BOSS): From a different plant indigenous to the Southwestern Cape region of South Africa, rooiboss is considered an herbal tea, not a true tea. It produces a rich-flavored brew. Other teas are made from fruit, herbs, spices or flowers. These are called tisanes or herbal teas.

# A Guide to Wine

## WINE IS TO BE ENJOYED

The most important thing to know about wine is that it is meant to be enjoyed. Drink what you like and with what you like. Life is complicated enough without having to make a big deal about the one and only perfect wine to go with a food. If you enjoy red wine with fish, drink it, and if you enjoy white wine with beef, drink it. But if you are unsure, following the old adage will rarely mislead you: Red wines generally are best served with red meat and firm cheese; white wines are best served with fish, poultry and light vegetable dishes. Sweet white wines are served with dessert.

So how do you go about finding wines that you like? Try new ones. Keep an informal record—especially of wines you don't like so you won't buy them again—that includes the price and place of purchase to simplify reordering. Get to know your local wine merchant or the manager of the wine department in your supermarket. Let him or her know what you like (and don't); over time it will become simple for the two of you to find something you'll prefer.

So where to start? If you are serving a Spanish dish, try an Albarino from Spain to go with it. Match a Malbec wine from Argentina with steak served with a chimichurri sauce, a French Chablis with a French dish. Excellent wines are being produced not only in France and the U.S. (especially the northwest regions), but also in Australia, Italy, Germany, Chile and New Zealand, as well as many other places.

A particular wine's quality depends on several factors, the most important being the skill of the winemaker and the quality of the grape that year, which depends as much on the weather as farming practices. This explains why some vintages (years) are better than others—even those coming from the same winery.

Wines are named after the predominant grape used or the region that produces them. Some of the world's finest wines are made in the Burgundy region of France, where both red and white wines are made. Champagne is produced in the Champagne region of France. Sparking wines produced elsewhere cannot be called Champagne

Knowing a little about the character of the grapes that produce wine helps in the selection, too.

Following is a list of some of the most popular types of wine:

## WHITE WINES

**BLANC FUMÉ:** A light wine with herbal, grassy overtones; slightly acidic. Many California vintners reverse the name, calling this type of wine Fumé Blanc. Made with the sauvignon blanc grape and therefore very similar to that wine.

**CAVA:** A sparkling wine from Spain, usually made using the same method as Champagne. It can run from dry to sweet and is popular as an aperitif, a lunch or dinner wine, and as a dessert wine.

**CHAMPAGNE:** Sparkling wine from the Champagne region of France that undergoes a secondary fermentation in the bottle. The wine of celebrations, but also good as an aperitif or with dessert. Sweetness varies from extra dry to slightly sweet.

**CHARDONNAY:** A full, rounded wine with toasty, buttery, vanilla and green apple flavors. Made from white burgundy grapes and produced in all major winemaking regions of the world.

CHARMAT: Not a wine but a method for making sparkling wines, developed around 1910 by a Frenchman, Eugène Charmat. While it is a faster and less expensive method than "méthode Champenoise," it can still produce excellent wines, far superior to "bulk process," where carbon dioxide is simply pumped into still wine (the way carbonated soft drinks are made).

GEWÜRZTRAMINER: A fruity, medium- to full-bodied wine with the flavors of coconut, papaya, and lychee, as well as allspice. Made from grapes of the same name, the pungent wine is also popular in Alsace, Germany and Eastern Europe. California makes good Gewürztraminer wine.

PINOT BLANC AND PINOT BIANCO: Citrus-tasting, medium-bodied wine with slightly nutty, spicy flavors. The grape used to make this wine is related to the famous pinot noir grape. California winemakers use this pinot grape to make Muscadet.

PROSECCO: Sparkling wine made in Italy. Excellent as an aperitif, at a celebration or with food.

RIESLING: Light- to medium-bodied wine with overtones of green apples, lime, honey and sometimes mint. Made mostly in Germany from Riesling grapes, but also made in Alsace, France, Austria, Eastern Europe, Australia and California, as well as elsewhere.

SAUVIGNON BLANC: Light-bodied, herbal-tasting, acidic wine with overtones of green peppers and limes. The sauvignon blanc grape is mixed with others to make wines such as Graves and Pouilly-Fumé.

SPUMANTE: The Italian word for sparkling.

## RED WINES

BEAUJOLAIS: A light-bodied wine with fruity flavors, reminiscent of summer berries, plums, cherries and spices. Made mostly in the Burgundy region of France, Beaujolais is one of the best-known wines in the world. Beaujolais Nouveau is a new wine bottled without aging and should be consumed within a few months of bottling.

CABERNET SAUVIGNON: A medium-bodied, woodsy wine with the flavors of blackberries, vanilla, herbs and Cassis—sometimes with hints of chocolate. Some of the best California wines are made from cabernet grapes. Also made in Australia, South America and Eastern Europe.

CHIANTI: A light to medium, earthy wine, tasting of oak, cedar, black cherries and spices. It is made with a blend of grapes, primarily sangiovese, and named for the Chianti region of Tuscany in Italy. It is made also in California and Argentina.

MÉDOC: A medium-bodied wine with earthy, cherry flavors and smoky overtones of herbs and spices. This wine is from the Bordeaux region of France.

MERLOT: A medium- to full-bodied wine, tasting of plums, cherries and herbs, as well as vanilla and smoke. Wine made with merlot grapes come from France, California, Washington state and Australia. The wine is often used for blending.

PINOT NOIR: Medium- to full-bodied earthy wine with flavors of cherries, plums, leather and spices. Wines made with the pinot noir grape are among the most lauded wines of Burgundy. This wine is also made very well in California, the Pacific Northwest and Australia.

ZINFANDEL: A medium- to full-bodied wine with flowery overtones, also tasting of spices, berries and prunes. Nearly all are made with zinfandel grapes from California.

Most red wines taste best at room temperature but take the temperature of your room into consideration. Bottles of red wine left in an ultra air-conditioned room for several hours might be too cool for full flavor. The same wine stored in a hot kitchen might not be at its best, either.

Should you open red wine ahead of pouring to let it breathe? Today most experts believe many red wines are made to be opened and poured right away. Very old wines may benefit from being allowed to breathe for an hour or so before drinking, but sometimes the flavor changes quickly and for the worse. Ditto very young wines. If you do take a first sip and think the wine needs a little time to open up, a gentle swirl in the glass and 5 or 10 minutes should do it.

Chill white wines for an hour or so before serving, taking into consideration how many bottles you are putting into your refrigerator at once. Champagne, which goes well with nearly every-thing from a main course to dessert, is best chilled.

Stemmed glasses look festive and are especially good for white wine since you can hold the glass by the stem and avoid warming the wine with the heat of your hands. Stemmed glasses with a bowl shape allow you to swirl the wine gently and admire the color and then the bouquet.

Small, so-called European wine glasses have no stems and are an excellent choice for a casual lunch or get-together.

## STORING WINE

Store all wine at cool room temperature. Try to find a cool cupboard or area of the cellar, pantry or utility room. Distance the wine from the oven and stove, where temperature fluctuations are most likely. It's equally important not to store it near the furnace or hot water heater.

# Table of Equivalents

Many recipes from other parts of the world measure ingredients in metric units. This chart will help convert recipes from standard U.S. measurements. The numbers in the chart have been rounded slightly.

## Abbreviations

| | |
|---|---|
| Teaspoon: tsp | |
| Tablespoon: Tbsp | |

| U.S./U.K. | METRIC |
|---|---|
| ounce = oz | milliliter = ml |
| pound = lb | liter = l |
| quart = qt | gram = g |
| | kilogram = kg |
| inch = in. | millimeter = mm |
| foot = ft | centimeter = cm |

## Volume

| U.S. | METRIC |
|---|---|
| ¼ tsp | 1 ml |
| ½ tsp | 2.5 ml |
| ¾ tsp | 4 ml |
| 1 tsp | 5 ml |
| 1¼ tsp | 6 ml |
| 1½ tsp | 7.5 ml |
| 1¾ tsp | 8.5 ml |
| 2 tsp | 10 ml |
| 1 Tbsp | 15 ml |
| 2 Tbsp | 30 ml |
| ¼ cup | 60 ml |
| ⅓ cup | 80 ml |
| ½ cup | 120 ml |
| ⅔ cup | 160 ml |
| ¾ cup | 180 ml |
| 1 cup | 240 ml |
| 1½ cups | 355 ml |
| 2 cups (1 pint) | 475 ml |
| 3 cups | 710 ml |
| 4 cups (1 quart) | .95 l |
| 1.06 quart | 1 l |
| 4 quarts (1 gallon) | 3.8 l |

# Weights

| U.S./U.K. | METRIC |
|---|---|
| .035 oz | 1 g |
| ¼ oz | 7 g |
| ½ oz | 14 g |
| ¾ oz | 21 g |
| 1 oz | 28 g |
| 1½ oz | 42.5 g |
| 2 oz | 57 g |
| 3 oz | 85 g |
| 4 oz | 113 g |
| 5 oz | 142 g |
| 6 oz | 170 g |
| 7 oz | 198 g |
| 8 oz (½ lb) | 227 g |
| 10 oz | 315 g |
| 12 oz (¾ lb) | 375 g |
| 14 oz | 440 g |
| 16 oz (1 lb) | 454 g |
| 2.2 lbs | 1 kg |

# Length measures

| U.S./U.K. | METRIC |
|---|---|
| ⅛ in. | 3 mm |
| ¼ in. | 6 mm |
| ½ in. | 12 mm |
| 1 in. | 2.5 cm |
| 2 in. | 5 cm |
| 3 in. | 7.5 cm |
| 4 in. | 10 cm |
| 12 in. (1 ft) | 30 cm |

# Oven temperatures

| FAHRENHEIT | CELSIUS | GAS |
|---|---|---|
| 250 | 120 | ½ |
| 275 | 140 | 1 |
| 300 | 150 | 2 |
| 325 | 160 | 3 |
| 350 | 180 | 4 |
| 375 | 190 | 5 |
| 400 | 200 | 6 |
| 425 | 220 | 7 |
| 450 | 230 | 8 |
| 475 | 240 | 9 |
| 500 | 260 | 10 |

# Index

# Credits

Almost all of the recipe development and food styling for photography is done by the *Woman's Day* Food Editors but sometimes there is just too much to be done in the time available. Then we turn to other experts whom we would like to thank for their invaluable contributions.

| RECIPE DEVELOPMENT | FOOD STYLING |
|---|---|
| Helen Jones | Margarette Adams |
| Frank P. Melodia | Frank P. Melodia |
| Sarah Reynolds | Karen Tack |
| Karen Tack | Diane Simone Vezza |

PROP STYLING

The prop stylist plays an important role in the way our photographs look by choosing the linens, dishes and flatware that showcase the food.

| | |
|---|---|
| Margarette Adams | Betty Alfenito |
| Stephanie Basralian | Betty Blau |
| Cathy Cook | Cynthia DiPrima |
| Debrah Donahue | Ingrid Leess |
| Marina Malchin | Jennifer Pracht |
| Karen Quatsoe | Loren Simons |
| Gerri Williams | Lynda White |

THE FOLLOWING RECIPES WERE ORIGINALLY CREATED BY *WOMAN'S DAY* READERS:
Thai Chicken Curry (page 49): Meghann Foye
Chicken, Tomatoes & "Breadsticks" Italiano (page 51): Rosemarie Grieco
Sweet & Spicy Wings (page 70): Jennifer Greer
Jambalaya (page 105): Julie Carpenter
Baked Tilapia with Avocado & Tomato (page 113): Lisa Miller
Poached Salmon with Dill Sauce (page 114): Ellen Greene
Saucy Salmon Grill (page 119): Lynette Kittle
Pork Pozole (page 127): Nancy Stanley
Pork Chops with Tomato Sauce (page 130): Chela Colon
Mixed Vegetable Frittata (page 177): Marisa
Slow-Cooker Mushroom-Herb Bread Stuffing (page 217): Brandy Hopwood
Pizza in a Bowl (page 226): Jennifer Rock
Mediterranean Pasta Salad (page 248): Marisol Vera
That Illinois Salad (page 249): Carole Faxon
Grilled Vegetables on Garlic Toast (page 267) Barbara Edwards